THE COMING OF GOD

Works of Jürgen Moltmann

Available from Fortress Press

The Church in the Power of the Spirit
The Coming of God
The Crucified God
God in Creation
Jesus Christ for Today's World
The Source of Life
The Spirit of Life
Theology of Hope
The Trinity and the Kingdom
The Way of Jesus Christ

JÜRGEN MOLTMANN

——

The Coming of God

CHRISTIAN ESCHATOLOGY

——

Translated by
Margaret Kohl

FORTRESS PRESS
Minneapolis

THE COMING OF GOD
Christian Eschatology

First Fortress Press edition published 1996.

Translated by Margaret Kohl from the German *Das Kommen Gottes: Christliche Eschatologie*, published by Christian Kaiser Verlag, Gütersloh, 1995. English translation © 1996 Margaret Kohl. All rights reserved.

ISBN 0–8006–2958–2

Manufactured in Great Britain   AF 1–2958

00   99   98   2   3   4   5   6   7   8   9   10

CONTENTS

PREFACE

In the end is the beginning: Eschatology is generally held to be the doctrine of 'the Last Things', or of 'the end of all things'. To think this is to think in good apocalyptic terms, but it is not understanding eschatology in the Christian sense. To think apocalyptically means thinking things through to their end: the ambiguities of history must sometime become unambiguous; the time of transience must sometime pass away; the unanswerable questions of existence must sometime cease. The question about the end bursts out of the torment of history and the intolerableness of historical existence. To echo a German proverb: better a terrifying end than this endless terror.

Eschatology seems to search for the 'final solution' of all the insoluble problems, as Isaiah Berlin indignantly remarked, playing on the phrase used at the Wannsee conference in 1942, where the SS decided for a 'final solution' of the Jewish question in the camps of mass annihilation. Theological eschatology seems to present the 'Endgame' of the theodrama World History. This was Hans Urs von Balthasar's view, when he took over this title as a legacy from Samuel Beckett. If we look back to the history of eschatology, we see it pictorially represented as God's great final judgment of the good and the wicked, with heaven for the one and hell for the other. Is the Last Judgment God's final solution for human history? Other people have dreamed about Armageddon, the final duel in the struggle between Christ and Antichrist, or God and the Devil – whether the duel be fought out with divine fire or with modern nuclear armaments.

Eschatology is always thought to deal with the end, the last day, the last word, the last act: God has the last word. But if eschatology were that and only that, it would be better to turn one's back on it altogether; for 'the last things' spoil one's taste for the penultimate ones, and the dreamed of, or hoped for, end of history robs us of our freedom among history's many possibilities, and our tolerance for all the things in history that are unfinished and provisional. We can no longer put up with earthly, limited and vulnerable life, and in our eschatological finality we destroy life's fragile beauty. The person who presses forward to the end of life misses life itself. If eschatology were no more than religion's 'final solution' to all the questions, a solution allowing it to have the last word, it would undoubtedly be a particularly unpleasant form of theological dogmatism, if not psychological terrorism. And it has in fact been used in just this way by a number of apocalyptic arm-twisters among our contemporaries.

But *Christian* eschatology has nothing to do with apocalyptic 'final solutions' of this kind, for its subject is not 'the end' at all. On the contrary, what it is about is the new creation of all things. Christian eschatology is the remembered hope of the raising of the crucified Christ, so it talks about beginning afresh in the deadly end. 'The end of Christ – after all that was his true beginning', said Ernst Bloch. Christian eschatology follows this christological pattern in all its personal, historical and cosmic dimensions: *in the end is the beginning*.

That is how Dietrich Bonhoeffer took leave of his fellow prisoner, Payne Best, in Flossenbürg concentration camp, as he went to his execution: 'This is the end – for me the beginning of life.' That is how John on Patmos saw the Last Judgment of the world – not as annihilation, a universal conflagration, or death in a cosmic winter. He saw it as the first day of the new creation of all things: 'See, I am making all things new' (Rev. 21.5). If we perceive it in remembrance of the hope of Christ, what is called the end of history is also simply the end of temporal history and the beginning of the eternal history of life. Christ can only be called 'the end of history' in the sense that he is the pioneer and leader of the life that lives eternally. Wherever life is perceived and lived in community and fellowship with Christ, a new beginning is discovered hidden in every end. What it is I do not know, but I have confidence that the new beginning will find me and raise me up.

Because of this, I have deliberately avoided calling this book about Christian eschatology 'The Last Things' or 'The End of All Things', but have given it the title: *The Coming of God*. In God's creative future, the end will become the beginning, and the true creation is still to come and is ahead of us.

This eschatology, written thirty years after the *Theology of Hope* (1964; ET 1967), is entirely in line with that doctrine of hope. Even then my Bonn colleague Philipp Vielhauer penned the ironical lines:

> The old opinion is no longer 'in',
> that end means end, beginning means begin;
> for this is now re-Blocht, and so we roll on
> from Althaus via Kreck to Moltmann.*

The Adventure of Theological Ideas: At that time I was trying to find a new fundamental category for theology in general: the theology of love in the middle ages and the theology of faith at the Reformation was be followed in modern times by the theology of hope. My present concern is the doctrine of hope in a special sense – i.e., the horizons of expectation for personal life, for political and historical life, and for the life of the cosmos: what *is* hope for eternal life, and what is its effect? What is hope for the kingdom of God, and what is its effect? What is hope for the new heaven and the new earth, and what is its effect? What is the hope of glory for God himself, and what is its effect? In accord with the new fundamental theological category, I said then, with the young Karl Barth: 'Christianity is wholly and entirely eschatology, not just in an appendix. It is hope, a vista, and a forward direction, and it is hence a new departure and a transformation of the present.' Now I am concerned with the content of that vista and that forward direction.

In the last thirty years I have travelled a long theological road, a road with many surprises and many bends. Very little that actually happened was planned. But since the beginning of the 'systematic contributions to theology' which I began in 1980 with *The Trinity and the Kingdom of God* (ET 1981), and continued most recently with the fourth volume on *The Spirit of Life* (1991, ET 1992), a certain programme has emerged. I have followed up particular lines. For me these lines point, first, to a trinitarian thinking about God; secondly to an ecological thinking about the community of creation; and thirdly, to an eschatological thinking about the indwellings of God in his people, in his Christ, and in our hearts through his life-giving Spirit. In this book on eschatology, the

*In the original: Die alte Meinung findet nicht mehr Anklang,
   dass Ende Ende sei, und Anfang Anfang.
   Man Blocht sie um und also rollt man
   von Althaus über Kreck zu Moltmann.

different horizons of eternal life, the eternal kingdom and the eternal creation draw together to a single focus: *the cosmic Shekinah of God*. God desires to come to his 'dwelling' in his creation, the home of his identity in the world, and in it to his 'rest', his perfected, eternal joy. In 1985, in the doctrine of God (*God in Creation*), the goal and culminating point was God's sabbath; in this doctrine about the future I am focussing attention on the goal of God's eschatological Shekinah, in which the whole creation will be new and eternally living, and every created thing will with unveiled face arrive at its own self. In my christology, *The Way of Jesus Christ*, I used messianic dimensions, and in my pneumatology, *The Spirit of Life*, I came back to the vitality of Yahweh's *ruach*; so it is easy to see how much Israelite and present Jewish thinking has influenced me, and how profoundly. For this I should like to mention with particular gratitude Ernst Bloch and Franz Rosenzweig.

None of us are given hope just for ourselves. The hope of Christians is always hope for Israel too; the hope of Jews and Christians is always hope for the peoples of the world as well; the hope of the peoples of the world is always also hope for this earth and everything that lives in it. And hope for the whole community of creation is ultimately hope that its Creator and Redeemer will arrive at his goal, and may find in creation his home.

Theological Method: Suggestions in a Community: I am often asked about my theological method, and seldom provide an answer. At a time when so many colleagues are concerned solely with questions of method, what interests me are theological ideas, and their revision and innovation. There is a personal reason for this, among other things. As a child I underwent no very profound Christian socialization, but grew up with the poets and philosophers of German Idealism. When I was forced to become a most unhappy soldier, at the end of 1944, I took with me Goethe's poems and his *Faust*, and Nietzsche's *Zarathustra*. I only acquired a Bible when one was given me by an American chaplain, in a prisoner-of-war camp in Belgium, and it was there that I began to read it for the first time. Since the moment when I began to study theology (first in England, in the prisoner-of-war camp at Norton, near Nottingham, and then, from 1948, in Göttingen) everything theological has been for me marvellously new. I have first to discover everything for myself, and understand it, and make it my own. Right down to the present day, theology has continued to be for me a tremendous adventure, a journey of discovery into a, for me, unknown country, a voyage without the certainty of a return, a path into the unknown with many surprises and not without disappointments. If I have a theological virtue at all, then it is one that has never hitherto been recognized as such: curiosity.

I have never done theology in the form of a defence of ancient doctrines or ecclesiastical dogmas. It has always been a journey of exploration. Consequently my way of thinking is experimental – an adventure of ideas – and my style of communication is to suggest. I do not defend any impersonal dogmas, but nor do I merely express my own personal opinion. I make suggestions within a community. So I write without any built-in safeguards, recklessly as some people think. My own propositions are intended to be a challenge to other people to think for themselves – and of course they are a challenge to objective refutation too. Theologians also belong to the *communio sanctorum*, the communion of saints, provided that the true saints are not merely justified sinners but accepted doubters too, thus belonging just as much to the world as to God.

Theology is a community affair. Consequently theological truth takes the form of dialogue, and does so *essentially*, not just for the purposes of entertainment. There are theological systems which are not only designed to be non-contradictory in themselves, but aim to remain undisputed from outside too. They are like fortresses which cannot be taken, but which no one can break out of either, and which are therefore starved out. I have no desire to build any such fortress for myself. My image is the Exodus of the people, and I await theological Reed Sea miracles. For me theology is not church dogmatics, and not a doctrine of faith. It is *imagination for the kingdom of God* in the world, and for the world in God's kingdom. This means that it is always and everywhere *public* theology, and never, ever, a religious ideology of civil and political society – not even so-called Christian society. Some people think that I say too much theologically, and more about God than we can know. I feel profoundly humble in the face of the mystery that we cannot know, so I say everything I think I know.

The Aim: Integrating Eschatology: With this eschatology, I am aiming at an integration of perspectives which so often diverge: the perspectives of 'individual' and universal eschatology, the eschatology of history and the eschatology of nature too. The traditional mediaeval, Protestant and modern eschatologies concentrated on the individual hope with which the questions of personal living and dying were answered. What is going to happen to me when I die, at the Last Judgment and afterwards? Where can I find enduring certainty in my living and my dying? The salvation of the individual and, in the individual, the salvation of the soul, was so much at the centre of things that the salvation of the body, human society and the cosmos were pushed out on to the sidelines, or did not receive any attention at all. But if the Christian hope is reduced to the salvation of the soul in a heaven beyond death, it loses its power to renew life and change the world, and its flame is quenched; it dies away into no more than a gnostic yearning for redemption from this world's vale of tears.

Ever since Augustine, 'God and the soul' have gone together and, following his lead, people have put the fate of the soul at the centre of the ultimate questions. There are two reasons for this. On the one hand, we have the well-known condemnation of the millenarian historical hope by the mainline churches. If there is no longer any historical future worth hoping for, all that is left is the vista of eternity, an eternity equally close to every time, and equally far off. But on the other hand, the Constantinian imperial churches condemned early Christian millenarianism only because they saw themselves in the Christian imperium as 'the holy rule' of Christ's Thousand Years' empire. So every future hope for a different, alternative kingdom of Christ was feared and condemned as heresy. The completion of history was pushed out by the completion of the individual life in death. Universal eschatology lost all its relevance. If the church as the kingdom of Christ is the last thing in history, then all that can come after the church is the end itself. So universal eschatology was found only as an apocalyptic expectation of the end directed to the era after that symbolic thousand years of the church's holy rule. In order to bring individual and universal eschatology into a living relation to one another, therefore, the presentative millenarianism of the holy rule, the holy empire and 'the Christian era' must be dispelled. Hope as the embracing theological category has to be freed from the wreckage of Christian history.

We shall only be able to overcome the unfruitful and paralysing confrontation between the personal and the cosmic hope, individual and universal eschatology, if we neither pietistically put the soul at the centre, nor secularistically the world. The centre has to be *God*, God's kingdom and God's glory. The first three petitions in the

Lord's prayer make this clear. What do we really and truly hope for? We hope for the *kingdom of God*. That is first and foremost a hope for God, the hope that God will arrive at his rights in his creation, at his peace in his sabbath, and at his eternal joy in his image, human beings. The fundamental question of biblical eschatology is: when will God show himself in his divinity to heaven and earth? And the answer is to be found in the promise of the coming God: 'the whole earth is full of his glory' (Isa. 6.3).

This glorifying of God in the world embraces the *salvation* and eternal life of human beings, the *deliverance* of all created things, and the *peace* of the new creation.

Christian eschatology has four horizons:

1. It is hope in God for God's glory.
2. It is hope in God for the new creation of the world.
3. It is hope in God for the history of human beings with the earth.
4. It is hope in God for the resurrection and eternal life of human people.

That is the *ontic* order of the different horizons of Christian eschatology. But because the *noetic* order is always the reverse of the ontic order of things, our perception has to begin, not with the cause, but with the effect. So in eschatology it makes sense to begin with the personal hope, then to advance to the historical hope, and finally to pass on to the cosmic hope, so as to end with God's glory for God's sake. The first effect of eschatology is personal faith. New life in this world follows. And out of that springs the hope for the redemption of the body and the expectation of the transformation of this whole world into God's kingdom.

I have put forward the ideas in this book in lectures given in recent years in Tübingen and at Emory University, Atlanta. I should therefore like first to thank the students who listened to me with patience and criticism and also, as I sensed, with enjoyment. The books I have published grew out of lectures; they were therefore written for students and professional theologians, but not least for all who love or are interested in theology.

The individual chapters of the present book were discussed with my last three assistants, Carmen Krieg, Dr Claudia Rehberger and Dr Thomas Kucharz, and with my doctoral students Dieter Heidt-mann and Steffen Lösel. I should like to thank them for their help and for many corrections. Gisela Hauber has undauntedly typed the manuscript many times. Let me take this opportunity of expressing my sincere thanks to this last 'seminar family' of mine in Tübingen.

Earlier, when I was writing on other subjects, I had a picture before me on my writing desk. And during my work on this eschatology of 'the coming of God' I have again had a picture in front of me: It is the Angel of the Annunciation, by Simone Martini, painted in 1315 and now in the Galleria Uffizi in Florence. The angel is not looking back to the wreckage of history, as does Paul Klee's 'Angelus Novus', which Walter Benjamin called the Angel of History. This angel of the future is gazing with great eyes towards the messianic Child of the coming God, and with the green branches in his hair and in Mary's hand proclaims the Child's birth. The tempest of the divine Spirit is blowing in the angel's garments and wings, as if it had blown him into history. And its meaning is the birth of the future from the Spirit of promise.

Tübingen, Advent 1994   Jürgen Moltmann

ABBREVIATIONS

AAS	Acta apostolical sedes. Commentarium officale, Rome
ASm	Smalcald Articles (1537)
AWA	Archiv zur Weimarer Ausgabe der Werke M. Luther
BöT	Beiträge zur ökumenische Theologie, Munich
BSLK	*Die Bekenntnisschriften der evangelisch-lutherischen Kirche*, Göttingen 1930, 10th ed. 1986
BTh	*Bulletin de Theologie Ancienne et Medievale*, Louvain
CA	Confessio Augustana (Augsburg Confession)
CD	K. Barth, *Church Dogmatics*, ET Edinburgh and Grand Rapids, 1936–69
Com.	Communio: International Catholic Review (Eng. ed., Edinburgh)
DS	H. Denzinger and A. Schönmetzer, eds, *Enchiridion symbolorum definitionum et declarationum de rebus fidei et morum*, 36th ed., Freiburg 1965; see also R.J. Deferrari, *The Sources of Catholic Dogma*, trans. from 13th edition of Denzinger/Schönmetzer, St Louis and London 1955
Eranos	Eranos-Jahrbuch, Zürich
ET	English translation
EvTh	*Evangelische Theologie*, Munich
FThSt	Freiburger theologische Studien, Freiburg
FGLP	Forschungen zur Geschichte und Lehre des Protestantismus, Munich
HWP	*Historisches Wörterbuch der Philosophie*, ed. J. Ritter, Basel etc., 1971 ff.
HZ	*Historische Zeitschrift*, Tübingen
KJV	King James' Version
MQR	*Methodist Quarterly Review*, New York
MThZ	*Münchener theologische Zeitschrift*, Munich

NTA.NS	Neutestamentliche Abhandlungen, neue Serie, Münster
NZSTh	*Neue Zeitschrift für systematische Theologie und Religionsgeschichte*, Berlin
PhB	Philosophische Bibliothek, Hamburg
Philologus	*Philologus. Zeitschrift für Klassische Philologie*, Berlin
QD	Questiones Disputatae, Freiburg
RE³	*Realenzklopädie für protestantische Theologie und Kirche*, Leipzig, reprint Graz
RGG³	*Die Religion in Geschichte und Gegenwart*, 3rd ed., Tübingen 1957–65
TDNT	*Theological Dictionary of the New Testament* (trans. of *ThWNT* by G.W. Bromiley), Grand Rapids and London 1964–76
ThG(B)	*Theologie der Gegenwart*, Bergen-Enkheim
ThQ	*Theologische Quartalschrift*, Tübingen
ThWNT	*Theologisches Wörterbuch zum Neuen Testament*, ed. G. Kittel et al., Suttgart 1933–79
TRE	*Theologische Realenzyklopädie*, ed. G. Krause and G. Müller, Berlin 1974ff.
TTh	*Tijdschrift voor theologie*, Bruges etc.
WA	M. Luther, *Werke*, Weimarer Ausgabe, Weimar 1883ff.
WuG	*Wissenschaft und Gegenwart*, Frankfurt
ZKG	*Zeitschrift für Kirchengeschichte*, Stuttgart etc.
ZNW	*Zeitschrift für die neutestamentliche Wissenschaft*, Berlin
ZThK	*Zeitschrift für Theologie und Kirche*, Tübingen

TRANSLATOR'S NOTE

Biblical quotations have been taken from RSV unless a change of wording was required to bring out the author's point. Where English translations of books referred to exist, references to these have been given, but in some cases quotations have been translated directly from the German. The absence in the relevant note of a page reference to the existing translation will make this clear. An exception is Ernst Bloch's *Principle of Hope*: here page references have been given to the English translation, but quotations have nevertheless been translated directly from the German.

A few minor changes have been made to the German text for the benefit of the English-speaking reader. These were made in consultation with Professor Moltmann. In this volume, as in those preceding it, his help has been of inestimable value. For his generous kindness I can only once again express my gratitude. The translator who has such a text and such assistance is privileged.

Margaret Kohl

I

The Coming God

Eschatology Today

I

The Coming God

Eschatology Today

The nineteenth century was 'the Christian era'. In North America the settlers pressed westwards and colonized the continent. In Russia Siberia was conquered, and the continent settled as far as Vladivostok. The European powers set up their empires in Africa, Asia and Latin America, disseminating European civilization with messianic zeal. For Christianity, the evangelization of the whole world seemed within reach, so missionary societies in considerable numbers were founded, most prominent among them the British ones. At the end of the century it looked as if 'the Christian world' would irresistibly prevail. The Ottoman empire disintegrated. India was in British hands. Japan and Korea were opened up for European missions and European trade. China was declared the last great Christian mission field. It is easy enough to understand why Christian millenarianism should have offered itself as universal interpretative historical framework for this unheard-of advance, and for the optimistic faith in progress of the people captured by it: 'The final age of history has begun, and it will be our age, the Christian age.' 'The Christian world' is the kingdom of Christ, in which his saints will rule with him.[1] In this kingdom, immeasurable progress in every respect is still to be had – everything in it is perfectible; but there are no fundamental, revolutionary changes any more. The final revolution took place with the seizure of technological and political power over the whole world. Now everything is simply a matter of evolution and proper development. The kingdom of God is so near that it has already become the highest good of morality and the goal of historical development. Humanity can almost arrive at everlasting peace simply by its own efforts.

I

The Coming God

Eschatology Today

ıe nineteenth century was 'the Christian era'. In North America the
tlers pressed westwards and colonized the continent. In Russia
ıeria was conquered, and the continent settled as far as
adivostok. The European powers set up their empires in Africa,
ia and Latin America, disseminating European civilization with
ssianic zeal. For Christianity, the evangelization of the whole
rld seemed within reach, so missionary societies in considerable
nbers were founded, most prominent among them the British
es. At the end of the century it looked as if 'the Christian world'
uld irresistibly prevail. The Ottoman empire disintegrated. India
s in British hands. Japan and Korea were opened up for European
ssions and European trade. China was declared the last great
ristian mission field. It is easy enough to understand why
ristian millenarianism should have offered itself as universal
erpretative historical framework for this unheard-of advance, and
the optimistic faith in progress of the people captured by it: 'The
ıl age of history has begun, and it will be our age, the Christian
.' 'The Christian world' is the kingdom of Christ, in which his
·s will rule with him.[1] In this kingdom, immeasurable progress in
 respect is still to be had – everything in it is perfectible; but
 are no fundamental, revolutionary changes any more. The final
 ution took place with the seizure of technological and political
power over the whole world. Now everything is simply a matter of
evolution and proper development. The kingdom of God is so near
that it has already become the highest good of morality and the goal
of historical development. Humanity can almost arrive at everlasting
peace simply by its own efforts.

Christian millenarianism spread the bow of its hope over the great syntheses of the Christian world in the Christian century – over church and culture, throne and altar, mission and conquest, science and world domination. It bolstered up European, Russian and American imperialism through the messianic sense of its mission to redeem the world. It elevated historical self-confidence with the solemn rhetoric of the perfecting of the world at the end of history.

The millenarian hope transported what was eschatological into history and imbued what was historical with a messianic passion. Divided though the Christian churches and nations were in the nineteenth century, political millenarianism possessed them all. What mobilized millions in the USA as the American dream of 'the New World'[2] became in Tsarist Russia the Russian dream of the world's End-time redemption. Moscow was 'the third Rome' and there was to be no fourth.[3] The messianism of the Byzantine empire became the matrix for Orthodox eschatology.[4] This forged the Russian idea that, after the fall of Constantinople, Moscow had taken over leadership of the one Christian-Orthodox empire, and with it had inherited the Byzantine claim to world hegemony too. In the British empire, the claim to sovereignty was in many ways religiously transfigured, and motivated by missionary zeal. In the Spanish empire, subjugation and baptism were one and the same, in the spread of *cristiandad*. In Prussia's Germany, 'culture-Protestant-ism' drew eschatology into history. Kant's ethics and Hegel's philosophy of history provided its framework and justification. In a secular way, France saw herself as the pioneer and guardian of civilization for the peoples of her African colonies.

I have painted with these few strokes this picture of the messianism of the Christian world, and the millenarianism of the nineteenth century 'Christian age', as a reminder of the background to the problems of Christian eschatology in the century that followed. It was not just theoretical problems that elicited a new formulation of eschatology – problems about the relationship between history and eschatology, completion within history and at its end, millenarianism and apocalyptic. The deadlocks arising from the historical experiences of the first half of the twentieth century also led to this reinterpretation.

Between 1914 and 1918, in the annihilating battles of the First World War, the messianic dreams of England, Germany, Russia and France turned into apocalyptic nightmares of death. The fall of the

Tsar in the October Revolution of 1917 and his murder led to the secularization of the Russian idea, and to Soviet millenarianism in the form of Stalinism. The United States decided the conflict when it entered the war, and it passed on its vision of humanity to the League of Nations. But 'the American century' that followed did not last long either. In Germany, the collapse of the Kaiser's empire and the entr'acte of the Weimar democracy were succeeded by the political messianism of 'the Führer', national 'rebirth' and the dream of the Third Reich of the Germanic race, the Thousand Years' empire, and the nihilistic will for 'the final solution' of the Jewish question. Only the destruction of Europe and the unconditional capitulation of 1945 brought the definitive end of the German dream.

The Christian world with its Christian age came to a terrible end, destroying itself in two world wars. The colonized peoples freed themselves from the colonial empires. Auschwitz extinguished the Jewish and Christian dream about the assimilation of the Jews into the Christian world. With Hiroshima, humanity lost its atomic innocence, and with Chernobyl its ecological innocence too. The terrors of twentieth-century history irrevocably shattered all nineteenth-century chiliastic and messianic projects, in both their religious and their secular form. What took their place? In many countries and in many sectors of life they were replaced by apocalyptic, whether in its religious or its secular form. Just as millenarianism draws eschatology into history in a positive sense, in order to establish the kingdom of God 'already here on earth' (Heinrich Heine's phrase), modern apocalyptic draws eschatology into history in a negative sense, in order 'already here on earth' to enact the nuclear 'Armageddon' and the ecological 'Chernobyl'.

Consciously or unconsciously, the eschatological thinking of the present day is determined by the messianic visions of the nineteenth century, and by the apocalyptic terrors experienced in the history of the twentieth. What hope can be justified, once we wake up out of the messianic dreams and resist the apocalyptic anxieties? What can eschatology mean, if it cannot be drawn into history, either chiliastically or apocalyptically, without destroying the world? In this first chapter we shall be looking not only at theological eschatology, but also at the way the philosophers grapple with messianism and apocalyptic. As we have seen, the eschatological problem of the present day is not merely theological; it is political too. It is the problem of history itself. In the present crises of our human world, End-times are heralded. Every eschatology in its own way plays a part in the judgments which we ourselves bring upon our world.

§1 THE TRANSPOSITION OF ESCHATOLOGY INTO TIME

There are already so many general surveys of contemporary eschatology, and so many classifications of their different trends, that it seems superfluous to add to them here.[5] Because ever since 1964 my own *Theology of Hope* has itself been the subject of accounts of this kind, in this chapter I shall merely try to clarify the category of Christian eschatology. If as category for 'the Last Things' we take present and future *time*, the category becomes difficult to maintain in the face of time's transience. If we take *eternity* as category for 'the Last Things', it is difficult to relate the category specifically to the present and the future, since eternity is simultaneous to all times, and is equally indifferent towards them. Here, in dispute with consistently futurist eschatology and the absolute eschatology of eternity, I propose to follow the line taken in *The Theology of Hope*, and put forward *Advent* as eschatological category, and the category *Novum* as its historical reverse side.

The tension of modern theological eschatology is generally said to be the antithesis between futurist eschatology and presentative eschatology. 'The end of all things', it is said, must either lie wholly and entirely in the future, or have wholly and entirely already come, and thus be present. According to this viewpoint, future and present lie along the same temporal line. So it is then also easy to find a reconciling solution when distinguishing in temporal terms between that which is 'now already' present and that which is 'not yet' present. If the kingdom of God is the quintessence of Christianity's eschatological message, then according to this viewpoint it is 'already there' in a hidden sense, but is 'not yet' present in the sense of being already manifest. The hope is then that what is *not yet* can after all still *be*. But this is only an apparent solution. Resignation knows that everything which 'now already' exists will 'no longer' exist tomorrow; for everything that comes into being passes away, even that which does 'not yet' exist. With these notions of linear time – the 'now already' and the 'not yet' – eschatology cannot be comprehended at all; it can only be dissolved altogether. How did this transposition of eschatology into temporal terms come about?

1. Prophetic Theology

Its *initial form* can be found in the 'prophetic theology' of the seventeenth century.[6] Here the Bible was no longer read as a document of God's self-revelation. It was viewed as a divine prophecy of the future history of the world. The subject of the historical testimonies of the Old and New Testament scriptures is the sovereignty of God, and the realization of that sovereignty in history. Scripture is inerrant, for all prophetic predictions have been fulfilled in Israel's history, and in the history of Christ and the church. So the eschatological prophecies which have not yet been fulfilled will be fulfilled too, in the End-time.

The great theme of this 'prophetic' exegesis was the recognition of the *series temporum*, the stages of time; through this the faithful were to be given the correct insight into God's redemptive plan: this is to be fulfilled successively in the different phases of salvation history, the seven ages of the history of the world. *Prophetia est quasi rerum futurarum historia*, declared Cocceius: prophecy is, as it were, the history of future things. All prophecy is *anticipata historia*, said van den Honert. In the nineteenth century Gottfried Menken maintained, somewhat more simply, that the Bible was 'a divine commentary on divine acts' in history.[7] If the rule of God is the scarlet thread running through the writings of the Old and the New Testament, then the *mysterium salutis* – the mystery of salvation – is one and the same as the *mysterium gubernationis Dei* – the mystery of God's providence; for salvation is effected in a redemptive history in accordance with God's salvific plan. The Revelation of John, which Luther brushed aside, becomes as the last book in the Bible the most important, for it contains the prophecy of the End-time, the beginnings of which can already be detected in the present. The interpretation of this secret revelation in terms of contemporary history stems from the tradition of this 'prophetic' theology. Prophetic theology tacitly assumes that history and eschatology, experienced present and predicted future, lie along one and the same temporal line.

2. Albert Schweitzer

A *second form* can be found in what is known as consistent (in English sometimes 'thoroughgoing') eschatology. This began with

Albert Schweitzer's famous *Quest for the Historical Jesus* ([1906]
1913, ET of 1906 ed., 1910). Schweitzer described research into the
life of Jesus from its beginnings in the early years of the Enlightenment down to his own day, in order to show the futility of this
'mighty act of scientific honesty'. The idea was to pierce through the
dogmatic icons of the church's christology with the help of modern
historical-critical methods, in order to discover Christianity's primary historical rock in 'the life of Jesus'. The dogmatically conceived,
divine human being Christ was to be replaced by the true Jesus of
Nazareth, the Galilean, whose historical personality would be
understood in human terms, and who would be willingly followed
out of personal conviction. Historical studies were to bring modern
men and women to the point where they would encounter Jesus
directly, as the disciples did long ago.

But then, as early as 1894, the young Schweitzer discovered from
Mark 10–11 that this real Jesus is someone totally alien. Researchers
into the life of Jesus set out to find the Jesus of history, and thought
that he could then, as he really is, be set in our own time as teacher
and saviour. They loosened the bonds which for centuries had
fettered him to the doctrine of the church, and saw coming towards
them the historical person of Jesus. But Jesus did not stop. He passed
our time by, returning to his own.[8] 'The Jesus of Nazareth who came
forward publicly as the Messiah, who preached the ethic of the
Kingdom of God, who founded the Kingdom of Heaven upon earth,
and died to give His work its final consecration, never had any
existence.'[9] For, so Schweitzer maintained, his message was not a
message about ethics at all. It was an apocalyptic message. He
preached the kingdom of God, not as an amelioration of the world
but as its downfall and end. The one who stands before us is not the
moral teacher of the Sermon on the Mount; he is the apocalyptic
proclaimer of the End-time catastrophe. The dreamed-up ideals of
the modern world's culture-Christianity have nothing in common
with either Jesus or early Christianity. The kingdom of God which
Jesus proclaimed as near, is not the goal of moral or historical
development. It breaks into this world out of the transcendence and
puts an end to it.[10] From this Schweitzer drew his conclusion:
'Eschatology makes it impossible to attribute modern ideas to Jesus
and then by way of "New Testament Theology" take them back
from him as a loan, as even Ritschl not so long ago did with such
naiveté.'[11]

Although he wanted to put an end to the quest for the true 'life of Jesus', Schweitzer himself unwittingly wrote just such a life himself: If Jesus' life and death are entirely shaped by his eschatological, apocalyptic expectation of the kingdom of God, then the history of his life is an 'eschatological' history. It is constituted by an eschatological hope and by three historical disappointments:

1. Jesus expects the transcendent break-in of the kingdom of God in the near future, and according to Luke 10 hastily sends out his seventy disciples into Israel's towns. He does not expect them to return.

2. When, contrary to expectation, they do return, Jesus arrives at the conviction that, according to the divine will, believers would be spared the tribulations of the messianic age if he were to take these upon himself. So he hastens to 'compel' the coming of the kingdom by himself assuming the messianic suffering (see the saying in Matt. 11.12 about 'taking the kingdom by force'). He goes to Jerusalem in order there to constrain the divine verdict. 'This imperious forcing of eschatology into history is also its destruction; its assertion and abandonment at the same time.'[12] But when the End-time still failed to materialize after his death on Golgotha, this meant that his eschatological expectation of an imminent end was disappointed for a second time.

3. On the basis of the Easter appearances, the disciples acquired a new, assured hope and new expectation that the end was imminent. But when that end still failed to come even in the second generation (II Peter 3.4), they took their disappointment to be final. They stripped the Jesus religion of all further eschatological expectation, and transformed it into a religion that was ecclesiastical and sacramental. The messianic hope for God's future was replaced by the presence of eternity, mediated by the church.

To sum up the argument: 'The delay of the parousia' which has continued for two thousand years makes Christian eschatology impossible. Jesus's eschatological expectation of an imminent end did violence to history. But the wheel of history turned on un-moved, and world history will 'continue to run its course as every sane person knows'.[13] Schweitzer then abandoned his 'historical Jesus's, the Jesus who had come to grief over his eschatological enthusiasm, and behind Jesus' eschatology sought for his 'moral will' and his hope for 'the final moral perfecting of the world'.[14] We can forget the imaginative eschatological imagery, but 'we bow before the mighty will that lies behind it, and seek to serve it in our own time'.[15]

Like Johannes Weiss, Schweitzer shrank back from insight into the eschatology of Jesus, turning away from the early Christianity that was so strange and alien, to the nineteenth-century culture-Christianity with which he was familiar. Drawing on the notion of the infinite temporal line and the history which 'will continue to run its course' (a notion based on an optimistic faith in progress), he rebutted the eschatology of Jesus and the early Christians.

But is his own confidence in time not a utopia? How can world history 'continue to run its course' if there is no longer any world? After Hiroshima and Chernobyl, 'every sane person' knows that limits have been set to our time, and that we are living in the 'End-time' in which the end of humanity and all higher forms of life on earth is possible at any moment. Schweitzer, and the 'consistent eschatology' school of Martin Werner and Fritz Buri that followed him, consistently abolished eschatology altogether. Their error was to transpose eschatology into time, instead of seeing in eschatology a transformation of time itself. But true eschatology is not about future history; it is about the future *of* history. Anyone who, like Schweitzer, 'imperiously forces' eschatology into history has already abandoned it. Apocalyptic within history is no more eschatology than is millenarianism within history. But it is millenarianism within history which is inherent in the idea to which Schweitzer turned – the notion of a 'final moral perfecting of the world'. The struggle about theological recognition of the eschatology of Jesus and the early Christians was nothing other than the struggle of culture-Christianity against the withdrawal by historical criticism of the basis for its own legitimation in the early Christian faith. 'The historical foundation of Christianity . . . no longer exists.'[16] We can see in Johannes Weiss and Albert Schweitzer how culture-Christianity was cut adrift from the early Christianity that had now been rediscovered, and from Jesus himself; and with this, Protestant culture-Christianity became inwardly eroded and untenable, only to founder altogether in the terrors of the First World War.

3. Oscar Cullmann

A *third form* of this transposition of eschatology into time can be found in the salvation-history theology of Oscar Cullmann.[17] His theological work on the New Testament is directed towards the discussion about the disclosures of consistent eschatology on the one hand, and 'the radical solutions' offered by Bultmann's demythologization on the other. He tries to mediate between the two concepts – the 'not yet' of consistent eschatology and the 'now already' of the existentialist interpretation; and for this he takes as basis the linear concept of time. If the kingdom of God is 'at hand', then it is neither wholly present, nor wholly not-present. With his message, Jesus has rather inaugurated a 'new division of time'.[18] Since the coming of Christ, we have been living in a new section of time. As Christians see it, Christ is 'the mid-point of time'. So we rightly count time chronologically as 'Before Christ' and 'After Christ'. 'The fullness of time' – which is also called 'the turn of the age' – is no longer in the future, as in Jewish apocalyptic. It is to be found in the Christ event – i.e., in the past. Time after the coming of Christ must be seen as 'fulfilled but not yet completed time'. It is no longer a time of pure expectation, nor is it as yet the eternal present of the time of completion. That is why Christians live between the 'now already' and the 'not yet'.

According to Cullmann, the differentiation of the times into different sections is conditioned by salvation history. Time takes its quality from the things that God allows to happen in it. Since Christ's coming, the time of the Holy Spirit has begun. This is the time of the church, between Christ's ascension and his parousia – that is to say, it is a transitional time between the fulfilment in Christ of the Old Testament time of promise, and the manifestation of the salvation that has taken place in him. 'The delay of the parousia' which Schweitzer conjured up was not for early Christians a disappointment for their faith. It was merely 'an error in perspective, which in isolated passages is corrected in the New Testament itself (II Peter 3.8)'.[19] With Christ, time did not come to an end, but a new division of time began, and the end of time came closer. The early Christians thought in terms of decades, a measurable time. But that is not the essential point. It was not expectation of an end imminent in a temporally measurable sense that provided the foundation for Christian faith; it was faith in the salvation already accomplished in Christ that evoked this expectation of an imminent end. For the temporal tension between the 'now already' and the 'not yet', Cullmann repeatedly uses the image about the decisive battle in a war and V-day, the day of victory. As Stalingrad and El Alamein showed in 1943, during the Second World War, the decisive battle can already have taken place, and yet the defeat of the enemy can still take its time. 'The hope of the final victory is so much the more vivid because of the unshakably firm conviction that the battle that decides the victory has already taken place.'[20] Christ has already won the decisive battle, but the day of victory will come only when the Holy Spirit has interpenetrated the whole world.

Cullmann's basic conception is the salvation-history theology which was widely held in the nineteenth century and which has its roots in the 'prophetic theology' of the seventeenth. Consequently at the centre of his theology is the link between prophecy and history: 'The redemptive history as a whole is "prophecy".'[21] Prophecy is fulfilled in history, since it is 'history viewed from the prophetic point of view'.[22] So Christ is both fulfilled prophecy and the prophetic beginning of the End-time. The concept upon which Cullmann draws to help explain this salvation-history complex is the idea of linear time. Inherent in the 'revelatory history' of the Bible is a linear view of time, over against the cyclical view of Hellenism.[23] But the linear view of time is simply calendar time, BC and AD. This now brings us daily closer to Christ's parousia. From Christ 'the mid-point of time', Cullmann then develops his insights into God's redemptive plan, on which salvation history is based: from creation it passes to humanity; from humanity to Israel; from Israel to the remnant of Israel; then comes the One Christ; from him come the apostles; from the apostles the church; from the church the new humanity; and then the new creation. From the many to the One, from the One to the many.[24]

This salvation-history eschatology is probably the Christian eschatology most widely held. Its thesis is that salvation history determines time, so that the continuance of time does not destroy the eschatological hope. But the weaknesses of this thesis are obvious:

1. If the time between the decisive battle and V-day lasts too long, it gives rise to a justifiable doubt as to whether the decisive battle really has taken place, and whether the enemy has not been underestimated. After the victory of the French campaign in 1940, many people in Germany thought that the war had been decided. Their error was a fatal one.

2. The notion of linear time is not in fact biblical, as Cullmann maintains. It is a modern scientific concept, although it can actually already be found in Aristotle's *Physics*. Because it quantifies the

times, it is impossible to qualify them in terms of salvation history. Past and future are merely segments on a parameter without any direction, and are equal in quality. Only when a pointer or time index is added, is time given a particular direction. Because the future can become past, while the past can never become future, time 'flows' out of the future into the past. But for all that, we count the years from the past to the future, and thereby unconsciously declare future to be the future past. Cullmann imagines the salvation-history future of Christ in measurable time. 'The Last Day' (which is also a German term – *der jüngste Tag* – for the Last Judgment) must then in foreseeable time be the final page of the calendar. This may surely be called in his own words 'an error in perspective', an error due to his concept of the linear nature of time.

3. A theology of salvation history which is based on God's pre-programmed 'redemptive plan' is Enlightenment theology. It is nothing other than historical Deism. God becomes the watchmaker of world history and the author of a master blueprint of foreknow-ledge. Once this has been drawn up, he has no further need to intervene. The calendar will one day bring 'the day of Jesus Christ'. Where is God's freedom in all this? Where can his living presence be experienced? Is not the very opposite the case – that it is not 'the Last Day' that brings Christ's parousia, but Christ's parousia that brings 'the Last Day'? For Christ surely does not come 'in time'; he comes to transform time.

The reduction of eschatology to time in the framework of salvation history also really abolishes eschatology altogether, subjecting it to *chronos*, the power of transience. Is 'temporality' really 'the essence of eschatology'?[25]

§2 THE TRANSPOSITION OF ESCHATOLOGY INTO ETERNITY

1. *Karl Barth*

According to Schweitzer, the 'consistent eschatology' of Jesus – that is, his expectation of the imminent coming of the kingdom of God – was crushed by the silent wheel of destiny, which drives forward the history which continues to run its course. After the catastrophe of Christian history in the First World War, a completely new interpretation of eschatology emerged in what was called 'the

theology of crisis'. It was put forward by Karl Barth and Rudolf
Bultmann, but also, independently of these two, by Paul Althaus. It is
not the history that continues to run its silent and inexorable course
which plunges every eschatological expectation of the future into a
destructive crisis; it is the transcendent breaking-in of eternity that
plunges all human history into its final crisis. It is not history that
puts an end to eschatology; it is eschatology that puts an end to
history.[26]

'The ultimate questions and answers, the final decision and the
sound of the last trump' are not going to take place in the never-
never, at some illusory end of history. They happen 'here and now',
when eternity breaks into time, when the call of decision in God's
kerygma brings men and women face to face with the decision that is
final, when people think the idea of God radically through to the end.
The eschaton which Christian eschatology talks about is not the
temporal end of our historical days, as in Karl Kraus's drama 'The
Last Days of Mankind' (1918–19). It is the presence of eternity in
every moment of this present history. 'Over against the Eternal One
there is only one time: eternity', said Kierkegaard. And this was
Barth's understanding too in his second (1922) commentary on
Romans, the fundamental document of 'dialectical theology'. 'Being
the transcendent meaning of all moments, the eternal Moment can
be compared with no moment in time.'[27] Anyone who hears the
thunderous word of the eternal God in the moment, loses interest in
the future. Of course there can be catastrophes in history and nature;
the human race can become extinct. But what has that got to do with
eschatology? 'The end of history' cannot be experienced in future
history, but only at the frontier of time which is eternity. It becomes
present in the moment which lies 'between the times', because it is 'an
atom of eternity', not a moment in time.

Every moment in time can take on the dignity of this eternal
moment, for every moment in time is 'a parable' of the eternal
moment. 'Every moment in time bears within it the unborn secret of
revelation, and every moment can be thus qualified.'[28] To every
moment qualified by the presence of eternity we can say 'the end is
near'. It is not a temporal end that limits time and makes it finite; it is
this presence of eternity. Barth also calls the eternal moment between
the times *nunc aeternum* – eternity is now. In the Christian sense
Christ's parousia takes place in this eternal moment, for the parousia
is the presence of Christ. Barth no longer thinks of 'the frontier of

time' temporally in quantifying terms, but as time's qualitative limitation through eternity. This is God's 'overhanging rock-face', 'the abolition and gathering up of all time and of all that time contains'. It is here that the human being of 'the last' hour stands, the human being who awaits Christ's parousia. 'Far too nigh at hand is the Kingdom of God, far too near is the overhanging rock-face of eternity – in every stone and flower, in every human face! – far too oppressive is the boundary of time – memento mori! – far too insistent and compelling is the presence of Jesus Christ as the turning point of time . . .'[29]

If eschatology has to do with the presence of eternity in the moment, and therefore with this limitation and abolition of time, then the problem of 'the delay of the parousia' collapses of its own accord. For this problem resulted from 'consistent eschatology' and its 'experiences of disappointment' in history. And 'How shall the coming of that which doth not *enter in* ever be *delayed*?'[30] 'This tension of the times has as much or as little to do with the well-known nineteen hundred years of the history of the Church – which quite obviously have "not yet" ushered in the Parousia – as it had with those weeks or months during which the Epistle to the Romans lay in Phoebe's trunk (xvi.1).'[31]

If eschaton means eternity and not End-time, then eschatology has no longer anything to do with the future either. Its tension is not the tension between present and future, the 'now already' and the 'not yet'; it is the tension between eternity and time in past, present and future. When Jesus proclaims that the kingdom of God is 'at hand', he is not looking into the future in the temporal sense; he is looking into the heaven of the present. The kingdom does not 'come' out of the future into the present. It comes from heaven to earth, as the Lord's Prayer tells us.

This view is also maintained by the New Testament scholar C. H. Dodd, in his doctrine of 'realized eschatology'. Jesus's message about the kingdom has no prototype in apocalyptic, as Weiss and Schweitzer asserted. It derives from rabbinic theology.[32] The message is: the kingdom has arrived! According to the rabbinic view, the person who obeys the Torah assumes 'the yoke of God's rule'. This presupposes that God's rule is present. If the person who 'receives it like a child' enters the kingdom of God (Mark 10. 15), then the kingdom must be already present. The call to repentance also presupposes the presence of the kingdom. For Jesus and the early Christians, the kingdom of God has moved out of the sphere of expectation into the sphere of experience.[33] Only its universal manifestation is still to come. This is expected on the basis of what has been experienced. For Dodd too the kingdom of God has a particular closeness only to the present, not to the future. So he integrates the futurist pronouncements of the New Testament with its declarations about the past: 'Many will come and sit at table with Abraham, Isaac, and Jacob' (Matt. 8.11). The kingdom of God embraces both the future and the past because God is king in heaven from all eternity. Jesus proclaims that the kingdom of heaven is now to be revealed on earth. It comes from eternity into time, not out of the future into the present.[34]

2. Paul Althaus

What Karl Barth put forward in 1922 as a transcendental eschatology of eternity, was called 'axiological eschatology' by the young Paul Althaus in the first edition of his book on 'The Last Things' (1922). His book did not cause such a furore in the theological world of the time as did Barth's second exposition of the Epistle to the Romans; but the fact that by 1933 he had revised the book as many as four times is particularly striking evidence of the inward movement of the new eschatology from a time-eternity dialectic towards a future-present dynamic. In order to round off the picture of 'eternity' eschatology, we shall initially look only at the first edition.

Althaus maintains just as radically as Barth that 'The fruit of history is not to be found in history's final temporal condition, but is ascertained from what is beyond history . . . "The Last Things" have nothing to do with the final epoch of history. Eschatology is not interested in the question about a final historical condition.'[35] 'We arrive at the completion not by traversing the longitudinal lines of history to their end, but by erecting everywhere in history the perpendicular line. That is to say, just as every time is equally close to the primordial state and the Fall, so every time is also equally immediate to the completion. In this sense every time is the last time.'[36] Every wave of the sea of time breaks, as it were, on the shore of eternity. With this North-German shore image, F. Holmström complements Barth's Swiss image about the overhanging rock-face. For Althaus, the eschaton is eternity, the completion, Christ's parousia; and it is supra-temporal. That is to say, it does not enter time and cannot therefore 'fail to appear' in time. For this he uses the neo-Kantian value-term 'axiom', constructing from it his concept of 'axiological eschatology'. 'The axiological concept of the Last Things emerges when in the midst of life we encounter the norm' – and by that he means the absolute norm. Then the eternal encounters us as the unconditional in the conditional, and as what is supra-historical in the midst of history.[37]

Like Barth, Althaus was convinced by the experiences of the First World War that all human values and conditions are without exception doomed to die, because they are historical, and are subject to the judgment of eternity. Like Barth, he condemned culture-Christianity and looked for the true origin. Like Barth, he wanted to cut Christian eschatology free from the faith in progress cherished by modern culture-Christianity, bringing it back to its own divine truth. That is why it was necessary to condemn the link between 'the last things' of eschatology and 'the historical things' that belong to belief in progress, to Christian chiliasm, and to the Jewish messianism that was its forerunner and accompaniment.

Because of this opposition to faith in progress and to Hegel's system of the consummation of world history, no saying was so frequently cited by Barth and the dialectical theologians, as well as by Althaus and the theologians of the Luther renaissance, as the famous dictum levelled by von Ranke, the historian, at Hegel, the philosopher of history: 'But I maintain that every epoch is immediate to God, and its value depends not on what emerges from it, but on its own existence, on its own self.'[38] Barth accordingly called eschatology 'the supra-historical', 'unhistorical' and 'primordially historical', and later, in the *Church Dogmatics*, was still saying that in its immediacy to God all history is actually unhistorical.[39] Althaus then maintained the value of every epoch in itself, in contrast to belief in progress: 'Every time is immediate to judgment, immediate to the completion. In this sense every time is last time. All time, not just the last time, will be perpetually ended and gathered up by eternity . . . Every time is to be found in the twilight of Rom. 13.12: "The night is far spent, the day is at hand." '[40]

Barth later criticized what he himself had said, and in 1948 regretted that in 1922 he had put only the 'supra-temporality' of God at the centre, and not his 'post-temporality' too, ' . . . that although I was confident to treat the far-sidedness of the coming kingdom of

God with absolute seriousness, I had no such confidence in relation
to its coming as such' and 'with all this art and eloquence missed . . .
the teleology which it [i.e., Rom. 13.11f.] ascribes to time as it moves
towards a real end'; so that 'in my exposition the one thing that
continues to hold the field as something tangible is the one-sided
supra-temporal understanding of God which I had set out to
combat'.[41] Barth reproached himself because – although he had
fundamentally disrupted the optimism of the neo-Protestant concept
of time – he had then, contrary to his intention, actually confirmed it
by way of a radicalization. But is it really progress if, while ceasing to
understand the frontier which eternity sets to time solely as 'supra-
temporality', we now see it as 'pre-temporality' and 'post-temporality' as well?[42] So that eternity then surrounds time from all sides,
and is contemporaneous with all times, not just to the present? No
eschatological tension as yet enters time just because God's 'post-
temporality' is added to his 'supra-temporality'; nor does this lend
any precedence to the future over against present and past. Even in
his own self-criticism of 1948, Barth did not rediscover that access to
the eschatological hope which he had encountered early on in the
two Blumhardts. His time-eternity dialectic remained stuck fast in
the Platonic thinking about origins pursued by his brother, Heinrich
Barth. It is impossible to see how the *kairos* philosophy of Tillich and
the existential theology of Bultmann can have escaped him, after he
had provided them both in 1922 with the keywords for their zest for
the eternal moment.

Paul Althaus tried to complement his early presentative eschatology by a futurist one in a similar way, adding a teleological
eschatology to his axiological concept. Axiologically, we experience
in the midst of time the timeless validity of absolute value;
teleologically, we perceive it as the goal for our desires and will.
Althaus therefore increasingly taught eschatology in double form:
the presence and future of the kingdom, the believing and hoping,
possessing and awaiting of human beings. 'In the one case eternal life
is a present possession, God's Today, in which the soul is happily at
rest; in the other case it is the goal of hope towards which our
Christian life, bound to the world though it is, presses forward in the
extreme tension of longing.' In just the same way Emil Brunner
added together 'the Eternal as Future and Present'.[43]

The dynamic metaphor which Paul uses in Rom. 13.11f. about the
night being far gone and the day being at hand is pressed by both

Barth and Althaus into the statics of the time-eternity dialectic. It is a contradiction in terms if 'every time' is supposed to lie 'in the twilight of Rom. 13.12'. It confuses God's kairological Today for gospel and faith with the eschatological 'moment' of the raising of the dead (I Cor. 15.52) when Barth talks about the eternal moment which every moment of time can become. Even his own metaphors betray this: the image of the overhanging rock-face which he uses for eternity points to the limit and end of the way, and if 'every wave of time breaks on the shore of eternity', we no longer have to do with a river, not even with a 'river of time'. We are then dealing with the eternal return of the same thing, in the tides, with their ebb and flow. Here time is understood neither eschatologically nor historically, but naturalistically, as transience. To the Eternal One, all times are simultaneous and of equal validity. This view is in line with the blithe resignation of Ecclesiastes, but not with the messianic passion of Isaiah.

3. Rudolf Bultmann

Rudolf Bultmann's eschatology also has to do with the eternal moment, only he puts it to the proof anthropologically, and interprets the Bible's eschatological statements existentially.[44] Eschatology is not an apocalyptic press-report; it teaches us to be aware of the eschatological moment. Because in the *kairos* of God's revelation human beings are faced with 'the ultimate, radical decision' to understand themselves in the light of God or in the light of the world, this moment is 'the final hour'. Because in the kerygma's call to decision, the Last Thing, as the Absolute, has become present, this present is eschatologically qualified. Just as Christ is 'the end of the law', he is also 'the end of history' – not in the temporal sense, but existentially. Through the kerygma, we will in faith be free from the past. The possibility of a true historical mode of existence is thrown open to us here and today. Existential eschatology is not about the future end of the world. It is about 'depriving the world of its worldhood'* in the present. Future is that which comes to meet human beings in the kerygma, and faces them with the final decision. It has nothing to do with calendar time, but is an existential impending condition:† *nunc aeternum – futurum*

---

*'Entweltlichung' – a Heidegger term (Trans.).
†'Bevorstand' – again a Heidegger term (Trans.).

aeternum. The proclamation of Jesus and the Christian kerygma point human beings to the fact of their standing before God and hence that God 'stands before' them. They 'direct [the human being] into his Now as the hour of decision for God'.[45] 'He who hears my word and believes him who sent me has eternal life' (John 5. 24).

Bultmann's eschatology is presentative in the eternal sense not the temporal one, so there is no way in which it can be complemented by a futurist eschatology. His explicit counter-thesis to Schweitzer's consistent eschatology is therefore: 'History is swallowed up by eschatology.'[46] We can nowhere detect any significance in history as a whole, or any finale to world history. For every individual person 'the meaning of history' is to be found in his or her own present existence. So at the end of *History and Eschatology* (1958) he writes, clearly echoing the early Barth: 'Always in your present lies the meaning in history, and you cannot see it as a spectator, but only in your responsible decisions. In every moment slumbers the possibility of being the eschatological moment. You must awaken it.'[47] This pushes aside the problem of 'the delay of the parousia'. Because faith is the practised end of history, in that existence is deprived of its worldhood, there is no need to look for an end of history in the future. Nor should we do so, for if we do, we lose sight of God's present *kairos*, which Bultmann calls 'the eschatological moment'.

With this concentration on the historicity and futurity of present human existence, an apocalyptic end of the world disappears from view. 'Talk about the Last Day must be replaced by talk about *thanatos*' (death).[48] Death as the existential impending condition compels human beings to arrive at their own selves, individualizes them, and brings them to the resolute decision to become themselves. At this point Bultmann is following Heidegger,[49] but Johannes Weiss had already offered this individual eschatology in place of the early Christian eschatology of the end of the world. We no longer believe that 'the world will pass away'. 'The world will further endure, but we, as individuals, will soon leave it. Thereby, we will at least approximate [to] Jesus' attitude in a different sense, if we make the basis of our life the precept . . . "Live as if you were dying." '[50]

Bultmann's existential interpretation of eschatology is correct in its concentration on our own individual existing, but it is unhelpful in its blinkered disregard of world history and the history of nature. To replace world history by the historicity of existence does not make world history disappear. To perceive the future as individual futurity does not disperse the future. To replace 'the Last Day' by my own death does not provide an answer to the question about the future of those who have died.

People are not just individuals for whom only what can be related to their own existence has any relevance. As every glance at the newspaper shows, people are also objects in the struggle between the forces of world history. Men and women do not only individualize history; they participate in it too. So they do not merely ask about themselves. They also enquire about the future of the world in which they participate, and whose object they are. If history is supposed to be based on historicity, then the reverse is, at the very least, just as true: historicity is based on participation in history. The same may be said about futurity. Future is subjectively perceived in the openness to the future of human existence. But this personal openness to the future depends on the prospects of human history and the history of nature. Human beings do not exist only in relation to themselves; they exist too, and first of all, in relation to others and to nature. It is too narrow to view existence solely in the relation of human beings to themselves, not in their social relations as well, and in their bodily, sensory relation to nature.

Christian eschatology teaches hope not only for the soul – the word used for existence in earlier times – but also for the body; not only for the individual but also for the community; not only for the church but also for Israel; not only for human beings but also for the cosmos. This supra-individual horizon of hope can then only be called mythological if one has no concern for the conditions over which this horizon spans its bow. The resignation which confines people to their own selves can hardly be called Christian. To say this does not rule out the fact that 'my decision' plays a decisive part even if the whole world is against me: on the contrary. But the Christian rebellion of conscience which leads to personal consequences in the form of resistance, persecution and suffering is a public rebellion against public demons, injustice and acts of violence; it is not a retreat into an individual chimney-corner.

The eschatology of 'the eternal moment' was not as new as its discoverers and advocates proclaimed it to be. Schleiermacher had already said: 'In the midst of finitude to be one with the Infinite and in every moment to be eternal is the immortality of religion.'[51] And even before him Angelus Silesius wrote:

I am eternity when, from time free,
I join myself in God with God in me.[51a]

Only Schleiermacher and Angelus Silesius did not call this eschatology. They called it mysticism.

§3 THE ESCHATOLOGY OF THE COMING GOD

The eschatology put forward here accords with the *Theology of
Hope* in that it starts from a concept of the future which neither
allows the history 'which continues to run its course' to swallow up
every eschatology, nor permits the eternity that is always present to
put an end to every history. The eschaton is neither the future of time
nor timeless eternity. It is God's coming and his arrival. In order to
express this we shall take an *Advent-like* concept of the future that
springs from the history of God, from the experiences and expectations of God as these are recorded in the biblical writings. We shall
develop this concept philosophically, in an understanding of time
which sees the future as the origin and source of time in general –
time *per se*. We shall take the category of the *novum* – the new thing
– as the historical category which characterizes the eschatological
event in history.

'Interruption' is not an eschatological category. The eschatological category is conversion.[52] An interruption certainly deranges
the normal course of things and the desired goals of our own
affairs, for it disrupts the notion of linear time, the causalities and
homogeneous temporality of 'the river of time'; but it interrupts
only 'for a time'; afterwards everything goes on as before, and the
general run of things remains completely unchanged. But whenever
the eschatological event interrupts the conjunctions of time, these
are changed fundamentally. The prophets 'interrupt', but not just
for a moment; they call the people to the conversion of the courses
of time. Conversion and the rebirth to a new life change time and
the experience of time, for they make-present the ultimate in the
penultimate, and the future of time in the midst of time. From this,
surprising partings of the way emerge, and new ramifications of
time, as the historical narratives of the Old Testament show. The
future-made-present creates new conditions for possibilities in
history. Mere interruption just disturbs; conversion creates new
life.

1. The Coming God

'Peace to you,' says Rev. 1.4, 'from him who *is*, and who *was* and who *is to come*.' We should expect '. . . and from him who *will be*', since according to Greek ideas the presence of God in all three modes of time is an expression of his timeless and simultaneous eternity: Zeus was, Zeus is, Zeus will be: Zeus is eternal. The gods exist in the eternal present of Being, and everything that was, that is, and that will be, is in their eyes present. But here instead of the future of the verb to be (εἶναι), we have the future of the verb to come (ἔρχεσται).[53] The linear concept of time is broken through in its third term. This has a considerable significance for the understanding of God and of time. God's future is not that he will be as he was and is, but that he is on the move and coming towards the world. God's Being is in his coming, not in his becoming. If it were in his becoming, then it would also be in his passing away. But as the Coming One (ὅ ἐρχόμενος), through his promises and his Spirit (which precede his coming and announce it) God now already sets present and past in the light of his eschatological arrival, an arrival which means the establishment of his eternal kingdom, and his indwelling in the creation renewed for that indwelling. The coming of God means the coming of a being that no longer dies and a time that no longer passes away. What comes is eternal life and eternal time. In the eschatological coming, God and time are linked in such a way that God's being in the world has to be thought eschatologically, and the future of time has to be understood theologically.

'The God of Abraham, Isaac and Jacob' is the God of history. Experiences of this God are experiences with a remembered past and an expected future. The God of the Exodus whose appearance Moses experienced on Horeb is not a local God belonging to that particular mountain. He is a God who leads his people forward into liberty as 'a pillar of cloud by day and a pillar of fire by night'. He leaves his holy place and becomes the God who goes ahead of his people, and journeys with them. He sets out with his people in order to arrive at his rest. His name is declared in the mysterious 'I am who I am' or 'I will be the one who I will be' (Ex. 3.14). Whereas the first rendering stresses the reliability of the God who remains true to himself, the second emphasizes his futurity. Ernst Bloch therefore talked about a God 'who has future as the essence of his Being'.[54] Both renderings say that God is there, and will be there, in the place to which his promise calls men and women. God does not need any name in order to be invoked and to be present. God is there. That is enough. All the individual promises in history point beyond their particularity to the universal appearance of God himself: 'The whole earth is full of his glory' (Isa.6.3). All God's individual acts in history point towards 'the day of the Lord'.

The God of hope is himself *the coming God* (Isa.35.4; 40.5). When God comes in his glory, he will fill the universe with his radiance, everyone will see him, and he will swallow up death for ever. This future is God's mode of being in history. The power of the future is his power in time. His eternity is not timeless simultaneity; it is the power of his future over every historical time.[55] It is therefore logical that it was not only God himself who was experienced as 'the Coming One', but that the conveyers of hope who communicate his coming and prepare men and women for his parousia should also be given this title: the Messiah, the Son of man, and Wisdom.[56] The coming God is older than the various expectations of the messiah and the Son of man. These live from the hope for him. By virtue of hope for the coming God, the expected future acquires an inexhaustible 'added value' over against present and past in the experience of time. *Sub specie aeternitatis* not all times are of equal significance. Nor is time experienced as the power of transience, like Chronos, who devours his own children. If God's being is in his coming, then the future that comes to meet us must become the theological paradigm of transcendence.

Entering into God's coming future makes possible a new human becoming: 'Arise, *become* light, for your light *is coming*, and the glory of the Lord is rising upon you' (Isa. 60.1). The proclamation of the near – the coming – the arriving kingdom of God makes human conversion to this future possible. 'Be converted, for the kingdom of heaven is at hand' (Matt. 4.17). This unity between the divine coming and human conversion is 'fulfilled time' (Mark 1.15). The First Epistle of John also links human becoming with the divine coming: 'It does not yet appear what we shall be, but we know that when he appears we shall be like him, for we shall see him as he is' (I John 3.2). The writer is talking about the Christ of the parousia. The eschatology of the coming God calls to life the history of new human becoming, which is a becoming without any passing away, a becoming into lasting being in the coming presence of God.

2. Future or Advent?

European languages generally have two possible ways of talking about what is ahead. *Futurum* means what will be; *adventus* means what is coming. The two words go together with two different conceptions of time.[57]

Future in the sense of *futurum* develops out of the past and present, inasmuch as these hold within themselves the potentiality of becoming and are 'pregnant with future' (Leibniz's phrase). Only that can become which is already implicit or dormant in being, and is heralded in the trends and latencies of the historical process. In the Greek myth, Physis is the eternally fruitful womb of Being. Physis is Being that brings forth. But that is only one side of her: if future (*futurum*) is her eternal process of becoming, past is her eternal process of dying. Matter is both matrix and moloch, the mother who bears and devours, like the Indian goddess Kali in Calcutta. In the process of the ever-recurring 'die and become', the times are equal. The future offers no special reason for hope, for the past predominates, inasmuch as that which is not yet, will one day no longer be. Because what is future is already latent in the tendencies of process, these tendencies cannot, either, bring anything astonishingly new. In this concept of time, the future enjoys no primacy, there is no category *novum*, and really no 'principle of hope' either.[58]

The German word *Zukunft* is not a translation of the Latin *futurum*. It is a translation of *adventus*. But *adventus*, in its turn, is a rendering of the Greek word *parousia*. In secular Greek, *parousia* means the coming of persons, or the happening of events, and literally means presence; but the language of the prophets and apostles has brought into the word the messianic note of hope. The expectation of the parousia is an advent hope. For in the New Testament the past presence of Christ in the flesh, or the present presence of Christ in the Spirit, is never termed *parousia*. The word is kept exclusively for Christ's coming presence in glory. There are not three parousias: in the flesh, in the Spirit, and in glory, as later theological tradition said, in an attempt to put the advent hope on ice. Although *parousia* means arrival, Luther was right when he translated the word as 'Zukunft Christi', the future – or rather the future coming – of Christ, thus bringing into the word the messianic note of hope. To translate *parousia* as 'coming again' or 'second coming' is wrong, because that presupposes a temporary absence.

What happens when we carry this concept of the future into the usual linear notions of time? We then find that we are dealing with two different concepts of the future: on the phenomenal level – the level of everyday experience – we are conscious of past time – present time – future time. But on the transcendental level we then presuppose the future as the necessary condition if time is to be a possibility at all.[59] The future as God's power in time must then be understood as the source of time. It then defines the past as past-future and the present as present-future and future time as future-future. Historical time is irreversible: the future becomes the past, but the past never again becomes future. That is because reality emerges from potentiality, all past and present realities being realized potentialities; but reality never again turns into potentiality. Just as potentiality surpasses reality, so the future exceeds the present and the past. Of course this is true only of the transcendental future of time, not future time in the phenomenal sense. If transcendental future is the source of time, then it does not abolish time as does timeless-simultaneous eternity, nor does it lose itself in the maelstrom of the general transience of all temporal being. It rather throws open the time of history, qualifying historical time as time determined by the future.

The 'eschaton' of an eschatology which works with the concept of God suggested here, and with this advent understanding of the future, is not an eternity which can neither *enter* time, nor remain *outside* time. This eschaton means a change in the transcendental conditions of time. With the coming of God's glory, future time ends and eternal time begins. Without a transformation of time like this, eschatology cannot be thought. This actually already emerges from the idea of the resurrection of the dead and the life of the world to come, in which death is no more; for all reflections about time here and now are determined by the *memento mori*, the remembrance of death.

Futurist eschatology is a contradiction in terms, because the future (in the static sense of *Futur*) cannot be an eschatological category.

An eschatology of the eternal present is a contradiction in terms, because it abolishes time.

Only the idea of the coming God, and the advent concept of time which is in accord with him, open up categories for eschatology.

3. *The Category* Novum

'Newness is not a category which is determinative for the divine. That category is eternity', said Bultmann.[60] This may be applicable to deity in Greek religion but it is not true of the messianic religions of biblical origin. For them the category *novum* – the new thing – is the historical side of their eschatological openness to the future. It is not without good reason that Gerhard von Rad headed his account of the 'Theology of Israel's Prophetic Traditions':

> Remember not the former things, nor consider the things of old. For behold, *I* purpose to do a new thing (Isa. 43.18f.).[61]

The category *novum* emerges theologically among Israel's prophets first of all. To put it briefly, after the destruction of Jerusalem and the temple in 587 BC, the God of history, known from the remembered past of the Exodus and the settlement of the promised land, became 'a hidden God', a 'God who was far off', and who 'had turned his face away from Israel'. The prophets taught that the catastrophe of 587 had to be seen as God's judgment, and that the people had to hold fast to Israel's God in this light. In proclaiming the judgment on God's people, the prophets also proclaimed a new act on God's part. True, they interpreted the ancient traditions about God, but over against these they also brought something new to expression. They proclaimed the God of history as the creator of a new future. In this way the foundation of salvation shifted from the experienced past to the expected future. The remembrance that had been severed turned into new hope. Hosea promises a new settlement of the land, Isaiah the new David, Jeremiah the new covenant, Deutero-Isaiah a new Exodus, and Ezekiel a new temple. In Isa. 43.18 the breach between the old and the new becomes so deep that hope takes over from remembrance altogether.[62]

In prophecy the category *novum* acquires at least two typical characteristics:

1. What is new announces itself in the judgment on what is old. It does not *emerge* from the old; it makes the old obsolete. It is not simply the old in new form. It is also a new creation. That is why *barah* is used – the word employed exclusively for the divine creation. *Creatio ex vetere* – creation out of the old – stands in analogy to *creatio ex nihilo* – creation out of nothing; for it is *creatio nova*, a new creation.

2. The first anticipatory reaching out to the new future which God has promised to create casts back to the analogies of history. In the images of the new Exodus, the new settlement, the new covenant, the new Jerusalem, what is new is presented as a return of what has been lost and as a renewal of what is past. But the images of the new Exodus and the new Jerusalem always hold within themselves more than was ever contained in the old, for the old is past, and for remembrance now only has the significance of being the advance radiance of what is new, or its prototype. For hope, what God sent forth in the past becomes the prologue to the future.

The category *novum* dominates the eschatological language of the whole of the New Testament. The reason for this is probably to be found in the Easter appearances of the crucified Christ. They point the men and women concerned towards an eschatologically new intervention of God's creative activity. The raising of Christ from the dead has no analogies in experienced history, and is comparable only with the miracle of existence itself (Rom. 4.17). Consequently the future of the risen One is nothing less than new creation. The person who is 'in Christ' is already here and now 'a new creation'. For that person, as Paul says, echoing Isa. 43.18, 'the old has passed away, behold, the new has come' (II Cor. 5.17). From this follows 'the new commandment', 'the new obedience', 'the new song', 'the new people of God' made up of Jews and Gentiles, and the finale: 'Behold, I make all things new.' The new thing, the καινός, the *novum ultimum*, is the quintessence of the wholly other, marvellous thing that the eschatological future brings. With the raising of Christ from the dead, the future of the new creation sheds its lustre into the present of the old world, and in 'the sufferings of this present time' kindles hope for new life. Again we find the two characteristics which make the category *novum* the eschatological category:

1. Just as the raised Christ does not *develop* out of the crucified and dead Christ, the *novum ultimum* – the ultimate new thing – does not *issue* from the history of the old. Between the old and the new, the New Testament sets the death of Christ, and the dying-with-Christ-to-this-world symbolized by Christian baptism. The new thing is the surprising thing, the thing that could never have been expected. It evokes unbounded astonishment, and transforms the people whom it touches.

2. Yet even the eschatological 'new thing' is not without analogy. If it were completely incomparable, as Marcion said, it would be

impossible to say anything about it at all. What is eschatologically new, itself creates its own continuity, since it does not annihilate the old but gathers it up and creates it anew. It is not that another creation takes the place of this one: '*this* perishable nature must put on the imperishable, and *this* mortal nature must put on immortality' (I Cor. 15.53). The raised Christ is the crucified Christ and no other, but he is the crucified Christ in transfigured form (Phil. 3.21). The coming God is not *Deus novus*, a new God, as Marcion maintained. He is the God who *is faithful to his creation*. The *creatio nova* is therefore the new creation of this one, the creation which is perishing from its sin and its injustice. The images of redemption and consummation used to describe the new creation are drawn from this impaired life here, and are hence incommensurable. But they fill this impaired life with hope and turn it into an experienceable promise of the life which will be transfigured and eternal.

In the time-transposed eschatology which called itself 'consistent', the future was equated with future in the static sense we have described. The category *novum* was unknown to it. But with time, life only becomes old, never young and never new. For that it needs hope in the God who promises: 'Behold, I make all things new.' Those who 'wait for' this God 'shall renew their strength, they shall mount up with wings like eagles' (Isa. 40.31).

In the eschatology that is transposed into eternity, the present 'moment' is 'the sudden', the what-can-never-be-expected, the leap, the miracle. But it is not 'the *eschatological* moment', and is not set within the category *novum*. It remains the exception, the interruption. The concept of eternity on which it is based makes perception of the category *novum* impossible.

But to the experience of the coming God, and the advent concept of time, the category *novum* belongs of necessity; for it is through this category that the experience is disclosed and deciphered.

§4 THE REBIRTH OF MESSIANIC THINKING IN JUDAISM

The appalling self-destruction of Europe in the First World War brought Jewish thinkers in Germany, with wholly unusual sensibility, back to their own Judaism, and in Judaism to Jewish messianism. These thinkers came from assimilated Jewish families. They had found their spiritual home in the humanism of the European Enlightenment, and had made their own contribution to

German culture. The disintegration of that culture in the empire of Wilhelm II, and the necrophilic enthusiasm for war displayed in 1914 – an enthusiasm which in the 'Ideas of 1914' (see n. 75) captured even the intellectuals, philosophers and poets – caused these Jewish thinkers to revoke the expectations which they had invested in the 'enlightened' culture of the West, and led them to rediscover the Jewish sources of their messianic hope. They condemned the ideas about educating the human race towards a condition of moral perfection, and rejected the notion of history's completion. Instead in their Jewish religion they found the idea of redemption. After the catastrophe of 1914–18 they forsook the cultural faith in progress, with its unattainable goal of 'eternal peace', and criticized its premise, which was the idea of time as a linear, homogeneous continuum, free of surprises. In its place they sought for a new, religiously defined and theologically reflected relationship to historical time – to the present, the Now. In place of the chiliastic 'self-realization of absolute Mind' in history (and, in its final phase, in Western history), they put the messianism which in Jewish thought had always been bound up with experiences of catastrophe. The Christian theodicy of Hegel's already 'reconciled world' had for them been shot to pieces at Verdun. In the sufferings of the present, theodicy once more became the tormenting question, a question unanswerable and yet irrelinquishable.

For the rebirth of messianic thinking out of the catastrophe of Christian humanism in the First World War, we are indebted to Martin Buber, Ernst Bloch and Franz Rosenzweig, Walter Benjamin and Theodor W. Adorno, Gershom Scholem and Margarete Susman, and – after the Second World War, which even outdid the catastrophe of the First – Karl Löwith and Jacob Taubes. They brought reason into the Jewish and Christian hope and – even more important – hope into the reason that was self-sufficient and hence self-destroying. Out of the ruins of historical rationality they rescued hope as a theological category. Without their messianic thinking, eschatology today is literally unthinkable. Here we shall be looking at only a few of their fundamental ideas.[63]

1. Ernst Bloch: 'The Spirit of Utopia' (1918)

In the 'Intention' with which he prefaced his *Spirit of Utopia* in 1918, Ernst Bloch describes his horror over the self-destruction of German culture in Prussian militarism and in the senseless slaughter of the First World War: 'Only an empty, gruesome remembrance still hangs in the air . . . What was young had to perish, forced to die for purposes so alien and hostile to the spirit . . . so great a flowering, so great a dream, such spiritual hope is dead . . . No war aim was ever more devoid of light than that of imperial Germany . . .'[64] Out of the ashes of that world Bloch tried in 1918 to find a new beginning in a search for 'the heritage that had not been lost', and found it in that which had been sought in all past civilizations as the One Thing, as salvation. That was for him at that time 'the ultimate possible self-encounter' on the inward path, and then, on the corresponding outward way, the utopia, 'clung to in the face of misery, death and the empty realm of physical nature'. '*Incipit vita nova*', he wrote at the end of the 'Intention' for his *Spirit of Utopia*: here a new life begins.

But where was the real movement of hope for this rebuilding of utopia on the rubble of the old world? In 1918 he answered: 'The war ended, the revolution began, and with the revolution the open doors.' For Bloch, the Russian October revolution of 1917 was a sign of hope in 'the decline of the west'. He maintained this belief to the end of his life, in spite of all the socialist disappointments which he was forced to see and to suffer. But this had not always been his view. In 1912/13, under the influence of Martin Buber's Jewish reform movement, he wrote an essay called 'Symbol: the Jews'. He included this essay as an excursus in the first edition of *The Spirit of Utopia*, but removed it again from the second edition of 1923, reprinting it only in 1964, in his essay volume *Through the Wilderness*.[65] In this essay it is not the proletariat who carry the messianic hope into the world; it is the Jews. He accordingly declared, with superlative 'Jewish pride': 'In the face of a great Jew, the great men of all other nations are, as it were, no more than bourgeois geniuses.'[66] Newly awakening Judaism was losing its fear of Christian dominance: 'At last Jesus is returning to his people', and the Jews will take over what has come to the nations in the form of Christianity, and the remnants of Christianity. What this is, he follows Joachim of Fiore in calling the Tertium Testamentum – a third testament reaching out beyond Jews and Christians, the messianic testament. In good Jewish and Christian fashion, he sees this in the *kiddush ha-shem*, the sanctification of God's Name by human beings; and at the end he has a vision of a union of Judaism and Germanic culture with Russia in 'the bringing forth of God and messianism', as a preparation for 'absolute time'.[67]

Bloch's Judaism was never Zionist, like the Judaism of Martin Buber and Gershom Scholem. He always expected more of the advent of the messiah than merely the ending of the dispersion (the *galuth*) and the return home to a kind of 'Asiatic Balkan state' in the Middle East. He was proud of 'my ancient, mysterious people', but saw its world-wide mission in the very dispersion itself: the Jews were scattered among the nations in order that they might everywhere kindle the messianic spark of hope for justice, freedom, democracy, and harmony with nature. From the sources that were specifically Jewish and Christian, he developed a general philosophy of hope, 'a metaphysics from messianic springs'.[68]

Bloch did not cast away the cultural link with the better German tradition, but he tried to establish it on a new level. The insane European-Christian delusion that the world was moving towards perfection perished in the First World War, but out of the debacle Bloch rescued that hope for a possible future salvation on which the modern world is based. He therefore continued to stand by Hegel, instead of casting him off, as did Rosenzweig, Löwith, Buber and Taubes; but with Marx's help he broke open Hegel's closed system of world history so that it became a process dialectic open to the future – a view which in fact accorded with the younger Hegel too.[69]

For Bloch, there is no theodicy within the world system; what there is, is enduring indignation over injustice and the suffering of the poor and weak. His real utopias about social justice and human dignity spring from this indignation, in which hope takes practical and efficacious form in the present. His later philosophy of hope has its shifting horizons and goals, and its 'concrete utopias' for each given present. But from the very beginning the foundation for hope is for him to be found in the inexhaustible depths of the immediately experienced moment. In that moment, both origin and goal are present. Its meaning is therefore to be found, not in the temporal transition from yesterday to tomorrow, but in what is eternal and primordial. In *The Spirit of Utopia* 'the darkness of the lived moment' is nothing other than 'the darkness of the lived God',[70] the *Shekinah*. If, one day, that which in hidden form drives us forward emerges, what will come into being is eternity, i.e., 'absolute time', time which does not pass away, life without death, the unveiled face in God.

In its final words *The Spirit of Utopia* expresses the new symbiosis of Jewish commandment and modern will: 'Only the wicked exist through their God; but the righteous – God exists through them, and in their hands is laid the sanctification of the Name, the naming of God itself, the God who moves and ferments within us . . .' In 1963 he wrote in a 'Postscript': 'The world is not true, but through human beings and through truth it strives to arrive at its homecoming.'[71] Here the Jewish *kiddush ha-shem* and the Jewish longing for a return home in the exile of the world are expanded into universal dimensions. With Moses and Jesus, Bloch links in a singularly characteristic way the 'theurgical titanism' of Nietzsche's Zarathustra. His later characterization of the great founders of religions as 'a human venture into the religious mystery' is also reminiscent of Nietzsche.[72]

Bloch's *Spirit of Utopia* did not look for redemption from history; it aimed at the consummation of history in the eternal kingdom, a consummation which had not yet taken place but which – as he believed – had not yet been finally thwarted either. It was this 'redemption from history', however, which became the fundamental idea of Bloch's contemporary, Franz Rosenzweig.

2. Franz Rosenzweig: 'The Star of Redemption' (1921)

Before the First World War Rosenzweig studied under the famous historian Meinecke at Freiburg university, writing a thesis on 'Hegel and the State', which was published in 1920.[73] He saw nineteenth-century world history from the viewpoint of the later Hegel's philosophy of history. But in the catastrophe of the war he recognized that the collapse of the old world also meant the burial of the dreams that had been invested in it. After some wavering in the direction of Christianity, after Eugen Rosenstock's conversion, he turned to Judaism, and in *The Star of Redemption* prepared the *dis*similation of Judaism from its *as*similation into the nineteenth-century bourgeois world. Through its election and in its religion, Judaism lives out a different history from that bourgeois world. In the star of David, Rosenzweig found redemption from the history whose consummation had found so catastrophic an end.

According to Hegel's philosophy of world history, reason in history means that the absolute Mind realizes itself in history through a process of self-emptying, in order to arrive at itself once more in knowledge of itself. The 'world mind' embodies itself in 'the minds of the nations'.[74] The nations who play a part in history assume their roles as preferred instruments of the world mind in the different epochs assigned to them. The final epoch of world history, and the highest realization of the world mind, is taken over by 'the Germanic world'. This epoch also brings Christianity, as 'the absolute religion' of all religions, into its final phase. 'The history of the world is progress in the consciousness of freedom – a progress whose necessity we are bound to recognize.'[75] Only in Western Christianity does the world appear as a reconciled world, in which reality has become reasonable and reason has become reality.

In *The Star of Redemption* Rosenzweig recognized the illusory nature of Hegel's 'reason in history'. The system as a whole is blind and indifferent towards the individual experience of existence. For Rosenzweig, Kierkegaard became the important alternative to Hegel. History itself has confuted 'reason in history' through the catastrophe – that is, through the barbaric nationalist consequences of the Hegelian ideology of 'the national spirit' in the German empire of Wilhelm II and 'the Ideas of 1914'. The sense of historical election and mission cherished by Prussian Germany, and the chiliastic deification of imperial policy, had confuted themselves in a catastrophic way.

Rosenzweig saw through this surface of world politics to the experience of time underlying them. If history is the medium through which the absolute Mind realizes itself, and in which humanity moves towards its preordained completion, then time is a homogeneous, linear continuum. Every given present acquires meaning in world history because it is a step on the road to completion. Here the consummation of history acts on instances of historical progress like an unattainable goal which every present approaches, and for which every present sacrifices itself, but which no present can ever reach. The linear pointer or time-index of history essentially knows no end, because the line of time stretches to infinity. But for progress in history, human beings need the ideal images of perfection, the end of suffering, and eternal peace. Regulative ideas of this kind are necessary, but they are utopias. And can we ever seriously hope for something which we know can never happen? Yet by virtue of their hope, the relationship of human beings to the future is one of 'messianic impatience'. They expect that what they hope for can, after all, happen at any moment.

Rosenzweig contrasted *utopia* as a category of purpose with *redemption* as category of the expectation of a total change possible at any moment. In his sense, 'redemption contrasts with utopia as an actual, present event contrasts with an ideal limit point that is continually deferred, as a standstill in time differs from an infinitely prolonged line, as a sudden illumination stands to an endless succession of moments'.[76] Time's homogeneous, linear continuum knows nothing of the surprisingly new event. But *redemption* is the thing that is surprisingly new.

Rosenzweig makes this clear from the double sense of the concept *present*. In the temporal sense, 'present' is the bridge between yesterday and tomorrow. This horizontal transition acquires its meaning as a progression towards something better, the end in view being time's completion. But in the vertical sense, the present is a 'springboard' to eternity.[77] Redemption takes place in the vertical sense as a standstill of time, or as a contraction of time into a new future qualitatively different from the linear future of time, which is a quantitative summation. Present as a springboard to eternity frees us from the endless sequence of time, and in the midst of time transposes us into a completely different reality. That is the religious dimension of time which, in *The Star of Redemption*, Rosenzweig rediscovers in practical terms in the Jewish holidays, or feastdays, and pre-eminently in the sabbath.[78] It is in accordance with these that he formulates what for him is 'the messianic moment' of redemption, for in Jewish interpretation sabbath and messiah belong together: when the whole of Israel keeps a single sabbath, the messiah comes; when the messiah comes, the End-time sabbath begins. Utopia is an enticing idea about progress and the moral completion of world history. But it is not utopia that constitutes the hope for the redemption of the world; it is the experience of redemption in the messianic moment. The ground of hope is not the furthest off, but the closest of all.

For Rosenzweig, what follows is a reversal of the objective relation of time: 'For whereas the past – what is already finished – lies there from its beginning to its end and can hence be told (and all telling commences with the beginning of the series) the future as that which it is, *as* future, can be grasped only by means of anticipation.'[79] For the past as it can be told, the pointer or time index moves from past to future, and future is the progression of the past. But for the anticipated future, the pointer moves from the future into the present and the past; for future becomes past, and potentiality reality, never the reverse. Rosenzweig's reversal of the relation of the times surmounts the historicism which essentially makes the future past, because it subjects the future to the power of the present. In Rosenzweig's critism of Hegel, 'the power of history' and 'the power of the logos' fuse into a single rule of violence.[80] With his reversal of the objective relation of the times he is also, finally, able to think together eternity and time in such a way that they do not put an end to one another: 'Eternity is a future which, without ever ceasing to be future, is yet present. Eternity is a Today, but it is aware of being more than Today.'[81]

Rosenzweig tried to renew German Judaism from its eternal sources. He did not become a Zionist, but joined Buber's *Lehrhaus* (or Jewish academy) in Frankfurt, and with Buber translated the Hebrew Bible into German.

3. *Gershom Scholem: 'The Messianic Idea in Judaism' (1959)*

Scholem belonged to the same generation as Bloch and Rosenzweig, and had similar experiences in the wartime Germany of 1914–18; but his conscious return to Judaism led him to different conclusions: he became a passionate Zionist, and emigrated to Jerusalem so as to go on with his research there, and to continue writing his learned treatises on mystical and messianic movements in Judaism.[82] In 1931 Scholem stated his opinion of *The Star of Redemption* in no uncertain terms.[83] He praised the renewal of Judaism out of the centre of its hopes, but complained that in his doctrine of 'the anticipation of redemption in Jewish life' Rosenzweig was blind to the fact that 'messianic apocalyptic was a theory about a catastrophe'.[84] The power of redemption is not merely an intrinsically liberating power; it is intrinsically destructive too. But Rosenzweig had 'the profound tendency to extract the apocalyptic sting from the organism of Judaism'.[85]

The First World War meant for Scholem too the death of Europe and its burial. From 1923 onwards he found his earthly home in Jerusalem and his spiritual home in Judaism's mystical traditions, which had been the subject of his study since 1918. His work is marked by an unusual wealth of knowledge and ideas, but here we shall pick out only his contributions to the understanding of history and redemption.

For Scholem, when Europe died the modern reinterpretation of messianism as faith in progress died too. He no longer believed that redemption could be an outcome of developments in the world itself, as liberal Jews had still taught (the Kantian Hermann Cohen, for example).[86] On the contrary, he saw redemption as 'a break-in of transcendence . . . in which history itself perishes.'[87] In Jewish history the messianic idea had always manifested itself in close association with apocalyptic; indeed it was itself by origin and nature 'a theory about a catastrophe'.[88] Among the prophets, the Day of the Lord already meant the end of the world, and the end of history in its previous form, so that an aeon which would be wholly and entirely new could dawn. For Scholem there is no transition from history to redemption. The apocalyptists have always stressed this lack of transition, thereby severing the messianic hope from all optimism based on belief in progress. In the Jewish traditions on which Scholem draws, the messiah comes unannounced and unexpected, and wholly unpredictably. His presence is the result, not of an evolution but of an explosion.

In spite of his stress on the catastrophic character redemption has for history, Scholem also brings out the utopian elements in Jewish messianism. This can be a longing for a restoration, 'a backward-looking hope', turned towards a reinstatement of an original state of things. But as 'a forward-looking hope' it can also be directed in a utopian sense towards a state of things which has never yet been. Scholem finely shows from the prophetic images that retrogressive messianism has utopian features, and that utopian messianism always has retrogressive ones too.[89] For this he invokes Ernst Bloch's *Spirit of Utopia* and *Principle of Hope*, whose 'mystical inspiration' he praises but whose 'Marxist rhapsodies' he condemns. At the end he describes critically as 'a deferred life' the influence of messianic expectation on the life of the present: 'To live in hope has a greatness, but it is also something profoundly unreal.'[90] That is the Jewish experience of life 'in exile'. Here everything is only for a time and provisional, nothing can be done wholeheartedly, no one can fulfil him or herself here, everything remains in a state of suspension, for: 'Next year in Jerusalem!' The 'preparedness for irrevocable effort towards a concrete realization' emerged for the first time 'in our generation', which began the return to Zion without subscribing to any meta-history. Whether it can sustain this effort without foundering in the crisis of the messianic claim remains in Scholem's view an open question in modern Jewish Zionism.

It is notable that, unlike Rosenzweig, Scholem does not see Jewish life in history as an anticipation of the redemption which ends history. If there is no transition from redemption to present-day history, but only the incalculable, catastrophic incursion, how can there be Jewish and Christian life in history at all? Scholem criticizes the Christian 'anticipation' of redemption in the invisible, inward realm of the soul as 'illegitimate', and stresses in contrast the Jewish view of a visible and practical redemption of this 'unredeemed world'.[91] But can there already be election and a life lived according to the Torah in this totally 'unredeemed world' without its also falling under the condemnation of being an 'illegitimate anticipation' of redemption? Can Israel celebrate the sabbath if the messiah can come only in the form of a historical catastrophe? How can this world be called an unredeemed world if the light of redemption does not yet shine at all, because it has not yet issued from its source? Whereas Bloch in 'the darkness of the lived God', and Rosenzweig in God's sabbath presence, found legitimate, necessary and incontrovertible 'anticipations' of 'absolute time' or 'the redemption of the world', for Scholem the very concept of anticipation itself appears to be illegitimate. He seems to see it as no more than 'deferred life'. Yet in Scholem the Zionist 'preparedness for irrevocable effort for a concrete realization' assumes precisely the place where Bloch and Rosenzweig talked about the presence of the eternal and the inexhaustible in the messianic moment.

4. *Walter Benjamin: 'Theses on the Philosophy of History' (1940)*

Out of the disaster of the First World War, Walter Benjamin also tried to find a solution in a new definition of the relationship between history as the nineteenth century understood it, and redemption as messianic faith expected it. In 1914 he was already criticizing 'the view of history which, confident of the endlessness of time, distinguishes only the rapidity of human beings and epochs, which roll on, either swiftly or slowly, along the path of progress'.[92] In his 'Theses on the Philosophy of History' (1940), he comes back to this.[93] 'History' only comes into being when we interpret a chaos of events. But how must we read the events so that for us they constitute history? Benjamin sets the materialist historian over against the positivist collector of facts. All generations seek their own happiness, and in this search wait for redemption from transience. Past generations therefore wait for the generations to come, and for their 'messianic power'. 'Only a redeemed mankind is given its past in all its completeness', because it has found what past generations sought for. 'Only for a redeemed mankind has every moment of its past become citable' – that is, present. Here Benjamin presses into service the category of *danger*. Just as particular memories 'flash up' at the moment of danger, so for the human being (as the conscious subject of history) at the moment of danger the past is present, because in the danger not only the present, historical subject is threatened but his past too. As a help towards understanding this, Benjamin reminds his readers of the biblical messiah, who does not come 'only as the redeemer' but also 'as the vanquisher of the Antichrist'. 'Even the dead will not be safe from the enemy once he is victorious.'[94] Consequently the (messianic) historian must 'fan the spark of hope for the past'. In the face of the apocalyptic catastrophe, the distance between the times of history disappears, the dead and the living are joined in a single fellowship: the fellowship of absolute danger; so they are joined too in their common hope for redemption.

Benjamin also makes this clear from the history written by 'the victors' and from the remembrance of suffering of the vanquished.[95] The victors desire the historical prolongation of their power, and develop a corresponding temporal continuum. But the oppressed desire redemption from the advance and temporal continuum of their victors, and wait for the break-in of a wholly different future. 'The consciousness that they are bursting apart the continuum of history is characteristic of the revolutionary classes at the moment of their action. The great revolution brings in a new calendar.'[96]

Like Rosenzweig, Benjamin tried to find a concept for the present that 'bursts apart the continuum of history'. This is not the transition from yesterday to tomorrow; it is something 'which enters time and has come to a stop'. It is a moment at which time itself stands still and is so contracted – as if through a time-lapse camera – that the whole past is present. Benjamin is thinking of the *revolutionary* moment but it is as the apocalyptic moment that he describes it. He also calls this present, the Now, which 'as prototype of the Messianic time, comprises the entire history of mankind in a tremendous abridgement.'[97] Into this Now, as prototype and anticipation of the messianic time, 'splinters' of the messianic time have already been exploded. And again he calls to mind the Judaism which was so strong in its remembrance of the past. Because the Jews were forbidden to probe into the future, they had to expect that in that future 'every second is the little door through which the Messiah could enter.'[98]

Benjamin saw 'the meaning of history' not in the connections of history as a whole, but in history's wreckages and fractures. There the unforeseen can appear and the primal truth be revealed as if in a lightning flash. Only the oppressed wait for 'redemption'. Consequently for them history is a discontinuity. Their redemption becomes possible when time's continuum and the advance of the victors crumble. In this sense Benjamin is as apocalyptic as Scholem, and at the same time, like Rosenzweig, he is turned towards the undeducible, sudden messianic presence of eternity. He is like Bloch in defining the moment 'when time stands still' not merely mystically, but always in a revolutionary sense as well.

In his 'Theological-Political Fragment' we find a kind of summing-up of his ideas about history and redemption.[99] In human history, striving aims at happiness. Yet in happiness everything that is historical also seeks its own downfall in the sense of its self-abolition and self-elevation into another order, and hence 'redemption'. 'Nothing historical (can) of itself strive to be related to what is messianic . . . Only the messiah himself completes all historical happening, by himself redeeming, completing and creating its relationship to his messianic future.' That is why 'the kingdom of God' as the quintessence of redemption is not the *telos* of historical dynamic but its end. As in Rosenzweig, we find in Benjamin two contradictory orders of time: the secular order, with its striving for happiness within history, and the messianic order of redemption, which runs counter to that. This is meant, not as a cleavage but as a counter-influence: Benjamin makes this clear by saying that he does not view 'the secular' as a category of the kingdom, but doubtless as 'its stealthiest approach'; and on the other hand sees 'the downfall of what is earthly' in fulfilled earthly happiness. Positive co-operation between human beings and the messiah, and a positive addition of happiness and redemption, are replaced by a dialectic of negative interactions. It is only here that Benjamin does justice for the first time to 'the catastrophic side' of redemption which Scholem stressed so emphatically. Downfall and redemption are two sides of the same thing.

That was written before Auschwitz, and yet it can be read as an anticipation of a downfall in which no 'redemption' could be perceived. After Auschwitz, Benjamin's friend Theodor W. Adorno summed up as a pure wistful longing what Jewish thinkers had sought for after the German catastrophe in the First World War: 'The only philosophy which can be responsibly practised in the face of despair is the attempt to contemplate all things as they would present themselves from the standpoint of redemption. Knowledge has no light but that shed on the world by redemption; all else is reconstruction, mere technique.'[100] 'The messianic light' shows the world as it will really be, lying there 'in its cracks and fissures', 'necessitous and disfigured'. Its utter negativity then becomes the mirror image of its redeemed positivity. But this redemption stand-point is impossible, because it would have to transport us out of the sphere of this present existence. As long as we are in that sphere, we ourselves are disfigured and necessitous too, and stricken by blindness. This means that the question about a future redemption of this 'unredeemed world' reverts to that present in which the Wholly Other suddenly lets time stand still, and for a moment does indeed 'transport us' out of the laws of our society and the compulsions of our history.

5. *Jacob Taubes and Karl Löwith: 'Western Eschatology' (1947) –* *A Theological Continuation or an Ecological Farewell?*

Soon after the end of the Second World War, two moving works appeared in Germany on the history of the eschatological thrust towards the end. In 1947, in Zürich, Jacob Taubes finished his doctoral thesis on 'Western Eschatology' (*Abendländische Eschatologie*, 1947, 1949), and Karl Löwith returned from his Japanese exile, bringing his book on 'the theological implications of the philosophy of history'. The book appeared in English in 1949 under the title *Meaning in History*, and was published in Germany three years later as *Weltgeschichte und Heilsgeschehen* ('World History and Saving Event').

The two books resemble one another in their historical content, and they treat the same thinkers, from Augustine to Hegel. But in their intention they differ fundamentally. Taubes turns back from Western eschatology to its Jewish roots, and from these develops post-Western apocalypytic, theological ideas. But in Tokyo Löwith had come to esteem Zen Buddhism's philosophy of nature, and with this book he intended to depart from both Christian and historical existence, in order to return to the circular courses of nature: 'At the end of the day, the proof of the theological significance of our reflections about the philosophy of history leads beyond all merely historical thinking.'[101] Taubes was looking for a history to come after the Hegelian and Western 'end of history'; Löwith asked about the nature of the human being within the framework of the natural world. But both really made the Christian eschatology of the West responsible for the revolutionary and catastrophic history of Europe and modern times.

Taubes was assistant to Gershom Scholem in Jerusalem from 1951 to 1953, and for him the Jews meant for Western eschatology what the Greeks were for Western ontology. Israel is 'the historical location of revolutionary apocalyptic', 'the restless element in world history', 'the ferment which really creates history'; for the hope for God's sole sovereignty and the experience of the present as conversion have broken through the cycle of the eternal return in which the nations live, and have actually disclosed the world as 'history' for the first time.[102] What interested him particularly in the realm of Jewish eschatology was the spiritual world of apocalyptic. He presents the historical viewpoint of the apocalyptic writers, their speculations about world eras, and their expectations of the End-time. But more important for Taubes himself is existential apocalyptic as limited time, End-time, disclosure, the world as exile, conversion in the moment of the present, perception in mirror and parable.

Taubes sets 'The Theological Eschatology of Europe' (the title of Book III) in the light of the Jewish 'History of Apocalyptic' (Book II), from which Christianity emerged. Here – unlike the theologians who in apocalyptic can discern only 'delays of the parousia' – he attaches importance to the millenarian, triumphalist interpretation of the present as the Thousand Years' empire, in the Holy Roman Empire and the holy Roman Church. Eschatology then provided a theologically legitimated horizon for the development of contemporary political and spiritual power. It was only with Joachim of Fiore that this became a horizon for the future of history, and a horizon of hope for modern times. For Taubes, the end of the era of Christian history had been thought through by Hegel. But where Hegel maintained that there was an End-time completion for world history, Taubes sees only the end of the Christian history of the West. It is understandable that, like others before him, he should have tried to rescue from the ruins of this triumphalist philosophy of history the original Jewish hope as theological category.

In apocalyptic Taubes perceived the pointer to the vertical rift through which the messianic event enters history, the history which can neither be brought to completion by human beings nor ended by them. Universal history is the meaning which the victors give to the result of their conquests. Their chronicles are nothing other than the parade of their spoils.[103] The dumb suffering of those who have been defeated and subjected finds no place in the annals of the ruling nations. Only apocalyptic, which sprang up out of Jewish and Christian martyrdom, lends these people a voice, a hope for redemption, and the power to rebel at the proper time. Taubes shows that Judaism's specific contribution to the history of humanity is to be found in the apocalyptic of the oppressed, and in the messianism of the conversion of time.

Löwith came from the Heidegger circle in Marburg. His writings after the Second World War all serve to confute the philosophy of history and the philosophy of historical existence through which 'history' is totalized and idolized. His book *Meaning in History*, which influenced theologians so greatly, lays bare the roots of the modern philosophy of history in Christian theology, only to condemn the one with the other, since for Löwith history has no meaning and no 'reason': 'Historical processes as such do not bear the least evidence of a comprehensive and ultimate meaning . . . Man's historical experience is one of steady failure. Christianity, too, as a historical *world* religion, is a complete failure.'[104]

Only theologians concerned to defend the secularization thesis have taken up Löwith's exposition favourably, as a way of proving that the modern philosophy of history is 'secularized theology'. And the misleading German title of his book ('World History and Saving Event') gives credence to this interpretation. But Löwith treated both 'world history' and 'saving event' as dangerous illusions, in the light of the history of 'failure'. For Löwith, 'belief in history' was not 'the final religion', as it was for the historicists Dilthey, Troeltsch and Croce; it was a deadly superstition. The modern over-emphasis on history which is reflected in the interpretation of 'me world as history' is for Löwith 'a product of our alienation from the natural theology of antiquity and from the supernatural theology of Christianity'.[105] The political messianism of the twentieth century had brought the human and natural world to the edge of the abyss, and Löwith was now concerned to rediscover 'nature', which was there before human beings, is there apart from them, and will still be there when they are gone – his purpose being to fit human history, with its unbridled will for power, into the conditions that provide its framework: nature, and the cosmos.[106]

Löwith followed Nietzsche, the modern 'prophet of post-modernity', who in place of advancing, purposeful time put 'the eternal return of the same thing' and with it 'the presence of eternity' in every fully lived moment: eternity as 'the eternal Yea of being'. In Nietzsche's post-Christian paganism, the old pre-Christian, pagan notion about the cosmic cycle returned, but with the difference that this new, post-Christian paganism is also lauded as 'the post-modern world', because – as Löwith never tires of demonstrating – the 'modern' world is the secularized 'Christian' world. The fact that with this view he was also spurning the Judaism from which Christianity emerged, and which, together with Christianity, moulded the European 'world of history', apparently never became a personal and practical problem for him.

6. *The Redemption of the Future from the Power of History*

If the present is no more than the bridge from the past to the present, then it has no inherent meaning of its own; it is only a step in the advance of history, and merely a rung on the ladder leading to the goal. The rediscovery of the present as a *moment* which towers out of the continuum of the times was the reason for Christian theologians and Jewish thinkers to ask no longer about the *completion of* history, but rather about *redemption from* history. The question about redemption pushed out the question about the utopian goals of historical progress. It emerged during the first catastrophe of Western eschatology and history in the First World War. Recent Jewish messianism is a modern 'theory about a catastrophe', as Scholem and Taubes stress; and historically they are correct. But this does not yet answer the question: redemption – for whom, and from what? For the dialectical theologians of the post-war era, it meant redemption from history and time, into the eternity of God. The historical 'moment' was for them, as it was for the anti-Hegelian Kierkegaard, 'an atom of eternity' and a standstill in the succession of the times. But for the Jewish thinkers, any such an 'eternal present' of redemption in this 'unredeemed world' was inconceivable. So by redemption they must have had something else in mind. In Bloch and Benjamin, 'the moment' seems to be something like a mystical *nunc stans*, and a gnostic spark of light which blazes up in time, as a 'messianic splinter'. Does the moment tower out of time so that in the light of that moment those touched by it can see the future of the redeemed world in God, and God in the redeemed world? Or do the times fall from the fulfilled present like withered leaves? Has 'the moment' come when time withdraws from life, and we are simply *there, wholly* there, and therein *eternal*? There is evidently this mystical interpretation of 'the moment' that 'leaves nothing more to be desired'; and there is the messianic interpretation, which throws open new perspectives, and discloses everything that is to be desired.

The messianic interpretation of the experience of the moment that ends and gathers up time is the *redemption of the future* from the power of history. The power of history is exercised by the mighty. They have to extend their victorious present into the future in order to augment and consolidate their power. *Their* future is without an alternative, and devoid of surprises. It is no more than the prolongation of the present state of possession, and its expansion. *Their* future is therefore extrapolated from the tendencies and trends of *their* past and present. *Their* future is planned and projected future, for only the person who has the power to implement and enact can plan and project. If the modern world itself is 'the modernity project' undertaken by the powerful people in Western society, then the future of this project will be perceived in two ways by those caught up in it: as a chance for permanent modernization, and as the compulsion to progress. 'The person who rides on a tiger can never get off again', says the Chinese proverb. It is true that today there is very little optimism about the future in the modernity project, but in science and technology the pressure for progress is still unchanged, under 'the compulsion' of competition.

The messianic interpretation sees 'the moment' that interrupts time, and lets us pause in the midst of progress, as the power for conversion. At that moment another future becomes perceptible. The laws and forces of the past are no longer 'compulsive'. God's messianic future wins power over the present. New perspectives open up. The deadliness of progress towards the economic, ecological, nuclear and genetic catastrophes is recognized; and the modern world's lack of future is perceived. The way becomes free for alternative developments. I should like to call this the redemption of the future from the power of history in the *kairos* of conversion. Only that will again make theological eschatology possible, for through that, hope as a theological category will be redeemed from the ruins of historical reason.

II

Eternal Life

Personal Eschatology

II

Eternal Life

Personal Eschatology

§1 LOVED LIFE AND DEATH

1. *Is Death 'the Finish'?*

Epicurus's famous answer seems a simple and handy one: if I am alive, I am not dead. If I am dead, I am not alive. Why should I think about death while I am still alive? It only spoils my pleasure in living and gets in the way of my work. For me, this life holds everything. For me, death is the end of everything. 'Death is not an event in life. No one experiences death', asserted Wittgenstein.[1] If my death cannot be anything I can experience while I am alive, then I can't talk about it, or about what may perhaps come afterwards. And if there is nothing we can say, all we can do is to hold our tongues. In any case, since in this life we have no sensory impressions of a possible world beyond death, and since parapsychological perceptions are unprovable, all we can do is to wait and see – or wait and not see.[2] What we don't know we can't deny – but we can't affirm it either. If we stick to facts, the vista beyond death is closed to us. The most we can do is to preserve a kind of childlike curiosity, and to wait and see whether anything will come 'afterwards', and what it will be. Perhaps that is what Paul Klee meant when – face to face with his own death – he painted angels and, leaving everything open, wrote:

> One day I'll lie nowhere
> by an angel somewhere.

The thought of death and a life after death is ambivalent. It can deflect us from this life, with its pleasures and pains. It can make life here a transition, a step on the way to another life beyond – and by doing so it can make this life empty and void. It can draw love away from this life and direct it towards a life hereafter, spreading resignation in 'this veil of tears'. The thought of death and a life after death can lead to fatalism and apathy, so that we only live life here half-heartedly, or just endure it and 'get through'. The thought of a life after death can cheat us of the happiness and the pain of this life, so that we squander its treasures, selling them off cheap to heaven. In that respect it is better to live every day as if death didn't exist, better to love life here and now as unreservedly as if death really were 'the finish'.[3] The notion that this life is no more than a preparation for a life beyond, is the theory of a refusal to live, and a religious fraud. It is inconsistent with the living God, who is 'a lover of life'. In that sense it is religious atheism.

But if we have ever been close to death and have escaped some deadly peril, we know the feeling that life has been given back to us. We feel new-born, and experience life here, in all its uniqueness and beauty, with freshly awakened and sharpened senses. We then suddenly realize with a blinding awareness what living really means. So the thought of death and a life after death doesn't have to deflect us from this life; it can also give this life a new depth. It doesn't have to make us 'absent-minded'; it can make us wholly present. It doesn't have to make us indifferent; it can make us fully and wholly capable of love.

To push away every thought of death, and to live as if we had an infinite amount of time ahead of us, makes us superficial and indifferent. Since we know in our heart of hearts that death can strike any day, we live with a repressed awareness of death, and that robs us of our contact with reality. The idea of living without death, and the theory that death 'is not an event in life' also act as briefs for a refusal to live, and are an irreligious fraud. They contradict our experience of life as it really is, and simply turn life into an idol. We all know that life is limited. To live as if there were no death is to live an illusion. Everyone who lives with awareness knows too that death is not only *an* event in life: it is *the* event – and that all our attitudes to life are attitudes to the death of this life of ours.

To draw a sharp line between life and death, as Epicurus counselled, does not lead to the life without death which is its aim; it merely evokes a feeling for life without an awareness of death. And this is only possible if the awareness of death is suppressed. For people in the middle ages, 'sudden death' was a terrible end, because it allowed no time to prepare for dying. Modern men and women desire nothing more than a quick, painless – in other words sudden – death. Because death cannot be suppressed, this is a way of suppressing at least the awareness of death. But like everything that is suppressed, the suppressed awareness of death is still there in the subconscious, acts on the consciousness, and influences all our feelings and actions. It paralyses our energies for living, because these energies are needed for the suppression; or it arouses a fear for life, so that we become hungry for it; or it leaves us no peace, so that we turn into workaholics and fussy activists. It makes us arrogant or depressive, it spreads indifference, coldness of heart, and spiritual numbness. The suppressed awareness of death buries us alive, killing us while we are still living through the force of its suppression. We become apathetic towards other people and ourselves. We shut ourselves up in prejudices that cut us off from new experiences, and wall ourselves up. To live as if there were no death is an illusion which is the enemy of life, and which cheats us of the mortal happiness this life offers. Epicurus was wrong. Life without death is not life 'here'. So he could be wrong with his converse too: death without life is not death 'over there'. Wittgenstein is confuted: death *is* an event in life. It is even *the* event in life. What kind of event could death otherwise be, and whose event? We experience death with this entire life – we experience this life with its entire death.

It seems to be the reduction of the consciousness to individual awareness, and the concentration of individual awareness on one's own life, which makes death so frighteningly 'the end of it all'. If the narcissism of modern men and women relates everything to their own selves, then of course the end of the individual self is 'the finish'. Individualization dissolves the sustaining relationships, making each of us the artificer of his or her own life, and exposing us to the pressure of growing competition.[4] To be lonely and isolated is in itself social death. That is why modern people, individualized as they are, no longer perceive the presence of the dead, which in pre-modern and non-modern (or more properly extra-modern) cultures was experienced as a matter of course, in ancestor cults and family celebrations at the burial places of the dead. Because individualized men and women know no life before birth in their ancestors, they know no life after death in their children either. If death is 'the finish', then it is the finish for the dead too. They must be forgotten, so that we can get on with our own lives unencumbered. Pre-modern and extra-modern awareness embedded individual awareness in the collective awareness of the generations, as the genealogical tables in the Old Testament show, or the ancestral tablets in Korea. This meant that the death of an individual was seen as a transition from the world of the living to the world of one's ancestors, not as the final rupture of life which puts an end to everything.

Today death 'is now rendered completely and utterly alien by the socially determined decline of continuous experience as such'.[5] For the individualizing of life is perpetuated in the fragmentation of experience. We live from moment to moment and from one day to another, because memory no longer fulfils its purpose, and hope is lost. The wider context, in life and beyond life, is only perceived again when we stop relating everything to ourselves and relate it to something that endures.

> Where do you come from?
> How long will you be here?
> How do you matter?
> The lime trees scent the air immortally.[5a]

For the dead and for one's own death this means that people who live in the presence of the dead will no longer suppress their own death; and people who accept their own death will also live with the remembrance of those who have died.

2. Was this life all there is?

> That surely can't have been all,
> that little bit of Sunday and children's voices,
> it's surely got to lead somewhere!
>
> . . .
>
> That surely can't have been all.
> There has to be something ahead – no,
> we have to get life into life, that's it.[6]

It is true that in this poem Wolf Biermann was not thinking of a life that will continue after death, but the question he puts – the question whether that was all, the question that can overwhelm us when we face the death of someone else, or our own approaching death – can no longer be answered with the experiences of this life. What do we ask for, out of a life unfulfilled or cut short? What are we asking for, and for which part of us, when we ask about a life after death?

The earliest idea found in our tradition is the notion of the immortal soul which, when the body dies, returns from the exile of this mortal life to its eternal home. In old pictures, the soul is shown as a tiny winged human being entering into the body at creation and leaving it again at death. Because the body is weighed down by the things of this earth, the soul was pictured winged – as a bird, a butterfly or an angel, so that after the death of the body it could take flight into the free world of heaven.[7] Underlying these images is the notion of the continuing existence of the bodiless human mind or spirit – if the soul is supposed to be our 'spirit'. Our real self is thought to go on existing after death, whether to be purified in purgatory, whether to experience a new reincarnation, or whether to go to heaven or to hell. But is the continuing existence of a disembodied mind – a mind without brain and cerebral activity – really conceivable? A human mind without a brain, or some physical equivalent, is merely an abstraction of a mind that thinks with a brain, and presupposes that.[8] A bodiless soul is inconceivable under the conditions of bodily thinking. It is a hypothetical assumption, like the one in the anecdote about the officer dying of his wounds in the Seven Years' War, who cried: 'O God, if there is a God, save my immortal soul, if I have one.'

But human life is livingness, and human livingness means to be interested, to be concerned.[9] Concern in life is what we call love. True human life comes from love, is alive in love, and through loving makes something living of other life too. 'A person's real identity, we may say, is his love: his concern: his minding, not just his mind.'[10] So soul or spirit is not something left over in the abstract, once we intellectually subtract everything physical, and with the physical forget the love out of which we receive life and give it. Our 'soul' is where our love is, and 'spirit' is the breath of the life that is loved and loving.[11] Our question about life, consequently, is not whether our existence might possibly be immortal, and if so which part of it; the question is: will love endure, the love out of which we receive ourselves, and which makes us living when we ourselves offer it. How should we really get involved in this life, with its conflicts, pains and disappointments, if we don't trust life more than death, and if we don't with every breath confess life, and stand up to the powers and conditions which disseminate death? It is the conflict between love and death which confronts us with the only real problem of life.

3. Suppressed Death – Reduced Life

Let us ask now about the connection between the affirmation of life and the awareness of death in modern society.

All human life advances towards its own death. That is something we cannot change. We have to die: it is this fact that distinguishes human beings from gods, and the fact that we know it is what distinguishes human beings from animals. 'Know thyself!' In Greece and Rome that meant: recognize that you are mortal, *memento mori*. 'Lord, teach us to remember that we must die, so that we may become wise', says Psalm 90.12 as Luther translated it. What kind of wisdom does this mean, and what kind of foolishness results if we forget it?

Unlike other living things, human beings know about their deaths while they are still alive, and adjust themselves to death. Death is not merely a medical fact. Since it is the death of the human person, it is an event belonging to his or her whole life – an event to which human beings have to adapt and in fact always do adapt. We can suppress the thought of our own death, and behave as if we were leading a deathless life. We can negotiate with death – we can protest against it in terror. We can accept it, and integrate it into our lives. We do these things, and much else, in order to attune ourselves to this event in life. Our attitudes to life always reflect our relationship to our death, and the way we die can make plain how meaningful, or meaningless, our life has been. Every civilization develops its own lifestyle, and its own sense of death too. This makes it difficult to generalize. As individuals, we live our own lives, and it is as individuals that we all have to grapple with our own deaths. But we don't live just for ourselves alone, and so we don't just 'die our own deaths' either, as the existentialists taught. Our personal life-style is moulded by the culture we live in, and so is our personal awareness of death. What do these two things look like in our modern society?

For any analysis and evaluation we always need criteria. My premise has always been that life and death are not merely biological facts; they are fundamental experiences which are inwardly connected with each other. They are fundamental experiences which we go through in the interest in life which we call love, that affirmation of the life which we receive and which we can give.[12] An affirmed, loved and accepted life is a happy life. An affirming, loving and accepting life is a truly human life. By virtue of this love we become living people – by virtue of this love we surrender ourselves to life – by virtue of this love we make others living people too.

But in what we love we are also vulnerable, for in this affirmation of life we open the door to happiness and pain, life and death. It is our love for life, our own life and the life of those we love, that makes us suffer and experience the deadliness of death. In love we surrender ourselves to life, and in surrendering ourselves to life we surrender ourselves to death. That means that love makes our life living, and at the same time consciously mortal. Love lets us experience the livingness of life and the deadliness of death. If the pain is paramount, if the disappointment is a torment, if we are afraid of death, then we surrender ourselves to life less and less. We withdraw our interest in life, so as not to be overwhelmed by pain and grief. But that means that we hold back, we retreat, we shut ourselves up in our own selves. The person who has seen too much bloodshed and too many dead becomes callous. People who have been continually threatened by death become indifferent. They 'couldn't care less', as we say. If we kill every feeling for life we become insensible to pain, and thick-skinned even in the face of death – our own death, and the death of other people. To let the flame of love for life die out means anticipating death. Feeling and thinking become numb and die, for that is what dying means: to become numb and insensible.

This intertwining of happiness and pain, the experience of life and the experience of death, doesn't only shape individual life. It puts its stamp on the life of society too.[13] Social life is moulded to a large extent by generally accepted rituals. Where do we encounter death in public life and in the awareness of modern society? To put it in a nutshell: we no longer encounter it publicly at all. When someone dies, it is seldom at home, in the circle of family and friends; it is generally in hospital, and even there often in an intensive care unit, or pushed away in a corner. The relatives can't do any more for them, so the dying are sent to hospital. The doctors can't do any more for them either; and because the other patients can't be expected to put up with the presence of people who are dying, they are pushed out of the general ward and die somewhere alone.[14] The dead are no longer buried in churchyards, in the centre of the village. Instead, cemeteries are established on the periphery of towns and cities. Undertakers and 'funeral parlours' cope with everything, so that the relatives are not required to give any thought to the funeral. When someone dies, most people retreat into an embarrassed silence; they can only shake the relatives warmly by the hand. There is nothing more one can 'do'. People don't mourn any more either, not because they don't want to, but because mourning rituals are obsolete, and no longer learnt. In public life the mourner has no longer any status. Women no longer wear black, and men are no longer seen with black armbands. 'Life goes on': that is the only comfort. It seems as if the dying and the grieving would like to apologize – 'please don't let me be in your way' – and disappear from sight.

Modern society knows no times and no spaces, no respect and no protection for the dying and the grieving. Dying and death are privatized (except for state funerals for well-known statesmen) and are pushed out of public life. The disruption which death brings in its wake is eliminated as far as possible. There is an unconscious suppressive tabu on dying, death and mourning. Whatever has to do with death is provided with a 'communication inhibitor'. In towns and cities, it has increasingly become customary for people not to be buried at all any more. Their bodies are cremated, and the ashes are scattered – thrown away. It is only at road accidents that we ourselves come face to face with death. But as swiftly as the accidents happen, just so swiftly are the bodies removed, and the ambulances and breakdown trucks driven away. A short time later everything looks as if nothing had occurred. 'The traffic must be kept moving.'

Illness, disability and age get similar treatment. If modern life only has a point as long as people fulfil some purpose or other, then people have to enjoy good health. In this meritocratic, consumer society, health means the ability to work and the ability to enjoy. Any impairment of these abilities counts as suffering, and is considered pointless. In spite of all the excellent protest movements and attempts at humanization, the trend of modern society is to push away the disabled into institutions, to look after the sick in hospitals, and to find places for the elderly in old people's homes. Anyone who can't keep up with this competitive society is pushed to the bottom, or out on to the fringe. 'He hasn't made it.'

And yet the death we push away from us is still there, and the dying and the grieving we suppress are present and in the midst of us. The suppressions of death make modern men and women callous, apathetic and infantile. They produce forced pretences of enjoyment, and fanatical performance neuroses. These suppressions kill the love for life as a whole. If we suppress our fears, and don't take time to mourn our dead, the pain of other people will leave us unmoved too. Suppressed death disseminates a paralysing indifference. We 'perceive' everything only in the technical sense, no longer in the human one. 'The inability to mourn'[15] becomes an inability to love.

Even our perceptions of reality are detached and distanced, as if they were communicated by way of the TV screen. We see things, but without apprehending them. We hear things, but without comprehending them. We experience, but the experience makes no impact. An unreal reality surrounds us which doesn't truly touch us, and to which we don't truly surrender ourselves. 'The real world' seems to have got lost. We see the world as if in a mirror, and don't know whether there is any reality that corresponds to the image in the glass. Secondary perceptions, no longer immediately communicated, push out our own experiences of reality. What is authentic? Where are we ourselves? Are we really there?

Another observation seems to me important too. Death sets a limit to our lifetime, and makes life short: *vita brevis est*. The unconscious, unassimilated fear of death shows itself in the pace at which we live: presto! If you want to get the most out of life you have to live fast! The modern world is the accelerated world. We 'modernize' faster and faster. We move about more and more. We rush from one place to another. We 'have' ever more experiences, and use up ever more life, without any apparent speed limit: fast food – fast life! And yet the truth of the matter is that it is only the person who lives slowly who really enters into life. That person can stand still in the moment, and experience eternity in it, able to enjoy the happiness and feel the pain. But doesn't this quietude in life presuppose a hope for a life that is eternal, whatever that hope may look like? Fear of death constricts, while hope for eternal life opens a wide space for living beyond death, and brings serenity into the soul: nothing will be lost, and you are missing nothing.

The person who retains a knowledge of death also cherishes the love for life – for every life, for the life of us all, for the whole of life. The remembrance of death makes us wise for living. But where is this wisdom to be found? How do we find the courage for a life on which death has set its mark?

§2 THE IMMORTALITY OF THE SOUL OR THE RESURRECTION OF THE BODY?

The history of European thought offers us two images of hope in the face of death: the image of the immortal soul, an image cherished by the ancient world; and the Bible's image of the resurrection of the dead. In the first image we have the self-assurance of the invulnerable soul; in the second faith's assurance that God will create new life out of death. Whereas the one puts its trust in the self-transcendence of the human being, the other relies on God's transcendence over death. Incomparable though the two ideas are, if we ask people in our own society what hope the Christian faith offers the dying, most of them will answer: hope for a life after death, hope for the immortality of the soul. For long enough, 'save your souls' was the cry of Christian revivalist movements. But the Christian creeds say: 'I believe . . . in the resurrection of the body and a life everlasting', or: ' . . . I look for the resurrection of the dead and the life of the world to come.' Let us first look at the difference between these two ideas, and then go on to develop the new version of the idea of immortality offered by the Christian hope for the resurrection.

1. *The Immortal Soul and the Unlived Life*

(a) *The soul as divine substance*

Every doctrine about the immortality of the soul begins with Plato. Here we shall confine ourselves to the sequence of ideas he develops in the *Phaedo*, because these ideas had – and still have – the greatest influence.

Plato describes the death of Socrates, so as to show from that what the immortality of the soul is, and the attitude to life and death which knowledge of that immortality induces.[16] In his first argument, Plato assumes that life and death are opposites, like waking and sleeping, and that they come into being from the antithesis between them. The living become the dead, and the dead the living: 'There really is such a thing as coming to life again, living people *are* born from the dead, and the souls of the dead exist.'[17] The second argument is the cognitive one: our learning is nothing other than recollection. All cognition is a re-cognition. Because like is only known by like, what the soul perceives in the world after birth must already have been implanted in it before birth.[18] This epistemological progression leads to the conclusion that the soul is pre-existent. The third argument starts from the experience of death. Death is the separation of the soul from the body. The soul becomes directly aware of itself in 'the right practice of philosophy', and that means 'the cultivation of dying' – that is, the remembrance of death.[19] If in its meditation on death (*meditatio mortis*) it anticipates the death of the body, it then becomes aware of its own immortality. We perceive everything through the mediation of our bodily senses, but in its anticipation of the death of the body and the extinction of all bodily senses, the soul ceases to become aware of itself through the mediation of the senses, and hence becomes conscious of itself through itself, without any mediation. To this immediate perception of its unmediated relation to itself belong inward concentration, the withdrawal from the body, and retreat from all the senses.

The post-existence of the soul corresponds to its pre-existence: before we are born, our soul *is*, and after we are dead our soul *is*. It is unborn and hence also immortal. If it clings to the 'region of purity and eternity and immortality and unchangeableness', then in all the vicissitudes of this transitory life it is that which remains the same. The soul is hence pre- and post-existent, because it transcends the birth and death of the body, and remains in its essence untouched by birth and death. It is the eternally existent side of the human being which is turned towards what is divine. Because it was never born, it cannot die either. Death reaches only what is mortal; what is immortal surmounts death. The death of the mortal body is thus the separation of the soul from the body. The more the thinking soul anticipates this separation from the body by turning to the divine and by detaching itself from the body, the more it will already be aware of itself even while it is still in the body. Plato undoubtedly identifies what is truly human with the soul. If human beings identify themselves with their souls, and detach themselves from their bodies, they will find that they are immortal, and immune towards death.

The doctrine of the immortality of the soul is not a doctrine about a life after death; it teaches that the human being possesses a divine identity which is beyond birth and death. What cannot die when the body dies, was not born when the body was born either, and has never lived in the life of body; for only what has never lived the life of the body can avoid dying the life of the body. The Indian *Bhagavad-Gita* says the same thing about the divine spirit in the human being:

'Never is it born nor dies; never did it come to be nor will it ever come to be again: unborn, everlasting . . .'[19a] It is not the lived life of the human being that is immortal, according to this doctrine; it is the unlived life. One might say that the soul is enclosed by a 'protective sphere of not-yet-living'.[20] This means that in the realm of death the soul is 'exterritorial'. It is then also supposed to withdraw into this transcendence, and concentrate itself. It should detach itself from the senses, 'gathered together alone into itself', 'separated from the body'.[21] It must therefore hold back from the life of the senses, which is transient and leads to death.

Because death means the liberation of the soul from the mortal body, death is the feastday of the soul. In dying, it celebrates its return to its eternal home. Death is the soul's best friend, liberating it from its bodily prison and from all its unloved bodily needs and pains. Out of its bodily exile, the soul returns home to the realm of the eternal divine Ideas.

Awareness of the unassailable freedom of the soul is the foundation for a particular attitude to life, an attitude of detachment towards happiness and pain, and of sovereignty towards birth and death. When Socrates saw how a pupil who loved him was suffering from the thought that he, Socrates, would soon be lying before them as a dead body, he said with sovereign irony: 'While they busy themselves about his body after his death, the true Socrates will surely have already escaped them.' The Middle Stoa trained its followers to be free from the emotions, and to achieve a state of *apathy*.[22] Only lack of passion can call forth the virtues of the wise man: tranquillity, imperturbability, and the lightness of heart that comes from being above things, and from not taking oneself too seriously. Those who love nothing earthly, and do not set their hearts on earthly things 'go freely through them'. But they have already spiritually anticipated the death of the body, because the soul has withdrawn into itself; and what has already died, can of course die no more.

For wise men there are, the same in pleasure as in pain, whom these (contacts) leave undaunted: such are conformed to immortality . . . The man who puts away all desires and roams around from longing freed, who does not think 'This I am', or 'This is mine', draws near to peace.

(*The Bhagavad-Gita*)[22a]

(b) The soul as transcendental subject

In accordance with the ancient world's metaphysics of substance, the soul was thought of as a fine, ethereal substance within the human being which has an affinity with the divine. With the transition to the modern metaphysics of subjectivity, this notion gave way to the idea of the thinking subject. Because the ego or 'I' as the subject of understanding and will is the presupposition for all experience, this 'I' has to be transcendentally defined. For this, we shall look at some ideas of the radical Kantian Johann Gottlieb Fichte, because they demonstrate the metaphysics of transcendental subjectivity particularly clearly.

For Fichte, the human 'I' is the moral 'I', which is possessed by its imperative, unconditional task, and through surrender to this task becomes itself absolute. 'Oh, this is the most sublime idea of all: if I assume that exalted task, I shall never have completed it; thus, since to assume this same task is undoubtedly my destiny, I can *never cease to effect*, and can hence never cease *to be*. That which is called death cannot cut short my work; for my work is destined to be completed, and it can never be completed in any time. Consequently no time is set for my existence – and I am eternal. In assuming that great task, I have simultaneously wrested eternity to myself.'[23] Fichte's 'exalted task' is the moral perfecting of the human race, its elevation above the animal world, and its approach to the divine. That is the meaning of world history. And to participate in this task is the meaning of every individual human life, for the essence of human beings is their will.

The final destiny of all reasonable beings is absolute unity, unbroken harmony with themselves – that is to say with their identity. This harmony is achieved when the empirical 'I' identifies itself with the transcendental 'I'. This comes about through commitment to that 'exalted task'. The pure 'I' (whose presence the empirical 'I' knows itself to be) is uncompounded, undivided, indivisible, and hence immortal. It transcends the world of phenomena or appearances, because it itself constitutes this world, and brings it to appearance. Death is a phenomenon, a phenomenon like all other phenomena; and no phenomenon touches the 'I'.[24] It follows from this 'that in every moment we have and possess the whole of eternity, and place no faith at all in the deceptive phenomena of a birth and death in time. We have hence no need of a resurrection, as deliverance from a death in which we do not believe.'[25]

In his 'Way towards the Blessed Life' (1806; ET 1849), Fichte expressed the same idea in the religious language of mysticism: 'There is with certainty no being and no life apart from the immediate divine life.' Unclouded and unveiled, 'it again emerges from the life and deeds of the one who has surrendered to God. In these deeds it is not the human person who acts; it is God himself in his primal, innermost Being and essence who acts in that person, and through that person works his work.'[26]

Anyone who is so in God that God is in him has no need to believe in God, for 'God continues to exist unceasingly in him for ever, just as he is'.[27] In indestructible peace, such persons can disregard the distress with which the contemplation of reality may fill them.

> A holy will lives,
> even when human will falters.
> High above time and space moves,
> living, the highest idea;
> and though everything circles in infinite change,
> there abides in the change an unwavering mind.[28]

Like Plato, from the transcendental presuppositions of perception Fichte deduces the immortality of the perceiving subject. Unlike Plato (and in this sense a philosopher of the modern era), he links the transcendental 'I' with the moral 'I', and the moral 'I' with the task of humanity. The transcendental presupposition of perception is immortal, and the moral 'I' will be immortal too if it commits itself to that 'exalted task'. The idea of immortality is therefore not related to any particular sectors of human existence, not even to a 'disembodied mind'; it is bound up with its eternal presupposition and its moral task. What is eternal is the transcendental dimension of life, and its moral qualification.

Whereas Plato deduced from this that the soul ought to 'separate itself' from the body, should 'have nothing in common with it', and should 'remain gathered together alone into itself', Fichte's motto was: 'the human being should always be one with himself.'[29] The pure, transcendental 'I' cannot contradict itself, for it is uncompounded – undivided – identical with itself. But the empirical 'I' is entangled and diffused by the flood of phenomena in all their multiplicity. Yet it should be in tune with itself in such a way that it could be eternally so attuned. If the empirical 'I' corresponds to the pure 'I', then human beings are at one with themselves. They are then unassailable, invulnerable, immortal. Death does not touch them, for only what is divided and at odds with itself is vulnerable and mortal.

(c) The soul as the kernel of existence

As a third version of the doctrine of the immortal soul we shall look at Ernst Bloch's materialist idea about the core or 'kernel of existence' which has not yet come into being; for in place of the Platonic anamnesis, or recollection, Bloch puts the messianic hope for the 'someday unveiled face', while he differs from Fichte's moral idealism in talking about revolutionary praxis.[30]

Bloch sees clearly that death is the problem for any thinking founded on hope: 'The jaws of death grind everything to dust, and the maw of putrefaction eats away every teleology.' Death is not just a reality on which utopias of the better life break, like waves on the shore. It is a true 'anti-utopia'.

After a critical analysis of the religious images of hope that gainsay death, Bloch expounds his own insight into the human being's 'exterritorial kernel of existence', and the hope for a *non omnis confundar* (a 'Let me never be confounded') which will counter death.[31] In 'the darkness of the lived moment' – that is, in ecstatic life – the human being approaches his 'kernel'. This most intimate element of our being is at the same time its defining foundation, the naked '*that* of our being'. In the Today of the lived moment, the kernel is dark – that is, it cannot be objectified. We cannot 'have' it, for we 'are' it ourselves. It is unmediated, and we are assured of it in the immediate experience of existence, of 'being there'. In this kernel, something is concealed which strives to emerge and to be materialized, but which has not as yet finally realized itself in any form of life. Its potentiality therefore transcends all its realities, thus making them supersedable, transitory and mortal. This 'fermenting', 'becoming' kernel of existence is not subject to transience, to 'dying and becoming', for it is itself that which makes the 'dying and becoming'. It is immortal just because it has not yet become.

With this Bloch gives the experience of transience a new interpretation, different from Plato's. Everything that comes into being must properly perish – not, however, because everything that is born is born for death, but because the true life, the full identity, was not yet born – not yet realized – has not yet appeared. Here the awareness of transience emerges, not out of the impact of grief at having to leave the beloved, but through the impact of the hope which supersedes and surpasses all its insufficient realizations. It is because that which can die is not yet the true essence that hope reaches out beyond death. Hope anticipates death itself, since it thrusts beyond present reality into the not-yet-realized potentialities in the world process. Only the realities which, as hope says, do not have the truth in themselves can die. But those still unborn, still unrealized potentialities to which hope is related cannot die because they are not yet there.

Transience and death therefore befall realized existence but not the kernel of existence, which is not yet realized. Over against death, the kernel is enclosed by 'the protective sphere of the not-yet-living'. Not because it lies in the higher, non-transitory sphere of the divine, as Plato said, but because – since it has not as yet become – it 'ferments' and is therefore, in confrontation with death, still future; that is to say, it cannot be killed. Its perfect realization is an eschaton in which inward and outward, kernel and shell coincide – which will hence be an eternal life without death. Death enters only at the moment of rupture, of dichotomy, in which the immediate being has not yet arrived at its consummated existence.

Because of this, Bloch can say that the utopia of the *non omnis confundar* gives the negation 'death' every shell to crack – but gives it that power only. The kernel of existing is not open to death's grasp, because it has not yet entered reality; and when the day comes that it is wholly there, in consummated reality, in a unity of essence and existence, death will in any case have lost its power. Consequently the promise follows: 'Wherever existence draws near to its kernel, continuance begins – not a petrified continuance but one which holds within itself the *Novum* without transience, without corruptibility.'[32]

In place of the distinction between the immortal soul and the mortal body, Bloch puts the distinction between the immortal kernel of existence and mortal existing. In becoming aware of this differentiation, human beings become conscious at the same time of the eternally creative wellspring of their existing. The kernel of existence cannot die because it is not yet alive. But then Bloch leaves Plato behind and turns to the Bible, in his hope for a consummated existing which will drive out death, and in his expectance of a life which 'will swallow up death' and therefore abide eternally. For our present existing, this hope certainly means merely a recourse to the not-yet-lived life in the kernel of existing. To counter death, the human being can only retreat into 'the protective sphere of the not-yet-living'. It is not the *lived* life that is to be exterritorial to death; it is the *unlived* life.

The attitude to living which follows from this concept can be called in Gershom Scholem's phrase 'deferred life'. Everything we experience is only for a time, everything we do is provisional. Everything remains 'in tremendous suspension',[33] nothing is final. Consequently there is no irrevocable venture into anything concrete. The world is 'an experiment'.[34] 'The kernel of existence' does not commit itself, and does not expend itself, because it hopes for a better future, and holds back, reserving itself for that. The dialectic of hope dissipates everything which thinks that it is finished and done with and purports to be 'fact', bringing it into the process of its potentialities; but this dialectic of potentiality remains potential and hence unreal. With this experimental attitude to life we do not truly live, do not expend ourselves, do not love life in such a way that with death everything is at an end; instead we keep our best back, guarding it for the future. But if death destroys only what is realized, does it not also make the possible impossible? It does not only condemn our existence to become a being-that-is-no-longer; it takes from us too the being-that-is-not-yet. I can see no *non omnis confundar* in recourse to 'the protective sphere of the not yet living'. I see it only in a life projected towards God: '*In te Domine, speravi* – in thee, O Lord, have I put my hope.'

2. *The Raising of the Body and the Life Everlasting*

The immortality of the soul is an opinion – the resurrection of the dead is a hope. The first is a trust in something immortal in the human being, the second is a trust in the God who calls into being the things that are not, and makes the dead live. In trust in the immortal soul we accept death, and in a sense anticipate it. In trust in the life-creating God we await the conquest of death – 'death is swallowed up in victory' (I Cor. 15.54) – and an eternal life in which 'death shall be no more' (Rev. 21.4). The immortal soul may welcome death as a friend, because death releases it from the earthly body; but for the resurrection hope, death is 'the last enemy'(I Cor. 15.26) of the living God and the creations of his love.

Just as death is not only the end, but an event belonging to the whole of life, so the resurrection too must not be reduced to 'a life after death'. The resurrection is also an event belonging to the whole of life. It is the reason for a full acceptance of life here, and means that human beings can give themselves up to the whole of life without any reservation. What is hoped for there, after death, as 'the raising of the dead', means here the life lived in love. 'We know that we have passed out of death into life, because we love the brothers and sisters' (I John 3.14). True life means here *love* and there *glory*. The resurrection hope is not a speculation about some far off, posthumous condition. Only the love which passionately affirms life understands the relevance of this hope, because it is through that that this love is liberated from the fear of death and the fear of losing its own self. The resurrection hope makes people ready to live their lives in love wholly, and to say a full and entire Yes to a life that leads to death. It does not withdraw the human soul from bodily, sensory life; it ensouls this life with unending joy. In expectation of the resurrection of the dead, the person who hopes casts away the soul's protective cloak in which the wounded heart has wrapped itself, so as not to let anything more come near it. We throw ourselves into this life and empty ourselves into the deadly realm of non-identity by virtue of the hope that God will find us in death, and will raise us and gather us.

Hope for 'the resurrection of the body' permits no disdain and debasement of bodily life and sensory experiences; it affirms them profoundly, and gives greatest honour to 'the flesh', which people have made something to be despised. In order to describe the relation between commitment to life here and the resurrection of the dead there, Paul uses the image of the grain of wheat: 'It is sown perishable, it is raised imperishable. It is sown in dishonour, it is raised in glory. It is sown in weakness, it is raised in power. It is sown a physical body, it is raised a spiritual body' (I Cor. 15.42–44, cf. also John 12.24; Matt. 10.39; Luke 17.33).

In the dialectic of the resurrection, the soul doesn't have to withdraw itself from the body. On the contrary, it will be embodied and become flesh. It doesn't have to deny the emotions. It will make them living in love. It doesn't have to anticipate death in the *memento mori*. It will overcome death in the midst of life, through love. In this resurrection dialectic, human beings don't have to try to cling to their identity through constant unity with themselves, but will empty themselves into non-identity, knowing that from this self-emptying they will be brought back to themselves again for eternity. Human beings find themselves, not by guarding themselves and saving themselves up, but through a self-emptying into what is other and alien. Only people who go out of themselves arrive at themselves. Life is not 'an experiment'. The resurrection hope, at least, does not leave life here in 'a state of suspension'. It permits no 'deferred life'. For the love of life which it makes possible, everything is singular, non-recurring and definitive. The transcendence of hope is lived in the incarnation of love. I shall live *wholly* here, and die *wholly*, and rise *wholly* there.

Following this link between love for life and the resurrection hope, we shall now look at the various ideas about resurrection. There have always been interactions between the great religions on earth. But when ideas were taken over they were integrated into the complex of the religion that adopted them. So in the Old Testament we find a number of different notions about resurrection taken over from other religions, from Egypt and Babylon. To some extent these are integrated into the Israelite belief in God, to some extent they are simply added on to it.

Israelite faith in God is determined by the Exodus experience. God is called 'the Lord' because he led the people out of slavery to freedom. Analogously, God was expected to act as deliverer from the exigency of death, as we see from the psalms of lament and thanksgiving.[35] Similar experiences led people to go a step further, and ask: 'Dost thou work wonders for the dead?' (Ps. 88.10). Or: 'If a man die, shall he live again?' (Job 14.14). For Israel as a whole expectations such as these also spring from remembrance of the Exodus. Ezekiel 37 puts it with particular force: 'Can these bones live?' As answer, the life-giving breath of God blows over the field of the dead: 'Behold, I will open your graves . . . I will put my Spirit within you, and you shall live again, and I will place you in your own land, and you shall know that I am "the Lord"' (37.12, 14). The passage is undoubtedly talking about a resurrection in this life. It comes about through Yahweh's *ruach*, and in this happening 'the Lord' manifests himself. 'The Lord' is the name of Israel's liberating God.

It is only in Israelite eschatology that expectations of the Lord of life reach out for the first time beyond the frontier of death to a raising of the dead to a life that is eternal, and consequently to the annihilation of death itself. The Little Apocalypse of Isaiah (chapters 24–26) says about Israel's dead: 'But thy dead shall live, their bodies shall rise. O dwellers in the dust, awake and sing for joy!' (26.19). From the great banquet of the nations on Zion the promise goes out to the whole human race: 'He will swallow up death for ever, and . . . will wipe away the tears from all faces . . .' (25.8). Here the resurrection is an unequivocal salvific hope.

In the Son of man apocalyptic in Daniel 12.2 it is a different matter: 'Many of those who sleep in the dust of the earth shall awake, some to everlasting life, and some to shame and everlasting contempt.' Here the idea of God's universal final judgment is in the forefront. Through his judgment God's righteousness and justice will be made to prevail in all things and among all people. The dead must rise so that they can take responsibility; they must rise body and soul so that they can take responsibility for everything that they have done in body and soul, and can receive eternal life or eternal shame according to their deeds. We find similar ideas about the judgment of the dead in Egypt.

These two ideas about resurrection can be found side by side in Israelite tradition, unharmonized.

In the books of Maccabees, the resurrection is thought of in order that the righteous who resist, and the fallen martyrs, can participate in Israel's End-time salvation. In the specifically apocalyptic literature the concept of the universal Last Judgment is developed further. Here resurrection is not a hope for salvation, but a two-edged expectation, because one does not know to which side one will belong. The idea of resurrection is used to show that everyone will be called to account on Judgment Day. If one takes this seriously, one does not know whether a resurrection is desirable at all, either for oneself or for other people. What is at the centre is not resurrection but the universal victory of God's righteousness and justice. Here resurrection is merely an auxiliary concept that makes it possible to think of the final judgment diachronically, as applying to all generations.

In both cases, resurrection presupposes the death of body and soul, and affects the complete person – that is to say, it is always thought of in physical terms. Is faith in the resurrection an essential part of Israelite faith in God? In the second of the Eighteen

Benedictions (the Amidah), the God of Israel is praised daily as 'Thou who revivests the dead', while the last of the Thirteen Principles of the Faith (which go back to Maimonides) affirms: 'I believe with perfect faith that there will be a resurrection of the dead at the time when it shall please the Creator, blessed be his name . . .'

Christian faith in God is shaped by the experience of the dying and death of Christ, and by the appearances of the Christ who was raised.[36] Resurrection is not a return to this, or another, mortal life. It is entry into a life that is eternal. Christ's resurrection is therefore not a historical event; it is an eschatological happening to the crucified Christ and took place 'once for all' (Rom 6.10). In the first commandment given to Israel, God identifies himself as the One who brought Israel our of Egypt; in analogy, God according to the New Testament is the One 'who raised Jesus from the dead' (Rom. 10.9). The God who raises the dead is the God who calls into existence the things that do not exist, and is faithful to his promise in history (Rom. 4.17). If Christ has been raised *from* the dead, then he takes on proleptic and representative significance *for* all the dead. He is 'the leader of life' (Acts 3.15), 'the first to rise from the dead' (Acts 26.23), 'the first-born from the dead' (Col. 1.18). He is therefore 'the resurrection and the life' in person (John 11.25). The process of the resurrection of the dead has begun in him, is continued in 'the Spirit, the giver of life', and will be completed in the raising of those who are his, and of all the dead. The eschatological question about the future of the dead is answered christologically. And yet even in the New Testament ideas about the resurrection are unharmonized: in community with the risen Christ, this hope is a living hope for eternal life; in expectation of the judgment of the living and the dead it remains an ambivalent and uncertain expectation, with fear and trembling.[37]

Like the raising of the dead Christ by God through his life-giving Spirit, the resurrection of the dead is also expected as a physical happening touching the whole person, namely as a 'giving life to mortal bodies' (Rom. 8.11). 'The raising of the dead' describes the event personally – as it affects the persons involved. The annihilation of death (I Cor. 15.26; Rev. 21.4) describes the cosmic side of that event. The two sides necessarily belong together: there is no resurrection of the dead without the new earth in which death will be no more. The very expression 'the resurrection of the flesh' (*resurrectio carnis*) reaches out beyond the human dead, according to Old Testament language; for the Old Testament formula 'all flesh' or 'no flesh' (Gen. 9.11; Ps. 65.3; 145.21; Joel 2.28 and frequently elsewhere) does not just mean human beings in their physical constitution; it means animals too – that is, 'all the living'. It is true that the patristic church's acknowledgment of 'the resurrection of the flesh' (or body) was always reduced to human beings alone. But the wording of the acknowledgment leaves it open for 'the resurrection of all the living'. 'Not only the present body but its matter, the flesh, is to partake in the future resurrection.'[38] With this, the 'identity' of the material body is maintained with anti-spiritualistic rigour.

Eternal life consequently embraces *this* person, and this person *wholly*, body and soul; and, beyond this person, it applies to all the living, so that in that future world the creation that 'groans' under transience (Rom. 8.19–21) will also be delivered, because there will be no more death. Hope for the resurrection of the dead is therefore only the beginning of a hope for a cosmic new creation of all things and conditions. It is not exhausted by personal eschatology. On the contrary, every personal eschatology that begins with this hope is constrained to press forward in ever-widening circles to cosmic eschatology.

If the dead are raised to 'eternal life', what can this eternal life mean? Is it another life, following this temporal one, or is this temporal life going to be different? If it were another life after this temporal one, then the expression 'raising' would be wrong, and death would be the birthday of that other life, so to speak. But the raising of the dead means that 'this mortal life will put on immortality' (I Cor. 15.54). So something happens to this whole mortal life. Will this life be 'immortalized', as obituary notices sometimes say? If that meant that this life from birth to death is recorded as if on a video, and stored up in the heaven of eternity, that would be anything but a joyful prospect: immortalized with all the terrible experiences, faults, failings and sicknesses? How would we imagine the immortalizing of a severely disabled human life, or the immortalizing of a child who died young?

The expressions which come closest to 'raising' or 'resurrection' in the New Testament are transformation (I Cor. 15.52) and trans-figuration (Phil. 3.21). Then 'raising' means that a person finds healing, reconciliation and completion.

To be raised to eternal life means that nothing has ever been lost for God – not the pains of this life, and not its moments of happiness. Men and women will find again with God not only the final moment, but their whole history – but as the reconciled, the rectified and healed and completed history of their whole lives. What is experienced in this life as grace will be consummated in glory.

Death is the power of separation, both in time as the stream of transience, materially as the disintegration of the person's living Gestalt or configuration, and socially as isolation and loneliness. The raising to eternal life, conversely, is the power to unite – in time, as the gathering of all temporal moments into the eternal present; materially, as healing for life's configuration in its wholeness; and socially, as a gathering into new community in the eternal love. Because here we lead social lives, there is no 'individual' resurrection, but always only a social resurrection into a new community. Otherwise 'eternal life' could not be love. Eternal life is the final healing of this life into the completed wholeness for which it is destined.

3. *The Immortality of the Lived Life*

If the Christian hope for resurrection is so totally different from knowledge of the immortality of the soul, is there nothing in this life – the life which runs its course towards death – that endures and sustains, and makes human beings invulnerable and immortal? According to Christian ideas, God will raise the dead through his Spirit of life. This Spirit, the life-giver, is in community with Christ already experienced now, in this life, as 'the power of the resurrection'. As this power, the Spirit of life is stronger than death and must therefore be called immortal. But the Spirit of life is the living Gestalt or configuration of life as a whole. In this Spirit, it is not just one part of life (whether it be the soul or the ego) that is already immortal here and now; it is the whole of this mortal life, because that life is interpenetrated by eternal life, as by the spring that is its source. The Christian experience of the Spirit means that we experience this life here as at once mortal *and* immortal, as at once transient *and* intransient, as at once temporal *and* eternal. In order to be able to think this paradox, we have to ask what conditions and what changes make it possible to integrate the ideas about immortality into the Christian hope of resurrection.[39]

According to Platonic dualism, the soul is immortal because it is divine. According to Christian understanding, God is the Creator and the soul is his creation, and as such is not divine.

According to Idealism's view, the ego or 'I' is transcendent, and death is merely a phenomenon in the world of phenomena. According to the Christian view, only God possesses that undivided identity with himself by virtue of which he can say 'I am who I am' (Ex. 3.14). The human 'I', on the other hand, is constituted by the 'Thou'. I am because you are.

According to Christian thinking, God's freedom is creative freedom, while the freedom of human beings is a freedom which God's freedom creates and permits.

Every theological concept of the soul or the 'I' has to start from the postulate that the soul is creaturely, finite, changeable, capable of love and suffering, and is in all these things human, not divine.[40] These definitions are not enough, however, because they merely establish the difference between Creator and creature, without considering the presence of God's Spirit in the human being. But the Old Testament says that the spirit of human beings enters them through the divine breath of life (Yahweh's *ruach*), making them live; and that after death this spirit returns to God: 'Into thy hands I commit my spirit' (Ps. 32.5; Luke 23.46). The Spirit of life which comes from God and goes to God is immortal.[40a]

How are we to understand this divine Spirit of life in human beings?

(a) It signifies a *relatedness that is immortal*. By creating his image on earth, the Creator puts himself in a particular relationship to this being. *Imago Dei* – the image of God – means first of all God's relationship to the human being, and then the relationship of human beings, women and men, to God.[41]

In God's relationship to human beings they are designated to be the image of God; and this relationship cannot be destroyed, either by the sin of human beings or by their death. Only God himself, if he 'repents' or 'is sorry' for having created human beings, can revoke his relationship to them, and put a term to his faithfulness. But as long as God holds fast to his relationship to them, their designation as the image of God is indissoluble, inalienable and immortal. If it were not, sin and death would be stronger than God, and God would not be God.

God's relationship to the human being, and the designation of the human being resolved on in that relationship, is occasionally called 'soul' in the biblical traditions (e.g., Matt. 10.28), but the word more generally used is 'spirit'.[42] In this relationship a distinction is made between God's Spirit and the human spirit, even though the same word is used. Psalm 104.29, 30 distinguishes between 'their breath' and 'thy breath', Rom. 8.16 between 'the Spirit' and 'our spirit'. We understand this to mean that God's Spirit signifies God's relationship to human beings, while the human spirit signifies the relationship of men and women to God. The second relationship depends on the first, but is the same in kind. 'In the Spirit' God is for human beings both transcendent 'opposite' and immanent presence. The human spirit is the immanence of God's Spirit, and God's Spirit is the transcendence of the human spirit. The relationship between Spirit and spirit can neither be described one-sidedly as God's relationship to human beings (as Barth depicted it[43]), nor one-sidedly as the human being's relationship to God, which is what Karl Rahner understood it to be.[44] It is a reciprocal, a two-way relationship between God and human beings in the same Spirit. We shall come back later to the divine Spirit of life, but for the moment we shall pause at the immortality of this two-way relationship between God and human beings in the Spirit.

(*b*) American process theology has also called this 'the objective immortality' of our life history. Death cannot undo what has once been done, and cannot erase it either. What has already happened, and what was once experienced or done, can no more be blotted out. It remains eternally, for it acts on God's 'consequent nature': 'There is a reaction of the world on God.'[45] Our life in time is once and for all and mortal, but we have an eternal present in God, by virtue of that two-way relationship in the Spirit of life (Ps. 139.5). Our life history is 'a book of life', to use Charles Hartshorne's fine image. When we die, the book is finished, but it will not be destroyed. It remains for eternity in the memory of the present God.[46]

God is 'the great companion – the fellow-sufferer who understands', said A. N. Whitehead, in a moving phrase.[47] God experiences us. God goes with us, God suffers with us, God rejoices with us, God understands us. So our life is eternally present to him, and remains eternally present for him. But the divine remembrance in which we are eternally held is not a photographic record 'which can be used in evidence against us', in judgment. Nor is it an unfeeling monitor. It is a loving and healing remembrance that puts things to rights: 'Remember me according to thy great mercy.' It must, however, be said that in strict process thinking the human being's 'objective immortality' is more often thought of automatically, as an objective registration, without these personal elements of God's rectifying and healing remembrance. And so the recognition of an 'objective immortality' of the lived life is an ambivalent recognition, and is by no means as yet consoling, let alone hopeful.

(c) According to the biblical traditions, God's relationship to human beings is not a silent one. It takes the form of dialogue. The people whom God makes his partners in his covenant remain God's 'conversation partners' as long as God desires it, whether they are living or dead. Otherwise God would not be God, and would have no power to fulfil his promise.[48] 'The one with whom God speaks, be it in wrath or be it in grace, that one is assuredly immortal', declared Luther.[49] Because this can be said about God, an objective immortality is inherent in this previously determined covenant partnership with men and women, whether the individual person is aware of it or not. Even if human beings do not answer God, they are still answerable to him. Their answerability to God cannot have bounds set to it by death. Otherwise God would not be God. Yet this immortality in dialogue is also an ambivalent and by no means consoling perception. It could be the worst thing for which the human being is destined. Death might be better.

(d) Anyone who lives in community with Christ believes in the God who raises the dead. According to Rom. 10.9, the acknowledgment of Christ and belief in the resurrection belong inseparably together. In both of them we experience the Spirit of life: the power of resurrection. In that we are assured that we are 'God's children' (Rom. 8.14) and so have a share in the Father's divine nature. As the divine power of resurrection, that Spirit cannot be destroyed by death. This power gives life even though we die (John 11.25, 26). Consequently the relation to God of sonship and daughterhood of which the Spirit assures us is an immortal relationship. This 'blessed' immortality of sonship and daughterhood in the Spirit is not ambivalent. It is unequivocally good and consoling.

(e) Does the resurrection hope premise the objective and subjective immortality of God's relationship to human beings, and of the Spirit in human beings? Of course the raising of the dead presupposes death; but it does not premise the annihilation of the dead's identity. On the contrary, God must be able to identify the dead in order to raise them, for it is not some other life that takes their place;

it is their own life that is raised. Raising is not a new creation; it is a new creating of this same mortal life for the life that is eternal, since it is the assumption of human life into the divine life.[50] The popular notion that people – especially little children – then turn into angels is not Christian, because it does away with the earthly creation. According to Luke 20.36, 'the children of the resurrection' resemble the angels only in so far as eternal life is immortal. They do not themselves become angels. 'It is not a self that is different from mine that is implied, but in "raising" God preserves my self in order to perfect it.' The 'preservation' of the person's identity includes 'the personal sexual characteristics, masculinity and femininity'.[51]

Everything that is bound up with a person's name – everything that the name means – is 'preserved' in the resurrection and transformed: 'I have redeemed you; I have called you by your name, you are mine' (Isa. 43.1). What is meant here is not the soul, a 'kernel' of the person's existence, or some inward point of identity, but the whole configuration of the person's life, the whole life history, and all the conditions that are meant by his or her name.[52]

Let us develop this Spirit concept anthropologically, and try out a line of thought. The Spirit brings God into relationship to the whole person, body and soul, past and future, and at the meeting point of that person's social and natural relationships. The Spirit brings the whole person into relationship with God, in the entire fabric of that person's life. In the Spirit we live 'before God', just as 'the light of God's countenance' is turned towards us in the presence of his Spirit.[53] In us, the Spirit of life shapes the mutual interdependence of body and soul, past and future, and the social relationships in the history of our lives. If 'our spirit' means the total configuration of our lives and our biographies, it also means our lives as a whole, which are qualitatively more than the sum of our members.

The human being lives *wholly*, the *whole* human being dies, God will *wholly* raise the human being. How ought we to understand this human *wholeness* in life, death and resurrection?

The *whole* is the form in which the different parts of an organism coalesce and co-operate. The whole is a new quality compared with the quantifiable sum of the parts. So human beings too as wholes are more than the sum of their organs, just as their organs are more than the sum of their cells, and the cells are more than the sum of their molecules, and so on. A person's total configuration or Gestalt is what we call that person's 'spirit'. If, now, the sum of the parts disintegrates in death, the new quality of the person's totality, as the outcome of a lived life, nevertheless remains in God's relationship to that person – not of course as the organization of the parts, which disintegrates, but none the less as the lived Gestalt 'before God'. In death, this Gestalt does not disintegrate into its several parts, but remains what it is 'before God'; for since the whole is more than the sum of its parts, it is also more than the disintegration of the parts. Through the disintegration of the parts – which we call dying, death and corruption – the person's lived Gestalt – will be transformed into the other form of living which we call 'eternal life'. For this reflection the category 'before God' is constitutive, since before the One God the human being always appears as a whole human being. Relationship in God is always a 'whole' relationship. Even if here people perceive only the fragments or ruins of their lives, they know that they are still perceived and loved by God as whole persons. It follows from this, according to the Sh'ma Israel, that those who pray should love God with all their hearts, and with all their souls and with all their might, since 'the Lord our God is one Lord' (Deut.6.4).

If these are the premises, what is death, and what happens to people in death?

We cannot then say: 'In death the whole human being is annihilated',[54] or 'In death human identity comes to an end'.[55] Death is not 'the end . . . of the whole person'. Nor is it an 'annihilation'. In death neither the life that has found its full fruition nor the life that has missed its mark will be 'annihilated'. Every life remains 'before God'. The person's 'continuance' is not something which human beings can claim over against death. God's relationship to people is a dimension of their existence which they do not lose even in death. The essence of death in the abstract and 'in itself' may be called 'lack of relationship'.[56] But this definition cannot be carried over to a human being's real, specific death. In that death the relationship in which God has put himself to the human being remains just as indissoluble as the relationship in which the human being has been put to God.

We cannot say either that death is the separation of the soul from the body, or that death is the separation of the human being from God. It follows from what we have already said that death has to be seen as a transformation of the person's spirit, that is to say his or her Gestalt and life history; and this means the whole person.[57] Through death, the human person is transformed from restricted life to immortal life, and from restricted existence to non-restricted existence. Death de-restricts the human being's spirit in both time and space. The dead are no longer there as temporally limited and spatially restricted 'contact persons', but we sense their presence whenever we become aware that we are living 'before God'; and wherever we sense their presence, we feel the divine 'wide space' which binds us together.

When we want to discover what death and resurrection really are, we have no need to search for an answer in ourselves, or from other people, or from past and future. We have to look at them in the death and resurrection of Christ. When they wanted to interpret the experiences of Christ's death on the cross and his appearances in glory, his men and women disciples talked about 'the *raising* of the crucified one', which is to say an act of God upon him through the Spirit; or they spoke about 'the *resurrection* of the Jesus who had died', that is a power of the Spirit in him; and they also used images about Christ's being *born again* from the Spirit to eternal life. So it is not enough just to talk about God's 'identification' with the crucified Jesus, and to perceive in the Easter appearances only the revelation of 'the meaning of his cross'. What happened to, and with, the dead Christ is a transformation and a transfiguration through and beyond dying and death, a transfiguration of his bodily form (Phil. 3.21), a *metamorphosis* from our low estate into the form of glory (Phil. 2.6–11). In analogy to this, believers will see their deaths too as part of the process in which this whole mortal creation will be transfigured and be born again to become the kingdom of glory. 'The resurrection of the body' means the metamorphosis of *this* transient creation into the eternal kingdom of God, and of *this* mortal life into eternal life. *Vita mutatur non tollitur* – life changes but it is not taken away.[58]

§3 IS DEATH THE CONSEQUENCE OF SIN OR LIFE'S NATURAL END?

The experience of death is always secondary. What we experience primarily is life and the love for life, and only after that the loss of life and the loss of the people we love. The way we live and the profundity with which we affirm life decides how we experience the deadliness of death. Death, frightening and mysterious, stares us in the face. We don't know what is ahead of us. We don't know where

we are going. Why this death? Why death in general, or at all? If it is
simply a fact of life that everything on earth oscillates in the great
cycles of die and become, then we ought to accept it, and stop asking
questions, because it is foolish to call in question what is self-evident
and a matter of course. But if death is experienced as a derangement
of life, and as a destruction of the love for life, then we are bound to
ask where this senseless happening comes from, and whether there is
any meaning in its meaninglessness. We shall then even call death
itself in question and say: death is not the end. But how *can* we call in
question the dead-sure fact which death undoubtedly is, and on the
basis of what hope?

In the first part of this enquiry we shall gather together biblical
traditions about expectations of life and the experience of death, so
as to bring out the diversity of the viewpoints. The Bible is a
collection of testimonies to the living God, testimonies too about life,
but it is not a theological textbook for conceptualities about life and
death. So there is no 'biblical concept' of death. We shall then go on
to describe the growth of a Christian theology of death, with its
consequences, and shall finally wrestle with its two main, contradictory theses: (1) death is the result of original sin; (2) death is the
human being's natural end. I believe that in the framework of
Christian theology these two theses are mutually incompatible, and
shall develop as alternative the idea of death as a characteristic of
frail, temporal creation which will be overcome through the new
creation of all things for eternal life.

1. Biblical Experiences

In Israel's early traditions, death was evidently imagined as it was in
Ugarit. It was an independent being which got hold of human beings
when they died, drawing them into its power (Ps. 49.14).[59] The
realm of the dead (Sheol) is death's kingdom. It lies in the earth, in the
waters below the earth, or in the darkness – or so it was supposed.
Although when human beings die they return to dust (Gen. 2.7; Ps.
90.3), they still go on living as the dead, having their own mode of
existence in death's kingdom. So when people died they were
'gathered to their fathers' in the family burial place and returned 'to
Abraham's bosom' (Judg. 2.10; Luke 16.22). Buried in the foetal
position, they also returned to the womb of 'mother earth' (Ecclus
40.1). When people die who have been blessed with a long life, they

die 'old and full of years', as is said of Abraham (Gen. 25.8), Isaac (Gen. 35.29) and Job (Job 42.17) – Luther translated the phrase as 'old and sated with life'. A death such as this is the natural end of life and is as such comprehended and accepted. It is of course only the end of the individual life, for this individual life partakes of the collective life of the generations. 'That your days may be long in the land which the Lord your God gives you' is the divine promise of blessing which rests on the commandment about honouring parents, and hence on the generation contract (Ex. 20.12). Even those who die 'old and full of years' go to their ancestors who – as the genealogical tables in the Old Testament show – are still present to the living. They are even called gods, *elohim* (Ex. 21.6; I Sam. 28.13; Isa. 8.19; 19.3). Because the early individual consciousness developed only in the framework of the collective consciousness of the family, the clan or tribe and the people, individual death is embedded in the securities of the collective life.

This general oriental view of death was taken over by the Israelite Yahweh faith, largely in the post-exilic period; but at the same time it was radically altered. 'The God of the fathers' is 'the God of promise'. His promise is fulfilled in the blessing of life. That is why this God is called 'the God of the living' and not the God of the dead. His presence blesses life, his absence is experienced as curse and 'death'. So everything that has to do with death – cults of the dead, food for the dead, invocations of the dead (necromancy) – counts as 'unclean' and far from God. For the special faith in Yahweh, true life is to be found in community with the living God, and real death is the loss of this community. 'For Sheol cannot thank thee, death cannot praise thee; those who go down to the pit cannot hope for thy faithfulness', prays King Hezekiah when death faces him (Isa. 38.18). Because praise of God is the elemental token of a blessed life and of awakened vitality, death and life are antitheses, like being able to praise and not being able to praise,[60] like being able to affirm and having to deny, like being capable of loving and no longer being able to love. Life and death are to one another like blessing and curse (Deut. 30.19). Here death is not experienced as the temporal end of life, or just as dying physically. It is felt to be a power in the midst of temporal life that is contrary to God and hostile to life. In every situation which stands in the way of God's blessing and hinders people from praising him – illness, for instance, or persecution, or imprisonment, or exile – death is experienced, if in these situations people feel that God is far from them. If living community with God in blessing and thanksgiving is the highlight of life, then every breach of this community will be understood as misfortune and curse. In death the human being is 'cut off from the hand of God' (Ps. 88.5) and experiences death as exile. God has 'hidden' or 'turned away' his face. In the transience of life, in the evanescence of labour, and in sudden death, God's wrath is experienced. Luther's translation of Psalm 90 brings out the point:

It is because of thy anger that we thus pass away,
and because of thy wrath that we are suddenly cut off.
For thou hast set our iniquities before thee,
our secret sins in the light of thy countenance.
So all our days pass away through thy anger,
our years are spent like idle talk.   (Ps. 90.7–9)

According to this belief, we can live only if God's face is 'turned towards us' or 'shines upon us', because this light is the source of the Spirit of life which makes us live. In Ps. 73.25f. we have one of the supreme utterances of personal trust in God in dying: 'If I only have thee, I ask not about heaven and earth' (again we are following Luther's translation): 'My flesh and my heart may fail, but thou God are my heart's comfort and my portion for ever.' Yet this does not say that God himself is the future of human beings, and that the hope placed in God himself is a 'pure hope'.[61]

Both ideas – death as the natural end of life and death as a cursed exclusion from lived community with God – can be found in Israel's traditions, side by side and unharmonized. Both experiences of death are possible, the experience of Abraham, old and sated with life, and the experience of Hezekiah, whom death appals. But the real riddle about Israel does not lie here. The puzzle is its refusal to give any positive meaning at all to death. Any comparison with Egypt's huge necropolises brings out the point. Here, just here, this people of promise and hope *par excellence* leaves everything open and does not 'cast a dream'[62] over death with images of a lovely fantasy. Like Rachel, in the face of death Israel 'refused to be comforted' (Jer. 31.15; Matt. 2.18). Death was a wound in life that would not heal. Only on the apocalyptic fringes of the prophetic writings do we find expectations uttered that God will make Israel's fields of the dead live again (Ezek. 37) and will raise the righteous to eternal life (Dan.

12.2). Otherwise the clash remains between the life in this world unreservedly affirmed in fellowship with God, and lament over the deadliness of death. Endured inconsolability in the face of death leads in Israel to an enduring 'remembering' of those who have died – evident today in the Shoah memorial Yad Vashem – and to the continual 'reminding' God of Israel's dead.

Christian ideas about life, death and resurrection presuppose these Israelite attitudes. But because of Christ's death and resurrection, and in the experience of the Spirit of life, views then changed. We have cited these Israelite ideas here because in their own way they played a part in the development of the Christian theology of death too.

The Christian *writings of the New Testament* all view death as a ruinous power contrary to God and hostile to life. In the rule of death over the world of the living, the godlessness of this world becomes manifest. There is no talk now about dying old and 'sated with life'. Instead faith in Christ picks up Israel's faith in Yahweh and, in contemplation of Christ's 'bitter death' on the cross, deepens the qualitative difference between life and death.

According to the stories in the synoptic Gospels, Jesus proclaimed the dawn of God's kingdom on earth (Mark 1.15). The kingdom comes to the sick as healing, to lepers as acceptance, to sinners as grace, and to the dead as resurrection. The raising of the dead is one of the signs and wonders of Jesus's messianic mission (Matt. 10.8; 11.5), for when the living God comes, death is forced to retreat (Isa. 25.8). But when Jesus raises the dead, he raises them into this life, which leads to death, and in so far this is merely an advance sign and heralding of the eternal life to come, which will drive death itself out of creation. The synoptic Gospels, which describe Jesus's messianic mission, did not develop any 'theology of death'. For them death is a power opposed to God whose end is at hand through the coming of the messiah. The 'meaning' of death is just that it will be overcome because through it the glory of the life-creating God is revealed.

It was Paul who first developed extensive reflections about death. As rabbi, he understood death to be a punishment for human sin: death is 'the wages of sin' (Rom. 6.23). We seldom come across this view in the Old Testament, but it is frequent in Jewish apocalyptic (Ecclus 25.24; II Esd. 3.7; 7.11; II Bar. 23.4; and elsewhere). This interpretation projects the familiar link between act and destiny into the metaphysical sphere. Death is not a heterogeneous divine punishment; it is simply 'the inevitable result of sin'.[63] Sin 'brings forth death' (James 1.15). As a Christian, Paul saw in the Christ surrendered by God 'for our trespasses and raised for our justification' (Rom. 4.25) the eschatological event of salvation. If Christ is experienced as the liberator from the power of sin, then he must also be expected as the conqueror of death. If he is the justifier of the godless, then he must also be the one who makes the dead live (I Cor. 15).

Paul sets this in the framework of the great Adam-Christ pattern: just as death came into the world through Adam's disobedience, so life comes into the world through the obedience of Christ (Rom. 5). In fellowship with Christ and in the power of the Holy Spirit, the new life that is eternal already begins in the midst of this life, marked though it is by death. The new eternal life will become universally manifest in the parousia of Christ and those who are his (Col. 3.3f.). According to I Thess. 4.13ff., at Christ's parousia the dead will be raised first. According to I Cor. 15.51, not everyone will die but everyone will be 'changed', the living and the dead both. The distinction between 'being raised' and 'being changed' was important for the Pauline expectation of Christ's imminent parousia. Once this expectation had been given up, the distinction lost its importance, because then the two things coincide.

In Johannine theology, death is the mark of this world, which perishes, while life is the new thing which the Christ sent by God brings into that world. John sees Christ and his mission so closely together that he can say of Christ that he is 'the resurrection and the life' in person. So those who believe Christ already pass from death to life (5.24) and will live even if they die (11.25). For John, the eternal life that overcomes death is a present experience of faith, whereas for Paul it is a hope for the future. For both John and Paul eternal life is experienced in the Spirit of life and is practised in love for life. 'He who does not love abides in death' (I John 3.14). If the present experience of eternal life is love, then the present experience of death is lovelessness and hate. This Johannine dualism corresponds very well to the dualism within Israel's faith in Yahweh between life and death, praising God and not being able to praise him.

Finally, we must look at the ideas about death in the book of Revelation. The Revelation of John distinguishes between a first and a second death (2.11; 20.6; 21.8). The first is physical – the death of the body and the severance of soul from body. The second death is eternal damnation after the Last Judgment – the final separation of God from the men and women who are damned. In Revelation, death once more takes on mythical dimensions. It is imagined as a personified power in opposition to God. Only at the end, after it has been forced to release the dead from its power for their resurrection, will death itself together with its kingdom, hell, be thrown into fire (20.14). Because death will finally be destroyed (I Cor. 15.26; Rev. 20.14), the new creation will know no death any more. This annihilation of death is anticipated in the Easter rejoicing of Christians: 'Death is swallowed up in victory . . . Thanks be to God, who gives us the victory through our Lord Jesus Christ' (I Cor. 15, 54, 57).

This brief survey of ideas about death in the biblical traditions is intended to show the following:

1. Death means on the one hand the temporal end of life. But on the other hand it also signifies the impairment of life through loss of community with God. The two experiences can coincide, so that when they are dying physically people can lose God and can feel forsaken by him. But they do not necessarily coincide. People can also experience this deadly God-forsakenness in other life-destroying experiences, while on the other hand they can die in serene trust in God. So what is the relation between the physical end and the experience of 'being at the end of one's tether' – the loss of life and the loss of God?

2. What has death got to do with sin? Is physical death the consequence of human sin, and not a fate which human beings share with all other living things that are ever born? Is sin the cause of physical death, or does it simply turn physical death into a mental and spiritual torment? Did the dinosaurs become extinct because of the sin of the human beings who did not yet exist? If a man or woman's sins are forgiven and they are freed from the burden of them, do they then die 'a natural death', or is death still, even then, 'the last enemy'?

3. What is going to happen to death? Is it going to be annihilated or transformed? Since death is experienced as 'the last enemy' of God and human beings, it will be annihilated, according to Paul (I Cor. 15.26). The power to destroy life will itself be destroyed. According to the great promise of Rev. 21.4, death 'shall be no more'. The power of transience and of no-longer-being is going to pass away and

will no longer exist. According to Hos. 13.14 (KJV), the living God says: 'O death, I will be thy plagues. O grave, I will be thy destruction.' In the image-world of apocalyptic, 'death and hell' are going to be cast into the 'lake of fire' 'that burns with sulphur' (Rev. 20.14; 19.20). That means that death will have to die and that hell will go to hell. In this language, the end of death is described with the logic of the negation of the negative. But that is not enough, because negative is simply countered by negative, and nothing positive ever emerges just from the mere negation of the negative. Death will die, not-being will no longer be, hell will go to hell.

The only possible basis for thinking the negation of the negative at all is a new position for 'being'. Because with the resurrection of the dead, eternal, intransient and immortal life comes into existence for created beings out of the divine life, death can no longer be. With eternal life, continuance without transience begins, and enduring present in the eternal presence of God. The picture language of the prophets talks here about death's being 'swallowed up' by the living God: 'He will swallow up death for ever' (Isa. 25.8); 'Death is swallowed up in victory. O death, where is thy sting? O hell, where is thy victory?' (I Cor. 15.54f.). In the presence of eternal life death loses its power, just as it already loses its power in the experience of passionate love, because this love is 'a flame of the Lord' (S. of S. 8.6). But will the death of this temporal life be 'swallowed up' by the life that is eternal? According to the hope of the first Christians, death will be 'transformed', just as this impaired, mortal life is going to be transformed into eternal, immortal life. 'The raising of the dead' is conceived of as a great metamorphosis of life: God who makes all things new is going to make out of life in its humble, frail and mortal form a transfigured, glorious Gestalt which will completely and utterly match his intention (Phil. 3.21). The negation of life, and the negative that thrusts from death into life, will be transformed into something wholly positive.

What is the difference between the annihilation of death and its transformation? An eternal life can proceed out of *annihilation* which has no knowledge of death at all, since death is no more; and so mortal life will be forgotten. But the eternal life that comes into being out of *transformation* carries the scars of mortality, because it is this frail, impaired and mortal life which is transformed into eternal life. Everything that has put its mark on this life remains eternally. Otherwise we should be unable to recognize ourselves in eternal life, and could never arrive at ourselves. But that 'everything' is no longer a torment and a fear. In the end all things will have worked together for good (Rom. 8.28), even things which have made us inconsolable, and which we shall never understand. The risen Christ could be recognized by the marks of the nails belonging to his death on the cross. And we too will still be recognizable from the configuration of our truly lived life. Just as his crucified body was transfigured in the glory of God through his resurrection from the dead, so too the Gestalt of our truly lived lives will be brought back, transfigured, and redeemed for God's kingdom.

2. The Church's Doctrine about the Death of the Sinner

The Fathers of the church followed apocalyptic and Pauline teaching for the most part: because of the link between act and destiny, death is the divinely decreed punishment for the sins of humanity. The fact that all human beings have to die is proof of the universality of Adam's first sin. Original sin is followed by hereditary death. Correspondingly, redemption takes place in two stages: sinners are reconciled by God through grace, and the dead are raised to eternal life. The fact that the conquest of sin has to be followed by the conquest of death is in line with the biblical traditions which interpret death as physical exclusion from fellowship with God because of the sinful breach of that fellowship. The patristic church's doctrine of physical redemption even puts the conquest of death in the foreground. The goal of salvation is intransience and immortality. But if death is the consequence of human sin, then when Adam and Eve were in the Garden of Eden they must have been immortal. That, however, makes their sexual reproduction impossible. Nor did their original immortality then shield them from mortality as a consequence of their sin. Other doctrines maintained that the sin of human beings resulted only in moral corruption without bringing about any change in their physical constitution; but these teachings were not admitted. In 418 the Synod of Carthage declared against the Pelagians:

> Quicumque dixerit, Adam primum hominem mortalem factum ita, ut, sive peccaret sive non peccaret, moreretur in corpore, hoc est de corpore exiret non peccati merito, sed necessitate naturae, Anathema sit.[64]

(Whoever says that Adam, the first human being, [was] created mortal so that he would have died physically whether he had sinned or had not sinned – that is, would have departed from the body not because of sin but out of mortal necessity, let him be anathema.)

The Councils of Orange (529)[65] and Trent (1546)[66] made this doctrine binding. According to Augustine, both forms of death, the death of the body (*mors corporalis*) and eternal death (*mors aeterna*), are causally derived from sin.[67] 'The wages of sin' is not only the 'eternal death' of damnation but the physical death of the body too. The Council of Orange called sin the death of the soul (*mors animae*), seeing the death of the body (*mors corporalis*) as the first penalty for sin (*poena peccati*), and eternal death (*mors aeterna*) as the second, final punishment. The question about the immortality or mortality of Adam was brilliantly solved by Augustine with the aid of a three-stage doctrine. In the Garden of Eden Adam enjoyed possible immortality (*posse non mori* – it was possible that he would not die). When he sinned, humanity lost this possible immortality and arrived at the condition of actual mortality (*non posse non mori* – it was impossible not to die). Grace, which abolishes sin and perfects nature, brings the elect the true immortality that cannot be forfeited (*non posse mori* – it is not possible to die). That is eternal life.

The early Protestant orthodoxy of the seventeenth century followed Augustine and the doctrine of the Catholic church, and distinguished three aspects of death: the death of the soul (*mors spiritualis*), the death of the body (*mors corporalis*) and eternal death (*mors aeterna*).[68] The origins of this threefold death are: (1) the temptation of the Devil; (2) the sin of human beings; and (3) the wrath of God.[69] Because these three forms of death are inwardly intertwined, God's wrath is already sensed in the death of the soul, and is then experienced in the death of the body. The eternal death of damnation is heralded in spiritual and physical death. As the hymnbooks show, the death of men and women was as a result deeply overshadowed by the terrors of the Last Judgment, and the curse of sin weighed tremendously on the dying. If the hour of death was the hour of God's personal judgment on a human being, it was essential to die believing in the forgiveness of sins through Christ.

3. The Modern Notion about a 'Natural Death'

Exceptions apart, and leaving aside so-called heretical Christian groups, it was the liberal Protestant theology of the nineteenth century which for the first time disputed the causal connection between sin and physical death, and cut loose physical death as something 'natural' from the religious framework of sin, judgment and punishment.

For Friedrich Schleiermacher, the Christian doctrine of faith had to do with the expression of the devout consciousness, not with dogmas about the constitution of the world: 'It is clear that in a system of doctrine the world cannot come under discussion at all except as it is related to man.'[70] Such doctrine does not talk about evil *per se* and death itself, but confines itself to the impression which both make on the believer's inward consciousness of self and God. Schleiermacher, and with him modern Protestant theology, distinguished strictly between person and nature; and he restricted himself to the religious and moral experiences of the human person. In the age of science and scientific medicine, religious statements about nature in general, and the nature of human beings in particular, were considered inadmissible, because they were 'speculative'; or they were demythologized and interpreted existentially.

With these presuppositions, it is quite logical that Schleiermacher should have declared death *per se* to be neither evil nor a divine punishment, but the natural end and temporal limit of the finite existence of men and women. It is only a God-consciousness* deranged by sin that will experience this natural death subjectively as an evil, and fear it as a punishment. Death is not caused by sin, but it is through sin that it acquires spiritual power over human beings, since 'it is not by death, but, as scripture says, by the fear of death, that we are subject to bondage'.[71] For if death draws up the final account of a life that has missed its mark, it will certainly be subjectively experienced as the consequence of these transgressions, and their punishment. Christ redeems human beings from sin by taking believers into his unremittingly powerful God-consciousness, thus strengthening theirs. His redemption is not a physical redemption for immortality, but a religious and moral redemption for perfect felicity. Those whose sins are forgiven and who believe in the

---

*This is the usual English translation of Schleiermacher's *Gottesbewusstsein*, though 'consciousness of God' would be more normal English usage.

Redeemer experience their deaths neither as evil nor as punishment, but as that which death really is: a natural end. The way death appears to believers differs from the way it appears to sinners. If they die 'a natural death', they also die without fear and trembling. Christ overcomes, not death but the fear of death. Redemption is related to the religious and moral life of humanity, not to the natural order.

Liberal Protestant tradition developed Schleiermacher's position further.[72] The underlying exegetical assumption was that the biblical traditions are talking about death both literally and in a transferred sense. In the transferred sense, 'the death of the soul' means a breach of fellowship with God, while 'eternal death' is its loss. These experiences in the God-conciousness must be uncoupled from physical death. The consequences of sin are spiritual disintegration, lack of inner peace, moral corruption, and fear of eternal damnation. To derive physical death from this source is nonsensical. Physical death cannot be put down to religious and moral causes. The transition from personal life to natural existence is a leap which is neither intellectually intelligible nor endorsed by experience. If we take a leap of this kind into a different category, we shall also have to make human sin the cause of other unpleasant natural circumstances. Where should we stop? Sin brings wretchedness and depravity: this assertion is valid as long as we are talking about the life of the moral person. As soon as we ascribe to sin consequences for natural life, we are on shaky ground. Sin has only subjective consequences and effects. We should not say either that through sin the objective 'character' of death has changed. It is only its character in human consciousness that changes, in the fear of death, the reproaches of conscience, and in contrition.

Liberal Protestant teaching concludes that the death of the soul and eternal death follow upon sin; but it removes the death of the body from this cohesion, because it distinguishes strictly between person and nature. For christology, it follows that Christ, by virtue of his 'unremittingly powerful God-consciousness' is the redeemer of *our* God-consciousness (which has been weakened by sin), but that his death and his resurrection have no special significance for our redemption. This of course gives rise to a further interesting question: being 'without sin', was Christ himself mortal or immortal, and what death did he actually die? As far as the old question about Adam and Eve is concerned, the answer is: they would have died even if they had not sinned, but it would have been 'a natural death', without 'fear and trembling'. Here hope for the resurrection of the body has to be replaced by the doctrine of the redemption of the immortal soul for blessedness. The body returns in a natural way to the earth.

Karl Barth adopted this view of Schleiermacher's in his own way: 'Death is not itself the judgment. It is not in itself and as such the sign of God's judgment.'[73] Death 'in itself' has only the character of the frontier of finite existence and as 'as such' belongs to human nature. Just as birth is the human being's 'step from non-existence into existence', so death is 'his step from non-existence into existence'. For 'finitude means mortality'.[74] So death 'in itself' belongs to the limited span of finite human existence, and is natural. Barth distinguishes '*de facto*' death from this character of 'death in itself'. It is indeed the death of the sinner, a death which the sinner fears as curse and experiences as punishment. Without Christ and faith, death in itself and *de facto* death coincide. But with Christ and in faith we have been freed from the curse of death for 'natural death'. 'This [liberation from unnatural death] obviously means that, as [the human being] is freed for eternal life, he is also freed for natural death',[75] which 'by divine appointment belongs to the life of the creature and is thus necessary to it.'[76]

So what, then, is the content of redemption, if natural death remains? Redemption means that God himself is the 'beyond' of human beings, and that these human beings, as those who 'one day will only have been', will share the eternal life of God, and that their finite life will be made eternal in God and will be glorified in him.[77] But does this not imply, on the other hand, that death, suffering and fear will be made eternal, simply because they in fact belong to the natural order?

Barth offers a christological justification for his view of 'natural death': so that Christ could die the accursed death on the cross vicariously for sinners, he had himself to be a human being 'without sin', but had at the same time to be mortal. If physical death in itself were the wages of sin, then the sinless Christ would have had to be immortal too. So Christ did not only die the accursed death of the sinner on the cross; he died his own natural death too. Consequently – so Barth concludes – finite human nature as such is already created mortal. The early Protestant doctrine of the two natures, on the contrary, held the human nature of Christ to be in itself immortal,[78] since as 'true man' – true human being – Christ is without sin and without death.

I should now like to offer the following train of thought for consideration, over against the Augustinian and the modern Protestant positions, and would suggest the following:

4. The Mortality of Temporal Creation

Is finitude simultaneously mortality?

1. Finitude is not always mortality. There are finite beings that are immortal – angels, for example, on the one hand, and stones on the other. Biologically, death came into the world of the living only with sexual reproduction.

2. Death may be called 'the wages of sin', but this can be said only of human beings. The angels remain immortal although according to II Peter 2.4 'they sinned'. Non-human living things, which have not sinned, are 'without their own will subject to transience' (Rom. 8.20) and die. Hence there is sin without death in creation, and death without sin.

3. Among human beings, there are sins against others and sins against the self leading to death. Through human beings, death is also unremittingly brought into the non-human creation. The ecological death of the earth is the work of human beings. According to the biblical stories about origins, sin is not merely rebellion against God; it is also violence against life (Gen. 6.5–7). Here we find true causation, but no causal connection beyond that in the metaphysical sense – the connection which Augustine asserted in his doctrine about original sin and hereditary death. It is a negative hubris for human beings to maintain that they are the origin of all unhappiness in the world. Psychologically, this is what Margaret Mitscherlich called 'the usurpation of guilt'.

4. According to the Priestly Writing, God's first commandment to human beings was: 'be fruitful and multiply.' Logically, this asserts that human beings were mortal from the beginning. Without dying and being born, there can be no sequence of generations. On the other hand the Yahwist's primaeval history (Gen. 3) seems to assume that death is the punishment for disobeying God's commandment. However we may view these biblical stories about the origins of the world, if we look to the end – the new creation of all things – we are told that there will be 'no mourning nor crying nor pain any more, for the former things have passed away' (Rev. 21.4). Since this is the new heaven and the new earth, we may assume that all death will be

expelled from God's new and transfigured eternal creation – not just the death of the soul but the death of the body too, not merely the death of human beings but the death of all living things. But that must mean that the eternal creation will perfect creation in time. The grace of God which overcomes sin and the consequences of sin does not lead back to the creation of the beginning, but completes and perfects what that creation was made and destined for. It is true that God judged the first creation to be 'very good', but the new creation for glory is more.

5. If death in general is part of creation in time, then the particular 'death of the sinner' has come into the world through sin. There is no causal connection between the two. But one could talk about a correlation between them. The frailty of the temporal creation of human beings is like a detonator for the sin of wanting to be equal to God and to overcome this frailty. Death is only the consequence of sin inasmuch as sin exists because of death: we cannot endure mortality, and by killing we can make other people die. The vulnerability of creation-in-the-beginning makes the act of violence against life possible. So there is a certain relationship between what we call sin and what we call death. Even if death is part of temporal creation, it does not have to be called 'natural' in the sense of being self-evident or a matter of course; and if it is called natural, this 'nature' by no means has to be taken as final.[79] If we turn back from the end to the beginning, then the death of all the living is a sign of the first, temporal and imperfect creation.

6. We do not die as a punishment either for our sin or Adam's. Nor do we die in the personal judgment of God. We do in fact die a 'natural' death, just as everything that is born someday dies. But we die in solidarity with the sighing and groaning community of all living creatures who are waiting for redemption (Rom. 8.19ff.), for we wait for 'the redemption of the body' (Rom. 8.23). What is natural is not something that is a matter of course – something that simply has to be accepted as an inevitable fate; it is that which is in need of redemption. Theologically, we call 'nature' the state of creation which is no longer creation's original condition, and is not yet its final one. 'Nature' is a time or season of creation which we might compare with winter. The new creation of all things is then the future of creation which, like Hildegard of Bingen, we can compare with the springtime when everything is green and fruitful,[80] and 'the earth opens and brings forth salvation' (Isa. 45.8). Our 'natural'

death brings us into the earth, and together with this earth we wait for the resurrection, and the springtime of eternal life. Even beyond human sin and violence, what Schelling called 'a veil of melancholy' lies over creation, and a strange sadness which Annette von Droste-Hülshoff apprehended so wonderfully:

> And yet there is a heavy weight
> which no one feels and each one bears,
> almost as dark as sin itself
> and fostered in the self-same womb.
> Each bears this weight as sickness knows
> The weight of air, by health unfelt,
> Unwitting, as cleft bears the rock,
> As coffin holds the mortal wounds.[80a]

The death of all the living is neither due to sin nor is it natural. It is a fact that evokes grief and longing for the future world and eternal life. The new creation will not only manifest the liberty of the children of God. It will also bring 'the deification of the cosmos'[81] through the unhindered participation of all created beings in the livingness of God.

7. The modern separation between person and nature (as in Schleiermacher) or between covenant and creation (as in Barth) does justice neither to human nature nor to the community of creation. It is an expression of the anthropocentricism of the modern world, an anthropocentricism destructive of nature. As persons, human beings share the nature of the earth, and as natural beings they are persons. The modern reduction of the expectation of salvation to the religious and moral personality is a deadly declaration of doom for the rest of the world. The patristic church's doctrine of physical redemption was more comprehensive in its cosmic dimensions. Today it must be transformed into an ecological doctrine of redemption. It could then be in a position to redeem the modern world from its deadly limitations and conflicts.

8. This has consequences for the understanding of the Redeemer. For it follows that several dimensions of his death have to be distinguished, and that none of them must be neglected. Christ died 'for us' the death of the sinner, vicariously, as our representative,[82] so as to bring us the divine reconciliation. But Christ also died in order to bring his fellowship with God not to the living only but to the dead too (Rom. 14.9). Finally, Christ died the death of all the

living in order to reconcile them all (Col. 1.20) and to fill them with the prospect of eternal life. Without these cosmic dimensions of his death, our understanding of sin and death remains anthropocentric. Christ's resurrection from the dead is not merely the endorsement of his death for the salvation of sinners; it is also the beginning of the transfiguration of the body and of the earth. The cosmic significance of Christ's resurrection has been retained in the Easter liturgies and Easter hymns.

9. *Faith* may be able to free us from the religious fear of death, if that means fear of judgment (although it must be admitted that in history the Christian faith has done more to spread the fear of death and judgment than to remove them). But *love* brings us into solidarity with the whole sad and sighing creation. We die into the earth, which is in need of redemption and awaits it. *Hope*, finally, means that we cannot come to terms with dying at all, or with any death whatsoever, but remain inconsolable until redemption comes.

5. Violent Death

Is death 'the wages of sin'? If we begin to doubt it, we have to ask whether the converse could not be the case too? Is sin not the wages of death? That would mean: sin presupposes the awareness of death. Animals and plants, which do not have any pronounced sense of death, and for whom, at least, death never becomes a problem, do not sin either. It is the awareness of death which first creates fear for life, the fear of not getting one's fair share, of not having enough from life, the fear that life will be cut short. This leads to a craving for life, and to greed. The person who senses death in the midst of life wants to live, and if not to be already immortal, at least to be invulnerable while living. People like this look at the immortal gods and want to be like them. They break away from their poor, frail, vulnerable and mortal human nature and want to be like God. They want to be rich, healthy, invulnerable and immortal. That is the origin of the sin that destroys life: not being willing to be what one is, but having to be something different. That is what H. E. Richter calls 'the God complex', and it is the source of all inhumanities against other people and oneself. For the knowledge of death also throws open the possibility of killing. Wild animals kill in order to eat. Among them too bloodthirstiness – killing for the sake of it – is a phenomenon. But out of their knowledge of the mortality of others, human beings contrive the art of murder, the art of the death threat and the death penalty, of war and mass killings. Human beings can use the threat of death because they know that other people are conscious of death and fear for their lives. Acts of aggression towards mortal life become deadly because killing is a possibility. Sin is the usurpation of life which springs from the awareness of death. Sin is the violence against life which springs from knowledge of mortality.

Sin is therefore 'the wages of death'. It originates in the covenant with death, and it disseminates death. According to the biblical traditions, human sin begins with the awareness of death (Gen. 3) and with Cain's fratricide (Gen. 4). According to the story of the Flood, the 'wickedness' of sin is its organized violence against life: ' . . . There were at that time tyrants on earth' (6.4) who thought that they were demigods, sons of male gods and human women, and who let themselves be worshipped as sons of the gods and divine emperors. They issued from the rape of women and became 'men of violence in the world'. They are 'flesh' and do not let themselves 'be punished by God's Spirit' (6.3). In other words, they make a covenant with death (for that is what is meant by flesh), and destroy the covenant of life coming from the life-giving Spirit of God. That is why their end is the Flood, in which the earth, corrupted by such iniquity, perishes, in order to come to life afresh in the covenant with Noah.

This ancient story uses mythical language, but its intention is political. The 'tyrants on earth' are the dictatorial empires, headed by their priestly kings, with their despotic rule. Israel viewed these 'kingdoms of peace' (as they called themselves) in Babylon, Egypt, Persia and Rome as the offspring of chaos and the enemies of life, and as murderous powers of destruction. This can be seen from the 'vision of the four kingdoms' in Daniel 7. In contrast, the kingdom of Israel's God is the humane kingdom of the Son of man (Dan. 7.13, 14) and 'the everlasting covenant between God and every living creature of all flesh that is upon the earth' (Gen. 9.16). It is the covenant between God and 'the earth' (Gen. 9.13). The iniquity of sin is therefore not so much personal rebellion against God and neighbour as the organized crime of the political despotisms which enforce obedience through the death penalty, and spread by subjugating other peoples and by genocide, tyrannies which do not just sacrifice human life but enrich themselves at the expense of nature, leaving deserts behind them. In a sovereignty of this kind, it is death that rules, not life. Under such a sovereignty life can be lived only at the expense of other people, not for their benefit. For persecuted Christianity too, in the pre-Constantinian era, the real Fall was to be found in the rise of demonic tyrants such as Genesis 6 describes: 'Justin turned Genesis 6, which tells of the fall of the angels, into an indictment of the Roman emperors and their gods; for these dignitaries were, Justin said, none other than the demon offspring of the fallen angels.' These demon offspring 'became the patrons of tyrants' and 'powerful and ruthless men', such as Gen. 6.4 talks about.[83]

The modern term 'structural sin' (a term which is also disputed because it is meant politically and economically) really says nothing other than what was already said in Genesis 6 and Daniel 7. There are political and economic structures which are unjust because they are used to enforce the domination of human beings over human beings, the exploitation of human beings by human beings, and the alienation of human beings from one another. Within these structures, violence is practised, not directly and personally, but indirectly, by way of laws and prices. Through structures of this kind, violence is legitimated. Through them, violent death is spread. Today impoverishment, debt and exploitation spread misery, disease and epidemics, and hence premature death, among the weakest of the weak in the Third World. The mass death of children in Africa is just the beginning. There, the number of people dying a violent death through structural violence is greater than the number of soldiers killed by military violence in the great world wars. 'The murder of millions through administrative methods has made of death something which people never before had to fear in just this fashion.'[84]

Death is not a consequence of these people's sin. A 'natural death' is rare among them: most of them cannot afford it. There, death through the indirect violence issuing from the wealthy countries is an everyday affair, just as everyday as hunger and disease. Because in the wealthy countries and richer classes of society personal possessions are of more value than a shared life, violent death in Africa and Latin America and in India is going to claim more and more victims. What were for ancient Israel the 'tyrants on earth', are for the poor today the wealthy countries, with their brutal structures. The violent death they spread is 'the iniquity of sin', and it reaches out not only economically to the dependent and subjugated peoples, but ecologically as well to every living thing on earth.

§4 WHERE ARE THE DEAD?

We experience what death really is from our love for life, and that means our love for the life of others, the people we love. It is true that modern individualism has privatized death – 'Everyone dies his own death', said Rilke – and modern existential philosophy has put its own 'Being-towards-death' at the centre of its thinking.[85] But in actual truth the death of others, the death of the people we love, is the real experience of death that we go through.[86] At the end of my own life I experience dying, but I don't experience my own death, because I don't on earth survive my own death. In the case of the people I love, on the other hand, I experience their *dying* only indirectly and 'sympathetically', by accompanying them and being beside them. The process of dying affects them themselves directly and personally. But their *death* is something I experience immediately and personally, for I have to survive that death, and mourn their loss, and go on living. The love that was happy in their presence must suffer their loss. How can it bear this without becoming numb and frozen?

How can I remain in my love for them without becoming bitter? Does my relationship to the dead change? Is there any lasting community with the dead? These questions burst from us when we experience death like this in the death of someone we love. They are questions that can now no longer just be answered personally, in the light of my relationship to God and to my own death. They have to find a social answer, in the light of God and the dead. I want to know where the dead are, and how I can hold on to my community with them. Are they sleeping, body and soul, in their graves, and will they sleep until the resurrection of the dead? Are their souls in the 'intermediate state' of a purgatory, where they will be purified through expiation of their sins before they are permitted to see God? Are they already risen, and now already with Christ in the bliss of eternal life? We shall look at these three ideas critically in order to see, first, whether they express a hope founded on Christ, and then whether they strengthen and consolidate our community with the dead, which is alive in love. Finally we shall enter into discussion with the Eastern and Western doctrines of incarnation.

1. *The Doctrine of Purgatory*

The pre-conciliar dogmatic theologian Michael Schmaus treats this doctrine with a detail that can only command admiration.[87] He is able to say so much about this individual eschatology that he has hardly any interest or space left for universal eschatology. The starting point of the dogma is to be found in the declaration of Pope Benedict XII of 1336. This rejects the teaching that the dead are asleep until their resurrection at the Second Coming of Christ, and it asserts that everyone is judged immediately after their own personal death.[88] In death itself 'the particular judgment' takes place, this being the individual anticipation of the Last Judgment; for with death, human beings acquire their final Gestalt or form. The decision for eternity has been made in their lifetime and becomes irrevocable through their death. In the 'particular judgment', human beings, in being known by God, are confronted by the whole and entire truth of the life they have lived, and are made 'their own judge'. If they die in faith in Christ, their sins, indeed, are forgiven, but they are not yet purged of their sins. They have not yet expiated them by suffering the necessary temporal punishments. The life of believers here on earth is a continual repentance and a permanent process of purification; and the same process will continue with their souls after death. The goal is the perfecting of the person, in accord with what God has designed and appointed.

'There is a purgatory, that is a state of punishment and purification, in which the souls which are still burdened by venial sins and the temporal punishment for sins, are purified.'[89] Purgatory is a divine grace through which God draws believing souls to himself after their death. There are two punishments in purgatory: *poena damni*, this torment consisting of the deferment of the ardently desired beatific vision; and *poena sensus*, an expiatory suffering for the rest of the sins that separate the soul from God. To put it in modern terms: after death, the believing soul experiences God's presence as the light and fire of love. The light of eternal love draws the soul to God; the fire of eternal love burns away the sins which cut it off from God. The fire of divine judgment is only the other side of the light of the divine transfiguration. Many people who once stood at the threshold of death and came back to life again tell of visions of this kind, visions of the light and fire of the unconditional divine love. For only the pure of heart will see God (Matt. 5.8).

Can the living do anything for the 'poor souls in purgatory'? 'We can efficaciously help the dead', says a tenet of faith, because of 'the communion of saints'. All those who are joined with Christ are joined with one another too. So in Christ we can pray for the dead and can vicariously offer God satisfaction on their behalf: 'Anyone who is granted an indulgence for sins is empowered to ask God to grant the promised remission of punishment to the dead.' The most efficacious help, however, is the celebration of the Eucharist on behalf of the dead – that is, the Mass for the dead. The communion of the living and the dead in Christ is a great, unique, 'expiatory community', so the living can intercede for the dead before God, and the saints can intercede before God for the living, and can be asked for their intercession. Where purgatory is located we do not know, nor do we know how long it lasts.

The finest literary expression of this teaching is the vision of purgatory in the second part of Dante's *Divine Comedy* (1319). There, purgatory does not lie beneath the earth. It is a mountain that reaches from earth to heaven. The mountain of purification is 'the second kingdom', where human beings are spiritually purified and are made worthy to ascend to heaven (Canto 1). It has seven overlapping circles or stages, in which the soul can purify itself from the seven deadly sins. Whereas hell is the place where all hope must be abandoned, purgatory is the path along which hope leads the soul: 'Beloved son, let your hope rise' (Canto 3). This path leads into the 'eternal living light' of the beatific vision, which Dante presents in trinitarian terms: 'O Light Eternal fixed in Self alone, / Known only to Yourself, and knowing Self, / You love and glow, knowing and being known' (*Paradiso* Canto 33). In this trans-figuration, Dante then also sees his transfigured Beatrice, and finds peace: 'O Triune Light which sparkles in one star / upon their sight, Fulfiller of full joy' (*Paradiso* Canto 31).[89a] Whereas hell and heaven are conceived of as closed and final stages, the one being without hope, the other without desire, the idea of purgatory throws open a prospect of a desirable future and a hopeful way forward after death.

Yet the content of the idea of a purgatory seems to be incompatible with the experience of the unconditional love with which God in Christ finds us, accepts us, reconciles us, and glorifies us. The notion of the continuance of bodiless souls does not satisfy our search for a fellowship with the dead whom we have loved body and soul. But the idea of an enduring communion between the living and the dead in Christ, and of the community of Christ as a communion of the living and the dead is a good and necessary one.

The Discussion:

1. Schmaus himself admits that the Bible contains no explicit evidence for belief in a purgatory. He therefore tries to prove it implicitly. As first biblical passage he cites II Macc. 12.40–46, although this text does not mention a purgatory at all. Matt. 12.32 talks about the sin against the Holy Spirit which will be forgiven neither in this world nor the next. Schmaus concludes from this that sins can be forgiven in the next world too – which is just what the text does not say. Finally, I Cor. 3.11–15 is adduced, according to which on the Day of the Lord every work will be 'revealed with fire'. Schmaus thinks this means the fire of final judgment on the evil and good works of men and women, and concludes that this must also be so in the 'particular judgment' at an individual death. But the text is talking about the true teaching of the gospel, which endures, whereas false teachings will be burnt in fire. His final argument, that Jesus presupposed the Jewish teaching about purgatory, and therefore did not talk about it, is a double *argumentum e silentio* – an argument from silence – because the Jews knew no such doctrine.

2. The real basis for the doctrine of purgatory is neither scripture nor tradition, but 'the church's practice of prayer and penance'.[90] Since the beginning – so the argument runs – there have been in the church prayers for the dead, good works, almsgiving, personal penitential practices, and the acquisition of indulgences, vicariously applicable to the dead, which free them from punishments for sin. The Letter of the Congregation for the Doctrine of the Faith on Certain Questions of Eschatology (17 May 1979) puts it even more clearly: 'The church rejects all ways of thinking and speaking through which its prayers, the burial rites and the cult of the dead would lose their meaning and become incomprehensible: for all this is in substance a *locus theologicus*.'[91] But that means in plain terms that theology is there in order to justify the existing practice of the church. Once this method is followed, there is no possible way of examining particular ecclesiastical and devotional practices for their conformity to scripture and the gospel.

3. The quotations which Schmaus cites from the pre-Augustinian Fathers do doubtless show that it was assumed that after death believers would undergo a purification process; but there is no question of satisfaction, achieved either through their sufferings or through vicarious penitential practices performed by the living on their behalf. The Orthodox Church therefore teaches that there is an

intermediate state in which souls can be completely liberated from the torments springing from their remoteness from God; but they are freed solely through God's mercy, not through 'satisfaction'. That is why the Orthodox Church has intercessions for the dead but no Masses for the dead.

4. For the Reformers, the real stumbling block was *the right-eousness of works* which was in this way projected beyond death. For purgatory after death is simply the prolongation of the path of penance followed before death. The end is moral perfection, the reward of which is the beatific vision of God. But if no one through their own achievements, merits and works can be righteous before God, but if 'we receive forgiveness of sin and become righteous before God by grace, for Christ's sake, through faith' (Augsburg Confession IV), then this must be even more true of life after death. In their fight against the traffic in indulgences, the Reformers therefore also condemned the doctrine of purgatory which was the basis for that traffic in the church. In 1530 Luther wrote his 'Disavowal of Purgatory',[92] and in the Smalcald Articles, Part II, Article 2, talked about the 'fair-ground trafficking in purgatorial Masses'. Calvin refuted the doctrine of purgatory in some detail: 'Purgatory is a pernicious invention of Satan, it makes the cross of Christ vain, it inflicts unendurable shame on God's mercy, it shakes and overturns our faith. For what is purgatory according to Romish doctrine but a satisfaction which the souls of the dead have to make for their sins after their death? So once the delusion that we must suffer punishment as satisfaction is destroyed, then purgatory is simultaneously destroyed to its very roots! . . . The blood of Christ (is) the sole satisfaction for the sins of believers . . . the sole atonement, the sole purgation . . . Purgatory (is) . . . a frightful blasphemy against Christ.'[93]

5. The theological arguments for the doctrine of purgatory are all strangely remote from christology, which is the centre of Christian theology. Only anthropological theses are put forward. But from an anthropological point of view, the assumption of the soul's continuing bodiless existence is inconceivable. And yet even today we can read: 'The church adheres to the continuance and subsistence after death of a spiritual element furnished with consciousness and will, so that the human self continues to exist, although in the intermediate period it lacks its full corporeality.'[94] The unity of body and soul in human beings makes this thesis untenable. It is refuted by a person's death, the death of the consciousness, perception and will. The soul

separated from the body is not a person. We can talk about a 'continuing existence of the human person' only from a theocentric viewpoint, because all finite beings are eternally present before the eternal God, and hence God's history with human beings can continue even after their death.

2. The Doctrine of the Soul's Sleep

After some initial wavering, Luther imagined the state of the dead as a deep, dreamless sleep, removed from space and time, without consciousness and without feeling.[95] He did not think anthropologically from here to there; he thought eschatologically from there to here: if the dead are raised by Christ 'at the Last Day', they will know neither where they have been nor how long they were dead. 'Therefore we shall suddenly rise on the Last Day, so that we know not how we entered into death, nor how we came through it.'

On the Last Day God will awaken the whole person, not just the soul-less body:

'We shall sleep until He comes and knocks on our little grave, saying: "Dr Martin, get up!" Then I shall rise up in a moment and shall be eternally merry with Him.'

'As soon as thy eyes have closed shalt thou be woken, a thousand years shall be as if thou hadst slept but a little half hour. Just as at night we hear the clock strike and know not how long we have slept, so too, and how much more, are in death a thousand years soon past. Before a man should turn round, he is already a fair angel . . .'

'Because before God's face time is not counted, a thousand years before Him must be as if it were but a single day. Hence the first man Adam is as close to Him as will be the last to be born before the final Day . . . For God seeth time, not according to its length but athwart it, transversely . . . Before God all hath happened at once.' 'For God, everything is on a single heap . . .'[96]

The idea that death has been made 'a sleep' has a double significance for Luther. On the one hand death has lost its power over human beings. On the other, it is no longer 'the last thing', the end. Both implications presuppose Christ's resurrection from the dead. Death has relinquished its power over human beings to the risen Christ. For believers, the form or character of death still certainly exists, but death's power has gone.[97] It is no longer the end; it is the gate to resurrection. With the help of the image of head and body, Luther compares death and resurrection to the process of birth; the head has already emerged, the body is drawn after the head and follows. Christ has already been reborn to eternal life. Those who are his, follow after him.[98]

How long is it, then, from the time of our own individual death until the eschatological raising of the dead? What ideas come to me when I think about 'death's long night', as the hymn puts it? Luther does not answer by projecting the time and space of the living on to the continuing existence of the soul, as does the doctrine of purgatory. He finds expressions for God's time: 'suddenly, in the twinkling of an eye' (I Cor. 15.52). The Last Day is the Day of the Lord, and God's time is the time of the eternal present. If the dead are no longer in the time of the living but in God's time, then they exist in his eternal present. So how long is it from a person's death in time to the End-time raising of the dead? The answer is: just an instant! And if we ask: where are the dead 'now', in terms of our time? – the answer has to be: they are already in the new world of the resurrection and God's eternal life. So Christ said to the man dying with him on the cross: 'Today' – not in three days – not at the Last Day – but: 'Today you will be with me in paradise' (Luke 23.43). And that today is the eternal today of God.

3. *Is there a Resurrection at Death?*

Modern Catholic theologians (Karl Rahner, Jacques Pohier, Gisbert Greshake, Gerhard Lohfink and others) have experimentally developed an interesting line of thought in this direction.[99] They have come very close to Luther. They start from the assumption that it is not the unlived life of the soul that God will reconcile, redeem and transfigure, but a person's real lived life, the life lived in body and soul, with all the senses. God is not interested in the unlived life of the soul; he is interested in the really lived life of the whole person. But during their lifetime, people grow out into the world, and the world grows into them. Salvation does not put asunder what God has joined in this life. So the visions of hope for salvation must embrace the world too: to understand salvation holistically means seeing it not as 'the soul's blessedness' but as 'the raising of the dead'. For the raising of the dead is part of God's new earth, in which death will be no more. Universal eschatology cannot be reduced to individual eschatology; on the contrary, it is the first that embraces the second.

But when does this holistic resurrection of the dead take place? The Dutch catechism of 1966 says: 'Life after death, therefore, is something like the raising of the new body. This resurrection body is not the same as the molecules and atoms that have entered the earth. We awake – or are woken – as new human beings.'[100] The 'New Book of Belief' (*Das Neue Glaubensbuch*) of 1973 puts it more precisely: 'The individual resurrection from the dead takes place with, and at, death.'[101]

But how ought we to imagine a 'resurrection at death'? The starting point must again be eschatology: the 'Last Day' is not just the chronologically final day in the calendar. It is eschatologically the Day of the Lord, and therefore the Day of Days. If this is the day when the dead are raised, then it appears to all the dead simultaneously, 'in a moment' – that is diachronically – irrespective of when in time they died. If this is correct, then we must be able to say the converse too: that the hour of every individual death in this present time leads directly into that eternal 'Day of the Lord'.

If with God there is no earthly time in which human beings succeed one another, then all human beings, at whatever earthly time they may have died, encounter God at the same time – in God's time, the presence of eternity.

This experiment in ideas overcomes the difference between the immortality of the soul on the one hand and the raising of the body on the other. The notion of a bodiless, intermediate state of the soul in purgatory become superfluous. But because indulgences on behalf of the dead, and Masses for the dead, then also become superfluous, the Congregation for the Doctrine of the Faith rejected this idea of a 'resurrection at death' in their Letter of 1979.[102] According to Karl Rahner, however, it is not a heresy to maintain the view 'that the single and total perfecting of man in "body" and "soul" takes place immediately after death; that the resurrection of the flesh and the general judgement take place "parallel" to the temporal history of the world, and that both coincide with the sum of the particular judgements of individual men and women'.[103]

But there are other objections too to the identification of personal death with the eschatological resurrection of the dead. Even if after death human beings are no longer subject to this life's categories of time and space, personal perfecting and the perfecting of the world still do not have to coincide. If we were already to rise at our own death, we should then be redeemed from 'this unredeemed world', and our bodily solidarity with this earth would be broken and dissolved. But is not every grave in this earth a sign that human beings and the earth belong together, and will only be redeemed together? Without 'the new earth' there is no 'resurrection of the body'. Only the new earth offers possibilities for the new embodiment of human beings. And if the individual 'resurrection at death' is called the historical 'anticipation' of the universal resurrection of the dead, and if the universal resurrection is said to be the completion of personal resurrection at death, then the very distinction which this line of thought was meant to overcome has after all once more been introduced.[104]

4. The Fellowship of Christ with the Living and the Dead

The deficiency of the ideas we have hitherto discussed about a life after death is that they start either from the human ego or self, or from the eternity of God. They do not begin with Christ. But it is essential to take Christ as point of departure, and to relate all the fears and all the desires of men and women to the One who can give us courage to live, and hope in dying, and consolation in grief.[105]

The centre of Christian eschatology is neither the human ego nor the world. It is God, who in Christ has thrown open to us his future. But Christ is *on the way* to God's kingdom. He himself is 'the way'. This means that Christian eschatology as a whole includes not only the anticipation of God's future in Christ, but also the distinction that has been called 'the eschatological proviso'. This 'proviso' says that although Christ has already been raised from the dead, we have not yet been raised. Through the strength of grace Christ has broken the power of sin, but the end of death's reign is still to come. So in Christ we are indeed already reconciled with God, but we still live and die in an unredeemed world, and together with this world look with longing for the new creation.

So there is after all an 'intermediate time' – the time between Christ's resurrection and the general resurrection of the dead. It is not empty, like a waiting room. It is filled by the lordship of Christ over the dead and the living, and by the experience of the Spirit, who is the life-giver. Christ's lordship begins with his death and resurrection. Christ's lordship will be completed when he annihilates our death and raises the dead and finally hands over the kingdom to the Father (I Cor. 15.28). So in history Christ is still on the road to his sovereignty over all things.[106] 'We do not yet see everything in subjection to him' (Heb 2.8). The rule of Christ is as yet only the promise of the kingdom of God; but the kingdom of God is the goal and consummation of Christ's rule. Anyone who dies in fellowship with Christ dies in fellowship with the One who is preparing the way for the coming kingdom. When poor Lazarus is safe 'in Abraham's bosom' he is hidden in the One who is the bearer of Israel's hope; but it is not yet a hope fulfilled in the world. In the same way, Christians know that they are safely hidden in Christ (Col. 3.3), the bearer or subject of hope for the peoples of the world; but they are not yet in the new world of the future.[107]

For Paul, this community with Christ, the subject of hope, extends to the dead as well as to the living. 'For to this end Christ died and lived again, that he might be Lord both of the dead and of the living' (Rom.14.9). I understand this in the following sense: In dying, Christ became the brother of the dying. In death, he became the brother of the dead. In his resurrection – as the One risen – he embraces the dead and the living, and takes them with him on his way to the consummation of God's kingdom. If I understand it rightly, this means that the dead are dead and not yet risen, but they are already 'in Christ' and are with him on the way to his future. When he appears in glory, they will be beside him and will live eternally with him. That is what Paul means too when he says that 'neither death nor life . . . will be able to separate us from the love of God that is in Christ Jesus' (Rom. 8.38f.), for the unconditional and prevenient love of God is the beginning of the divine glory that raises the dead and annihilates death.

The existence of the dead in the community of Christ is not yet 'a resurrection from the dead' but only a 'being with Christ': 'My desire is to depart and be with Christ', says Paul (Phil. 1.23). The dead are not separated from God, nor are they sleeping; and they are not yet risen either. But they are 'with Christ'. What can that mean?

(a) Do the dead have time in the fellowship of Christ?

If we understand time only as the linear time of human life – 'from the cradle to the grave' – then the dead no longer belong to the sphere of time. But if we understand time relationally as God's time *for* creation and as Christ's time *for* human beings, then the dead too have 'time' in Christ, because Christ 'has time' for them. The fellowship of Christ does not let them become iron-bound, or sleep, but has its own potentialities for them: 'The gospel is preached to the dead', says the First Epistle of Peter (4.6), for after death 'Christ went and preached to the spirits in prison' (3.19). The point of the talk about Christ's descent into hell (or into the realm of the dead, as the modern German version of the creed puts it) is to say that through his solidarity with the dead, Christ avails himself of his salvific possibilities for them, and thus brings the dead hope. In that world the gospel also has retrospective power. Those who died earlier can also arrive at faith, because Christ has come to them.

The fellowship of Christ encompasses this experience of the divine possibilities to which death can impose no limits. Who is more powerful, death or the risen Christ? So the dead also have time – not, certainly, the time of our present life, which leads to death, but none the less Christ's time, and that is the time of love, the accepting, the transfiguring, the rectifying love that leads to eternal life. That is a true element in the doctrine of purgatory.

(b)   Do the dead have space in the fellowship of Christ?

The fellowship of Christ consists of two semi-circles, so to speak. The one is the community of the living, the other the community of the dead. The living space of those who are alive has open frontiers, and so does the space of the dead. Certainly, we who are living cannot imagine the space of the dead in community with Christ, because we have not yet experienced it. But we are confident ('I am sure', says Paul) that our death does not mean that we fall out of this community. We simply move to the other half of the circle, so to speak, and will then experience the fellowship of Christ from its other side.

In Christ's fellowship with the dead and the living there is an enduring and indestructible community of the living and the dead, one they share – not an 'expiatory community', but a community of love, because it is a community in the common hope. Before God, the living and the dead are in the same situation. The dead are not lost, but they are not yet finally saved either. Together with the living, they exist in the same common hope and in a common danger too. That is no doubt what Walter Benjamin meant with his dark and mysterious saying that 'Even the dead will not be safe from the enemy once he is victorious. And this enemy has not ceased to conquer.'[108] Not in us, not in the world, and not in the realm of spirits is the division into this world and the beyond which death brings with it overcome, but assuredly in the risen Christ. So in him we remain indestructibly and unforgettably joined with the dead in love for each other and in a common hope. In him the dead are enduringly with us who are the living. The common hope for the future of eternal life and the new creation binds us together. It is true that 'it has not yet appeared' what we – and they – will be, but when he appears we – and they – will see him as he is and be like him (I John 3.2). And I would add: we shall see one another as we shall then be in the all-pervading presence of God.

(c) The community with the dead

The hope for resurrection has not just a meaning for the dead. It has significance for the living too.[109] This has become a remote idea to us today. Of course today too we are tormented by pain and sorrow. We suffer almost dumbly under the unreconciled hurts of the past. But we hardly perceive any more the sufferings of the dead which cannot be made good. A wall of silence, hard to break through, has been built up between us and the dead. Who feels the silent protest of the dead against the indifference of the living? Who is still conscious that the dead cannot rest as long as they have not received justice?

It was these experiences which led to the emergence of a 'political theology' in postwar Germany. We perceived the long shadows of Auschwitz, and heard the cries of those who had been silenced. We became aware that we have to live and act in community with the victims of the Holocaust and in their presence. The classic question here was the question posed by the critical theory of the Frankfurt school: Are the murderers to triumph irrevocably over their victims? Can their death be their end? 'Theology', said Max Horkheimer at that time, 'is the hope . . . that injustice will not be the last word . . . [It is] the expression of a longing, a longing that the murderer may not triumph over the innocent victim.'[110]

It is profoundly inhumane to push away the question about the life of the dead. The person who forgets the rights of the dead will be indifferent towards the life of his or her children too. Nor is there any present happiness or any social progress towards a better future for humanity which could compensate for the injustice suffered by the dead. The person who is indifferent towards the dead will ultimately be cynical towards the children.

In this situation, to acknowledge hope for the resurrection of the dead means preserving community with the dead and deepening it in recollecting solidarity. The community of Christ has always been understood as a community of the living and the dead. Many ancient rituals testify to the fact. In Germany, on All Souls' day Catholic Christians visit the graves of the dead, and on the last Sunday in the church's year (in Germany known as the Sunday of the Dead) many Protestant Christians do the same. On Easter morning many Christians, Catholics and Protestants both, celebrate Christ's resurrection at sunrise in the graveyards where the dead lie. The church used to be built in the centre of the village, with the churchyard round it. When people went to church on Sunday morning, they visited the graves of those belonging to them, and their worship took place in the presence of the dead.

Where, then, do we discover the proximity of the dead, and how do we experience it? In the community of Christ. Wherever this unconditional divine love comes close to us, there the dead whom we love are close too. The closer we come to Christ the more deeply we enter into community with the dead. But Christ is present in the gospel, in the Eucharist, and in the community of brothers and sisters. In the worship of the Latin American base communities, when the roll is called of the dead, of the people who have disappeared, and the martyrs, the whole congregation calls out: 'Presente!' They are present in the community of Christ. But Christ is present too in the least of his sisters and brothers, in the poor, the hungry, the prisoners (Matt. 25.31–46). The person who becomes the sister and brother of these grows into the fellowship of Christ, and in that fellowship comes close to the dead. We have no need to do anything for the redemption of poor souls in purgatory, for Christ has done it all, and they are already safe and hidden in his love. But we must not forget them or suppress the remembrance of them. This may be the deeper sense of the church's tradition of intercession for the dead, and almsgiving on their behalf. We come close to the dead in the eucharistic fellowship and in fellowship with the poor. They are beside us wherever the Spirit of life lays hold of us and makes us happy. The community of the living and the dead is the praxis of the resurrection hope.

If we see the personal hope for the future in this exclusively christological way, we are of course faced with the question: does this then apply only to Christians, who through their faith are already 'in Christ', and so may hope to be 'beside him' in the future as well? Or is it also universally true for everyone else as well?

In modern theology, the distinction is often made by saying: if you believe, you can have this hope; if you don't, you can't. Only believers are 'hidden in Christ' and will be with him in the future of his kingdom. Those who don't believe, or who rest their personal hope on something or someone different, will not see Christ's future. To each his own. All human beings must not be turned into Christians against their will *post mortem*.

The Lausanne Covenant of evangelical theologians says: 'Those who reject Christ repudiate the joy of salvation and condemn themselves to eternal separation from God.' They will therefore not only be damned by God. They also damn themselves. Is this theologically conceivable? Can some people *damn themselves*, and others redeem themselves by accepting Christ? If this were so, God's decisions would be dependent on the will of human beings. God would become the auxiliary who executes the wishes of people who decide their fate for themselves. If I can damn myself, I am my own God and judge. Taken to a logical conclusion this is atheistic. There is a more modern evangelical idea about a *conditional immortality*, according to which no one finds a life after death without believing and unless God confers eternal life; all the rest simply remain dead. But I do not find this very helpful either, because it excludes God's judgment. Mass murderers might possibly welcome this solution, because they would then not have to answer before God's judgment for what they had done. The *annihilationists* think that unbelievers do not go to hell eternally but are simply destroyed and fall into an eternal nothingness; but this too does not seem to me compatible with the coming omnipresence of God and his faithfulness to what he has created. For the lost to 'disappear' conforms to the terrible experiences with the murder squads in military dictatorships, but it does not accord with God. The God of the Bible is the Creator, not simultaneously the Destroyer, like the Indian god Shiva.[111]

Christian tradition occasionally introduced a distinction here between the first resurrection (Rev. 20.6) and the second. Believers will appear with Christ at his parousia (Col.3.4) and will reign with him in his kingdom. But all human beings will be raised later for God's eternal judgment. The first resurrection is therefore called 'blessed' but not the second. The raising of believers for the kingdom

of Christ is a resurrection *from* the dead; it is only the second that
will be the resurrection *of* the dead. This distinction presupposes an
intermediate, millenarian kingdom of Christ before the universal end
of the world. But it leaves unchanged the universal resurrection of
the dead 'for judgment' in the legalistic form of Daniel 12.2, so that
the gospel of Christ is for believers only, while the law of God applies
universally to everyone. This is a profoundly unsatisfactory solution,
because on the one hand it shakes the certainty of the hope of
Christians (who knows whether he or she really belongs?) and on the
other hand it surrenders not only the rest of the human race but
everyone who lived before Christ to the divine judgment, without
hope.

But the distinction can also be seen as meaning that 'the first
resurrection' is the beginning of the general resurrection of the dead,
and that the second is the goal of the first. Because cosmically the
personal resurrection of the dead means the annihilation of death –
that it will be 'swallowed up' in the victory of life – death's
subjugation begins with the eternal life already lived with Christ here
and now; it is experienced in the Spirit of life here by those who are
his, and in the life given to their bodies there. This is how Paul
described it in I Cor. 15.23–26, unfolding it as the 'order' of the
resurrection process: Christ 'the first fruits' – then at his coming
those who belong to him – afterwards the end . . . the last enemy to
be destroyed will be death.

If we follow this processual thinking, the hope of Christians is not
exclusive, and not particularist either. It is an inclusive and universal
hope for the life which overcomes death. It is true not only for
Christians but for everything living that wants to live and has to die.

5. Do we Live on Earth only Once?

Although a soul that cannot die is not born either, from time
immemorial the idea of the immortal soul has often been coupled
with the notion of the soul's transmigration, its rebirth and
reincarnation in ever new forms. Everything living comes into being
and passes away. Why should it not come into being afresh, and pass
away again? If one ceases to look at the individuality of a life, but
observes its natural participation in the wider complexes of the
earth, then it is rather the idea of the irrecoverable uniqueness of
every life that is new and strange, not the impression of the eternal

return of life in ever new forms. The so-called doctrine of reincarnation – the term is not particularly apt – belongs to the lore of pre-
modern and non-modern (more properly 'extra-modern') societies.
It is at home in Hinduism, Buddhism and Jainism, as well as in the
more recent doctrines of spiritism, theosophy, anthroposophy,
transpersonal psychology and the New Age movement. Plato and
Plotinus, Lessing and Goethe supported it. Today it suggests itself to
people who research into death and try to interpret the visions of
reanimated men and women. Did we live before this life, once or
many times? Will we live again after this life, once or many times? Or
does the ego or self die too when this life dies, so that if a
reincarnation were to take place, no re-identification would be
possible for us? In our present context we shall not offer a survey of
the various doctrines of reincarnation – there are surveys in plenty[112]
– but shall confine ourselves to a theological discussion about the
substance of these doctrines.

1. Every doctrine of reincarnation sets the individual life in a
wider community of generations, often in a cosmically conceived
community of solidarity shared by all living beings and things.
Everything is related to everything else. Don't kill any animal
because the soul of one of your ancestors could be within it! Don't
act unjustly towards any living thing because in your next life you
could be that living thing yourself! If the souls of human beings,
animals and plants are seen in the broad context of the great world
soul, then we are living in an ensouled cosmos. Every individual can
return in everything else, because it is out of that 'everything' that it
has come into being. So every individual must be able to recognize
itself in all other individuals. There are certainly teachers who
restrict rebirth to human beings, but the basic assumption from
which one has to start is that 'everything is at heart related', and that
everyone and everything can therefore be re-embodied in everything
and must consequently also recognize itself in everything. Every
spiritual life is lived in the presence of spirits, for they are everywhere
and present in everything.

The Abrahamic religions, in contrast, deduced from the vis à vis
of a personal God the uniqueness of the human person, and the
conviction that that person's individual life is once and for all, and
can never be brought back. Human beings are not, it was thought,
'part of nature'. They are 'the image of the invisible God'. By virtue
of their relation to God, they are set above the natural cohesion that

binds them to the rest of the living (Ps. 8.5f.) and are furnished with a charge to rule over the earth (Gen. 1.26). In the light of this view, the 'mother earth' idea, which is behind the impression of the eternal return of birth and death, was suppressed. 'Before God' every life is unique, and is God's own unique idea. God creates originals, not replicas. God creates uniquely and never repeats himself. This premise leads to the concept of the individuality of every human person, the originality of every form of life, and the uniqueness of every lived moment.

From this standpoint, those who believe in reincarnation must be asked whether their doctrine does not considerably reduce the number of souls, and whether the claim to have lived often, and to have continually been reborn, does not mean a tremendous ousting of people from their own lives. Who is meant by a person's name? Does the impression that life is repeatable really awaken sympathy for all other forms of life, or is the result in-difference, since there is then no-difference in the status of these forms?

On the other hand, the doctrine of reincarnation challenges the Abrahamic religions with the question: does the prominence given to the personhood of human beings not destroy the natural warp and weft of life as a whole, making men and women the destroyers of the earth, the mother of all the living? The harsh distinction between person and nature is hostile to life. As a person 'before God', a man or woman is also part of nature, representing nature before God. The modern individualist concept of person ought to give way to the earlier hypostatic concept of person, so that the person and nature of the human being can be seen together again. For the idea of community goes beyond both. As persons, men and women are persons in community. Personhood and sociality are two sides of human nature. But as beings in community people are natural beings too, and exist in the community of other natural beings on earth. The idea of the community of creation shared by all created beings expresses this fact in terms of space. Underlying the doctrine of creation is a corresponding concept in terms of time, the concept of the sequence of generations – and not just human generations at that.

These fundamental ideas do not seem to me incompatible. Today it is actually vitally necessary to mediate to each other in a fruitful way the Eastern understanding of nature and the Western under-standing of person.[113]

2. Every doctrine of incarnation is faced with the question of how

to preserve the identity of the soul in the mutability of the forms which the soul assumes.[114] If I am born again as a human being, the human identity of my soul must be preserved. But if I am born again as an animal, or if I once died as a plant, then this identity cannot be preserved. It comes into being or passes away with the human form of life. If I have the impression that 'I have been here before', I must be able to identity this 'I' of mine. So it cannot be mortal. But if my 'I' belongs to this life, then it passes away with this life too, and I shall not be able to recognize myself if I should be born again. If my feelings of happiness and my experiences of pain go back to experiences in a former life, then that former life – and not just my soul – would have to repeat itself in my life now. But then that former life cannot be dead.

According to ancient Indian teaching, the soul too does not really 'migrate'. That is a personal concept. If my 'atman' – the essential principle of my life – is immortal, then in its truth it is also immovable and always the same. The Bhagavadgita certainly says (II.22):

> As a man casts off his worn-out clothes
> and takes on other new ones,
> so does the embodied [self] cast off
> its worn-out bodies and enters other new ones.[114a]

But if the soul is in fact without individuality and personhood, then there is no determining subject that can 'migrate' or exchange its 'worn-out clothes' either. On the contrary, the determining subject itself is part of the cycle of rebirth, and must be dissolved in order to find redemption. In Buddhism the idea of a 'transmigration of souls without a soul' has been thought through further: 'Is the one who is born again the same as the one who departs, or different? Neither the same nor another . . . One appearance emerges, another disappears, yet they all range themselves to each other without interruption. In this way the final constitution of the consciousness is attained neither as the same person nor as another.'[115]

In the ancient Indian world, reincarnations were viewed as a curse for the souls bound to this meaningless wheel of rebirth. There is only redemption once they cease to be reborn, in Nirvana. It is only in the personal thinking of the Western world and – under its influence – through new Indian thinkers too that reincarnations have come to be conceived of as marvellous extensions of the potentialities for life which reach beyond death. But this thinking presupposes the identity of the soul and its power to identify itself in ever new forms of life. The Western lust for life which finds expression here is completely un-Indian, not to say 'unenlightened'.

3. In the ancient Indian world, reincarnation belongs to 'the wheel of rebirth', and according to karmic teaching is the requital for the good and evil deeds in a life. In the European world of today, reincarnation belongs to the modern world's principle of education and evolution. The ancient karma doctrine expresses the inexorable and inescapable cohesion of act and destiny. 'As one acts, so one will be after death.' 'If one steals corn one will become a rat.'[116] The coherence is merciless because it cannot be broken by any power in the world, or by any God. But in the Western interpretation, reincarnation is supposed to give us 'a second chance' to fulfil the tasks which in this life we could not, or would not, complete – which is what Elisabeth Kübler-Ross desires.[117] If we do better next time, we shall advance along this path towards perfection. 'Little by little they raise themselves and climb higher and higher up the ladder of progress. This advancement comes about through the incarnations as human being, which can also be experienced as atonement or as mission. Material life is a test which spirits have to pass again and again, in order to reach a certain degree of perfection', says the spiritist Allan Kardec.[118]

If this life is subject only to the curse of the evil act, then it is a place of punishment. If it is subject to the compulsion to be tested, it is a purgatory. In both cases the achievement principle destroys the fragile beauty and happiness of this earth. If every human body is no more than a transitional stage and a husk for the migrating soul, how can I love my existence here and now? Am I, with my soul, not then always somewhere else? If this life is no more than just a means to an end, does it not cease to be lovely and meaningful in itself?

4. The doctrine of karma is both close to the Abrahamic religions and remote from them. The law of act and destiny was so generally recognized and accepted that it can be found everywhere. 'As one acts, so one will be.' 'As a man sows, that he will also reap' (Gal. 6. 7f.). The law spans the generations too: 'The fathers have eaten sour grapes, and the children's teeth are set on edge' (Jer. 31.29). Like karma, the biblical link between act and destiny is a law immanent in the world, not a divine punishment for human guilt. Acts recoil on the doer of them, and beyond that on the community

of family and generations. Modern indologists have called karma a 'retribution causality' or 'a cosmic principle of retribution'.[119] It can be understood as a cosmic principle which keeps the cycle of rebirth going. But – if it is linked with personalized, Western ideas – it can also be seen anthropocentrically. Then we carve out our own destinies and dig our own graves. We are all responsible for our own fate in this world and beyond. We can save our souls or destroy them. Because, according to karma doctrine, acts mould the doers of them, this ultimately means that everyone is his own creator. No distinction is made between being and act, between the person and what the person effects. Finally, the cosmic law of karma traces back the disabilities, diseases and distresses of the present to the 'karmic guilt' of the incarnate soul or its ancestors. All suffering must derive from some previous act. Belief in karma has nothing to do with belief in God. Human beings are alone with what they do and suffer, and with its preconditions and consequences.

When theologians set over against karma the Christian 'principle of grace',[120] they must say what this means. For me it means the following:

1. The creative God acts contingently and historically, and in history creates 'a new thing'. He continually interrupts the chain of act and destiny, and repeals the law of karma. This interruption, in which something new happens, is what we call grace: 'His grace is new every morning.'

2. Forgiveness of sins does not mean dispensing with punishment. It means repealing the law of act and destiny. That is why in this creative happening men and women become 'righteous without the works of the law' and are saved without the consequences of their works.

3. It also means that the judgment that consists of the consequences of evil action does not take place. Anyone who teaches 'the principle of grace' cannot at the same time teach 'the Last Judgment' as apocalyptic karmic law. If at 'the Last Judgment' we were to be judged only according to what we have done, then the outcome of the proceedings would be in our own hands; it would then be we ourselves who decided on our salvation or our damnation. We could then do what we wanted with judgment, and should need no God for it. We should only have to know the law, in order to will, or not to will, the consequences of what we do. A God who is bound to this law, and who can do no more than implement it, is neither free nor godlike. He is a

slave of his law and the execution officer of our decisions. But the final
verdict is the word of the free, creative love of God.

4. The principle of grace, finally, distinguishes very clearly
between person and act, and does so qualitatively. According to this
principle, evil action is condemned, but the person is pardoned.
People are no longer nailed down to what they have done and judged
according to their works. They are freed from them in all their
dignity. People are more than the sum of their works, and more than
the sum of their sufferings. That is why being is more important than
doing and having.

6. *The Future of the Spoiled Life:* *Some Personal Thoughts*

1. Much of our life remains unfinished. We have started something,
but have never completed it. We have tried to map out a plan for our
lives, but the plan was spoiled. Life was promised us – we promised
life – and both promises remained unfulfilled. We have failed. The
pain has left wounds which have healed only on the surface. The
moments of happiness have fled, and we wished so ardently to hold
on to them, to tarry in them. But we can only mourn their passing.
How can life here ever be finished and complete? For in the end
everything is still open and unconcluded. We die with the un-
answered question which we ourselves have been, our whole life
long. However we imagine eternal life, it cannot be the eternalization
of our beginnings, our attempts at life and life's abrupt endings,
experienced or willed. Can resurrection into the life of the future
world really already take place at death, as Luther and the modern
Catholic theologians we have cited believe? It would then seem as if
with death this earthly, fragmentary life would be broken off, and
would be absorbed into a different, divine life. But we should then
still not have coped successfully with this life. 'Hell', 'heaven' and 'a
future world' are expressions that mean final states which themselves
have no further future but which are an eternal present, and hence
offer no further history either.

It is impressions of this kind which make us after all think about an
on-going history after death with our lives as we have lived them.
Purifying fire, transmigration of souls, the soul's journey, an
expiatory passage through the faults and omissions of this life are all
images for this. If we leave aside the external ecclesiastical and

political motives that were often bound up with ideas of this kind, and look simply at what is meant, we could then after all say: I shall again come back to my life, and in the light of God's grace and in the power of his mercy put right what has gone awry, finish what was begun, pick up what was neglected, forgive the tresspasses, heal the hurts, and be permitted to gather up the moments of happiness and to transform mourning into joy. That does not mean wishing to lead this life all over again. Nor does it mean being punished by recapitulations, according to the merciless law of karma. And finally, it certainly does not mean catching up, at some new stage of development, with the tasks left unfulfilled in this life. But what it does mean is being given the chance to become the persons God meant us to be. If everyone is a unique idea on God's part, as we like to say, then God will think it important for this idea to find its own proper realization, and its successful and completed form. Should our death hinder him? Jörg Zink puts it this way, speaking for himself and in his own language:

> I think, according to what the gospel suggests, that I will have to re-suffer much and re-live much, will have to bemourn much that was neglected; but that I shall not perish of it all, because God's goodness will hold me fast. I think that I shall have to suffer a transformation into the one I was really destined to be, until . . . harmony with the nature and will of God is finally attained, and the forgiveness takes place which must be pronounced before existence can achieve the fullness and power for which it was really intended. Until that Figure, that great counterpart God, says: it's all right – everything is all right. Now come and fill the place and take up the tasks intended for you, for the great future of my kingdom.[121]

2. It is not just the harsh caesuras in the history of our own lives, and our life's unfinished beginnings, that make us pose this question. Think of the life of those who were not permitted to live, and were unable to live: the beloved child, dying at birth; the little boy run over by a car when he was four; the disabled brother who never lived consciously, and never knew his parents: the friend torn to pieces by a bomb at your side when he was sixteen; the throngs of children who die prematurely of hunger in Africa; the countless numbers of the raped and murdered and killed. Of course their lives can take on a considerable meaning for others. But where will their own lives be

completed, and how? Can they somewhere be healed, complemented, lived to the full and completed after they have died?

The idea that for these people their death is 'the finish' would plunge the whole world into absurdity; for if their life has no meaning, has ours? The notion of a 'natural death' is appropriate only for the life-insured denizens of the affluent society, who can afford a death in old age like this. Most people in the Third World today die an unnatural, premature, violent, and by no means affirmed death, like most of the people of my generation who died in the Second World War. Their life is broken off short before it has really been lived at all. The idea of 'the eternalization of life as it has been lived' does not take in those who were neither permitted to live nor able to do so. Must we not think the thought of an on-going history of God's with this life, if – in this world of disappointed, impaired, sick, murdered and destroyed life – we are to be able to affirm life and go on loving it notwithstanding?

I would think that the Spirit of eternal life is first of all a further *space for living*, in which life that has been cut short, or was impaired and destroyed will be able to develop freely. Even in this life before death, we experience the Spirit of life as the wide space in which there is no more cramping. And how much more will this be so after death.

To every space for living which is an invitation to an unfolding and to movement, there belongs a *time* for living which allows growth and completion. Even before death we experience the Spirit of life as the power of the divine hope which leaves us time, because it gives us future. And how much more will this be so after the end of this restricted time, however short or long it may be.

The eternal Spirit is experienced as *the well of life*. Even before death, people are newly born from the streams of this living spring, life is given back to them, and is filled again and again with fresh energies. How much more, after death, will the Spirit of eternal life lay hold of those whose life here was cut short, impaired or destroyed.

So I would think that eternal life gives the broken and the impaired and those whose lives have been destroyed space and time and strength to live the life which they were intended for, and for which they were born. I think this, not for selfish reasons, for the sake of my personal completion, and not morally, for the sake of some kind of purification; I think it for the sake of the justice which I believe is God's concern and his first option.

§5 DEATH, MOURNING AND CONSOLATION

We began this chapter about personal eschatology by describing the love for life which makes life so alive, and which therefore also makes death seem so deadly. So we shall end the chapter with some ideas about the mourning and the pain with which we react to the death of people we love, and shall look at the consolations in the mourning process which make it possible to start living again.[122]

What is mourning and how do we mourn? Is mourning the reverse side of love, and is its pain the mirror-writing of love's delight? The greater the love, the deeper the grief; the more unreserved the surrender, the more inconsolable the loss. Those who have given themselves utterly in love for someone else die themselves in the pains of grief and are born again, so that life can be given to them afresh, and so that they can again find the will to love – or so one can say out of one's own experience, and from experiences with other people.

But if this is true, then we shall have to take, or leave ourselves, just as much time for the mourning as for the love. It is only the grief that is accepted and suffered-through that restores the love for life after a death. People who shut themselves off from the mourning process or who cut it short will discover in themselves insurmountable depression and increasing apathy. They will lose contact with the reality of the people around, and will fail to find new courage for living. The person who mourns deeply has loved greatly. The person who cannot mourn has never loved. Admittedly, in our age and culture we are so conditioned that we want to have happiness without pain, and love without grief. We flee the grief and seek a painless happiness. What is on offer in modern society, culturally and medically, is designed to accommodate this personal wish. But if it is true that mourning is not the farewell to love, but love's reverse side, then we can explore the mystery of grief without fear, and surrender ourselves to mourning without being afraid of losing ourselves in it.

1. Experiences of Mourning in Modern Society

For every individual, the process of mourning has a very intimate and personal side. This is shaped by the experiences in which we have lived and are living. But it has a social and public side too. Gone from 'a culture of narcissism'[123] are the old familiar mourning rituals, which were the condensation of the experience of past generations with death. Our society, with its multifarious suppressions, is not willing to permit experiences of death and mourning. But people who in their grief are not prepared to let society push them on to the sidelines, will have to set out on their own path into the experience of mourning. They may find most help in the self-help groups for the bereaved.[124] These do not offer therapy. What they do offer is mutual help, and a new experience of the self.

Because the old rituals and attitudes no longer carry conviction, there is really no pre-packaged 'ministry of the church'[125] to the bereaved either, even though funerals are announced at church services, and many pastoral 'manuals' are on offer. The situation of the bereaved is not a chance for mission. And the expression 'pastoral care' sounds paternalistic, as if priests and minsters could really take over the care of souls assailed by grief. In the self-help groups for the bereaved, comfort is discovered mutually, in shared conversation. This is very much in line with the ancient concept of the religious communities, which Luther took over, the *mutua consolatio fratrum* – the mutual consolation of the brethren.[126] People enter mutually into the situation of others as brothers and sisters, and combine the trust which loosens dumb tongues with respect for the intimate mystery of other people. Here no one talks down to anyone else. People speak or are silent, weep and laugh with other people in the same situation. For those who arrange self-help groups, the aim is not to be theologically correct, but to be personally concrete. What is 'correct' cannot always 'be applied'. The word which meets the special situation, releasing and consoling, has to be sought. To find it requires awareness and sensitivity, and not least one's own assimilated experience, particularly the experience of things left undone and the things in one's own life that have never found completion.

Anyone who is profoundly affected by a death – the death of a child, a wife or husband, a mother or father – is generally subjected to pain of such violence that even if they are mentally and spiritually strong, they lose their foothold and are overwhelmed. In this situation, it is only out of the solidarity of suffering that they can be talked to at all. And yet people who are close to the bereaved person must keep their heads above water, and look beyond the moment of pain. Often the pain comes over the grieving in waves. If this is so, the ability to weep is better than dumb, frozen calm.

Even to lose consciousness can be a blessing in the pain of mourning.

If the pain comes in waves, the intervals between them must be used to find a foothold from which lines of resistance can be built up. One can try to evoke stories and pictures in which the pain can find expression and the mourners composure. This comfort is entirely tied to the moment, and will generally be washed away by the next wave of pain. A long accompaniment is always needed, and best of all a firm enfolding community, before the reality of the beloved person's death can be accepted without those who mourn being overwhelmed by pain, and without their suppressing the pain, so that in their inconsolability they can be consoled, and in a reawakened courage for living can, in the very feeling of loss, keep the lost person present to them. 'Nothing can make up for the absence of someone we love, and it would be wrong to try to find a substitute, we must simply hold out and see it through. That sounds very hard at first but at the same time it is a great comfort; for because the gap really remains unfilled, we remain bound to one another.'[127]

In talking together, both the accompanying and the accompanied experience something new. The accompanying persons help the grieving, supporting and encouraging them, and those accompanied teach the others by telling their experiences. So the first question is not: 'How can I help?' or 'What shall I say?' but 'What does he or she want to tell me?' Listening to each other and talking to each other generates a dialogue in the face of death and with the pain of grief, until the loss can be accepted and – through the transformation of the mourner – a new community with the dead emerges. Grief for those who are lost can be transformed into gratitude for what has been experienced. The fellowship with the beloved dead does not have to be broken off; it can be so transformed that we live with them, because they were part of our own lives, and the community shared with them must not be forgotten.

Only people who have addressed and assimilated their own experiences of grief and leave-taking can accompany other mourners, and arrange self-help groups with them. Behaviour in grief varies greatly from individual to individual, according to circumstance. For some people, the way the beloved person died is important – whether it was after a long illness, or suddenly and unexpectedly, whether death was a painful struggle or a peaceful end. The depth of the relationship to the person who has died is reflected in the pain of the grief. The reactions of family, friends and neighbours influence behaviour in grief, as well as the financial situation of the survivors and their status – whether they are now 'singles' with children still unprovided for, whether they have a job or are unemployed.

2. *Mourning and Melancholia:*
A Discussion with Sigmund Freud

'People who have lost someone intimately connected with them suffer a bereavement which for them can never be made good. They feel incomplete, left behind, and incapable of living alone. Through the death of a person close to them, which they often experience as an amputation, they have lost part of themselves. Not only half of life but half of their soul too has gone from them.'[128] In order to take this apt description further, and to find ways leading out of this loss of the self, we shall look at Freud's ideas about 'Mourning and Melancholia'.[129]

'Mourning is regularly the reaction to the loss of a loved person, or to the loss of some abstraction which has taken the place of one, such as fatherland, liberty, an ideal, and so on . . .'[130] It does not occur to us to regard mourning as a morbid condition. We feel sure that after a certain time it will be overcome. Consequently interference with mourning must be viewed as inexpedient and harmful. 'The distinguishing mental features of melancholia are a profoundly painful dejection, abrogation of interest in the outside world, loss of the capacity to love, the inhibition of all activity, and a lowering of the self-regarding feelings which finds expression in self-reproaches and self-revilings, and culminates in a delusional expectation of punishment.'[131] According to this distinction between mourning and melancholia, there is mourning if a partnership existed and the person was loved for his or her own sake. Mourning means a slow detachment of the cathectic energies from the lost object of love. After the completion of what German calls *Trauerarbeit* – 'the work of grief' – the ego is once again free and able to choose a new object for its love.

In the case of someone suffering from melancholia, the experience of an unusual lowering of the ego-feeling indicates that the choice of object was made on the basis of narcissistic self-love. The object of love was not loved for his or her own sake, but was the object of the projected needs, cravings for power, and wishful thinking of self-love. The narcissistic ego therefore reacts to the loss of the object of love with a sense of personal injury or affront, feeling that it has been left in the lurch and betrayed by the dead person. The libido's cathectic energies are withdrawn into the ego. Dissociations of the ego result, these expressing themselves in self-hatred and melancholy. If they are repressed, the mental operations involved in the process of detachment from the beloved object take place mainly in the subconscious. This impedes the mastering of the conflict that has arisen in the self.

A first important point about Freud's distinction between mourning and melancholia is his distinction between a love which loves the object for its own sake, and the narcissistic love which in the object of love, loves and enjoys only him or herself. This conforms to the ancient theological distinction between love of one's neighbour and self-love. The pschoanalytical figure of Narcissus, who fell in love with himself, corresponds to the figure of the *homo incurvatus in se* – the person turned in on himself – which was used by Augustine and Luther. People who are in love with themselves are permanently afraid for themselves. They use all objects and experiences, and every other person, as mirrors of themselves, and for the purpose of self-endorsement. The object of love is viewed merely as a possession that 'belongs to me'. What they love in others is only the resonance of their own selves. They only love people who are like themselves, not people who are 'other'. They love what corresponds to themselves and increases their experience of themselves, and their opinion of themselves; they do not love the other person who seems to them merely strange and hostile. It is clear that loss of the object of love is then taken as a personal injury. In contrast, those who love others for their own sake can mourn without melancholia. They accept the beloved person for his or her own sake, and make no possessive claims. In the language of faith: the people they love are accepted as a gift of God's love, so they can also be left to that eternal love when death comes. Through this gratitude, the joy of experiencing the happiness of love becomes a protection in the experience of grief. In the very consciousness of the loss, gratitude keeps the fellowship with the beloved person alive.

Freud thought that in 'the work of grief' the libido is withdrawn from the lost object of love, until the ego is capable of choosing something new to love. That sounds very mechanistic, and is not an adequate analysis of the complexity of human relationships. This pattern of thought leads to the conclusion that in love we should surrender ourselves only up to a certain point, so that we can withdraw our love again, after disappointments, separations, or in the case of death, in order then to choose a new object of love. This idea, again, presupposes a stable and at heart untouchable ego, which only gives itself up to relationships incidentally, or to a subsidiary degree. But is this not an extremely narcissistic picture of the ego, and one which leads to a kind of permanent melancholia in the unloved and unlived life?

According to the accounts of the bereaved, however, and from my own experience, it would seem to me that when so-called 'objects of love' die, part of those who loved them dies too in spirit; in the death of those they love those who are left experience what death really is. Here it is not a matter of an injury to a narcissistic self-love, so this is not melancholia; it is part of the mourning process itself. 'The work of grief' does not merely serve to detach love from the 'object' it has lost, so that it is able to choose a new love. Of course that is also part of it. But at heart it is a matter of the renewal of the self which, by virtue of the love, has died with the beloved person. In the mourners themselves 'the well of life' opens again. They acquire a new will to live, and courage for new experiences of life. They will not forget the dead, but they can remember them without sinking into the bottomless pit of grief. Remembrance of the dead changes. The feeling of loss and the gap left in one's own life remains, but it is joined by the feeling of gratitude for the life shared and the happiness experienced. There is even a growing certainty that what has been, after all endures and cannot be destroyed. The past is past, and at the same time is still in its own way present, so that it becomes intransient. In the grief we realize, not only the present loss, but also that the dead have become an integral component of our own life history. Of course in our grief we take leave of them. But in faith we know that death is not final, and therefore discover that the parting too does not have to be absolute. If we part from someone in the face of God, then it is a parting in the enduring presence of eternity. We express this by saying that God has taken the person we love to himself when we take leave of them, 'for all live to him' (Luke 20.38). But then our leave-taking becomes different. It loses its tragic quality. In the grief we do not only take leave of the dead; we also participate in their transformation into that other world of God's, and that other life which we call eternal.

If death is not the end, then the grief and the mourning do not have to be endless either. If death is the side of the transformation to eternal life that is turned towards us, then our grief is transformed from mere lamentation over the loss into a new community with the dead. If we believe that the dead experience resurrection, then hope leads us out of the abyss of fear, and makes us free. We look beyond the graves and the partings in our life to that future of God's in which 'every tear will be wiped away' and 'death shall be no more' (Rev. 21.4).

To keep company with the dead in retrospective gratitude and forward-looking hope does not mean clinging to memories and holding fast to the dead in such a way that we no longer have an independent life of our own. It is rather that the dead are present in a kind of second presence. In this singular presence they do not bind life to themselves, but let it go free, where it knew itself to be bound to them. On the other hand the survivors must not forget the dead, or withdraw their love from them so as to lead an independent life.

We have extended Freud's analysis by drawing attention to the link between grief and gratitude on the one hand, and between mourning and hope on the other. This brings us to the difference between mourning and melancholia, for in Freud's analysis of melancholia we find elements which can be found in every grief as well.

Human love for others is always bound up with self-love, for not all self-love is narcissistic. The command to love our neighbour presupposes self-love – 'as your self'. How can those who hate themselves love other people? Moreover love is a mutual affair. If I love her for her own sake, I know I am also loved by her for mine. True love is more than an association for reciprocal use or mutual possession. The ego-impoverishment and the loss of self felt at the death of the beloved person are inescapable elements in the mourning process and are by no means in themselves symptoms of melancholia. Of course all self-love, even the self-love experienced in being loved, also contains narcissistic elements of self-endorsement, vanity and fear. It would be inhuman to exclude them, and to consider them as being inherently pathological.

The process of mourning and talk with other mourners will then make those concerned aware of what true love of others for their own sake is, and what being truly loved for one's own sake is, and what simply ministered only to self-endorsement, vanity and fear. Grief leads the grieving to self-examination. It can make us aware of the things where we fell short towards the dead, and where they fell short towards us, aware too of what we had wanted to say to them and never did, what we wanted to thank them for, or to ask their forgiveness for, and so forth. Every partnership always remains incomplete. But self-examination can also make us conscious of the aspects of our love which were true and enduring, and the aspects which were part of our narcissistic lovelessness, and should therefore disappear.

3. The Rebirth to Life

The pain of grief lies in the sense of loss and of being lost oneself. So comfort in grief is to be found in the experience of indestructible community, in the knowledge that the dead person is in safe-keeping with God, and in the awareness of being oneself in God's safe-keeping. But this is only possible if the deity is not an unfeeling, indifferent, heavenly power called 'fate', but is the eternal love that feels with us and suffers with us. We can then experience that our sorrow is God's sorrow too,[132] and that hidden in the pain of our own love there is a divine pain as well. God loves with the lovers. God weeps with those who weep. God grieves with the grieving. So whoever remains in love even in the midst of grief, and does not become bitter, remains in God.

> And when human hearts are breaking
> under sorrow's iron rod,
> then we find that self-same aching
> deep within the heart of God.[133]

If the experience of losing a beloved person and the experience of our own lostness are joined by the feeling that God has forsaken us, and if these two experiences are intensified to such a degree that we can only sigh 'my God, why have you forsaken me?', then we can be comforted by the awareness of the crucified Christ, who died on the cross with this cry. He brings God into our most profound forsakenness, and brings our forsakenness to God.[134] The crucified Christ consoles us by bringing the love of God and the fellowship of the Holy Spirit into the abysses of our suffering and the hell of our lostness, so that we do not drown in pain but with him take heart again, and get up, and believe in the victory of life over death: 'I live, and you shall live also' (John 14.19).

'The ministry of the church' in the process of grief should not be understood in a clerical sense. Its ministry consists simply in the fact that the community of Christ understands itself as a community of the living and the dead, of lovers and mourners. It is for that reason that it arranges the self-help groups with the bereaved which we have mentioned. 'Blessed are those who mourn, for they shall be comforted' (Matt. 5.4). According to this Beatitude, the grieving are Jesus's brothers and sisters, and fellow citizens of the kingdom of God, whether they know it or not.[135] So the community of Jesus Christ belongs at their side and in their company. In company with the grieving, the community of Christ will fight against the melancholia which springs from that narcissistic self-love which is in fact lovelessness, and it will fight against the repressions which make life sterile and incapable of loving. On both sides it is a matter of a personal and a social venture *for* life and *against* the paralysis which death spreads. If fellowship with the dying and the dead takes the pain of its love seriously, it will also protest against the conditions in public life which do not allow people the liberty and the free space to mourn, but compel them to repress their grief, because mourning is considered illegitimate. Narcissism is always a social phenomenon too, a question of public recognition and respect, a standpoint to which individuals adapt themselves in their personal attitudes to life and death. In 'a culture of narcissism', those who accompany the dying and the grieving will build up a counter-culture, because they deal with death in a totally different way, and from this develop a new life style.

- The grieving are Jesus's brothers and sisters, as the Sermon on the Mount says. If they are going to be comforted, then we shall find God's comfort in their society. The community of Jesus lives in the community of mourners, who no longer enjoy any status in our society. It will listen to the grieving, and accept them.
- The community of Jesus resists the culture of narcissism by

standing up publicly for recognition and respect for those who mourn, and by resisting the cult 'forever young', confronting it with the resurrection hope and the experience of the rebirth to life.

III

The Kingdom of God

Historical Eschatology

III

The Kingdom of God

Historical Eschatology

§1 THE APOCALYPSE OF HISTORY

1. *Political Eschatology*

In Chapter II, the personal hope for eternal life led us of its own accord from the personal experience of the human self out into the sphere of community between human beings, and between human beings and nature. Men and women are social beings, and as social beings they are natural beings. So it is not enough to grasp the eschatological hope solely in the symbol of *eternal life*, nor is it sufficient to reduce eternal life to the soul, or to individual human existence, as did the liberal theologian Adolf von Harnack, when he wrote: 'The kingdom of God comes by coming to the individual, by entering into his soul and laying hold of it.'[1] Personal hope in the face of one's own death and beyond is certainly the beginning of eschatology, when the Spirit of life lays hold of people personally, and makes them living people. But *as* beginning, it is an integral component of the universal hope for the whole creation in its present misery. Eternal life is 'the life of the world to come', as the Nicene Creed says, so it means not just human life but the life of all the living – of 'all flesh', as our Bible puts it. There is eternal life only in God's kingdom. No one possesses, or is given, eternal life for him or herself alone, without fellowship with other people, and without community with the whole creation. So *the kingdom of God* is a more integral symbol of the eschatological hope than eternal life. Of course the different hopes complement one another and merge into each other; but the two also say something different. So just as we draw on the symbol 'eternal life' to meet our experience of a life loved and a death suffered, so we talk about 'the kingdom of God', and with it 'the judgment of God', pre-eminently in our experiences of history and our sufferings in history.

And yet even the kingdom of God is still not itself 'the integral hope of Christians'.[2] For human history is embedded in nature, on which it is dependent and from which it lives. Consequently cosmic eschatology's symbol of *the new creation of all things* is more integral than the historical symbol 'the kingdom of God'. We shall see that there can be no historical eschatology without cosmic eschatology, just as there is no personal eschatology without the transformation of the cosmic conditions of the temporal creation. This became clear from the experience of death (Ch. II, § 3.4). So with historical eschatology we find ourselves in the middle between personal hope and cosmic expectation.

We are stressing this mediate position here, because historical eschatology too has repeatedly been viewed as 'the integral hope', and 'history' has continually been made the quintessence of the whole of reality. But if 'history' is no more than the field of human interaction, the result is an eschatology forgetful of nature, or even hostile towards it. If God's future, as the future of the Creator, has to do with the whole creation, then wherever eschatology is narrowed down to merely one sector of that creation, whether it be the individual sphere or the historical one, that contraction has a destructive effect on the other sectors, because it deprives them of every hope. The eschatological field of human hopes and fears, longings and desires, has always been a favourite playground for egocentricism and anthropocentricism, and for the exclusion of anything strange and different. But true hope must be universal, because its healing future embraces every individual and the whole universe. If we were to surrender hope for as much as one single creature, for us God would not be God.

In this chapter we shall be looking at history only in so far as the eschatological symbols 'judgment', 'kingdom', 'end' and 'consummation' can be related to it. For other theological aspects of history and time I must refer to earlier books.[3] 'Judgment' and 'kingdom' are ideas taken from the political world. The historical eschatologies whose focus is 'the eternal kingdom' are explicitly political eschatologies. But the apocalyptic eschatologies which focus on the end of the world and the divine judgment are no less political. As I hope to show, all eschatologies of world history have grown out of political experiences and intentions. It is true that the modern concept of history goes beyond the political concept: history is political, but not just political. Nevertheless, all modern political concepts are 'secularized theological concepts',[4] just as, conversely, all theological concepts of historical eschatology are political concepts that have been lent a theological colouring.[5] We shall pay particular attention to these interactions, and shall demonstrate them in both political messianism and in political apocalyptic, down to the present day.

The relationship between the eschatology of hope and historical experience is more complex and more ambivalent than we once assumed. At the beginning of modern eschatological thinking in Germany we find Karl Löwith's thesis that 'modern philosophy of history originates with the Hebrew and Christian faith in a fulfilment and . . . ends with the secularization of its eschatological pattern'.[6] By this he meant that Jewish and Christian eschatologies made possible the experience of reality as a purposeful history open to the future; and that the ancient orientation of human civilization towards the eternal orders and cycles of nature had been replaced by 'the eschatological compass [which] gives orientation in time by pointing to the Kingdom of God as the ultimate end and purpose'.[7] Löwith meant this in anything but a positive sense; in opposition to Hegel, he made it the peg on which to hang his criticism of 'historical' and 'Christian existence',[8] pointing explicitly to the ecological orientation of human civilization towards nature, which is external to human culture and prior to it – an orientation which is essential if humanity is to survive.

In Germany, however, modern thinking about the theology of history picked up only the positive side of Löwith's thesis, and developed from it the theological programme of 'revelation as history',[9] and 'the experience of history'[10] in the context of eschatological revelation. 'Universal history' is only comprehensible against the eschatological horizon of the final revelation of the One God, which is the goal. The experience of reality as history is only possible, and can only be endured, if we trust its ultimate meaning and purpose. That is why, ever since Hegel, the experience of reality as history has always gone hand in hand with ideas about 'the end of history'.[11] Only the idea of history's ultimate goal makes the experience of the transitoriness of all things endurable. The hope for a good finale to history makes the ancient fear of fate or karma just as superfluous as the gamble with fortune and kairos. Historical eschatology has de-fatalized the experience of history.

'Not only does the *eschaton* delimit the process of history by an end, it also articulates and fulfils it by a definite goal.'[12] This goal is in theological eschatology the kingdom of God and divine glory – in secularized modern eschatology, the kingdom of human beings and the home of human identity. In both cases the eschaton is viewed as the *telos*, the goal and purpose of historical developments and struggle, but not as the *finis*, the rupture of history and its end. The apocalyptic expectations of rupture and end do not 'articulate' the course of history, nor do they fulfil it. They do not lend history any meaning, but withdraw from it every legitimation. Löwith's thesis was one-sided because it took up only the inner-worldly hope, the teleological nature of the kingdom of God and the messianic side of Christian eschatology. It neglected the other side of this hope for 'the end of history' and 'the end of the world', that is to say, the eschatological character of God's kingdom and the apocalyptic nature of Christian eschatology. The German title of Löwith's book was *Weltgeschichte und Heilsgeschehen* – 'World History and Saving Event' – not 'World History and the Event of Disaster', although the latter would surely have been considerably closer to the experiences of the Second World War, Auschwitz and Hiroshima. But only through this affirmative conviction was it possible to interpret as 'the secularization of an eschatological model' a modern world voracious of power, obsessed with growth and with a credulous faith in progress.

Although Löwith also meant his thesis critically, it could nevertheless be taken up by theologians as an *apologia*, in order to prove to the modern world its Christian roots, and thus to justify its foundations theologically. But this theological justification of 'the modern world' with its intentions and hopes overlooks the victims on the underside of its history – in the Third World, in nature, and among women. It turns 'the modern world' into a secular millennium. Its most recent prophet, Francis Fukuyama – after the end of Marxism – then also elevated liberal democracy and 'the global marketing of everything' into 'the end of history'.[13]

2. Apocalyptic Eschatology

Politically speaking, history is always a struggle for power and for domination over other people and over nature.

The person who possesses power is concerned that history should continue to run its course towards the goal he has designed for it. He understands future as the prolongation of his own present, so he swears by economic growth and scientific progress, and seeks the increase of the power he already has.

But the people who are dominated and powerless have no interest in the long-term prolongation of this history. On the contrary, they are concerned that it should find a speedy end. Better an end with terror than a terror without end, says a German proverb. Those who are dominated, hope for an alternative future, for liberation from present misery and deliverance from their helplessness.

Like all other knowledge, eschatology is always determined by its concerns, while at the same time it also determines those concerns. *Cui bono?* is a critical question put to all eschatological symbols and images. The person who possesses power fears the end of that power; the person who suffers under it hopes for its end. The people who enjoy the modern world because they live 'on the sunny side of the street' fear the downfall of their world; the people who suffer on the underside of this world hope for that very downfall. For the one group, apocalypse is a word for the catastrophe that brings their world to an end; for the others it is an expression for the disclosure of reality, and the fact that the truth will at last emerge and liberate them.

Rudolf Bultmann still believed even in 1941 that 'mythical eschatology is untenable for the simple reason that the parousia of Christ never took place as the New Testament expected. History did not come to an end, and, as every sane person knows, it will continue to run its course'.[14] Today the notion that world history will continue to run its course is nothing more than wishful thinking.[15] 'Every sane person' is aware of the nuclear, ecological and economic catastrophes that threaten the modern world. The apocalyptic eschatology which Bultmann considered 'mythical' is more realistic than his faith in the inexorable onward course of world history. The belief that things will 'always go on' and that no end is in sight – at least not for us – is one of the fairytales of 'the modern world', the fairytale of its endlessness and its lack of an alternative. That is secularized millenarianism. Anyone who declares 'the modern world' to be his millennium, his 'golden age', in which it is only a matter of refining the methods of power, and approximating ever more closely to perfection, is really making the world for other people 'the beast from the abyss', 'the whore of Babylon', the voracious 'dragon' of Revelation 13; and that person is actually preparing the modern world's downfall. We shall see that the political apocalyptic which talks about the final battle of Armageddon is simply the reverse side of the political messianism of 'the Thousand Years' empire'.[16] But apocalyptic springs from messianism and is its necessary accompaniment, not vice versa.

The relationships between history and God's revelation are multifarious, and if we want to talk about the 'revelation of history' we must clarify the sense in which we mean the phrase. It has been pointed out often enough, and rightly, that the God of Israel revealed himself through the medium of the history which Israel experienced, not in the orders, rhythms and fertile forces of nature. The revelation of God in the event of the Exodus, it has been said, made Israel's faith a religion of history.[17] But now, for the modern world too, 'history' has increasingly become the quintessence of reality as a whole, and has pushed out 'nature', or historicized it. We must therefore ask self-critically whether, when we call Israel's faith a 'religion of history', modern experiences of history are not being projected into the testimonies of that faith. The difference between Israel's revelatory history and the praise of God's glory by the whole of creation is, at all events, not as great as the modern differentiation between history and nature.[18]

The revelation of God which the New Testament talks about when it proclaims the revelation of the crucified and raised Christ is not a historical revelation of God *in* history; on the contrary, the eschatological revelation of God is 'the end of history'. This eschatological revelation of God in the cross and resurrection of Christ has a final character and can never be superseded (Heb. 1.1f.). By this I mean that with the raising of the crucified Christ from the dead, the future of the new creation of all things has already begun in the midst of this dying and transitory world. But this presupposes that with the raising of the Christ crucified by the powers of this world, the end of this world and its powers has already become manifest.

A double revelatory process is inherent in the eschatological revelation: God reveals himself as the one 'who has raised Jesus from the dead'. God is the God who awakens the dead, and who creates everything anew. Before him, this world is manifested in its lack of orientation, its injustice and transience. For the first side of this revelation we have the expressions of epiphany: the risen Christ is 'revealed' and lets himself 'be seen'; the strength of his life is experienced in the Holy Spirit. For the second side we have the expression *apocalypsis* – that is to say the uncovering, unveiling, exposing of what has been hidden.[19] That is why the book of Revelation begins with the words: 'This is the revelation (*apocalypsis*) of Jesus Christ, which God gave him to show his servants what must soon take place' (Rev. 1.1). 'What must soon take place' are the so-called mysteries of the End-time: the collapse of the world systems that are at present dominant, the downfall of the bestial empire of Rome (ch. 13), the fall of the divine adversary 'the dragon', 'Babylon's' end and the liberation of the suffering, and the raising of the martyrs through the final victory of the crucified Lamb over the powers of sin and death which crucified him. The end manifests what the time of this world and its history is about: 'All's well that ends well.' The end reveals the instability of the powers, and lends support to those who resist. 'Look to their end', says the apocalyptic literature of resistance in Israel and Christendom, when it is talking about the great empires that seemed to have been built for eternity. They will perish in the sea of chaos out of which they rose. 'But he who endures to the end shall be saved.' The eschatological message of the New Testament – 'The end of all things is at hand' (I Peter 4.7) – is geared towards resistance, and against resignation. History is disclosed and known in the light of its end, and what history is really about, according to God's will, will then be understood.

What influence does this eschatological expectation have on the experience of history? 'Coming events cast their shadow before', says the phrase. If we understand the end of history in a one-sided sense as *history's goal* (as Löwith did, and with him the secularized millenniarists, with their credulous faith in progress), then history is 'articulated' into meaningful steps in the direction of this goal. Every historical epoch serves to prepare that final condition which is supposed to be history's goal, and as an intermediate stage acquires its meaning in the light of that goal. World history is then a giant, purposeful, providential sequence, and a tremendous realization of a divine master plan. The history of humanity is in this case a purposeful sequence of human plannings for final peace in humanity's body politic. Even if – in view of the inconceivable catastrophes of the modern world – ideas of this kind are no longer maintained as they were at the beginning of the Enlightenment and in the nineteenth century, the notion still persists that eschatological revelation has made *the linear understanding of time* prevail, over against *the cyclical understanding of time* held in nature-orientated cultures. The linear understanding of time no longer recognizes any qualitative difference between past and future, but reduces the different times to one and the same temporal line, distinguishing between them only quantitatively. But this concept of time is a modern scientific category, not an eschatological one.

It would seem much more obvious to perceive the shadows which the great eschatological event casts ahead of itself in *a rhythmicization of the times* of history. Rhythm and ecstasy condition each other mutually, analogously to the eschatological finale and the times which vibrate in it. Life-time is ordered, not in a linear sense but rhythmically. Only working-time and mechanical-time are linearly directed towards goal and purpose. But every living organism experiences the time in which it lives in the rhythm of its inward and outward movements, in tension and relaxation. For Israel, the general eschatological expectation of the future in which 'the whole earth will be full of God's glory' (Isa. 6) could be experienced practically in the weekly sabbath, in the sabbath (or seventh) year, and in every forty-ninth year, the Year of Jubilee. In the rhythm of the sabbath, which healingly interrupts the flux of time, God's rest is experienced, the rest which, as well as being the goal of creation, will also be the end of history. 'The messiah will come when the whole of Israel keeps a single sabbath – or when the whole of Israel keeps none.' This rabbinic saying shows the connection between sabbath and messiah. Every sabbath celebration is a messianic intermezzo in time, and when the messiah comes, he will bring the final messianic sabbath for all God's created beings.[20] Consequently the Adventists are the Christian community who observe the sabbath, by virtue of their hope. The Sunday worship of Christians too was originally, and is essentially, the eschatological celebration of Christ's resurrection in the in-streaming powers of the future world. Every Sunday points beyond itself to the first day of the new creation, on which the dead will be raised into the life of the future world. Here too the expectation of the final future of the world induces, not a linearization of lived time but its rhythmicization. In the expectation, time vibrates and dances.

Eschatology's most profound influence on the experience of history, however, is to be found in *the qualitative differentiation between past and future.* If the great eschatological event is the end of the time of this world, and the beginning of the new time of the world that is eternal, then its shadows already fall here and now on the experience of that which passes away and that which comes. 'Past' becomes the scheme of this old world, which will pass away because it has no permanence. 'Future' is filled with the image of the new creation, which will remain eternally. Those affected will therefore no longer conform to the pattern of the old world but will renew themselves in the in-streaming energies of the world that is new, saying with Paul: 'I forget what lies behind and strain forward to what is ahead' (Phil. 3.13, following Isa. 43.18f.). Past and future are then like night and day, and the chance of the present lies in that fact: 'Let us cast off the works of darkness and put on the armour of light' (Rom. 13.12).

This eschatological qualification of past and future is the heart of the eschatological experience of time. The experience of struggle in the antithesis between the powers of the past and the forces of the future calls forth the imaginative worlds of the apocalyptic scenario about the final contest. Of course these are mythical extrapolations and compensations for present experiences of strife and suffering. The worlds of apocalyptic fantasy are easy to decipher psychologically, easy too to criticize. But they should be read as subversive 'underground literature' with encoded messages for resistance groups.[21] Finally, the apocalyptic writings of Israel and Christianity are the testimonies of martyrs, not blood and thunder tales. This is true of the book of Daniel, which dates from the period of the Maccabees, as well as for the Revelation of John, which goes back to the persecutions under Domitian.

It is difficult enough to say anything at all about the future, especially if one has no power to implement what one predicts. How much more difficult must it be to say anything about the ultimate future of the whole world! Silence, or the not-knowing of a negative eschatology, would perhaps be an honest alternative to all eschatological dreams and anxieties, if silence and not-knowing were not to lead to the speechlessness with which we fall backwards upon the future, because we do not want to look it in the face. The impression of the qualitative difference between past and future must lead us to distinguish qualitatively too between types of utterance about past and future. Let us first follow up the clue offered by Franz Rosenzweig:

'The world is not yet finished. Laughing and weeping are still to be found in it. The tears have not yet been wiped away from every eye. This condition of becoming, of incompleteness, can now only be grasped through a reversal of the objective relationship of the times. For whereas the past, that which is already finished, lies open to us, from its beginning to its end, and can hence be re-counted – and all counting starts from the beginning of the sequence – the future can be grasped as that which it is – as future – only by means of anticipation. If we wished to recount the future too, we should inescapably turn it into the fixed and rigid past. The future has to be said-in-advance. The future is experienced only in expectation. Here the last must, in our thinking, become the first.'[22]

Of course the past too is not just told as something that is finished, and finally harmoniously disposed. The past contains so much that is unfinished, undone and unrealized that the way we deal with it goes beyond any mere telling. In so far as the historian concerns himself with 'the future in the past'[23] and with the possible in what has become reality, he is like a backward-facing prophet. 'In the Hebrew and Christian view of history, the past is a promise to the future', declared Karl Löwith. 'Consequently the interpretation of the past becomes a prophecy in reverse, demonstrating the past as a meaningful "preparation" for the future.'[24] If we dispense with Löwith's one-sided, linear understanding of time, and take the difference between past and future seriously, then dealings with the past are dealings with past future and with the recovery of lost potentialities.[25] Interaction with those who are past and dead is necessary in the name of the common future in the resurrection of the dead – necessary, and an expression of a community not merely in transience but in coming too.

On the other hand the relation to every future is certainly not that of a recounting; it is essentially an anticipation through the medium of the imagination, because that future has not yet happened. There can be no telling of the ultimate future, but only divine promises and human expectations. Nevertheless, just as there is future in the past, so there could also be past in the future. Can we not by way of scenarios describe what in the future will pass away? Can the Christian hope for the victory of God's justice and righteousness not 'tell' of the passing away of the powers of injustice and death? The apocalyptic writers, at all events, present the downfall of Babylon and the end of this world of injustice and violence as a narrative of that 'which will soon come about'. That too is an anticipation of something that has not yet happened, but it is an anticipation in the mode of the narrated past of what must pass away.

Here too we must distinguish: *the negation of the negative* can be told: to take up our German proverb once more, an end with terror ends the terror without end that has been experienced here and now. *The position of the positive* – the new heaven and the new earth, and the heavenly Jerusalem – are anticipated on the basis of the position already experienced – the goodly creation of heaven and earth and God's sanctifying presence in Jerusalem – but that position is broadened out into what is new and unimaginable. This is anticipation in the mode of remembered future, the mode, that is, of fulfilled promises, the promise of creation and the promises in history. Telling and anticipation are interlaced, and cannot be distinguished as easily as Franz Rosenzweig would have us believe. We shall keep these interlacings in view by continually relating the messianic anticipations of the future in what was promised beforehand to the apocalyptic narrative of the future past of the godless powers; and vice versa.

3. Eschatological Orders of Time in History

Eschatologies that are orientated towards a goal have always tried to order history by distinguishing periods, epochs and times. They have assumed that the course of world history is articulated in a unified way.

Nebuchadnezzar's dream in Daniel 2 and the image of the monarchies in Daniel 7 were examples of this. This is *the pattern of the four empires,* which rise out of the sea of chaos and rule in bestial form. The fourth empire will be 'strong as iron' (2.40) and will 'devour the whole earth, and trample it down, and break it to pieces' (7.23). But then 'the God of heaven will set up a kingdom which shall never be destroyed . . . It shall break in pieces all these kingdoms . . . and it shall stand for ever' (2.44). This is the humane kingdom of 'the Son of man' (7.13f.). It will be given to 'the saints of the Most High' (7.27). In Cromwell's time, the people who considered themselves to be these saints called themselves 'Fifth Monarchy men'. In this first pattern of world history, the question is: *to whom does sovereignty over the world belong?* It is, that is to say, a question about power. Because in Daniel the different empires are only named in code-form, ever new attempts at world hegemony could be identified with them: Rome, Napoleon, the USA, communist and capitalist supremacy.[26]

The theopolitical interpretation of the image of the monarchies in Daniel chapter 7 wavers between apocalyptic rejection and a justification of the empires in the context of world history. The original meaning of the chapter can be explained by the struggles of the Maccabean period. The purpose is to expose the godlessness and wickedness of the empires, and to predict their final downfall, brought about by the God who by ending the empires will set up his own kingdom of justice and peace. But in the realms of Christendom, from Constantine onwards, the chapter was read very differently. The sequence of the empires determines world history, and divine providence orders the kingdoms of the world in the direction of the final goal of the kingdom of God. 'World history' was always – as it still is – an intellectual and interpretative framework for the imperial powers which considered themselves to be 'universal' empires, and allowed themselves to be revered as such. According to their own claim, these empires are the determining subjects of world history and make of the earthly universe their own world history, by way of their universal imperial policies. Appealing to Daniel 7, the Christian empires saw themselves as preliminary stages for the universal kingdom of God, for they were not revolts against that kingdom but purported to be its pre-forms and the means to its implementation.

The idea was as follows: every empire is a new 'centralization' of the many peoples into a single humanity. At the climax of the self-integration of human beings into humanity's body politic, the kingdom of God can then come into being, as the divine universal realm. Of course the climax of humanity's integration is also threatened by the danger of humanity's absolute *dis*integration.[27] The utmost concentration of power can lead to humanity's self-destruction; this is already so in the case of the nuclear powers and the ecologically destructive industrial countries. But for that very reason, this self-integration of humanity, which is necessary for peace, has to be legitimated and safeguarded by the expected divine state which will be universal and final.

We find this scheme of the four kingdoms or ages in the chronicles of world history written in the middle ages and the Reformation period. The Lutheran *Magdeburger Centurien* is constructed on the same pattern, as is the *Chronica Carionis* of 1532, which was revised by Melanchthon in 1558 and later by his pupils Caspar Peucer and

Christoph Pezel.[28] Although the picture of the monarchies in Daniel is meant apocalyptically and subversively, in the Christian chronicles of universal history it was understood as a positive revelation of God's plan for the world, and was used to discover for the present what 'the state of the times' was.

Another scheme originated in the rabbinic transposition of the seven days of creation into the *seven ages of world history*. If symbolically speaking a thousand years are 'as a day', then the history of the world from creation to the end lasts for six thousand years. Afterwards comes the end-time, eternal sabbath. In the middle ages, Rupert van Deuz and Anselm von Havelberg presented world history in this way. Luther and Melanchthon were convinced that the world would end in the sixth millennium. Church history too was repeatedly presented according to this pattern, so as to announce the advent of the End-time and its events at the end of the sixth millennium, and so as to hope for the eternal sabbath.

For the Christian chroniclers of world history and for the apocalyptists, a Talmud passage also played a part that should not be underestimated: 'In the school of Elijah [Rabbi Elijah ben Solomon, the Vilna Gaon] it is taught: the world will endure for 6,000 years: 2,000 years chaos, 2,000 years Torah, 2,000 years messianic time; but because of our many sins some of these (years) have already lapsed.'[29] Melanchthon, Carion, Osiander and Pezel already quoted this passage, and made use of it.[30] They reckoned that the 2,000 years after the birth of Christ would be shortened, and assigned their own contemporary period to the apocalyptic events of the End-time.

The *trinitarian periodization of history* into the kingdom of the Father, the kingdom of the Son, and the third kingdom of the Holy Spirit goes back to Joachim of Fiore.[31] Whereas for Thomas Aquinas and the Catholic tradition there was only one decisive transition in God's history with human beings, the transition from the old law to the new and from Israel to the church, Joachim expected a further transition in history from the word to faith, from Christ to the Spirit. It is true that Joachim was always so understood as if these three ages were self-contained stages, separate from one another. But that is incorrect. As his *Liber Figurarum* shows, the three conditions intersect, like three intertwining rings, so that the Spirit is also present in the kingdom of the Father, and the Father is also present in the kingdom of the Spirit, and the Son is also present in both.

Joachim's idea about the dawning kingdom of the Spirit is inconceivable 'without Christ'.[32] In this respect he was no free-thinking, Enlightenment spirit, like Lessing, who sought the fulfilment of the Christian age in a post-Christian era.

Finally, it must be stressed that according to Joachim, even the kingdom of the Spirit is a historical kingdom, not yet the eternal kingdom of the triune God. What is meant is a qualitative leap in history, not history's end. The era of the Holy Spirit is 'new time' compared with the ecclesiastical era of Christ, but in respect of the end of history it is simultaneously 'End-time'. The pattern of the three ages, however their content is defined, is a picture of progress in the positive sense, not of the apocalyptic overthrow of power; so from the beginning of 'the modern world' onwards, and especially in the nineteenth century, it was a pattern that was applied in ever new variations to the present.

For many millenarianists, the expected Thousand Years' empire of Christ also has a cosmic significance, for it is identical with the seventh age of the world, the End-time sabbath year. If the millennium is the End-time sabbath of the world, then at that time 'everything will arrive at what is its own' and there will be 'a great year of jubilee and release for all creatures.'[33] Then nature will blossom again as it did in paradise, and peace will dwell in the fields, because during this time Satan has no power. Every creature that is sighing and groaning now (Rom. 8.19ff.) looks forward to the Thousand Years' empire, the sabbath of the world.

The 'seven' scheme and this 'triple' pattern are combined in an interesting way with the help of a Talmud saying: if twice a thousand years are added together in each case, the result is three plus one. The thousand years that is left over is the world sabbath. It is quite possible that Joachim had come across this Talmud saying in Spain, in the Jewish Kabbalah of his time.

The connection with classic Christianity can be found in the ancient doctrine about Christ's threefold parousia: Christ came in the flesh – he comes in the Spirit – he will come in glory. Flesh – Spirit – glory characterize the three different presences of Christ, and succeed one another in history.

Generally speaking, Christian theology has always distinguished, both substantially and in time, between three levels or kingdoms: nature – grace – glory. This triad has put its impress on both the theological and the philosophical way of thinking about history in modern times: *regnum naturae* (creation), *regnum gratiae* (history), *regnum gloriae* (future).

The real problem of these different periodizations of world history is posed by their theological premise: does world history really unveil successively a predetermined 'divine plan for the Kingdom'? *Is* the Bible 'the divine commentary on divine acts in history'?[34] Is prophecy nothing other than 'antecipata historia',[35] and history consequently simply fulfilled prophecy? In that case the testimonies of the Bible would in no way be the self-revelation and self-communication of God; they would merely be the revelation of God's providence. Biblical research would be for the knowledge of history what research into nature is for the knowledge of nature.[36] The deistic doctrine of God as the Creator of a 'universal machinery' which functions in a self-contained way according to its inherent laws is generally considered to be a product of the Enlightenment and rationalism; but in fact it dominated the Pietism of the Enlightenment era as well. With the help of his interpretation of the Bible as prophetic history, Johann Albrecht Bengel explained God's plan of salvation, and calculated the course and end of the history of the world. His pupil, Philipp Matthäus Hahn, built his astronomical clocks as the 'sensory presentation of the 7 Chief Eras of the world age' (*Tabula Chronologica qua aetas mundi septem chronis distincta sistitur*, 1774). The big hand shows the millennial age of the world. The first Thousand Years' kingdom of Christ is shown as beginning on 18 June 1836. The deistic 'world machine' is nothing other than the apocalyptic world clock. The astronomical view of history held by Bengel, Oetinger and Hahn corresponds precisely to Newton's mechanistic picture of nature.

The 'prophetic interpretation of scripture' began in the Protestantism of the post-Reformation period in Holland, England and North Germany. Just as for Catholic theology scripture and tradition belonged together, so for prophetic theology the Bible and world history were to correspond. The Reformation principle *sola scriptura* was turned into the biblicistic and salvation-history principle *tota scriptura*. It is obvious that this meant promoting the book of Revelation to be the 'prince of the New Testament writings', no longer – as for Luther and Calvin – the Epistle to the Romans, with its doctrine of justification. But – to express immediate criticism at this point – the Bible is the book of God's promises, not of God's providence. It is the source for a historical theology in testimony, assailment, struggle and suffering, not for a speculative theology of universal history and a divine plan of salvation. The theology of hope is not a theory about universal history, nor is it an apocalyptic prediction. It is a theology of combatants, not onlookers.

In this chapter about historical eschatology we shall first look at millenarianism (which is also known as chiliasm or messianism) and then at apocalyptic. Millenarianism stresses history's goal, apocalyptic its end. In millenarian eschatology I am distinguishing between *historical millenarianism*, which interprets the present as Christ's Thousand Years' empire and the last age of humanity, and *eschatological millenarianism*, which hopes for the kingdom of Christ as the future which will be an alternative to the present, and links this future with the end of 'this world' and the new creation of all things. In apocalyptic eschatology, I am correspondingly distinguishing between *apocalyptic interpretations of annihilating end-times* in human history, and *the eschatological exposure* of the powers of this history in the divine judgment, which prepares for the new creation of all things. Historical eschatology is political eschatology, and more than that. Consequently I shall end the chapter with some thoughts about the Last Judgment and its justice, and about the restoration of all things in the new creation.

§2 MESSIANIC ESCHATOLOGY: 'THE THOUSAND YEARS' EMPIRE'

No eschatological hope has fascinated men and women as much as the idea of a Thousand Years' empire in which Christ and those who are his will reign on earth before the end of history – and yet no hope has caused so much unhappiness.[37] Seers, thinkers and enthusiasts have all seized hold of this idea. For the sake of the Thousand Years' empire people have left house and home, and have gone out to meet it.[38] For the Thousand Years' empire, martyrs have suffered and given their lives. For the Thousand Years' empire people have been persecuted, driven from their homes, and murdered. For long stretches, the history of Christianity has been identical with the struggle for the Thousand Years' empire, writes Norman Cohn. In its purely religious form this expectation is cherished by the sects which separate themselves from this world as far as possible – the Adventists, for example, or the Mormons, or Jehovah's Witnesses. The idea has been implicit in the missionary consciousness of a church that sets out to convert the nations of the earth. It exists in the form of the Christian imperialism that subjugates peoples and sets out to rule the world. Finally, it can be found in the guise of Christian restorationism, which expects the Thousand Years' empire to take the form of a union between Christians and Jews on Zion.[39] Religious, ecclesiastical and political messianism has been fired by this idea. We therefore have to take it seriously, and consider it theologically without brusquely pushing it away into the history of heresies, citing the condemnation of millenarianism by the mainline churches.

By excluding the future hope for Christ's coming kingdom in history, the established Christian churches condemned part of their own hope too, so that all that was left to them was hope for souls in the heaven of a world beyond this one.

It could also happen that the churches of the Christian imperium condemned the hope for a coming kingdom of Christ because they thought that they themselves were already that kingdom; so the hope that the kingdom was still to come, and would replace them, had to be viewed as subversive criticism of their own authority.

1. *Pre-millenarianism and Jewish Messianism*

The expectation of the Thousand Years' empire is called millenarianism or millennialism (from the Latin word) or chiliasm (from the Greek one). In everyday language the words 'messianism' and 'messianic' are often used. In continental literature on the subject, the Greek word is preferred; in English and American the Latin one. We are using the American word here, not just for international reasons but because today the United States is the country par excellence of millenarian thinking and hoping. It is America, too, that has given us the important distinction between *pre-millenarianism* and *post-millenarianism*.[40] Pre-millenarianism is the belief that the Thousand Years' empire is a period in the future, *after* Christ's second coming, his coming in glory. *Post-millenarianism* is the belief that the Thousand Years' empire is a historical era *before* his second coming. *A-millenarianism*, finally, is the denial of any millennium at all. Occasionally this takes the one-sided form of denying only a future millennium, while viewing some great period in the past or present as being that millennium; but generally the time-eternity dialectic takes the place of historical dynamic. Because in the light of eternity all times are con-temporaneous, the future enjoys no preference. The theological divides along the line of Christ's second coming sound like hairsplitting, but for the eschatological history of Christianity they are of very considerable consequence religiously, ecclesiastically and politically. For the eschatological history of Christianity is not a history of disappointed hope or the delay of Christ's parousia; it is a history of prematurely fulfilled hope in presentative millenarianism. It is not the disappointment that was for two thousand years Christianity's chief problem; it was the fulfilment.

The word *messianism*, which is also used, shows that the roots of the millenarian hope are to be found in the Old Testament and in Jewish writings. It is the theopolitical hope for the kingdom of God, which is going to put an end to the human kingdoms of the world (Dan. 2 and 7). This divine kingdom can – following Isaiah – be thought of as a messianic kingdom of peace for the peoples of the world, with Zion as its centre. But following Daniel 7, it can also be imagined as the Son of man's eternal kingdom of peace for all human beings. When, later, the this-worldly figure of the messiah and the next-worldly figure of the Son of man were fused, a balance was struck between an Israel-centred messianism and a human universalism. Inner-Jewish messianism can be confined to the idea that the messiah will one day end the *galuth*, Jewish existence in exile and in foreign lands.[41] But universal Jewish messianism can also be a hope that the remoteness and alienation from God of all the nations will be ended. If messianic hope is linked with Israel's sense of mission, then the fulfilment of that hope must also mean the fulfilment of Israel's mission for the nations, and hence the abolition of that particular historical role. The messianic kingdom includes Israel, and more than Israel in its historical form.

Religious Zionism in both its Jewish and its Christian form has interpreted in a messianic sense the return of the Jews to the promised land from their exile. Judaism in exile has existed ever since the exile in Babylon, and more generally since the annihilation of Israel and the destruction of Jerusalem by the Romans in 70 and 134 AD. It has seen its exile as a judgment on Israel's sins and as atonement for the sins of the world. All prayers in exile are directed towards the return home. The founding of the state of Israel and the capture of the whole of Jerusalem in 1967 have to be viewed as fulfilments of the prayer for the return home – 'next year in Jerusalem'.

In the wake of the cultural fusion of Judaism and Hellenism, the messianic hope was also linked with the Greek idea about the Golden Age, the age of felicity in which that which has hitherto failed to be realized in other ages of history will at last succeed, as Virgil predicted in his Fourth Eclogue about 'the return of the age of gold'. In Christianity these two dreams were linked from the beginning: the Thousand Years' empire of Christ, and the golden age of the world.[42]

The biblical roots can be discovered, not only in Dan. 7.18: 'The saints of the Most High shall receive the kingdom and possess the kingdom for ever', and in 7.27: 'The kingdom and the dominion and the greatness of the kingdoms under the whole heaven shall be given to the people of the saints of the Most High.' We find them too in Ezekiel 37, the vision of Israel's raising and reunification: 'I will make them one nation' (v.22) and 'My servant David shall be king over them' (v.24) and 'I will set my sanctuary in the midst of them for evermore' (v.26). But afterwards, 'in the latter days' (38.16), the enemies 'Gog and Magog' will attack Israel, the last struggle for Zion will be fought, and God will be finally victorious. The symbolic number 1,000 probably derives from Ezek. 38.8: 'many days' (similarly Isa. 24.21f.), and from the rabbinic transposition of the days of creation in Genesis 1 into God's history with the world according to Ps. 90.4: 'a thousand years are as a day'. The Thousand Years' messianic empire is, accordingly, the final age of the world before God's eternal sabbath in the new, eternal creation. The lordship of the messiah belongs within the history of this world; the new creation of all things, which begins with the Last Judgment, only comes afterwards.[43]

These messianic hopes cherished by Israel are certainly related to crises in its faith, following the theopolitical catastrophes and the experiences of exile. They provide an answer to the besetting questions: why must the righteous suffer so much, and why do the godless have it so good? Where is God's justice? The hopes are certainties about the future born from the trust that 'God will remain faithful to his promise'. In this way they keep faith alive in suffering, and encourage inward and outward resistance to the powers of this world. I do not believe that messianism, either Jewish or Christian, can be explained as a mere 'theory about a catastrophe',[44] unless history in general is interpreted as crisis and catastrophe. But it is true that the messianic hope, which designs to lead people out of catastrophe, is always linked with apocalyptic, which perceives that catastrophe. There is, indeed, apocalyptic without messianism; but there is no messianism without apocalyptic.

2. Christian Millenarianism

Did *Jesus* proclaim a messianic hope of this kind, and was he a millenarianist? According to the account in the synoptic Gospels, Jesus's message about the kingdom, and his behaviour to the poor and the sick, sinners, tax collectors and others certainly has messianic features. If the indirect identifications of Jesus with the Son of man go back to Jesus himself, then the hope of Daniel 7 is part of his message too. When the disciples expect that when his kingdom dawns they will sit at his right hand this is good messianic thinking. When Satan falls 'like lightning from heaven' (Luke 10.17ff.) he loses his power, which according to Rev. 20.3 is what is expected of the millennium. The expulsion of demons is a sign of the arrival of the messiah on earth. According to Mark 10.30, what Jesus promises is 'now in this time . . . and in the age to come eternal life'. The complaint of the disciples on the road to Emmaus 'But we had hoped that he was the one to redeem Israel' (Luke 24.21) is just as messianic and millenarian as the rejoicing of the people on Jesus's entry into Jerusalem: 'Hosanna! Blessed is he who comes in the name of the Lord! Blessed is the kingdom of our father David that is coming!' (Mark 11.9f.). Jesus's message of the kingdom was also confined to Israel (Mark 7.27). On the other hand, outside the framework of the messianic hope for victory are the announcements of suffering, the conversion from lordship to servanthood, and the cross of Christ, as well as the discipleship of the cross assumed by his followers

Did *Paul* maintain millenarian expectations of the future? 'The Thousand Years' empire' is certainly not a feature of his message, but he did use millenarian ideas. The idea that those who suffer with Christ now, will one day reign with him is a millenarian idea: 'Do you not know that the saints will judge the world?' (I Cor. 6.2). 'If we endure, we shall also reign with him' (II Tim. 2.12). The notion that the end of this world will not come with one great stroke but in a series of End-time events is also millenarian: 'Each in his own order: Christ the first fruits, then at his coming those who belong to Christ. Then comes the end, when he delivers the kingdom to God the Father after destroying every rule and every authority and power . . . The last enemy to be destroyed is death' (I Cor. 15.23ff.). I Thess. 4.16f. is similar: 'The dead in Christ will rise first; then we who are alive shall be caught up together with them . . .' Paul distinguishes between the eschatological, general 'resurrection *of* the dead' and a series of anticipatory resurrections *from* the dead. The process of the eschatological raising of the dead begins with the raising of Christ '*from* the dead'. That makes him, as the first fruits of those who have fallen asleep, the leader of life (I Cor. 15.20; Col. 1.18). The expression 'resurrection *from* the dead' is used by Paul (Phil. 3.11) and Luke (20.35) for believers, who are to be raised ahead of the other dead in order that they may be with Christ and appear with him when he comes (Col. 3.3f.). This 'resurrection *from* the dead' is a raising analogous to the raising of Christ, not a mere prolepsis of the general raising of the dead.[45]

Astonishingly enough Paul describes the redeeming future for Israel in very similar terms: 'For if their rejection means the reconciliation of the world, what will their acceptance mean but *life from the dead*?' (Rom. 11.15). Resurrection from the dead points towards a future of resurrection and life with Christ before the eschatological end of history, and can only be understood in a millenarian sense. The fact that this messianic hope of those who believe in Christ opens up an analogous future for Israel, seems to be the special mark of Christian pre-millenarianism. It is the Christian dream for the Jews – not for their conversion to the church, but for their resurrection into the kingdom of their Messiah.

For millenarianism, the most important New Testament passages are Revelation chapters 7 and 20. According to Revelation 7, 'the sealed' – that is, the elect – will be called together for the End-time, 144,000 from the twelve tribes of Israel, and afterwards 'the great multitude' from every nation, and together with the angels they will adore God and 'the Lamb' Jesus Christ. These are those who 'have come out of great tribulation', those, that is to say, who have withstood the godless powers and have not worshipped the beast from the abyss: Israel's martyrs and the martyrs of the Christian faith.[46] According to Rev. 20.4, the martyrs 'who had been beheaded for their testimony to Jesus and for the word of God' because they 'had not worshipped the beast or its image and had not received its mark on their foreheads or their hands' will live, reign and judge with Christ for 'a thousand years'. This is 'the first resurrection'. The martyrs will become 'priests of God and of Christ'. For these thousand years Satan will be 'bound'. After the thousand years he will be loosed for a short time. Then the final battle with Gog and Magog for the saints and the beloved city Jerusalem will follow. And after that will come the end, in the great divine Judgment.

The seer John evidently took over the Jewish apocalyptic tradition about the messianic kingdom before the Last Judgment and the new creation of all things (a tradition found in Ezek. 37 and 38, II Bar. 40.3, II Esd. 7.28f. and b.Sanh.99a); but he gave the concept a new function. He used this messianic idea in order to present the victory of the martyrs over 'the beast', that is the Roman empire.[47] Those who are judged here will judge with Christ there; those who die with Christ here will live with Christ there; those who are defeated with Christ here will rule with Christ there. Because he concentrates solely on this martyr eschatology, he does not say *whom* the martyrs will then judge, reign over and rule. We have to go back to the Jewish models and draw on Daniel 7 if we wish to turn Revelation 20 into the vision of a Christian empire. John wants to say that the martyrs of the Roman empire will be justified by God. His Thousand Years' empire is the pictorial presentation of their justification and the divine counter-image for godless Rome. It cannot be sufficiently stressed that – contrary to the speculative misuse of these passages – the millenarian hope is a *hope for martyrs*. The praxis of this hope is resistance in the godless kingdoms of the world, and the refusal to conform to their idol worship and cults of power. It is not just the hope that must be called messianic and millenarian; it is the resistance and martyrdom itself that precedes the hope. For in that resistance the relative, conditioned and often so ambivalent Here and Today is made the point in time of an eschatological, absolute and unconditioned decision.

That those who suffer martyrdom in history should be promised a future in history is quite logical. 'For it is equitable that in the selfsame creation in which they laboured and suffered tribulation, in all ways tested in endurance, they should also receive the fruits of their patience', wrote Irenaeus.[48] It would be a confutation of their martyrdom if God were not to show his power at the very point where, for him and with him, they suffered in his helplessness, and if God were not to assert his rights in the very situation in which they were executed. Even critics of the messianic, millenarian hope in Christianity have recognized this: 'The most important theological justification of chiliasm is that it points to the necessary this-worldly character of the Christian hope.'[49]

But every hope is equivocal. It can fill the present with new power, but it can also draw power away from the present. It can lead to resistance – and also to spiritual escape. The countless interpretations of the book of Revelation, and especially the fundamentalist and the new political interpretations of the apocalypse, make this plain. If the call is no longer to resistance against the powers and their idols, but if instead escapades into religious dream worlds are offered in the face of a world destined for downfall – a downfall that is even desired – the meaning of the millenarian hope is turned upside down. This is always the case when it is no longer resistance that is at the centre, but 'the great rapture' of believers before the annihilation of the world in the fire storm of nuclear bombs.[50] But Revelation was not written for 'rapturists' fleeing from the world, who tell the world 'goodbye' and want to go to heaven; it was meant for resistance fighters, struggling against the godless powers on this earth, especially the nuclear powers; it was written, that is, out of love for this world of God's.

The distinction between pre-millenarianism and post-millenarianism should not be underestimated, for the place given to the present in the history of salvation and in world history depends on whether one sees the kingdom of Christ ahead or whether one looks back to it. In the pre-Constantinian church, *pre-millenarianism* was dominant in Christian eschatology (cf. Barn. *bt*. XV 3–8; Justin, *dial. cum Trypho* 80; Irenaeus, *adv. haer.* V, 30.4; 33.2). 'So-called chiliasm – the term is not entirely apt – can be found wherever the gospel is not yet hellenized . . . and must be considered one of the main elements of the earliest proclamation', declared Arnolf von Harnack. '. . . It was there that part of the power of Christianity in the [first] century lay, and it was one of the means by which it outdid Jewish propaganda in the empire.'[51] Harnack argued that belief in Christ's second coming necessarily implies a kingdom of glory for Christ. Since this millenarianist expectation is martyr eschatology, in the era of Christian persecutions in the Roman empire it was undoubtedly the eschatology that was dominant. It was therefore also a reason why many Christians, together with Eusebius of Caesarea,[52] welcomed the turning point under Constantine as the transition from suffering with Christ to ruling with him, and hence as the dawn of the Thousand Years' empire.

When the Roman empire transformed itself from 'the beast from the abyss' into the *imperium Christianum*, and persecuted Christianity became the empire's dominant religion, *presentative millenarianism* sprang up: the *Imperium Sacrum* was held to be already the Thousand Years' empire of Christ heralded in Revelation 20, and the divine universal monarchy of Daniel 2 and 7. The church's theology turned into an imperial theology, because it was no longer just Christ's church which represented God's rule on earth; it was the Christian emperor and the Christian empire too. Salvation and sovereignty fused into a unity. The result was the mission to the nations by way of cross and sword, but above all through their subjugation and incorporation into the *imperium Christianum*. We shall look at this political millenarianism in the following sections. At this point we must simply establish that people who think that they are living in an already fulfilled hope cannot tolerate any still open hope for the future. It was therefore quite logical that in 431 the imperial Council of Ephesus should have condemned the hope for the millennium, maintaining – contrary to I Cor. 15.28 – that the lordship of Christ, which is now already a hidden reality, 'is eternal' and without end. In this way the present representation of Christ's kingdom through church and emperor was secured.[53]

After the fall of Rome, another form of presentative millenarianism developed in the western part of the empire. Here Tyconius and Augustine interpreted the era of the Thousand Years' empire as the era of the church, from Christ's ascension until his coming again. Baptism is 'the first resurrection'; the rule of the saints lasts from the first coming of Christ until his second coming. Through the church, Christ already exercises *now* his sovereignty according to Revelation 20. We shall discuss at a later point what this presentative millenarianism means for the church. Here it may suffice to point out that every hope for a kingdom of Christ in the future withdraws all legitimation from this chiliastic concept of the church. The premillenarian communities were therefore bound to be condemned as a danger for ecclesiastical rule, just as were the Jews, with their expectation of a future messiah.

It is obvious that once the 1,000 years in their chronologically and literally understood sense had passed, apocalyptic crises about how to define the present position in salvation history were bound to arise, both in the Christian empire and in the ruling church. In Europe, post-millenarianism spread. But what happens after the millennium? 'Satan' will be let loose once more, and Gog and Magog will storm Christianity and the holy city. As the middle ages drew to a close, post-millenarian apocalyptic dominated hearts and imaginations. The end of the millennium will be followed by the tribulations of the End-time, by the final struggle between Christ and Antichrist, and then a short time afterwards by 'the Last Day', with the Last Judgment. In the late middle ages, that is to say, we find ever more post-millenarian eschatology and an interpretation of the present that is now solely apocalyptic.

The Reformers were also convinced that the millennium was a historical era in the past, and that with the manifestation of the pope as Antichrist this era had come to an end. It is understandable that Luther should have believed that he lived at the end of the times, that in the struggle with Rome he was involved in the struggle with the Antichrist, and that he should have seen ahead only 'the dear Last Day', the general resurrection of the dead and the great Judgment.[54]

The Protestant condemnations of 'chiliasm' are condemnations of pre-millenarianism.

The Confessio Augustana (the Augsburg Confession), Article XVII, runs: 'Damnant et alios, qui nunc spargunt iudaicas opiniones, quod ante resurrectionem mortuorum pii regnum mundi occupaturi sint, ubique oppressis impiis.' ('Rejected, too, are certain Jewish opinions which are even now making an appearance and which teach that, before the resurrection of the dead, saints and godly men will possess a worldly kingdom and annihilate all the godless.'[54a])

And the Confessio Helvetica posterior of 1566 (the Swiss Confession), Article XI, reads: 'Damnamus praeterea judaica somnia, quod ante judicii diem aureum in terris sit futurem seculum, et pii regna mundi occupaturi, oppressis suis hostibus impiis.' ('Moreover we condemn the Jewish dreams that before the Day of Judgment on earth there will be a golden age, and the devout will capture the kingdoms of the world and will suppress their godless enemies.')

Right down to the modern confessions written after the Second World War, these are the only passages in Christian confessions of faith in which Jews are mentioned at all. Historically, one can point to messianic movements in European Judaism in the Reformation period, in order to explain why millenarianism should be termed here a 'Jewish opinion' or a 'Jewish dream', but these historical explanations are not sufficient. What is also being theologically condemned is the idea that the Christian hope includes a future for the Jews as Jews.

When the Swiss identify Jewish messianism with the Greek hope for a golden age, this goes back historically to an early Jewish-Christian humanism such as we find in Reuchlin. In essence, they are identifying the millennium with a whole world era, and are universalizing it. If the eschatological mediation between history and eternity in 'the Thousand Years' empire' is dropped, then history continues right up to the general resurrection of the dead and the Last Judgment. When Christ comes again, he will come for the great Judgment over all human beings. Here there is no special future for believers in his kingdom. The premise for this viewpoint can be found in the authors' post-millenarianism. If one lives in the Thousand Years' empire or at its end, then all that can be seen ahead is the Last Judgment and eternity.

3. The Post-Reformation Rebirth of Messianic Eschatology

Protestant post-millenarianists defined their position on the basis of either political or ecclesiastical millenarianism.[55] If they assumed the *political millennium of Christ*, they calculated that the 'thousand years' began with Constantine (324), coming to an end in 1324. Just as before Constantine there had been an era of Christian martyrdom, so after 1324 there was a new period of Christian martyrdom, with the persecution of Wycliffe and the burning of Jan Hus – signs that the Antichrist had arisen in the Christian empire. Other people connected the struggle with the advance of Islam, and linked the Mongol incursions into Christian Europe with the End-time struggle of Gog and Magog. For West European Protestants, the Reformation and post-Reformation periods were full of the ecclesiastical and political struggle against the Antichrist in Rome. The defeat of the Catholic Armada in 1588 made England the 'chosen nation' in this struggle. When the Protestant post-millenarians took up the ecclesiastical millennium, they calculated the Thousand Years' empire from the year of Christ's death and resurrection (33 AD), and arrived at the year 1033. They dated the papal apostasy from the pontificate of Silvester II. Since that time two churches had fought with each other, the church of Christ and the church of the Antichrist, in other words: the one is persecuted, the other persecutes. The new era of the martyrs will last until the end of the world.

Characteristically, with the beginning of so-called modern times, a new *pre-millenarianism* also developed, one which again allowed people to hope for the future of the messianic kingdom, or – more simply – for 'better times to come'. The beginning of modern times brought a rebirth of messianic and millenarian hope, in spite of all the condemnations of that hope in the Lutheran and Calvinist confessional writings. The new messianic hopes awoke first with Thomas Müntzer and the peasants in 1525, and with the Anabaptists in Münster in 1534, Joachimite expectations reaching Germany and England from Italy by way of the late Renaissance humanists.[56]

Within pre-millenarianism the Lutheran tradition distinguishes between a *chiliasmus crassus* – i.e., the expectation of a 'worldly kingdom' (*regnum mundi*, in the Latin of the Augsburg Confession, XVII) in which the saints will reign and the godless will be destroyed; the 'Mohammedan realm of lust and pleasure'; and a *chiliasmus subtilis*, the expectation of a spiritual kingdom in which Christ will reign from heaven over human beings and the earth, through the Holy Spirit. Because Satan is for this time bound, during this era the good will be able to spread unhindered.

With the post-Reformation rebirth of chiliasm, especially in England, the suppressed spirit of Joachim of Fiore returned too. His works were printed for the first time by Anabaptists in 1519, in Venice. Of great influence on Christians in Europe was Manasseh ben Israel's book 'The Hope of Israel' (*Spes Israelis*, Amsterdam 1650). In Protestant England it evoked a wave of philosemitic feeling. In Germany the rebirth of chiliasm began in the Calvinist Academy in Herborn through Johann Heinrich Alsted's *Diatribe de mille annis apocalypticis* (Frankfurt 1627, 2nd ed. 1630).[57] Philipp Jacob Spener took ideas from him for his influential book *Behauptung der Hoffnung künfftiger Besserer Zeiten* (Frankfurt 1673), also drawing on the new 'prophetic theology' of Dutch writers belonging to the circle of Campegius Vitringa, and on the salvation-history federal theology of Johann Cocceius. Spener was followed by Johann Albrecht Bengel's *Erklärte Offenbarung Johannis und vielmehr Jesu Christi* (Stuttgart 1740).[58] and by Friedrich Christoph Oetinger's *Die Güldene Zeit oder Sammlung wichtiger Betrachtungen von etlichen Gelehrten zur Ermunterung in*

diesen bedenklichen Zeiten zussamengetragen (I, Frankfurt and
Leipzig 1759, II and III, Frankfurt and Leipzig 1761).

With Oetinger the mediaeval theology of love and the Reformation's theology of faith was followed by a deliberately modern
'theology of hope': 'In the time of Luther and Arnd, faith and love
were taught for the most part, and for the least part hope. But now
comes the time when, following Bengel's representations, we also
proclaim hope more fully.'[59] Friedrich Hölderlin aptly summed up
the existential significance of the new chiliastic eschatology in his
words:

> Near / and hard to grasp the God,
> but where danger is / deliverance also grows.[60]

In the seventeenth century a new optimistic kingdom-of-God
theology developed, with a missionary hope for a springtime of the
heathen, a new *diakonia*, a new school, a new kindergarten and, for
the first time, a readiness for dialogue with the Jews. The movement
of the mystical messiah Sabbatai Zwi met this halfway. The
amelioration of the world in view of the coming kingdom of Christ
motivated many Christians, among them Johann Amos Comenius,
the last bishop of the persecuted Moravian Brethren, and one of
the universal scholars of his time: 'I venture to declare true chiliasm
to be true Christianity, anti-chiliasm, conversely, to be anti-
Christianity . . . The general amelioration of things will be the work
of Jesus Christ, who will renew the condition from which everything
has drifted away; in spite of that he requires our assistance, but that
will no longer be difficult in the present state of things.'[61] Comenius
saw 'the present state of things' as determined by the new chiliastic
horizon of the future. We need not pursue further here the link
between this new kingdom-of-God theology and Enlightenment and
humanism.[62] Until the French Revolution, the messianism that was
dominant in the pietistic movement was open to the world and
orientated towards a positive future. It was only the apocalyptic
interpretations of the French Revolution that made pietism and
biblicism conservative and anti-modernist.

In England and the United States, the 'prophetic' and 'salvation
history' interpretation of the Bible of the early seventeenth century
developed into an antimodernist, fundamentalist *apocalypticism*.
'Dispensationalism' was spread by John Darby, D.L. Moody and
C.I. Scofield, with his famous Scofield Reference Bible. In their view,

God's plan of salvation can be perceived from the seven dispensations or periods to which the Bible witnesses, for the Bible is the divine testimony of a successive salvation history. God's final revelation is consequently the revelation of the end of history in the book of Revelation. The Bible is essentially prediction, and world history is essentially the fulfilment of the divine predictions. The Bible is God's word, and hence inerrant. But in what sense inerrant? All biblical predictions are free of error. They will come about sooner or later.

Right down to the present day, this new apocalyptic is spread in the United States through Bible institutes and prophecy conferences and end-of-the-world announcements in all the major newspapers. Its theology resembles the early prophetic theology of the kingdom, but its function is the precise opposite. The messianism there finds its correspondence in the apocalyptic here. The historical involvement in resistance there is paralleled here by the apocalyptic flight from the world. Here 'the great rapture' is at the centre of eschatological interest: will it save believers before 'the great tribulation', in the midst of it, or only afterwards? There are 'pre-tribulationists', 'mid-tribulationists' and 'post-tribulationists' – for the initiated: 'pretrib premils', 'midtrib premils' and 'posttrib premils'.[63] They are politicized through 'the moral majority' of Jerry Falwell and others, who since the time of Ronald Reagan have linked this apocalyptic fundamentalism with the political right in the USA, and with the preparation for a nuclear Armageddon.

§3 POLITICAL MILLENARIANISM: 'THE HOLY EMPIRE'

1. *The Messianic Turn from Persecution to Domination: Constantine and the Consequences*

The initial fulfilment of messianic hope in Christianity was political in nature. As consequence of the turn of events under Constantine, the old apocalyptic martyr eschatology was transformed into a millenaristic imperial theology. This transposition can only be understood apocalyptically, even if historically speaking the early Christian apologists had already prepared the way. Those who with Christ had fought against the political demons and had suffered under them, began in the Roman empire after Constantine, with

Christ to be victorious politically and to rule religiously. The Constantinian turn of events made of once-persecuted Christianity, first the permitted, and then the dominant religion in the Roman empire. From this there developed Byzantinism, from Byzantinism Tsarism in the east, and in the west the theo-political ideal of the Holy Empire which was supposed to endure to the end of time.

This Christian imperialism has endured under ever new names down to the present day, whether the name given to it is Christendom, Christian civilization or the Christian age, or whether secular names are found for it, the modern world, for instance, or modern times, or scientific and technological civilization. Whatever the names, it is always the old idea of a political fulfilment of the messianic hope for Christ's Thousand Years' empire of peace, the golden age of humanity, and the End-time sabbath of nature.

We find the first and enduringly influential imperial theology in Eusebius of Caesarea, who is hence often apostrophized as Constantine the Great's court theologian.[64] But he is only one among many theologians of the Constantinian era who made of ecclesiastical theology a political, imperial theology, in order to constitute 'the Holy Empire'. Here we shall take up only a few basic ideas which became important for the political history of Europe.

With his victory over Licinius in 324, the Emperor Constantine restored the Roman monarchy, and with it the unity of the empire. His theologians interpreted this event to mean that what the Emperor Augustus had begun, Constantine had now completed. Augustus surmounted the plurality of the nations in the unity of the Roman empire. In the political imperial cult he also overrode the polytheism of the different peoples and established political monotheism. 'According to this viewpoint, monotheism had in principle begun with the monarchy of Augustus. The *imperium Romanum* dissolved the nationalities, and metaphysically, monotheism was an essential part of it.'[65] Nationalities are always pluralistic, and are hence the cause of wars among themselves. The one imperium, in contrast, meant universal peace.

For Eusebius, the prototypes for Constantine and the church were Augustus and Christ, and these prototypes were providential, being linked with each other in salvation history through the so-called census: the Saviour was born when 'a decree went out from Caesar Augustus that all the world should be enrolled' (Luke 2.1). 'But when the Lord and Saviour then appeared, and when at the time of his coming Augustus, as the First among the Romans, became Lord over the nationalities, the pluralistic rule by many was dissolved and peace embraced the whole.'[66] The messianic hopes were thus fulfilled: 'But when God's Messiah appeared, about whom the prophets had once said: . . . They shall beat their swords into ploughshares and their spears into pruning hooks . . . the fulfilment followed in exact correspondence to the prophecies. For among the Romans every rule by many was at once abolished, since Augustus assumed sole rule at the very point in time when our Redeemer appeared.[67]

Constantine was therefore chosen by God to realize the divine plan of salvation, which purposes to fulfil the promises of peace in the messianic kingdom. Constantine brings this time of salvation to the peoples of the earth, and himself has messianic significance.[68] 'In the darkness of the night God let a great light shine out to all, with a strong arm bringing forth his servant Constantine as deliverer.' In his oration at the *tricennalia*, Eusebius interpreted Constantine's rule in an entirely apocalyptic sense by citing the words of Dan. 7.18: 'The saints of the Most High shall receive the kingdom.' The Roman empire which had now become Christian was itself nothing less than the universal kingdom of Christ.

2. Political Millenarianism: 'The Holy Empire'

The *pax Romana* instituted by Augustus and completed by Constantine is the realization of the *pax messianica* and therefore of the 'Thousand Years' empire'. Christianity's link with political power was now no longer by way of Pontius Pilate, under whom Christ suffered and who had him crucified, but through Augustus, who by means of his 'tax' made him a Roman subject. In this way Rome lost the character given to it in Revelation 13. It was no longer anti-God and Antichrist. It now became a power in salvation history, an instrument for realizing the kingdom of Christ on earth. The apocalyptic city of the godless became the city of eternal salvation.

This was the beginning of the theo-political doctrine of 'the eternal city': first Rome, second Byzantium, third Moscow. The monarchy of the One Roman Emperor became the guarantee for the unity of the empire, and had to receive a religious legitimation. This legitimation was offered by Christian monotheism, according to which the one earthly monarchy of Caesar corresponded to the one divine monarchy in heaven.[69] 'One God, one Logos, one emperor.' Imperium, peace, monarchy and monotheism forged the new theopolitical unity of the empire. There is always only One Christian Emperor, for – so the argument ran – scripture says 'Fear God and honour the emperor' (I Peter 2.17), not 'the emperors'. The emperor's kingdom can have no end as long as Christ reigns in heaven, and as long as the emperor judges the whole earth in his name. If his kingdom is supposed to represent the universal monarchy of the One God, it cannot acquiesce in any limits presented by other kingdoms or nations. It must therefore be imperialist in principle, to the ends of the earth and to the end of time; in no other way could this kingdom be seen as the fulfilment of Daniel 2 and 7 and as the Thousand Years' empire of Revelation 20.

When the imperial theologians transferred these apocalyptic promises to the *imperium christianum*, which came into being before their very eyes, they conferred upon that kingdom a messianic sense of mission which has never wholly disappeared from the political or civil religions of Christianity down to the present day. It is the apocalyptic calling of this kingdom to ward off the end of the world and to keep down Satan – that is, to be the *katechon* of the End-time. The imperial church no longer prayed 'May thy kingdom come and this world pass away.' It prayed *pro mora finis*, for the delay of the end. As that naive cultural milleniarist Johann Weiss wrote in 1892 (contrary to his own better exegetical knowledge): 'We no longer pray, "May grace come and the world pass away" but we pass our lives in the joyful confidence that *this* world will increasingly become the showplace of the people of God. But another attitude has silently come among us in place of the strictly eschatological one . . .'[70]

Like the kingdom of Christ, the kingdom of Constantine began with a cross; but it was not the cross on Golgotha. It was the dream cross that promised him 'In hoc signo vinces' – 'in this cross you will conquer'. With Constantine's victory over Maxentius in 312, the martyr cross of Christ became a sign of imperial victory. That is why decorations conferred in the Christian empires also point, not to Golgotha, but to Constantine: the Cross of St George, the Victoria Cross, the Iron Cross, and so forth. In all the European national flags that carry the cross, the cross is the symbol of victory.[71]

The messianism and apocalypticism of the Byzantine Christian imperium can best be seen from its symbols. These images and symbols were taken from the adjacent Christian empires in Europe and America. The famous Easter icon links the resurrection of Christ with the beginning of the Thousand Years' empire. Christ can be seen rising from the tomb, with both hands drawing Adam and Eve out of the realm of the dead, and with them the whole of humanity. Below, Death and the Devil can be seen as now tiny figures, chained and guarded by angels. Here I Corinthians 15 and Rev. 20.2 are combined in a single happening, and framed in a single picture.

The next symbol is the image of the fight with the dragon.[72] According to Eusebius, in his palace Constantine had himself portrayed as dragon-slayer.[73] In Byzantium the dragon counted as the foe of both faith and empire,[74] that is to say, as the enemy of the Christian millennium. The archangel Michael, as warrior and victor in the heavenly struggle against the dragon, was considered to be the guardian angel of the Christian imperium, and his picture was carried into battle on the imperial banners in the forefront of the troops. St George was turned from a Christian martyr into a warrior for the empire, and a victor in the earthly fight with the earthly dragon. He became the patron saint of the Christian imperium. From Byzantium, St George passed to Charlemagne and Otto the Great, then to the crusaders and, from the crusades onward, to England, while after the fall of Byzantium he found his way into the Moscow coat of arms. The legend telling how St George delivered the royal virgin from the dragon's den was often also interpreted as the deliverance of the church by the Christian imperium and its warriors. The Cross of St George was everywhere the supreme military decoration for the soldiers of the Holy Empire.

According to Revelation 13–19, the fight with the dragon is the beginning in heaven and earth of what is described in 20.2f.: the binding of the Dragon, the old Serpent, the Devil or Satan for the Thousand Years of the kingdom of Christ and his people on earth. Here the Christian imperium is interpreted as the End-time power which holds down evil so that the good can develop. That is the interpretation of the Holy Empire in terms of salvation history.

According to Constantinian imperial theology, Christ already reigns in heaven now as Pantocrator, the form in which he is often depicted in the domes of Byzantine churches – in Daphni, for example. So the reign of his earthly representative, the emperor, must be universal too. The Byzantine royal ritual and court ceremonial are an evident and visual demonstration of this imperial liturgy. The royal rituals and court ceremonials in the Holy Roman

Empire (the designation generally used for the Empire in the period from Charlemagne until 1806) hardly fell short in this respect.[75] The liturgy of the Mass is marked by Byzantinian court ceremonial down to the present day.[76]

What began with Constantine reached its brilliant climax with Justinian (527–565). State and church fused into a millenarian unity. The 'symphony of the two powers' was formed from the ecclesiastical and imperial charisma of the one Corpus Christianum. The Hagia Sophia in Byzantium (532–537) was built as the mighty symbol of Christ's earthly political governor and his world-wide imperial claim.

It has often been supposed that in the long run this messianic, imperial claim overtaxed Byzantium's political and military potentials and, as religious factor, brought about the collapse of this first Christian empire. Christian triumphalism destroyed itself, because the Christian emperors themselves were unable, even in human terms, to fulfil the expectations of a world-wide Christian empire. In Byzantium, political theology in fact linked the idea of oriental world rulers, for whom domination is really one and indivisible, with Christianity's messianic claim to redeem the world. This Holy Empire itself was viewed as the final goal of the divine plan for the nations, and hence as the completion of world history. The claim of this Holy Empire was directed not only towards domination but also towards salvation through true faith. Consequently the empire put itself under the protection of the heavenly hosts, the angels and saints, first and foremost the archangel Michael, and effected salvation through rule, and the conversion of the peoples of the world through subjugation. It is obvious that all religious and political power had to proceed from God's single representative on earth and from the one Lord's Anointed. The political monarchy itself was understood as *imitatio Dei* and adorned with supernatural pomp and glory. The emperor in his orthodoxy is the sole source of all power on earth and the sole fount of justice. He hence rules with unlimited power.

This autocratic absolutism was the hallmark of the political system and the political history of Byzantium, and after the fall of Constantinople in 1453 it continued until 1917 in 'the Third Rome', through the autocracy of the Russian tsar in Moscow.[77]

For Orthodox theology, the fusion of the church with the Greek and Roman empire created the 'Christian world' that was its starting point and to which it related itself. It was a special organism in which neither the church nor the state owned any separate existence distinguishable from that of the other. The political collapse of these 'Orthodox worlds' in Byzantium, Bulgaria, Serbia and Russia profoundly transformed the political self-awareness of the Orthodox church and Orthodox theology. Reactions varied, and still do: they range from an idealization of the past by way of the apocalyptic demonization of the present, down to a new eschatological orientation. The collapse of the Byzantine symphony of church and state in 'the Christian world' could also be simply ignored. Then even atheistic governments were offered the symphonic co-operation of the church, while the nationalism of 'an Orthodox country' or 'an Orthodox people' was viewed as the common bond of church and state.

If one takes the historical breakdown of 'the Christian world' seriously, however, it has to be replaced by a new eschatological orientation on the part of the church. It is not 'the Christian world' that mediates between church and world; it is the kingdom of God, which the church awaits for itself and the world both. As epiphany of the kingdom of God in history, the church frames the vision of the world's future, and takes it seriously in its dynamic, which is the dynamic of the provisional.[78]

3. *Millenarian Christianity and its Mission of Violence*

When it was surrounded by a pagan world, Christianity had organized itself in congregations. In 'the Christian empire' the church was organized in parishes and dioceses, provinces and nations, in accordance with the population areas and the governmental organization of the people; for now Christian and civic communities, ecclesiastical and governmental provinces, coincided. Church occasions became part of public, political life, for the worship of God is the supreme purpose of the state. Consequently church attendance became the first civic duty. The offices of priests and bishops took on the character appropriate to a state church. This finalized the division between clergy and laity and meant the final separation of the church from the people. The shared sacraments of baptism and Lord's Supper were replaced by 'the ministrations' of priests. Community *with* the church took the place of fellowship *in* the congregation. The church became more and more clerical, as a hierarchy chiliastically understood as 'holy rule', and in the 'Christian empire' acquired an unusual public influence. It permeated all the official functions of the *imperium*'s political religion. In this way the *imperium* was indeed 'christianized', but Christianity for its part became in the political sense 'religiofied' and subjected to political interests. Christian *diakonia* faded away, dissolving into charitable care by the state. The mission of faith degenerated too, and was replaced by state coercion.

In the Byzantine empire, Christianity surrendered the congregational form of living and interpreted its celebration of the divine liturgy as the true, public worship of God in empire and region. That is really the picture of the self-dissolution of the church in the Christian state, conceivable only in the symbolic 'Thousand Years' empire' of Christ. Only in the kingdom of Christ does the Christian spirit abandon its special form of life in the church, and acquire its universal political form of living. Only in the messianic kingdom will the body politic become the body of Christ. Wherever political communities, whether they be empire or nation, are viewed as the body of Christ, and the church is supposed to be merely the soul of this Christian polity, we have to do, not only with a millenarian concept of the state, but with a millenarian concept of the church too.[79]

Was the church as Christian community entirely lost in the 'Christian empire' after Constantine? It is remarkable that the transformation of the Christian church into an imperial religion also saw the beginning of the heyday of the monastic life. The more a secular, 'worldly' Christianity in the form in which we have just described it took shape, the more vigorously the voluntary Christian monastic communities flourished. Here was lived what the major churches could no longer give: a common life in the discipleship of Jesus, freedom from possessions and public regard, life in contemplation and neighbourly love. Without the numerous new monastic communities, the mainline church would probably have been unresistingly transmuted into the political religion of the Christian empire, and would have forgotten both Christ's cross and the liberty of faith. Of course there had been monasticism and voluntary virginity earlier, but from Constantine onwards, Christianity consciously existed in the double role of Christianity-in-the-world, and monastic Christianity. One cannot say that Christianity-in-the-world took its bearings from this life, and was turned towards this world, whereas the monastic Christian life was orientated towards the world beyond, and away from this one. The distinction is rather this: where Christianity-in-the-world sought to realize the messianic kingdom of Christ in the Christian *imperium*, monastic Christianity preserved the apocalyptic proviso, in opposition to the powers of this world.[80] As church history shows, its influence was thereby no less political than that of Christianity-in-the-world; it was simply completely different.

How long will the Holy Empire endure? The millenarian hope says that it will last until the world's end. For this, Christian imperial theology developed the idea of the *translatio imperii*.[81] Jerome already made use of this concept in his interpretation of the vision of the four kingdoms of the world in the book of Daniel: the Holy Empire will not perish but will be transferred from one nation to the other until the appearance of the Antichrist. The empire has the power to keep the Antichrist down. It is the *katechon*, the power of order against apocalyptic chaos. Once it is no longer able to do this, the end is near. This was the conviction behind the Catholic imperial theology of the 1920s, which was pursued in Germany in the monastery of Maria Laach.[82] Carl Schmitt's 'political theology' and his apocalyptic friend-enemy thinking was fed by this concept.[83] It was in this sense that the ill-fated Vietnam war was interpreted in the United States by the religious right: when the Western (Christian) states are no longer able to 'hold down' the powers of evil (communism), then the end is near.

The gospel is supposed to be proclaimed to the ends of the earth (Acts 1.8). What does that mean for the religious mission of the Holy Empire? It gives the Christian rulers of the empire an apostolic mission and makes them – like the Hapsburgs in Vienna – 'apostolic majesties'. The mission of the gospel turns into the theo-political charge to missionize and subjugate the nations, subjecting them to Christ's End-time kingdom of peace. Charlemagne's mission to the Saxons, Otto the Great's mission to the Slavs, and the 'conversion' of the Baltic peoples by the German orders of knighthood were just such millenarian disseminations of Christ's kingdom by way of sword and baptism.

The conquest and missionizing of Latin America by Spain and Portugal were not an evangelization designed to awaken faith; they were propagations of the kingdom of Christ in which subjugation brought salvation, and resistance led to death. The question on which the decision rested was not belief or unbelief; it was baptism or death. The conquerors came from an empire which was equally represented by the pope and the emperor, or the king of Spain. It was the idea of a religiously and politically unified *orbis christianus*, a 'christiandad', which as theological and political unity claimed to be the messianic age that would bring salvation to the nations. When he conquered Mexico, Herman Cortés then deliberately cast back to the Emperor Constantine, and when he stormed Tenochtitlan (Mexico City) adorned his banners with the cry: 'Brothers, let us in believing trust follow the sign of the Holy Cross! In this sign we shall conquer!'[84]

The Protestant missions of the eighteenth and nineteenth centuries were never pure missions of the gospel either. They were kingdom-of-Christ missions, and therefore spread, not only the Bible, but 'Christian values' too, which meant European, American and modern culture. Christianization and civilization often went hand in hand. In the Victorian age these cultural missions were deliberately pushed forward in Africa and Asia.

It is the millenarian character of the Christian imperium and its mission that also explains the messianic motivation of the mediaeval crusades which set out to reconquer the holy city of Jerusalem. In the vision of hope, Jerusalem always counted as the capital city of the Thousand Years' empire, and as the place of Christ's second coming. So what is a Christian imperium with a millenarian sense of mission without Jerusalem? And where, if not in Jerusalem, can the Christian nations await Christ's coming? If the end is approaching, it is to Jerusalem that one must go! The messianic myth told that the last Christian emperor will be the emperor of the End-time, who will defeat the Antichrist in the final battle, and will enter the holy city in order to lay his crown at the feet of the returned Christ on the hill of Golgotha. The famous, mysterious rider in Bamberg cathedral probably represents 'the End-time ruler on his entry into Jerusalem'.[85] In all likelihood this prophecy came from Byzantium and was transferred by the Frankish kings to the German kings and emperors. At all events, it stems from the millenarian interpretation of the Christian imperium.

§4 POLITICAL MILLENARIANISM: 'THE REDEEMER NATION'

Another kind of political fulfilment of the millenarian hope in Christendom is the idea of *the nation* whose destiny, according to

God's salvific plan, is the redemption of the world. Ever since the disintegration in Europe of the Holy Roman Empire, religiously inspired nationalism has existed among nearly all European peoples. Hitler's political messianism and his 'thousand years' empire' was the terrible but short-lived German caricature of this idea. Even today, Poland and Serbia cherish the myth of 'the redeemer nation'.

What has to be taken seriously is the USA's strange millenarian mythology, because it has a genuine basis. Through immigration, European and, more recently, Hispanic and Asiatic peoples have created the United States, have shaped its multicultural civilization, and have made it the central country of the world. The Afro-Americans have contributed quite considerably to this through their enslavement and their liberation. The country of Indo-Americans, Euro-Americans, Afro-Americans, Hispano-Americans and Asio-Americans is settled by a people drawn from all nations, and is hence the unique modern experiment in the universal representation of humanity.

Ever since the time of the Pilgrim Fathers, America's political philosophy has been determined by messianic faith. What Robert Bellah has called the civil religion of the United States, and has deduced from the inaugural addresses of American presidents, from the national holidays, and from the interpretations of political history,[86] breathes the messianic spirit of world redemption. Woodrow Wilson assured his people that 'America had the infinite privilege of fulfilling her destiny and saving the world'. John F. Kennedy and Lyndon B. Johnson invoked 'the messianic faith' of 'our forefathers'. Richard Nixon insisted that the faith of the American nation must be filled with crusading zeal, in order to change the world and win the battle for freedom. Franklin D. Roosevelt wanted to 'save the world for democracy'. In 1993 Bill Clinton proclaimed that 'our hopes, our hearts, our hands' were with all men and women in every continent who were building democracy and freedom. Their cause, he said, was the cause of America. Quotations could be multiplied at will.[87] They all display a special messianic sense of America's mission and its End-time role in world history.

Hand in hand with this political messianism goes the end-of-the-world apocalypticism, the expectation of the final struggle of good against evil, and the total destruction of the world on the day of Armageddon, a destruction which President Ronald Reagan

prophesied to 'our generation' would follow the nuclear catastrophe.[88] Nowhere else in the world is this doomsday apocalyptic
so widespread, and apparently so firmly held, as in the United States.
'The doom boom' is evidently the inescapable reverse side of the
political messianism in the USA's political mythology.[89] We shall
first look only at the political messianism, picking out some essential
aspects, in so far as these are typical.

1. 'The Chosen People'

The confidence of being God's chosen people and thus 'new Israel'
came to America from England with the early Puritans. Between
1629 and 1640 more than 20,000 Puritans emigrated to New
England. They took with them the apocalyptic images of the fight
between Christ and Antichrist, the true and the false church, and the
prophecy about the imminent advent of Christ's Thousand Years'
empire. They were also convinced of the inescapably military nature
of the final life and death struggle. Did not the Puritan preachers even
in 1644 bless Cromwell's troops as 'soldiers of Christ' in the fight
against the forces of the Antichrist? That was 'the revolution of the
Saints'.[90] When 'the great revolution' in England ended in 1660, the
emigrants had the impression that now Protestant destiny was in
America's hands, and they resisted English attempts at a restoration.
Through the conversion of the New World, Jonathan Edwards, the
great revivalist preacher, wanted to pave the way for 'that glorious
future' of the church, in which the kingdom of Satan would be
overcome on the whole inhabited globe.[91] White, Anglo-Saxon,
Protestant America (WASP) saw itself as 'the millennial nation'. This
was the dream of Anglo-Saxon superiority.[92] 'The Battle Hymn of
the Republic', published in 1862, then also saw the apocalyptic
'glory of the Lord' in the march of the Union troops: 'Our God is
marching on.'

Just as God had liberated Israel from Egyptian slavery, so the
emigrants from slavery in feudalist, absolutist Europe, with its state
churches ('Pharaoh's Britain' was a catchword) felt liberated for a
free life in the New World: 'A new nation conceived in liberty.'
Europe is Egypt – America the promised land. Liberty and self-
government are the new American achievements, and hence also the
political salvation which this chosen nation had to bring the world.[93]
The Puritans already gave the biblical prototype, the Exodus, a topical

and also a political application. Ever since then, 'Exodus' has been the motif of liberations in shifting contexts – the liberation of the black slaves, the liberation of the oppressed peoples in Latin America, the liberation of unjustly treated women everywhere. But the Exodus motif has another side too: Pharaoh and his army must perish. The God who frees his people will destroy his people's enemies. In the world of apocalyptic images, both sides of the Exodus story are clearly evident: the redemption of the chosen for the messianic kingdom, and the annihilation of the realms of violence that are anti-God – Egypt, Babylon and Rome. The chosen people always fights the battles of the Lord; so its wars are really crusades in a divine mission, rather than mere struggles for power.[94]

Not the least of the elements that gave 'the chosen people' its self-confidence is the feeling of *political innocence*. Compared with the old, sinful European nations, America is a young country. The other nations are out for conquest – America is a country for immigrants. They expel – America invites. It is hence a country that is politically innocent. Only the sense of political innocence makes America able to judge the nations. In 1813 John Adams wrote to Thomas Jefferson: 'Many hundred years must roll away before we shall be corrupted. Our pure, virtuous, public spirited, federative republic will last forever, govern the globe and introduce the perfection of man.'[95] Jefferson himself saw the young republic as 'the innocent nation in a wicked world'. Of course this led to the idea that 'the saints will rule the world' here and now. If the saints are not necessarily saints in a religious sense, today they are still 'the good guys' who will defeat 'the bad guys'. Here is 'the free world' – there the sombre 'world of evil'. 'The goodies' are clean and wear light-coloured clothes. 'The baddies' are dirty and dark. This dualistic and apocalyptic picture of history is disseminated from Westerns to science-fiction films. Whether it is Christ, Superman, Batman or He-man, there is always the same victorious end.

2. *The Rebirth of the Nation out of Sacrificial Death*

Together with Thanksgiving Day, Memorial Day is the most important festival in America's civil religion. It is a sacred ceremony, a religious ritual, a modern cult of the dead.[96] Flowers are put on the graves of the fallen, the veterans and the American Legion parade through the streets. The nation remembers those who have 'died for their country'. The first Memorial Day was celebrated in 1864 and commemorated the dead who had recently fallen in the battle of Gettysburg. The meaning of this death in battle was interpreted by Abraham Lincoln in his famous Gettysburg address on 19 November 1863: 'They gave their lives that the nation may live.' And he went on to draw the conclusion: 'That we here highly resolve that these dead shall not have died in vain; that this nation under God shall have a new birth of freedom, and that this government of the people, by the people, and for the people shall not perish from the earth.'

When 'this nation under God' wins the rebirth of its liberty from the sacrificial death of those who have died in battle, it becomes the enduring End-time nation. The echoes of Christ's sacrificial death for the redemption of the world are unmistakable – the apocalyptic echoes of the martyrs who died for Christ's kingdom cannot be overlooked. But they are carried over to those who have died in war, and to the chosen nation of liberty whose destiny it is to redeem the world. The public ritual of America's Memorial Day then also binds together Protestants, Catholics, Jews and atheists in a national religious community. Because Lincoln was murdered on a Good Friday, some people have seen his murder as his own sacrificial death for the nation, and for the self-government of the free American people. The funerals of the murdered John F. Kennedy, Robert F. Kennedy and Martin Luther King were staged according to the pattern of this ritual: rebirth to liberty out of sacrifical death.[97] The connection we have pointed out between martyrdom and millennium in the book of Revelation shows that it is not difficult to interpret death for one's country and the rebirth of that country's freedom in the millenarian sense. And the honorific title 'the nation under God' suggests this interpretation.

Only the memorial for the Vietnam dead in Washington escapes this framework, because it permits public mourning and does not proffer any heroic, national significance. It is for that very reason that so many people visit it. Here the tragic limits of millenarian optimism become evident, politically and in human terms.

3. *'The Manifest Destiny'*

In the nineteenth century America's sense of mission was determined by its expansion westwards. This began with Jefferson's Louisiana

Purchase of 1803, when the territory acquired from Napoleon doubled the extent of the United States at a single stroke. The Mississippi was made navigable, and the great trek westwards began. The Christian interpretation of this story cast back to Israel's occupation of the promised land: the Indians were driven out following the pattern of the Canaanites and Amalekites. The subjugation of nature through axe, plough and railway heightened the American sense of dominance. The old notion of the chosen people and its religious mission was transmuted into the concept of 'the favoured people' and its God-given successes.[98] The Wild West was to become a Garden of Eden, and the barbarism of the original inhabitants was to be overcome by the superior white civilization.

Famous preachers founded seminaries and schools in the newly won West. In his famous address 'A Place for the West', Lyman Beecher declared that the United States was destined 'to lead the way in the moral and political emancipation of the world' and that the necessary resources could be found in the west of the continent. The phrase 'manifest destiny' became a popular cry in the nineteenth century, and meant that the fulfilment of the United States' divine mission included the appropriation of the continent.[99] The successes in expansion and conquest made manifest the destiny conferred on America by divine providence. 'Manifest destiny' was the justification for the wars against the Indians and the later Mexican war, for the conquest of Cuba and the annexation of the Philippines. 'Manifest destiny' was supposed to explain the expansion of the United States in North America, then its domination over America as a whole – 'America for the Americans', as the Monroe doctrine put it – and not least American imperialism in the wider world.[100] In 1941 the magazine publisher Henry Luce proclaimed 'the American century', and in 1988 President George Bush made the claim his own.

Why did divine providence assign this country to the United States? The reason given was always the successful political experiment in 'liberty and self-government'. The idea that divine providence manifested itself in the successes and conquests of the USA, meant the loss of the ancient biblical picture of 'the chosen people' and its election, an election apprehended in faith and clung to in suffering. The hidden election apprehended in faith was replaced by the destiny in world history manifested in success. The appeal to divine providence then also served the apotheosis of America's own achievement. Walt Whitman's great poem 'Passage to India', published in 1871, lauded the discovery of America and its westward expansion by way of 'the mighty railroad'. Towards the end of the century the term 'republic' was then increasingly often replaced by the word 'empire'.[101] After his return from a journey to the Philippines and the Far East in 1900, Albert J. Beveridge gave a famous address, 'Westward the Star of Empire Takes its Way', in which he proclaimed that God had chosen the American people 'to finally lead in the regeneration of the world' and 'to civilize' it.[102]

From being a refuge for the persecuted saints and an experiment in freedom and democratic self-government, America turned into a world power with a world mission. The millenarian formulation of this world mission of course involves the danger of a messianically inflated nationalism. But it also contains the germ of criticism and resistance against all narrow nationalism – and the right to such criticism and resistance. If America has been chosen for the salvation of all nations and humanity in general, then its policies not only can but *must* be measured against their promotion of the liberty of other peoples, the self-government of these peoples, and their human rights. The idea of 'manifest destiny' is dangerous if it is used to expel, to conquer and, for the sake of America's own 'national security', to support dictatorships contemptuous of humanity. Its merit is to be found in the possibility of testing this power against its own claim. As a humane dream, the American dream is a good and necessary one; but if it is no more than an *American* dream, the humane dream turns into its very opposite.

Essentially speaking, this ambiguity is already present in Israel's sense of election and mission too. Is Israel chosen by God to be 'a light to lighten the Gentiles', or are the Gentiles destined to find their light in Israel? Is God concerned about Israel for the sake of all peoples on earth, or is he concerned about the peoples of the earth for Israel's sake? Behind this question is another, decisive one: how can a universal concern be represented by anything particularist without this particular concern either viewing itself as the universal one, or melting away altogether? If, in the context of world history, the United States is there 'to save the world for democracy', then American foreign policy cannot merely serve the nation's own personal interests, as it does in Central America and the Caribbean. John F. Kennedy had in mind the humanization of the American dream when he talked about Americans being 'citizens of the world'.

And many peoples have certainly received from America liberty and self-government.

But the Americanization of this humane dream of liberty and human rights for each and every human being, makes the United States a burden for the peoples who have to help carry the load of this 'experiment' and bear its cost.[103]

4. The Great Experiment

As a self-governing people, America is what Franklin D. Roosevelt called 'the bold and lasting experiment' of modern Western times. This democratic commonwealth is indeed, as Bill Clinton has said, a human invention. Most other nations, on the basis of age-old traditions, see themselves as part of nature. Their present stands in the long shadows of their ancestors and is burdened by the sins of the past. But the United States was consciously 'founded' on the basis of the Declaration of Independence, the constitution and the Bill of Rights. American civil rights are derived from human rights, and themselves point to the fact that 'all men are created free and equal'. In this respect the United States is a country – and the first country – for all humanity. Its claim and its promise is a body politic for humanity founded on human rights for each and all, which will surmount national states, and guarantee world peace. Consequently the United States will remain historically unfinished and imperfect until this political experiment that humanity is making with itself succeeds or fails. American democracy remains incomplete as long as the whole world has not been won for democracy. That makes this political experiment a messianic experiment. If it succeeds there will be an era of peace for all human beings; if it fails the world of human beings will perish in violence, injustice and war – and not the human world alone, but the world of nature too. Such an experiment on humanity's part is probably unique and unrepeatable, and could be viewed as 'the end of history' if it were not that before our very eyes an equally universal experiment, humanity's experiment 'socialism', with its anticipatory messianic realization in the Soviet Union, miscarried without the world's having come to an end.

As the self-government of the people, America is what Franklin Roosevelt called it: a bold and lasting experiment. What America is to be, must therefore be continually re-defined, and what America is, must continually be reinterpreted. In January 1993, President Bill

Clinton stressed this aspect, and demanded 'the vision and courage to reinvent America'. It is true that in his inaugural address he stressed the inner political side of this renewal of America on behalf of the poor and the weak; but he also reaffirmed America's world-wide mission: 'America must continue to lead the world we did so much to make.' The greatest power was 'the power of our ideas' which, he said, were still new in many countries, the ideas of democracy and freedom. 'America's long heroic journey must go forever upward.'[104]

For a long time America saw itself as 'the land of unlimited opportunities', first in the open space of the West – then in the room opening on to the technological, industrial future – then in the wide forum of intellectual opportunities. Unknown possibilities must be tried out, so that their strength can be tested and the best of them implemented. The experimental attitude to life corresponds to the openness to the future of the personal history in which one believes. Life as an experiment means continually seizing afresh the chances it offers for the future. The experiment 'life' must certainly then be continually 'reinvented' in the face of changed situations. Scientific-ally this is the trial-and-error method – in human and political terms it is the method of 'challenge and response'. Life as an experiment and politics as an experiment rely on the dynamic of the provisional: everything is in the balance – nothing has been finally achieved – nothing has been finally lost – everything can be tried out again at any time, and afresh.

American life-style is to a great extent just such an experimental life-style, open to the future, hankering after no past, venturesome. So everything is staked on success, and is dependent on success. In this sense the trust in 'the power of positive thinking' which Norman Vincent Peale preached is typically American. America has always lived in the firm belief that something better could always be round the corner. So Americans were happy when they could let things grow, and could keep them on the move. When did human beings ever have so much confidence in the unexpected? And yet: in order to remain mobile and to keep things moving one must cut away one's roots, and live in relationships which are not too durable but can be terminated at any time. Life as an experiment demands a certain rootlessness and a projecting of the self towards the future. That is the essence of the inner unrest of the American soul. The dream of all Americans is to own a house of their own, on their own land; and on a national average every American moves at least every five years. Each year forty-two million people change their address. That is 25% of the population.

Life as experiment – the price has to be paid, and that price is not just the loneliness of personal life but the sacrifice of much other life too. An experiment is no more than an attempt. Setbacks have to be endured. We must be able to repeat the experiment – otherwise it is not an experiment at all. We must be allowed to make mistakes, so as to learn from them. Translated into practical existence, the limitations of this experimental attitude to life become plain. Medical experiments which leave behind them irreparable damage or end in the death of the patient are irresponsible. Politicians should dispense with political experiments with nations, because they do not have to bear the consequences. There are no military experiments, because no one can restore the dead to life. Catastrophes are not a field for experiment. A 'nuclear Armageddon' is not an experiment, because no one will be left whom the event can afterwards make wise. The same is true of the worst-case scenario in the sector of nuclear power. In the contaminated region round Chernobyl no one will be wise after the event. After this event they are merely sick. Both in the nuclear sector and in genetic engineering, experiments have arrived at the limit of their unrepeatability, and have hence come up against the limit inherent in themselves.

Politically this is true of the American experiment as well. It cannot be repeated. It cannot be transferred. For it cannot be universalized. Politically, humanity cannot afford more than 'one America', and the same can be said ecologically of the earth. If the whole world were 'America', the whole world would already have been destroyed. If all human beings were to drive as many cars as Germans and Americans, and drive them as much, the atmosphere would already be mortally poisoned. The American millennium can be the downfall of the world. There is awareness of this ambiguity in America, inasmuch as 'the American nightmare' (Malcolm X) is following hard on the heels of the American dream, and American messianism is closely pursued by American apocalyptic.

Today the messianic myth of the redeemer nation of the Endtime can be encountered in Europe too, and in particularly passionate form among two nations on the fringe of the ancient Christian imperium, Poland and Serbia.[105] In Poland it has been seen in the fight against the Asiatic attacks on the Holy Empire from the east, in Serbia in the fight against the encroachment of Islam.

In the West, the political millenarianism of the Constantinian empire broke up under the onslaught of the Germanic tribes on Rome, and the conquest of the city by the Western Goths in 410. The consequence of this fall of the 'Holy Empire' in the West was an enormous strengthening of the papacy on earth, and an other-world eschatology in which religious longings were to find their fulfilment in heaven.

1. *Roma aeterna*

In the political disintegration, the religious authority of the pope acquired undreamed-of political importance, especially under Leo I (440–461). Fundamentally speaking, the idea of the Christian empire was transferred from the Christian emperor to the pope. From Gelasius I onwards, both the kingdom of God on earth and the Christian empire were represented before God no longer by the holy emperor but by 'the Holy Father', as *pontifex maximus*. The pope became the successor of both Peter and the Roman Caesars, for he took over from the latter their imperial priestly functions. It might be said that the imperium as church in Byzantium, turned in Rome into the church as imperium. It is not the Holy Empire that brings salvation to the nations; it is Holy Church. So the church must be recognized and privileged as 'mother and preceptress (*Mater et Magistra*) of the peoples', to cite the words with which John XXIII's 1961 encyclical letter begins.

The political centralism of the *imperium Romanum* passed to Rome's ecclesiastical centralism. The development of canon law out of Roman law already makes this evident. Ancient Roman and new Christian promises have engendered the doctrine of the Holy City.[106] Early Christianity still saw in the domination of Rome the last of Daniel's four empires, which at Christ's second coming would be crushed as if by a stone, because it persecuted the saints; but now Rome became the central point of the future universal kingdom of peace, and the guarantor of the Golden Age. In the eyes of Christendom, the growth of papal power made Rome no longer the apocalyptic city of godless wickedness but the city of eternal salvation. *Roma aeterna* became the religious centre of the Christian church's world-wide claim, as the pope's annual solemn blessing *urbi et orbi* still demonstrates today. The structures of the imperial, universal monarchy were transferred to the universal episcopate of the pope and his *plenitudo potestatis*. The Christian church was romanized and became the 'papal monarchy'. This papal absolutism reached its climax in 1870, in the First Vatican Council.[107]

Whereas the political formula of unity and peace was 'one God – one emperor – one empire' (later, with Louis XIV of France, 'un roi – une loi – une foi': one king – one law – one faith), the church's formula of unity and peace was now 'one God – one Christ – one pope – one church'. Just as only One Emperor had ever been permitted in the *sacrum imperium*, so there was always only One Pope in the *una sancta ecclesia*. In its development, the 'monarchical episcopate' from Ignatius of Antioch onwards entirely followed in the footsteps of the political monarchism. In both spheres it was a matter of rule through representation, not through the self-government of the people.

For the church's own self-interpretation, this development means that it ceases to see itself as the struggling, resisting and suffering church; it is now the church victorious and dominant. It no longer participates in the struggle and sufferings of Christ, but already judges and reigns with him in his kingdom. The hierarchical concept of the church is a millenarian concept of the church. It was not until 1964, with the Second Vatican Council, that this concept was cautiously called in question, inasmuch as in the constitution on the church, *Lumen Gentium*, the church is certainly seen as the people of God, but not yet as the kingdom of God.[108] And yet the millenarian concept of the church lives on in Catholic traditionalism, and at the moment evidently still determines the Vatican's ecclesiastical policy, especially where episcopal appointments are concerned. The self-interpretation of the *ecclesia Romana* – 'that it is the fulfilment of the apocalyptic vision of the thousand-year reign of Christ on earth' – lends it in Paul Tillich's view both 'divine and demonic traits'.[109] Apocalyptic enthusiasm makes excessive demands on the church and causes it to despair over the enduringly unredeemed character of the world. In the past, both enthusiasm and despair have led to the ruthless persecution of the Jews, who still wait for the Messiah, and of dissidents unable to recognize in this Roman ecclesiastical rule Christ's messianic kingdom of peace. The legislation against the Jews promulgated by the Fourth Lateran Council in no way falls behind the Emperor Justinian's unjust and humiliating anti-Jewish edicts; indeed it even goes beyond them.

Ecclesiastical millenarianism was in vogue, publicly and officially, especially during the era of Pope Gelasius I. Even before that, the Donatist Tyconius had viewed the Thousand Years' empire as a spiritual reality, interpreting it as the era of the church, the sixth age of the world. This kingdom of Christ and the saints is 'the time of the church' from Christ's first coming until his coming again. Augustine took up this interpretation and developed it further. The church is 'now already the kingdom of Christ and the kingdom of heaven'. 'During the "thousand years" when the Devil is bound, the saints also reign for a "thousand years" and, doubtless, the two periods are identical and mean the span between Christ's first and second coming.'[110] Christ's saving work on the cross and in the resurrection is 'the binding of Satan'. Consequently the millennium begins with Christ's ascension and his enthronement 'at the right hand of the Father'. 'The first resurrection' is the resurrection of believing souls. It already takes place at their baptism, for they are raised by the Spirit. The general bodily raising of the dead will take place only at Christ's second coming 'to judge both the quick and the dead'. But through his church, the Lord already rules from heaven over his kingdom on earth here and now. That is why the church is universal in its scope. 'The priests of God and of Christ' judge and rule the nations, as Rev. 20.4, 6 says.

The apocalyptic symbols of the Roman Catholic Church are easily recognizable in the Mariology. Mary stands for the church as a whole. On the one hand there is the picture of Mary 'clothed with the sun, with the moon under her feet, and on her head a crown of twelve stars', following Rev. 12.1. Together with the Child, the Messiah-king, she is pursued by 'the red dragon' (Rev. 12.4) and flees into the desert.

On the other hand, there are the many statues of the Virgin in which Mary is shown treading the Serpent underfoot, the Serpent being the Dragon, the Devil, Satan. This image goes back to an incorrect translation of Gen. 3.15, but it is also linked with Rev. 12.7. According to this passage, it is the Archangel Michael who vanquishes the Dragon in heaven, but it is Mary who treads him down on earth.[111]

Because Augustine, leaving aside the individual apocalyptic ideas, viewed the Thousand Years' empire as already realized in the church now, in antithesis to the earthly empire which will perish, he was bound to conclude that the visible church with its judicial priests and its hierarchical order was the kingdom of God. This divine realm stands in opposition to the transitory, sinful kingdom of the world. Even though its perfecting is in heaven, and the church on earth is a *communio peregrinans*, a pilgrim people, it nevertheless contains the inherent trend towards theocracy. *Cogite intrare*! Only when it is subordinated to the church of grace can the state achieve a relative, natural justice, and arrive at its *pax terrena*, the earthly peace which is always contested.

It is true that Augustine confuted and rejected in no uncertain terms the 'millinarii' who dream of a future earthly and physical kingdom of Christ; but he did so only in order to maintain his spiritual and ecclesiastical present-day millenarianism. If millenarianism is understood to mean only the expectation of a kingdom of Christ in the future, it is then possible to maintain with Wilhelm Kamlah that millenarianism 'petered out' first in the East and then in the West, pointing for evidence to Tyconius's commentary on Revelation.[112] But in actual fact millenarianism neither petered out nor 'waned'. As we have seen, it was transformed into a political and ecclesiastical self-confidence and sense of mission. Once the Christian imperium and the Christian empires themselves become millenarian, they can obviously no longer tolerate any futurist millenarianism; they are bound to see this as profoundly calling in question their own existence, and put an extinguisher on such a hope as heretical.

2. Societas perfecta

According to this millenarian interpretation, the church is 'the crown of society'.[113] It is the *societas perfecta*, and secular society must be ordered according to the church's principles of solidarity and subsidiarity. The church is related to state and society as grace is related to nature. The one does not destroy the other but perfects it, because it interprets and regulates what is natural in the light of revelation. It is the church alone, therefore, which permits what is natural to arrive at its own truth.

As we have said, millenarianism shows itself not only in the ruling church's sense of mission and its own confidence in itself, but also in the form of its organization.

What counts as the church is now the *hierarchy*, no longer the gathered congregation which governs itself according to synodal principles. But hierarchy is the spiritual rule of the world on the model of Revelation 20. The very word 'hierarchy' as used for the church is itself millenarian. 'The holy rule' is the rule of the saints according to Daniel 7 and Revelation 20. Roman monocentralism and the authoritarian structure of command are supposed to be its implementation. Christian fellowship *in* the church is replaced by communion *with* the church and its head, who represents Christ: the *communio cum et sub Petro*. The dissolution of the church in the religion of the Christian world, and this elevation of the church to spiritual rule over the nations, are both millenarian dreams. They demand of politics and church more than they can give, and destroy the world. They want to end history within history by way of a centralistic integration of humanity, and founder on the unredeemed character of this world.

Another indication of a millenarian interpretation of the church in its present existence is the reduction of eschatology to the expectation of judgment, and the spiritualization of the Christian hope. If the church knows that it itself is already the Thousand Years' empire of Christ, then there can be nothing between its present existence and the other-worldly future of heavenly eternity. The church itself lasts to the end of the world and lives in the assurance that the gates of hell will not prevail against it. This other-worldly eschatology, which has increasingly come to prevail in the West ever since Augustine, is not due to the waning of chiliasm. Its cause is the ecclesiastical occupation of chiliasm. If the church in history reaches forward directly as far as the beyond of history, then it also has in its hands the keys of heaven and hell for human beings. If the church reaches directly as far as the end of history, then in salvation history there is only one great transition, the transition from Israel to the church, from the old law to the new; and the church of Christ now stands in Israel's place as people of God.[114]

3. *'Ruling with Christ'*

Every hierarchically organized church is a centralistic church, and a church with a claim to spiritual rule over the world: *extra ecclesiam nulla salus* – outside the church no salvation, only damnation and hell. This is undoubtedly an eschatological dualism carried by this church into the ambivalences and pluralities of history. Within this church the universal episcopate of the pope rules, and his claim to infallibility in doctrinal decisions. The structure of command runs from above to below and requires obedience – in case of doubt even blind obedience. After Vatican I, the monopolist claim was applied not only to the divine truth of revelation in matters of faith but to ethics too, and thus to the moral orders of society as well. Hierarchy has grown out of the monarchical episcopate and, from Dionysius the Areopagite (Pseudo-Dionysius) onwards, is an expression for the God-given order of the church: *ecclesiastica hierarchia* in the singular covers both the power to ordain (*potestas ordinis*) and the power of jurisdiction (*potestas juridictionis*). Both are based on the one ecclesiastical power of the pope, his *plenitudo potestatis*.

The monarchical structure of this chiliastic church is justified monotheistically and according to a subordinationist principle – One God – one Christ – one Peter. In this respect it stands in contradiction to the dogma of the Trinity. 'The church was presented as the work of Christ, as the fruit of his ministry, as his "sphere of rule". When Christ ended his earthly life, he installed as his visible representative on earth Peter, and Peter's successors, the popes; consequently, inasmuch as it represents Christ as the Lord of the church, the papacy is the principle of the church's unity and structure. This is, as it were, a closed system, like a pyramid, at the top of which is the pope. By virtue of his *plena potestas*, conferred on him by Christ, he ensures the unity of the church, which has in him its visible centre. But this is really an a-trinitarian, not to say an anti-trinitarian, understanding of the church. The starting point is an abstract concept of unity: one God, one Lord and Christ, one pope, one church.'[115]

The doctrine of the Trinity, in contrast, talks about the great, pattern community of the tri-une God, which is reflected and manifested in the community of Christ as a community of brothers and sisters. It is not the monarchical church which can be considered the image and icon of the triune God, and not the *communio hierarchica*; it is the community of free and equal men and women, for that is the community of believers and the baptized. The differences in the various charismata are part of this 'fellowship of the Spirit', but they justify no privileges, and no subjugations and submittances.

For their hierarchical view of the church, both Catholic and Orthodox theology make use of the 'totus Christus' ecclesiology. The crucified and risen Christ is the Christ who is now de-individualized and turned into a corporate person. The head and the body form the 'totus Christus'. This is a millenarian doctrine of the church. But the church is not yet the totus Christus, for it is not yet the kingdom of Christ. As yet it is only 'the bride of Christ' who looks for the coming of her bridegroom (Rev. 22.17) and awaits with hope the eschatological marriage. She is not 'the spouse of Christ'.[116] Totus Christus ecclesiology is an 'over-realized' eschatology – that is to say, it is a millenaristic doctrine of the church, a triumphalist, illusory and presumptuous ecclesiology. Before the millennium there is no rule of the saints. Only in the millennium will the martyrs rule with Christ and judge the nations. Before the millennium, the church is the brotherly and sisterly, charismatic, non-violent fellowship of those who wait for the coming of the Lord and in the power of the Spirit, who is the giver of life, enter into Christ's struggle and bear their cross in his discipleship.

§6 EPOCHAL MILLENARIANISM:
THE BIRTH OF 'MODERN TIMES' OUT OF THE SPIRIT
OF MESSIANIC HOPE

The Enlightenment believed that the world was capable of development, that the human race could be educated towards a state of humanity, and that history was open for completion. These ideas all had religious roots which can be found in the 'prophetic theology' of the seventeenth century,[117] in the return of millenarianism, in Jewish messianism, in the philosemitism of the Cromwell period,[118] in Puritan apocalypticism,[119] and in German reform Pietism.

The Reformation is the precondition for the modern world only indirectly, inasmuch as in the Protestant countries the Reformation put an end to the mediaeval world in a religious way. Where the modern world emerged in the Catholic countries of Italy, France, Spain and Portugal, its precondition was the Renaissance, which put an end to the mediaeval world in a way that was irreligious and humanist. Just as the Reformation stressed the subjectivity of justifying faith, so the Renaissance made the human being 'the measure of all things' – reason enough to elevate the European (which meant the European man) to be 'the lord of all things'.

In Europe, there were two significant, practical ventures in the direction of the modern world:

1. *The conquista, discovery and conquest of America* was the one European launch into modernity. The kind of reason that gave it victory was nothing other than 'modern reason', as Tzvetan Todorov has shown from the encounter between Hernan Cortés and Montezuma in Mexico.[120] The 'instrumental reason' of domination proved superior to the mythological reason of the Aztecs (which we should today call ecological), because it took account only of the opponent, but not of harmony with the stars and the earth. With the conquest of the American continent, European Christianity came forward to missionize the world through colonization, and Europe acquired the resources for its world-wide mercantile and capitalist economic system.

2. The scientific and technological *seizure of power over nature* was the other way in which Europe set out towards the modern world. In the century between Copernicus and Newton, the new sciences stripped the world of its magic and took from it the divine mystery, 'the world soul', so as to 'enslave' it (the purpose behind Francis Bacon's scientific theory), and in order to make the human being 'the master and possessor of nature', as René Descartes put it somewhat later in his *Discourse on the Method*. Both ideas were illusory from the beginning. People can dominate spaces but not time. There is space travel but no time travel. Unrepeatable and inexorable, time holds sway over us human beings.

Experimental reason now took the place of the reason guided by tradition. It is not 'what has been said from time immemorial' that is true, but that which can be proved by experiment. Modern instrumental reason pushed out the older, receptive reason, turning an organ of perception into an active and aggressive human potency. Faith in the reason that had direct access to God did away with the historically mediated faith of the church. In view of unimaginable successes in the subjugation of foreign peoples and a nature viewed as hostile, it is understandable that modern reason should see only 'that which it itself brings forth according to its own design', as Kant maintained in his *Critique of Pure Reason*.[121]

The religious interpretative framework for this double seizure of power over the world by European civilization could be found in the messianic hope that the saints will rule the world with Christ for a thousand years and will judge the nations, and that this (Jewish)

Christian messianic kingdom, or 'Christian age', will also be the final, Golden Age of humanity before the end of the world. *Now* that which had so long been promised could be fulfilled; *now* that which had so long been hoped for could be realized. That is the emotional messianic solemnity with which 'modernity' was greeted and baptized. What Joachim of Fiore had only prophesied is *now* going to happen: the Enlightenment is 'the third age of the Spirit'. *Now* human mastery of the earth will be implemented, and with it human beings will recover the likeness to God which they lost through their own guilt. The radiance of glory returns once more: Enlightenment. Now comes the final exodus of human beings from 'their self-inflicted tutelage' into 'the free and public use of their reason'.

This is not secularized eschatology, as Karl Löwith and Jacob Taubes thought. It is realized millenarianism, for only the millenarian hope can be realized in history, since only that is a hope for a future within history. Only millenarianism makes it possible to understand the kingdom of God not apocalyptically but teleologically, and allows it to be viewed, no longer as the catastrophic end of this world, but as a moral and political ideal which human beings can approach by working unremittingly on themselves and the world. Only millenarianism makes of eschatology teleology. Only millenarianism supplies humanist optimism – 'the human being is good' – with the theological ground that 'Satan is bound for a thousand years'. The Good can spread unhindered, and history, otherwise what Goethe called a 'hotchpotch of error and violence', can be perfected, becoming the eternal kingdom. 'A God without wrath brought men without sin into a kingdom without judgment through the ministration of a Christ without a cross': this was the dictum with which H. Richard Niebuhr described the modern Christianity of his country. That is the millenarian Christianity of modernity against which apocalyptic fundamentalism protested.

The return of theological millenarianism in the seventeeth century by way of 'prophetic theology' and pietistic messianism is demonstrably the source of the faith in progress and the humanitarian ideals cherished by the German Enlightenment. I have already drawn attention to the theological rebirth of millenarianism. The transition from prophetic theology to the Enlightenment's ideas about the future is palpable in the pietistic Lutheran philosopher Christian August Crusius, who taught in Leipzig round about 1750.[122] He was a pupil of Bengel's and a teacher of Lessing. Crusius came from theology to philosophy. It is true that in his system he did not use the expression 'thousand years' empire', but he had been convinced by Bengel's prophetic interpretation of the Bible that the history of humanity was based on a 'divine plan of salvation', the goal of which was the reign of Christ, and that all the kingdoms of this world were preliminary stages which would be ended and gathered up into that kingdom. 'The moral progress of the history of the visible world' is a divine work which will be advanced by means of revelation and reason.

Gotthold Ephraim Lessing's essay 'On the Education of the Human Race' (1770) counts as the foundational writing of the German Enlightenment, and as a successful translation of prophetic kingdom-theology into the faith in humanity and progress cherished by the modern world.[123] The 'divine plan of salvation' is replaced by educative providence, which can be perceived from the spiritual and moral development of the human race. 'Revelation is education' to reason and morality (§2) and makes itself superfluous once Reason itself comes to recognize the True and the Good. 'The cultivation of revealed truths into the truth of reason is absolutely necessary' (§76).

In the Thousand Years' empire Christ himself will be present. So the historical mediations of him through word and sacrament will cease. In Christ's parousia, no one will teach the other any longer, but all will know him as he is. In the realm of Enlightenment, traditions cease. Instead there comes into being an unmediated and direct relationship of enlightened reason to truth, and of the purified moral will to the Good.

Out of the millenarianism of prophetic theology Lessing takes his standpoint in the proclamation of the 'now' dawning 'realm of the spirit' in world history. 'Perhaps their "Three Ages of the World" were not so empty a speculation after all, and assuredly they [i.e., "certain thirteenth- and fourteenth-century Enthusiasts"] had no contemptible intentions when they taught that the New Covenant must become as antiquated as the Old has now become. There remained among them too the same economy of the same God' (§88). Lessing appeals to Joachim of Fiore and the thirteenth- and fourteenth-century Joachimites. The time was now ripe for what they had proclaimed – in his view too early and as too imminent: 'the time of the new eternal gospel' as they called it, 'the time of perfecting, when man . . . will do the Right just because it *is* right' (§85). It is the era in which humanity has come of age. It is the united world of perfected human beings with 'inward purity of heart'. Their 'world-wide alliance' will replace the kingdoms of the world which war among themselves, and will confer peace. This corresponds precisely to the millenarian reign of Christ and his latter-day saints. That explains why in 1793 Kant could call Lessing's idea about the evolution of the world 'philosophical chiliasm'.[124]

For Kant, this End-time concept about the evolutionary history of the human race had already become a matter of course. In addition, he saw the French Revolution as a 'historical sign' of the inherent moral trend of the human race towards improvement, and an eschatological sign of the times which he described in Thomist sacramental terminology as a *signum prognosticon*.[125] Talking about 'nature's hidden plan' for the development of the human race, he even used the words: 'One sees that the philosophers can have their chiliasm.' For Kant as for Lessing, this chiliasm consisted in 'the complete civil unification of the human species' in a 'league of nations' (*foedus amphictyonum*) and a state embracing all humanity, which will bring about 'eternal peace'.[126] According to Kant, enlightenment offers 'the hope that after many revolutions in organization, that which nature has as its highest intention, a general *condition of world citizenship*, as the womb in which all the primal aptitudes of the human species will grow, will one day at last come into being.'[127] This 'civil unification of the human species' is nature's plan, and the goal of world history; it is 'the final purpose of creation' itself.

Kant was aware that the fundamental ideas of the teleological philosophy of history – development, progress, goal – were derived from the salvation-history theology of chiliasm, and are translations of salvific plan, economy of salvation, world aeon, and the reign of Christ as the completion of history. He expressed very clearly the awareness of his age, its sense of being on the threshold of a new epoch: 'If one now asks, what period in the entire known history of the church up to now is the best? I have no scruple in answering, *the present*. And this, because, if the seed of the true religious faith, as it is now being publicly sown in Christendom, though only by a few, is allowed more and more to grow unhindered, we may look for a continuous approximation to that church, eternally uniting all men, which constitutes the visible representation . . . of an invisible kingdom of God on earth'[128] Kant saw the time for the entry of the kingdom of God into history in 'the principle of the gradual transition of ecclesiastical faith to the universal religion of reason.'[129]

The kingdom of God is coming, but it will not be the result of an apocalyptic revolution brought about by God; it will come through the growth of reason and morality among human beings. It will have no effect on natural life but will take place exclusively in the life of the human being. These postulates distinguish 'philosophical chiliasm' from theological chiliasm, but the underlying assumptions about the unified and planned course of history, its progress and its ultimate goal of completion, are the same.

For Fichte, Schelling and Hegel, these transferences from theological millenarianism into universal-history systems are already so much a matter of course that they no longer mention these roots at all. The emotional solemnity of the 'realization' of religion and philosophy in Feuerbach and Marx, and their faith in the oneness of idea and realization, are typically messianic and millenarian in the will towards the completion of uncompletable history. Inherent in this is the tendency towards totalitarianism. They all lived in the hope for the *now* possible, and hence necessary, liberation of the human race from its bonds with nature, a liberation which will make human beings the determining subjects of their own history; and they had before their eyes that glorious future in which history will arrive at its goal.

The *power* of modern European times was derived from the industrial revolution which first made England the imperial centre of the world. The *solemn emotional weight* of the concept 'modern times' derives from the emotional solemnity of the American Declaration of Independence and the French Revolution. It is an End-time solemnity. The judicial and social utopias which have been embodied in the declarations of human rights ever since that era – that 'all men (all human beings) have been created *free and equal*' – reflect the visions of the millennium and the Golden Age, the sabbath of world history according to the sabbath precepts of the Torah. 'Modern times' have always counted as the End-time, for on modern times no other time can follow. They are the final age of humanity. So there is no 'end of the modern world',[130] since the modern world is itself 'the end'.

In England and France there were comparable transitions from religious to political messianism, and from theological to philosophical millenarianism. In France the Age of Reason replaced the age of religion and metaphysics. The French Enlightenment was laicistic and anti-clerical, and thus atheistic. And yet it ended in Joachim's spirit in 'the law of the three stages' 'discovered' by Auguste Comte and Saint-Simon, according to which positivism is 'the third realm of the spirit' and the last, perfecting stage of human development. The English Enlightenment, in contrast, was religious and a domain of nonconformity. Only on the continent was English deism viewed as a polite form of atheism. In England deism was a form of sabbath theology in the anticipated kingdom of glory. There the Enlightenment still had an Old Testament impress and was determined by Judaism. In this way it was millenarian: the coming of the messianic kingdom is preceded by the enlightenment of humanity through the divine Spirit.

Rule over the peoples of the earth, the seizure of power over nature, and the project of a civilization that makes human beings the subjects of history: these things constitute the millenarian dream of 'the modern world'. The reality it takes is the scientific and technological civilization of 'modernity', whose inward and outward dissonances we are today experiencing and suffering in ever stronger form.

The most important achievements of modern times are:

1. the universal declarations of human rights;
2. the decipherment of nature according to mathematics;
3. the United States of America.

Ever since 1789, all declarations of human rights have begun with the tenet that 'all human beings were created *free and equal*'. Europe's rule over the world therefore abolishes itself, being gathered into the universalism of humanity. Ever since that time, the indivisible and universal right to liberty has motivated and legitimated all the liberation movements of the oppressed and despised: the black slaves, humiliated women, and the subjected peoples. The indivisible and universal right to equality has ever since that time motivated and legitimated all modern social revolutions. If the political form of liberty is democracy, the economic form of equality is socialism or communitarianism. If all human beings are created free *and* equal, then the task of modern societies is to harmonize between the right to individual freedom and the right to social equality. Without equal conditions and equal opportunities for living no democracy can function. Without the development of individual freedom no system of social justice can function. The universalism of these declarations can be put into practice only in a world-wide community of states which make these human rights the fundamental rights of their citizens. Of course this was, and is, largely a utopia but it will increasingly become a historical necessity if humanity is to survive. What began as a utopia of messianic humanism is becoming an ecological necessity: the unity of the human race is inexorably required by the unity of the earth as organism.

The decipherment of nature through 'l'esprit de la géométrie' provided the motivation and legitimation for the modern sciences. But is the reality of nature translucent? The intelligibility of nature that was premised incited the search for the all-embracing 'world formula'. Or is nature only 'calculable' to the extent to which it can be dominated? Does nature withdraw into her own mystery the more her phenomena are deciphered? The mathematization of nature through the sciences also includes the decipherment of human behaviour through the social sciences, and the application of those sciences to the bureaucratization of societies. The general thrust of human reason is directed towards the annihilation of chance, said Wilhelm von Humboldt rightly. That is an 'end of history' too, for with the elimination of chance, the future as 'the coming' is excluded, and the present is made endless. Wherever history is 'grasped' in this sense, it ceases to be history, for, as Hegel said, 'the concept obliterates time'.

The only new political foundation stemming from the Enlightenment is the United States. Its Declaration of Independence and its constitution are human constructions, drawn up without any recourse to traditions and nations, solely out of the 'messianic faith' of the founding Fathers: a 'new world', *e pluribus unum* – one out of many, as the United States seal says; a messianic *novus ordo seculorum* for the whole of humanity, as every dollar note proclaims, over against the feudalistic, nationalist and class divisions and conflicts of Europe; and the 'American dream' as a first step to the realization of humanity's dream of the modern world. The American experiment is in fact the political and social experiment of modernity. It has not yet succeeded, but it has not as yet failed either. It must, however, be said that human rights and mathematics can be universalized, but not 'the American way of life'.

Because the modern world was created out of the Enlightenment, and because the Enlightment was born out of the Jewish-Christian spirit of messianic hope, the religious question, according to Kant, is *'What can I hope for?'* That is new and without precedent in the history of religion. Earlier, the religious question was always directed to the sacred origin of the world, and was answered with myths of origin; or it was concerned about what was Eternally Abiding in the flux of the times, and was answered with symbols of heaven. Earlier, religion was supposed to give transitory life stability. But life in history is either enthused by the future or threatened by it. Only a redeeming and fulfilling future can give consolation and meaning to suffering and acting in history. With modern times, *future* therefore becomes the new paradigm of transcendence. Theological thinking becomes a reminder of hope: *docta spes*. Christian theology must expel the messianic presumption and the apocalyptic resignation from modern attitudes to the future, and must answer Kant's question by holding in living remembrance the resurrection of the crucified Christ Jesus.

§7 IS MILLENARIAN ESCHATOLOGY NECESSARY?

1. *Historical Millenarianism No –*
Eschatological Millenarianism Yes

I am distinguishing between *historical* millenarianism and *eschatological* millenarianism. Historical millenarianism is the millenarian interpretation of the present in its political or ecclesiastical aspect, or in the context of universal history. Eschatological millenarianism is an expectation of the future in the eschatological context of the end, and the new creation of the world. Historical millenarianism, as we have seen, is a religious theory used to legitimate political or ecclesiastical power, and is exposed to acts of messianic violence and the disappointments of history. Eschatological millenarianism, on the other hand, is a necessary picture of hope in resistance, in suffering, and in the exiles of this world. Millenarianism must be firmly incorporated into eschatology. Detached from eschatology, and simply by itself, it leads to the catastrophes of history. But incorporated in eschatology it gives strength to survive and to resist.

The dogmas of the Orthodox, Roman Catholic and mainline Protestant churches have condemned millenarianism, but in many nonconformist communities it has been maintained for centuries, and developed in ever new ways. Mediation between the non-millenarian and the millenarian eschatologies seems to be impossible. It is true that modern Protestant theologians acknowledge the realistic and real-futurist significance of millenarianism. According to Paul Althaus, the millenarians are right in stressing the 'this-worldly character of the Christian hope'; but all the same, in his view realism and this-worldliness 'can make their way by virtue of their essential truth even without millenarianism'.[131] Walter Kreck would like to retain in millenarianism as 'irrelinquishable aspect' the fact 'that it wards off a docetism in eschatology which abandons the earth', though he himself admittedly does not support a millenarian eschatology.[132] Yet these are not genuine acknowledgments of millenarian eschatology; they are actually a dismissal of it in various polite forms.

The young Karl Barth, on the other hand, said: 'Ethics can no more exist without millenarianism, without at least some minute degree of it, than without the idea of a moral personality. The man who claims that he is happily free from this *judaica opinio* has either not yet learned or has forgotten what the ethical problem really is.' He was talking about millenarianism because he viewed 'the moral object' as 'the goal of history'. Only millenarian eschatology understands the eschaton as the goal of history, as future history, as the consummation and final condition of history. Non-millenarian eschatology can only talk about a rupture of history, which can have no relevance for present ethics. For Barth too the millennium according to Revelation 20 is 'by no means an island of the blest, but the kingdom of saints and martyrs built over the bottomless pit in which the old dragon is chained. According to Kant it is the kingdom of practical reason. It is as a task and not as an object of desire, as a goal and not as a termination of the moral struggle . . . that Christian hope envisages reality here on earth. The cry of Western humanity is one: let freedom in love and love in freedom be the pure and direct motive of social life, and a community of righteousness its direct objective! . . . Let class differences, national boundaries, war, and, above all, violence and unrestrained power be done away! Let a civilization of the spirit take the place of a civilization of things, human values the place of property values, brotherhood the place of hostility!'[133]

As we have seen, the condemnations of eschatological millenarianism always have their basis in a historical millenarianism. Those who proclaim that their own political or ecclesiastical present is Christ's Thousand Years' empire cannot put up with any hope for an alternative kingdom of Christ besides, but are bound to feel profoundly disquieted and called in question by any such hope. We have seen that eschatologies developed in the context of a presentative reign of Christ, or at its end, can visualize only the apocalyptic catastrophe of 'Gog and Magog' and the great Judgment on the Last Day. But post-millenarian eschatologies of this kind are based on a false definition of the location of the present in the context of salvation history.

2. The Sufferings and Future of Christ

Every eschatology that claims to be Christian, and not merely utopian or apocalyptic or a stage in salvation history, must have a christological foundation. The first question we have to put to millenarianist eschatology is therefore not: can it be existentially verified, or is it pure 'enthusiasm' and hence a product of the fantasy? The initial question has to be: does it have its foundation in christology? By christology we do not mean: did the earthly Jesus express prophecies of this kind? We mean: is the Christian hope based on Christ's coming, his surrender to death on the cross and his resurrection from the dead? The fact that Christ came into this world and appeared in Jesus, the crucified and risen One, is the eschatological presupposition of the whole Christian faith. But to say this is to assert nothing less than that with the coming of Christ the new, eternal aeon has dawned in the midst of this old aeon which is passing away: 'The night is far gone, the day is at hand . . .' (Rom. 13.12). That is to say, the end of this world-time of sin and death is foreseeable by the people who believe, and who struggle against the powers of this world with 'the powers of the world to come', and who thus enter into Christ's struggle. The 'lordship' of the risen Christ is still disputed here and now, for 'we do not yet see everything in subjection to him' (Heb. 2.8); so life in the community of Christ must also be called participation in Christ's struggle.

This struggle has two sides to it. On the one hand believers participate in Christ's messianic mission, as did the disciples and apostles; on the other hand, through this participation they are led into 'the sufferings of Christ', which was the experience of Christ's martyrs. Christ's mission and his fate will determine their life and

death too. In his catalogues of tribulations, Paul describes the
manifesting in our bodies of 'the death of Jesus' and 'the life of Jesus'
(II Cor. 4.10ff.), the life of Jesus meaning not his earthly life but the
eternal life-giving life of the One risen.

What hope is awakened through this lived and suffered community with Christ? It is the hope that, just as we have participated in
Christ's mission and his suffering, we may also share in his
resurrection and his life: those who die with him will live with him
too. But what resurrection is meant? It is the special and messianic
'resurrection *from* the dead', not the universal and eschatological
'resurrection *of* the dead'. But the resurrection *from* the dead
necessarily leads into a reign of Christ *before* the universal raising of
the dead for the Last Judgment. That is to say, it leads into a
messianic kingdom in history before the end of the world, or into a
transitional kingdom leading from this transitory world-time to the
new world that is God's. This hope is clearly evident in Paul:

> . . . that I may know him and the power of his resurrection, and
> may share in his sufferings, becoming like him in his death, that if
> possible I may attain the resurrection *from the dead* (Phil. 3.10f.).
> (The 1611 Bible and Luther translate: 'if by any means I might
> attain unto the resurrection *of* the dead' – probably deliberately
> so, in order to exclude millenarianism.)

Ever since Daniel 12, the universal and final resurrection *of* the
dead has been the presupposition for the diachronic fulfilment of
God's righteousness and justice at the Last Judgment. That is why
Martha, talking about the dead Lazarus, says: 'I know that he will
rise again in the resurrection at the last day' (John 11.24). But
Christ's resurrection *from* the dead is his exaltation to be lord of the
divine rule, and his transformation into the Spirit who is 'the giver of
life' (I Cor. 15.45). That is why Jesus answers Martha by saying: 'I
am the resurrection and the life' (John 11.25) in person. The hope of
believers founded on Christ's resurrection is directed, as in Paul, to
the eternally life-giving life of Christ. It is not an ambiguous
expectation of judgment. It is an unequivocal hope for salvation. The
resurrection of the crucified Christ *from* the dead is more than just
the prolepsis of the general resurrection of the dead, as Wolfhart
Pannenberg teaches at the heart of his theology of history,[134] and is
something different. 'If we have died with Christ [i.e., in baptism],
we believe that we shall also live with him' (Rom. 6.8). So the special

hope of Christians is the expectation that they will rise with Christ
'*from* the dead', so as to live with him; their hope is not for the general
resurrection of the dead, for the expectation of which no Christian
faith is required, as John 11.24 shows. What is the relationship
between the resurrection *from* the dead in the case of Christ and those
that are his, and the general resurrection *of* the dead?

If we follow Paul in I Corinthians 15, Christ is 'the first fruits of
those who have fallen asleep' and 'the leader of life', and those who
are his are the men and women who have trod, and still tread, their
path with him. At the end, death will be 'destroyed' and swallowed
up in the victory of life (I Cor. 15.55), so that the life of God's new
world, which has already appeared now in Christ, and is experienced
in the presence of his Spirit, will interpenetrate everything. The
general resurrection of the dead is then only the final consequence of
that process of new creation which began with the coming of Christ.

If we follow the Revelation of John, we have the impression that
Christ's resurrection and the resurrection of believers are merely an
'anticipation' of the general resurrection of the dead on the Last Day,
and that the great Last Judgment has the final word. But then the end
of world history is a double one: eternal life or eternal damnation.

The first viewpoint leads to a christologically founded universalism of life; the second leads to an apocalyptic christology subordinated to the Last Judgment. The millenarianism founded on
Christ's resurrection *from* the dead has as result the universalism
of eternal life: 'Behold, I make *all things* new' (Rev. 21.5). The
millenarianism founded on legalistic, apocalyptic ideas of judgment
results in the separation of humanity into believers and unbelievers,
and ultimately into the saved and the damned. That means that it is
talking about three judgments: first, the Judgment Seat of Christ;
secondly, the judgment passed on the nations by believers with
Christ in the Thousand Years' empire; and thirdly, the Last
Judgment (Rev. 20.11ff.). In the first viewpoint christology
dominates the eschatology; in the second, the apocalyptic eschatology that is presupposed dominates the christology.

3. Hope for Israel

The essential indicator for the theological 'placing' of the present
was, and still is, the church's stance with regard to present-day Israel,
and the attitude of Christians to the Jews.[135] By 'Israel' I mean here

the biblical and theological view of the Jews before God as this is expressed today through religious Judaism in the synagogues and in the land of Israel.

The eschatological hope of the church and its relationship to Israel have always corresponded, whether in a positive or a negative sense. If the church hopes for something greater than itself, it can then draw Israel into its hope. If the church considers itself to be the fulfilment of all hopes, it then shuts Israel out. Significantly enough, the millenarian hope of Christians has maintained a future for Israel *as* Israel. That is the real reason why millenarianism was condemned by the churches of the Reformation as a 'Jewish dream'. 'We shrug our shoulders over the people of the election, and hence over chiliasm too', declared Carl Auberlen rightly.[136]

In positive terms this means that there is no affirmative community between the church and Israel without the messianic hope for the kingdom. And that then means that there is no adequate Christian eschatology without millenarianism. Eschatology is more than millenarianism, but millenarianism is its historical relevance. It is only the millenarian hope in Christian eschatology which unfolds an earthly and historical future for the church and Israel. Millenarianism is the special, this-wordly side of eschatology, the side turned towards experienced history; eschatology is the general side of history, the side turned towards what is beyond history. Millenarianism looks towards future history, the history of the end; eschatology looks towards the future of history, the end of history. Consequently the two sides of eschatology belong together as goal and end, history's consummation and its rupture.

The presuppositions for a Christian hope for Israel are these:

(*a*) Israel has an enduring 'salvific calling', parallel to the church of the Gentiles, for God remains true to his election and his promise (Rom. 11.1f.).

(*b*) The promises given to Israel are as yet only fulfilled in principle in the coming of the Messiah Jesus, and in him without conditions, and hence universally *endorsed* (II Cor. 1.20); and in the outpouring of the Spirit 'on all flesh' are as yet realized only partially, *pars pro toto*, and in trend. Through the gospel and the Holy Spirit, the divine promises given to Israel are extended to all the nations, for whom there has therefore dawned what Paul calls the time of the gospel – in the language of Maimonides, the *praeparatio messianica*.

(*c*) Christianity is God's 'other community of hope', parallel to

Israel, and over against Israel. Parallel to the people of God, it is the missionary and messianic church of the nations. It can therefore only remain true to its own hope if it recognizes Israel as the older community of hope alongside itself. In its hope for the nations the church also preserves the 'surplus of promise' in Israel's prophets, and therefore waits for the fulfilment of Israel's hopes too. In the very fact of turning wholly to the Gentile nations with the gospel, it confirms and strengthens Israel's hope: all Israel will be saved when the fulness of the Gentiles arrives at salvation (Rom. 11.25f.).[137]

The common focus of Jewish and Christian hopes is the coming of the Messiah to his messianic kingdom. Only *the Christ of the parousia* will save 'all Israel' (Rom. 11.26). The acceptance of all Israel will be 'life from the dead' (Rom. 11.15f.). Consequently Israel's Messiah must be the risen One.

Just as Saul the rabbi became Paul the apostle by *seeing* Christ, so all Israel will one day be redeemed through the seeing of the Christ of the parousia. That means that all Israel will not through faith become Christian but through sight it will be redeemed.[138] Yet even Israel's 'life *from* the dead' is not identical with the eschatological 'resurrection *of* the dead' on the Last Day, but is in line with the resurrection of Christ *from* the dead and the resurrection '*from* the dead' of those who live and suffer with Christ (Phil. 3.11); it must therefore be understood in a millenarian sense, in the framework of the end-time of history, not eschatologically as the end of history itself. Israel's resurrection and redemption belong to the great process of giving life to this mortal world, and the new creation of all things, a process which has begun with Christ's resurrection *from* the dead.

If the millenarian implication of Christian eschatology is the side of the Christian hope that is turned towards Israel, the 'Thousand Years' empire' of Revelation 7 and 20 must then be conceived of – in spite of the anti-Jewish utterances in Rev. 2.9, 3.9 and 11.8 – as the messianic kingdom of Jews and Christians. According to Revelation 7, the hundred and forty-four thousand 'sealed out of every tribe of the sons of Israel' will be joined by 'a great multitude from every nation, from all tribes and peoples and tongues . . . who have come out of great tribulation' (7.9 and 14). This corresponds to the list of martyrs in Hebrews 11, that 'cloud of witnesses' who have borne 'the shame of Christ' and have kept the faith. The list begins with Abraham and reaches down to the Christian martyrs. If the chosen and 'sealed' Christians are joined together with the chosen and 'sealed' Jews, together with them becoming the messianic people of the messianic kingdom, then it is not impossible also to think with J.T. Beck of Jerusalem and the land of Israel: 'the central people' and 'the land of the first fruits'.[139]

'This Israelo-centric kingdom of Christ forms the organic transitional link between the present state of the world and the completion of the world that will one day come about.'[140] Ever since Joachim of Fiore, many people have thought that before the dawn of the messianic kingdom on earth a new gospel will be proclaimed to all nations – the 'eternal gospel' (Rev. 14.6); for all acts of God are preceded by their announcement. If this is the End-time kingdom of Christ, then that gospel must be 'the universal *preaching of the kingdom*': a preaching which calls people, no longer to the church but to the kingdom – converts no longer to the Christian faith but to hope for the kingdom. Christoph Blumhardt understood his mission and his preaching as a mission and preaching of the coming kingdom of Christ: from faith to life, from the church to the kingdom. It is not surprising that the early Reformation 'located' the 'vocatio Dr Martini Lutheri' in the sending of the angel in Rev. 14.6, and justified it accordingly, declaring that the Reformations's gospel is 'the eternal gospel' and hence the 'preaching of the kingdom' that precedes the dawn of the messianic kingdom. The young Luther then also expected that the Jews would be converted to his gospel, and it was only out of disappointment that he turned into a critic of the Jews.

4. What is 'Timely' Today?

The most difficult problem of millenarian eschatology is *the time problem*. How can we think of a consummation of historical time *in* history before 'the Last Day' and the dawn of the new, eternal creation? In prophetic interpretations of scripture and those based on the concept of salvation history, this millenarian hope was hitherto thought of in terms of linear calendar time. It was this which gave Bengel his date of 18 June 1836, the date that caused so much trouble and distress in Württemberg. But with the parousia of Christ and his kingdom, not only will everything in time be different; time itself will be different. The whole situation of the world will change. It is therefore wrong to fit the messianic kingdom into calendar time, for that is the time of this transitory world. If God is the Lord of history, he does not make over his providence to the stars. Astrology has nothing to do with the providence of the Creator, and the promises of the coming God are not surrendered to a so-called divine historical plan or 'plan of salvation'. They remain in God's hand.

Time is determined by what happens in it. 'For everything there is a season' (Eccles.3.1). Theologically, time is determined by the presence or absence of God – that is to say, by the different modes of his presence in time. There is a 'time of the law', there is a 'time of the gospel', there is a 'time of the Messiah' and there is a time of 'the sabbath of the Lord'; and there is a 'time of eternity'.[141] Analogously, we talk about different epochs in which the whole paradigm of living, thinking and feeling changes: the ancient world – the middle ages – modern times, or modernity-postmodernity. Theologically we distinguish between 'the kingdom of nature', in which God is present as the creator and preserver of his creation, 'the kingdom of grace', in which God is present in Israel through his covenant and in the church through Christ, and 'the kingdom of glory', in which God himself will indwell his creation as in his temple. For the Christian faith, the present is shaped by the presence of Christ in the life-giving Spirit. Faith therefore expects a future of Christ in the resurrection from the dead and in 'the giving life to our mortal bodies' (Rom.8.11). This future is therefore a time which bears the impress, no longer of Christ's struggle but of his kingdom. This time is determined no longer by transience, but by a tarrying and abiding in the felicitous moment. No one participates in the messianic struggle of Christ against the powers of destruction and annihilation without a hope for such a 'fulfilled time' in a victory of life of this kind. Anyone who lives in necessary contradiction to the laws and powers of 'this world' hopes for a new world of correspondences. The contradiction suffered is itself the negative mirror-image of the correspondence hoped for.

Christian theology is not a theology of universal history. It is a historical theology of struggle and hope. It therefore does not teach the secular millenarianism of the present, as does the naive modern faith in progress, maintaining that in the future everything will get better and better. Nor does it teach that in the future everything will get worse and worse, like equally naive modern apocalypticism. But it does warn that in the future of this world things are going to become more and more critical. Danger grows with the growth of human power and the progressive concentration of that power, for with the constructive opportunities open to human beings the destructive opportunities open to them increase as well. Once the formulas for splitting the atom have been found, they can never be forgotten again. Since Hiroshima, humanity has lost its 'atomic innocence'. Humanity as a whole has become mortal. Our time has a time-limit, and we are fighting to survive, inasmuch as we are fighting to stave off the end. We can prolong the nuclear and ecological end-time in which we are living, but we and succeeding generations have to live our lives in this end-time. When things become more and more critical in history, they become more and more dangerous too. The growing danger to the world endorses the truth of both Hölderlin's chiliastic promise that 'where there is danger deliverance also grows' and Bloch's apocalyptic warning that 'where deliverance is near, danger grows'. I deduce from this that before the final end of history there will be a concentration of humanity's both constructive and destructive opportunities.

The Thousand Years' reign of Christ, 'the kingdom of peace', is hope's positive counterpart to the Antichrist's destruction of the world in a storm of fire, and is indispensable for every alternative form of life and action which will withstand the ravages of the world here and now. Without millenarian hope, the Christian ethic of resistance and the consistent discipleship of Christ lose their most powerful motivation. Without the expectation of an alternative kingdom of Christ, the community of Christ loses its character as 'contrast community' to society.[142] Because original Jewish and Christian millenarianism was a martyr eschatology, it is the precise opposite of every eschatological escapism, and of every know-all assumption based on a salvation-history concept.

Finally: the millenarian expectation mediates between world history here, and the end of the world and the new world there. It makes the end as transition imaginable: christocracy, as J. T. Beck said, is the transition from the world's present condition to its coming consummation. The transition will be brought about through a series of events and the succession of various different phases. If we leave out this transition, as the non-millenarian eschatologies do, then world history will end – according to modern fantasy – with an abrupt Big Bang, like the Big Bang with which it is supposed to have begun. These are Hiroshima images without any relevance for the way we live and act here, because they view life and

action here as irrelevant for the end of the world, even though the end
of the world caused by human beings will be brought about precisely
through unconscious and irresponsible ways of living and acting
here. 'Eat, drink and be merry for tomorrow we die' leaves
succeeding generations no chance. 'After us the Deluge' – life led and
actions performed according to this motto do indeed lead to deluges,
financial, nuclear and ecological. Succeeding generations will sink
under the mountains of debt, atomic waste and the ravaged
environment. The eschatology of the 'last Big Bang' is catastrophic,
and catastrophes are its result. Christian eschatology – eschatology,
that is, which is messianic, healing and saving – is millenarian
eschatology.

§8 END-TIMES OF HUMAN HISTORY: EXTERMINISM

Having looked at millenarian eschatology and its historical anticipations and secularizations, we shall now turn to its accompaniment,
apocalyptic eschatology, with its historical anticipations and secularizations. In the terrors which humanity has experienced in our
century, and which men and women are facing in the century ahead,
the word 'apocalypse' is on everyone's lips, and is applied to ever
new phenomena of 'the end'. During the Cold War, people talked
about the inferno of a 'nuclear apocalypse' of humanity, while
Ronald Reagan used the phrase 'nuclear Armageddon'. The
irretrievable annihilation of thousands of plant and animal
species through the ruthless industrial exploitation of nature was
accordingly understood as what Rachel Carson called 'the silent
spring', and as the 'ecological apocalypse'. Speculative practitioners
of biblical exegesis found apocalyptic names for the catastrophe of
Chernobyl, interpreting it as a sign of the approaching end of the
world. The mass death among the people of the Third World, where
a billion and a half go hungry and fifty million die of hunger and
disease every year, is today termed the 'silent apocalypse' of the
modern world.

But do these 'end-times' of human histories have anything to do
with an 'end of history' in general? We shall enter into discussion
with the secular prophets of the *post-histoire*. And if the end-times of
human histories do have something to do with the end of human
history in general (because they are the beginning of the end of the
human race, and its disappearance from this earth) what does this

end of history have to do with 'the future' in Jewish and Christian apocalypticism? Would it not be better to call the terrors of the present end-times of human histories 'exterminism', mass extermination through acts of military, economic or ecological violence?[143] Anyone who talks here about 'the apocalypse', or the battle of Armageddon, is providing a religious interpretation for mass human crime, and is trying to make God responsible for what human beings are doing. Even if the end result were to be the universal suicide of the human race, the apocalyptic interpretation would simply paralyse men and women and make them irresponsible, and themselves, consequently, a religious factor in such an ultimate exterminism. Nothing has a more fatal effect than the expectation of a fatal future.

It is true that the Jewish and Christian apocalypses speak to people in the terrors of historical and cosmic catastrophes, but they do not talk like Cassandra; nor do they interpret humanity's crimes and cosmic catastrophes religiously, so that people may accept them, collaborate with them, or simply resign themselves to them. They awaken the *resistance of faith* and the *patience of hope*. They spread hope in danger, because in the human and cosmic end they proclaim God's new beginning. The apocalyptic prophets were no doomsday prophets, like the self-styled prophets of today, who 'prophesy' future disasters; they were prophets of God's creative word and Spirit. In the experiences and forebodings of historical and cosmic terrors they proclaim God's future, his judgment, and his eternal kingdom.

We shall bring out the common ground in the historical experiences and forebodings, and stress this difference as clearly as possible, in order to spring the 'apocalyptic trap' which so many people fall into. The modern apocalyptic mood which journalists and, in recent times, interpreters of history and philosophers of the *post-histoire* like to spread, are entirely without practical consequences. They do nothing to detract from medium-term holiday planning. Many people, especially in the rich industrial countries of America and Europe, expect 'apocalyptic' terrors in this generation; but hardly anyone reckons with his or her own death. The apocalyptic mood remains diffuse; the profound and melancholy announcements of an apocalyptic era bring about no reversal of the trends leading to exterminism. The only result is a general alarmism and sense of catastrophe, while the general lack of resolution is fostered.[144]

People are paralysed; they do not arrive at the point of 'watching and praying' – which is the least that might be expected, if the mood is supposed to be taken seriously.

It is important to tear down the veil of this contemporary apocalyptic mood, and to go to the root of things as they really are. Only a clear perception of the situation in which we have put ourselves, other people, and life on earth will make us able to decide whether the apocalyptic categories are an appropriate way of interpreting this situation or not, and will allow us to evaluate what the Jewish and Christian traditions of apocalyptic hope said in the past, and say today.

1. *The Nuclear End-Time: Methods of Mass Extermination*

As long ago as 1946 Albert Einstein wrote the prophetic words: 'The power of the atom that has been unleashed has changed everything except the way we think. We need an essentially new kind of thinking if humanity is to survive.' Today, almost fifty years later, the exterminating power of ABC weapons has grown immeasurably and has been increasingly developed; but we are still searching for a 'new kind of thinking' in order to escape this deadly danger threatening humanity.[145] With Hiroshima, 'the bomb' changed the world at a single stroke, but Christian theology is only slowly becoming aware of the new situation which makes all its traditional concepts for dealing with power, with terror and with war obsolete.

Because we have not taken in the situation realistically, we cannot yet grasp the future in convincing visions of hope. Fear of the great catastrophe makes us incapable of doing what has to be done today so that our children can live tomorrow.

(*a*) Hiroshima 1945 fundamentally changed the quality of human history: *our time has become time with a time-limit*. The age in which we exist is the last age of humanity, for we are living at a time when the end of humanity can be brought about at any minute. The system of nuclear deterrence which has been built up and increasingly perfected has made it possible to end the life of a large part of the human race in a few hours. The nuclear winter which will follow a war with nuclear weapons will leave even the survivors no chance. This time of ours, when humanity can be brought to an end at any moment, is indeed, in a purely secular sense and without any apocalyptic images, the 'end-time'; for no one can expect that this nuclear era will be succeeded by another in which humanity's deadly threat to itself will cease to exist.[146] The dream of 'a world without nuclear weapons' is certainly a necessary dream, but for the time being it is no more than wishful thinking. No one seriously expects that people will ever again be incapable of doing what they can do now. Anyone who has once learnt the formula can never forget it again.

If the nuclear age is the last age of humanity, then today the fight for humanity's survival means *the fight for time*. The struggle for life is the struggle against the nuclear end. We are trying to make our present end-time as end-less as possible, by giving threatened life on this earth ever new *time limits*. This fight to stave off the end is a permanent fight for survival. It is a fight without victory, a fight without an end – at best. We can prolong this nuclear end-time, but it is an end-time in which we and all succeeding generations must live out our lives under the Damocles sword of the bomb. The lifetime of the human race is no longer guaranteed by nature, as it has been hitherto; it has to be created by human beings by way of deliberate survival policies. Up to now nature has regenerated the human race after epidemics and world wars. Up to now nature has shielded the human race from annihilation by individual human beings. From now on this will no longer be the case. Since Hiroshima the human race as a whole has 'become mortal', as Mikhail Gorbachev rightly observed. Ever since Hiroshima, 'immortality', as he thought, or – more modestly – 'life', has irrefutably become the primary task for human culture, and for political culture too. That means that all decisions today have to be thought through with an eye to the life of coming generations. That is a new, hitherto unknown responsibility for all human beings.

(*b*) The nuclear age is the first common age of all nations and all human beings. Since Hiroshima, the many different histories of the peoples of the earth have become a single, shared world-wide history of a single humanity – but initially this takes a merely negative form, in mutual threat and the shared danger of annihilation. The nuclear deterrent has created a situation in which no more movement is possible. The blackmailers have become the blackmailed. The situation of mutual deterrence restricts the scope for manoeuvre open to any large-scale policy. Already nuclear weapons can no longer be put to military use in minor conflicts. After the disintegration of the great mutual system of deterrence between the USA and the USSR, the danger has become no less, because the non-proliferation pact is ignored, and in the year 2000 more than twenty nations will possess nuclear weapons.

Today the peoples of the world have entered upon the first common age of humanity, because they have all become the possible common object of nuclear annihilation. In this situation, the survival of humanity is only conceivable if the nations organize themselves into a collective determining subject which will work for survival. So since Hiroshima, the survival of humanity has become indissolubly linked with the unification of the nations in joint defence against this deadly danger. Only the unity of humanity will guarantee survival, and the survival of every individual presupposes that humanity is united. The unity of humanity which will secure its existence in the age of nuclear threat means that the individual interests of the nations must be relativized, that ideologies with their potential for conflict must be democratized, that the different religions must acquire tolerance, and that everything must be subordinated to the common concern for life. Above all, what is required is the joint Yes to life, to the life shared by us all. The ongoing rivalry of the superpowers and the different social systems, still prevents the emergence of the world organization that we need. And yet, little by little, an international network of political responsibility for peace is possible, in partnerships for regional security. There are practical political steps to be taken from confrontation to co-operation.

(c) The military system of nuclear deterrence is ambivalent in itself. It does not merely secure peace; it also endangers peace in the highest degree. It can never be more than a transition to a different way of securing peace, a political one. But the nuclear deterrent endangers peace in two other ways as well:

The build-up of armaments in the northern hemisphere is at the expense of the peoples of the Third World, who are becoming poorer and poorer, and more and more encumbered by debt. It has led to the arming of the developing countries and to the waging of numerous wars in these countries, as the UNO Report on Disarmament and Development showed in 1986. During the last two decades, 75% of the arms trade was carried on with the developing countries. The two crises are in many respects mutually conditioning: without disarmament in the northern hemisphere there can be no justice in the southern one, and the reverse is equally true: it is only by building up 'sustainable development' in the southern hemisphere that we can arrive at disarmament and peace. But does disarmament in the countries of the Western world already benefit the Third World? A war with nuclear weapons is a potential danger for humanity. But the economic north-south conflict is a reality from which people are already dying today.

A nuclear war would be the worst environmental catastrophe which human beings could bring about. But the security policies of the industrial world – together with other factors – are already spreading the ecological catastrophes in the Third World, because of the debts with which those countries are encumbered. For exploitation creates poverty – poverty leads to debt – debt forces the sale and depletion of a country's own natural foundations for living. Humanity is losing the capital it needs, and the raw materials and manpower it requires, as well as the scientific intelligence that is essential for its own survival. Armament is theft, said President Eisenhower at the end of his period of office, in critical comment on 'the military and industrial complex' – and he was right, as the Brundtland Report 'Our Common Future' (1987) shows. The spiral of mutual fear has led by way of the mutual deterrent to the militarization of public awareness, and to the modern arms culture. But this is deadly for human beings and for nature. So we have to dismantle this civilization based on weapons and fear, and create reasonable confidence through democratization.

Not least, attention must be drawn to the human problem of nuclear technology. In the forced build-up of nuclear technology, both military and peaceful, the ecological problem of the disposal of radioactive waste and the scrapping of nuclear bombs was evidently overlooked, as was the human factor involved in the handling of this technology. Apparently radioactive material cannot simply be handed back to nature, for nature itself to degrade; it has to be stored and guarded somewhere or other for centuries. In addition, nuclear technology requires infallible human beings, because it reacts extremely disagreeably to human error.

Can this dangerous technology be contained by fallible and corruptible human beings? The catastrophes of Windscale/Sellafield, Harrisburg and Chernobyl, as well as the diverse international corruption scandals in the German nuclear industry, tell us that the answer is: no. The experimental method – the method of trial and error – is reaching its limits. We cannot afford any major error, neither a meltdown in nuclear power plants nor a nuclear war. But that means that we are unable to extend our experience any further. We only live once. There will be only one nuclear accident or nuclear war, and there will be no one left afterwards who can be wise after that event. But this means that either human beings must withdraw from this deadly nuclear technology and look for other sources of energy which are more environment-friendly and humane, or human beings themselves must be done away with or genetically reconstructed – the human beings of whom it used be said in so kindly and lenient a way that 'to err is human'.[147]

In genetic engineering too there are signs that the end of the experimentation is approaching: bacteria produced through genetic engineering cannot be recaptured once they have been released. An act of this kind will be once and for all, and irrevocable. We shall not be able to say: once bitten, twice shy. If decisions are final, irrevocable and unrepeatable, then it is no longer a case of experiment. There is then no more potential scope left. Truth and error can then no longer be distinguished from one another. This is the point of no return: all or nothing. But that brings us to the end of time and the eternal present of what has traditionally been called 'the Last Judgment'.

2. The Ecological End-Time: The Destruction of the Earth

The nuclear threat shows the end-time of human history in quick-motion, so to speak: the end can be brought about in a few hours through an exchange of intercontinental missiles. But there is another threat too, which shows the end-time in slow-motion, as it were, and that is the *ecological catastrophe*. This catastrophe is happening every day: in Seveso, in the oil pollution in the Persian Gulf, in the contamination of the soil through dioxin, in the dying forests, and the death of lakes and oceans, in the extinction of animal and plant species. We are still talking about an 'ecological crisis', and behaving as if this crisis will sometime or other go away, and will be dealt with by someone or other. But this is not a temporary crisis. It is a slow but sure and irreversible catastrophe, in which the weaker living things will be destroyed first, but then the stronger ones too, and finally human beings as well. 'The ecological crisis' is not a temporary crisis. As far as we can see it is the beginning of a battle for the life and death of creation on this earth. It is not something that might happen 'one day', like the nuclear catastrophe: we are involved in it now, it is creeping forward steadily, and we ourselves are part of it.[148]

The destruction of the environment which we are causing through the present world-wide economic system is undoubtedly going to endanger – and endanger seriously – the survival of humanity in the twenty-first century. Through modern industrial society the organism of the earth has lost its equilibrium, and is on the way to universal ecological death, unless we can change the way things are going. Scientists predict that carbon-dioxide and methane emissions are going to destroy the ozone layer of the atmosphere; that the use of chemical fertilizers and various pesticides is making the soil infertile; that the world climate is already changing, so that we are going to experience more and more 'natural' disasters, such as droughts and floods, forest fires and rain storms; that the ice layers in the Arctic and Antarctic are going to melt, so that coastal cities such as Hamburg, and coastal regions such as Bangladesh and many South Sea islands, will be under water in the next century; and that all in all, life on this earth itself is under threat. The human race can become extinct like the dinosaurs, millions of years ago.

What makes this idea so disquieting is the fact that we cannot retrieve the poisons which are rising into the ozone layer of the earth, and the poisons that are seeping into the soil, so we cannot know whether the die has not already been cast and the fate of the human race already sealed. The 'ecological crisis' of our industrial society has already become an ecological catastrophe, at all events for the weaker creatures: year for year, hundreds of plant and animal species become extinct, and we can never bring them back to life again.

The ecological crisis is first of all a crisis caused by Western scientific and technological civilization, which has meanwhile become the matrix for the civilization of the world. That is true. If everyone were to drive as many cars, and pollute the air with as many toxic emissions, as the Americans and the Germans, humanity would already have suffocated. The lifestyle of the Western world cannot be universalized, and can be maintained only at the expense of a Third World.

But it would be wrong to think that environmental problems are problems for the Western world alone. On the contrary, the already existing economic and social problems of the countries of the Third World are accentuated even more by the ecological catastrophes.[149]

The Western industrial countries can try by technological and legal means to preserve a clean environment in their own back yards, but the poverty-stricken countries cannot do so. The Western industrial countries can try to push away environmentally harmful industrial plants into the countries of the Third World, and sell the countries of the Third World dangerous toxic waste, and these poverty-stricken countries have no defence. But even apart from that, Indira Gandhi was right when she said that 'poverty is the worst pollution'. It is an increasing vicious circle which leads to universal death: everywhere impoverishment leads to overpopulation, because children provide people with the only security they have. Overpopulation leads to the depletion, not only of all foodstuffs but of the foundations from which people live. That is why the deserts are spreading more quickly in the poverty-stricken countries than anywhere else.

The world market also compels the poor countries to abandon their own subsistence economy and plant monocultures for the world market's use, as well as to cut down the rain forests and to overgraze their grasslands. They not only have to sell their products; they have to sell their means of production too – which is to say the foundation from which they live. It follows from this that they can only survive at the cost of their children. In this way these countries are being inexorably driven towards self-destruction. In countries with large-scale social injustice, ruthlessness is part of the 'culture of violence'. Violence against weaker people justifies violence against weaker living things. Social lawlessness reproduces itself in lawless dealings with nature.

Both worlds, the industrial world and the Third, are caught up in a vicious circle in which nature is destroyed. It is easy to see the interdependence of the different forms which this destruction takes. The Western world destroys the people of the Third World, compelling its peoples to destroy their natural foundations for living; but the destruction of nature in the Third World, such as the cutting down of the rain forests and the pollution of the seas, then reacts on the industrial world by way of climatic changes. The destruction which the industrial world causes is a boomerang. Would it not in the long run be more humane, and also cheaper, to fight the poverty in the Third World now, and to renounce our own growth, rather than in a few decades to be forced to combat world-wide natural disasters? Would it not be more sensible to restrict the driving of cars now, rather than to have to walk round in gas masks in the future?

Without social justice between the industrial world and the Third, there will be no peace, and without peace there will be no liberation of nature. This one, single earth cannot in the long run put up with a divided humanity. The organism of the earth is coherent in itself and can carry only a united humanity that is integrated in the organism.

The spreading ecological catastrophe is universal and makes no distinctions. Nature, living things and ecosystems, human beings – all are equally threatened. The catastrophe unites divided humanity in an undivided danger. It brings humanity and nature into the fellowship of a shared plight. In this respect too, it is essential for humanity to stop being the common object of this threat, and become the common subject of responsibility for life. It is only out of a community forged by the recognition of a shared danger that a common readiness for responsible action can come into being. But competitive struggles and battles for power hold humanity captive, and do not as yet allow it to act freely and responsibly. Consequently the mutual threat must cease, so that we can address in common our much greater collective peril.

I believe that the ecological crisis in nature is a crisis of modern scientific and technological civilization itself. That great project 'the modern world' is threatened with failure. So this is not not just a 'moral crisis', as Pope John Paul II said; it is deeper than that. It is a religious crisis of the paradigm in which people in the Western world put their trust and live.[150]

3. The Economic End-Time:
The Impoverishment of the Third World

With the beginning of modern European times and the development of the modern world in the northern hemisphere, what has come to be called the Third World came into being in the south, in Africa and Latin America. The two worlds emerged simultaneously, stood in a causal relation to each other, and conditioned one another mutually. It was the modern enslavement of Africans and the modern exploitation of the American sub-continent which first made available the capital and resources required for the development of Western industrial society.

The destruction of Africa began with the slave trade.[151] Apart from North Africa, the slave trade south of the Sahara extended to almost all African peoples, the hunter and herdsman tribes in the

African interior being least affected. To give some figures: between 1575 and 1591, 52,000 Africans were shipped to Brazil from Angola alone; in 1617, 28,000 from Angola and the Congo; between 1680 and 1700, 300,000 were carried on English ships; between 1680 and 1688 the English Royal African Company had 249 slave traders in their employ, shipped 60,783 Africans, and unloaded 46,396 who had survived the voyage. During the sixteenth century as a whole, 900,000 were sold from all parts of Guinea to the New World; in the seventeenth century the number was 2,750,000 – that is 27,500 annually. Together with the industries producing goods for trade, and the plantations and mines where the slaves in the New World worked, this was probably far and away the biggest international trading enterprise. A worldwide triangular commerce came into being: weapons and industrial products for Africa – slaves from Africa for America – gold, silver, lead, sugar, cotton and tobacco from America to Europe. The merchantmen were never empty. All in all it is thought that twenty million Africans were enslaved, and that fifty million died in the slave hunts and in transport. In Europe these opportunities for trade gave rise to mercantilism and industrialization, for which the necessary investment capital could be made available out of income from the slave trade.

In America and Europe, slave-trading companies were formed. In the Caribbean and in Central and South America the subsistence economy was destroyed and the colonial economy built up, with monocultures for the export of cotton, sugar-cane, rice and tobacco. Africa was 'de-developed' economically and politically through the slave trade. 'It had lasted the better part of four centuries, during which it had involved, by a conservative estimate, the forced migration of fifteen million Negroes, besides causing the death of perhaps thirty or forty million others in slave raids, coffles, and barracoons. What it had produced in Africa was nothing but misery, stagnation, and social chaos. In England and France – also at a considerable cost in lives – it had created greater accumulations of wealth than had been known in previous centuries, and thus it had played its part in the Industrial Revolution. In the Western Hemisphere, besides introducing a vigorous new strain of immigrants, it had created the plantation system, it had opened vast areas to the cultivation of the four great slave crops – sugar, rice, tobacco, and cotton – and it had also encouraged the fatal and persistent myth of Negro inferiority. The trade itself was almost impossible to suppress as long as chattel slavery flourished in a powerful country; in fact it was being revived in the 1850s. It helped to bring about the Civil War, and nothing less than a war could end it. One might say that the doom of the slave trade was sounded by the guns at Fort Sumter and was sealed at Antietam and Gettysburg.'[152]

For the abolition of slavery in modern times (the struggle was carried on between 1840 and 1850, and was in full force only in the second half of the nineteenth century) a number of factors must be mentioned. These varied in weight in differing situations:

Industrialization displaced the plantation economy. Industry needs paid labour but not slaves. The worker sells his working capacity but not his body, even though the two can be closely connected. In the nineteenth century, the American Civil War was a battle between the industrialized North, with a work force of voluntary immigrants from Europe, and the agrarian South, with non-voluntary slave labour. The struggle between liberty and slavery was a struggle between the principles of capitalism and feudalism. When cheap wage-earners were brought to Trinidad from India, the black slaves were no longer needed. A different kind of labour grew up, and a different system of domination. It is true that in white literature the black slaves were always depicted as docile, obedient and subservient, as *Uncle Tom's Cabin* shows. But in reality the enslavement of Africans is an endless history of mutiny on the ships, of revolts, of flight, of active and passive resistance.

Religion is not the least of the factors which should be mentioned on both sides. The biblical stories about Israel's slavery and Moses's liberation, about Exodus and homecoming, put their stamp on the Christian 'religion of these oppressed people', as blues and spirituals still show today; while religious and humanitarian motives also fuelled the movement first to contain slavery, and then to emancipate the slaves.

The exploitation of Latin America began with the 'gold fever' of the Conquistadores.[153] Gold was and is a means of payment; in itself it has hardly any value. The greed for gold is the greed for power, nothing else. Marco Polo's accounts tell us that the countries of the Far East were thought to possess gold galore, and to have inexhaustible gold mines. It was the gold fever that impelled Columbus's voyages to the Indies. After the war against the Moors, the Spanish treasury was empty. The acquisition of gold was therefore the royal concern behind Columbus's voyages. The first enquiry among the natives was always the question about gold. The myth of Eldorado grew up, the golden land with the city of gold. Expeditions to look for it were sent to Florida, to the Amazon, and into the Andes. People probably assumed that the Garden of Eden could be found somewhere in America too. With gold, the ragged soldiers and the indebted Spanish officers could become effortlessly rich.

For the Indians, the greed for gold and talk about the Christian God made the conquerors' God and their gold two sides of the same thing. 'The real reason why the Christians murdered and ruined so terrible a number of innocent people was simply this', wrote Las Casas: 'that they were trying to get possession of their gold.'[154]

After gold came silver. The richest silver city in the world was Potosi, in Bolivia, where even the pavements are said to have been made of gold. In 1573 the city had a population of 120,000, as many as London, Rome or Paris at that time. The mountain where the silver mines were located was over 15,000 feet high, and today, five hundred years later, it looks like a pierced antheap. It is now an exhausted refuse dump. In the seventeenth century silver exports edged out the export of gold from America to Europe. It is difficult to arrive at figures. According to Galeano, the silver brought to Spain between 1503 and 1660 was more than three times all European reserves. Gold and silver from America generated an accumulation of capital in Europe which was used for investment in industrialization. 'The metals seized from the new colonies promoted the economic development of Europe – one could even say they made it possible.'[155] The Spanish crown was deeply in debt, and pledged the gold and silver deliveries in advance to Italian, German, Flemish and English banking houses. The crown waged wars, and the nobility wanted to retain its luxury. As a result, industrialization did not develop in feudalist Spain and Portugal. At the end of the seventeenth century, Spain was in control of only 5% of its trade with its own colonies. 95% was in other European hands.

The colonies did not profit from their wealth either. It was in Europe, and later in North America, that the capital was accumulated, not in Latin America. The colonies delivered what Europe needed and wanted. Thus the Latin American peoples became 'sub-modern', 'underdeveloped' so that the European countries could develop into 'modernity'.

After gold and silver came King Sugar. Huge latifundia and monocultures grew up in the islands of the Caribbean, to produce sugar for the European market. The need for black slaves and landless farm labourers for the sugar-cane plantations grew enormously in the eighteenth century. The native subsistence economies were driven out. Together with sugar came cotton, with the same effect. Venezuela produced cocoa, the highlands of Columbia coffee, the Amazon region rubber, Argentine meat, and so forth. 'The greater the demand for a product in the world market, the greater the disaster for the Latin American people, who have to sacrifice themselves to produce it.'[156]

To the exploitation of the colonies through their 'mother countries' was added the enrichment of the colonial aristocracies, the 'oligarchies'. Third World is not just a geographical expression; it is a class term too. Since these ruling aristocracies, for their part, secured and invested their wealth in Europe, the poor in Latin America were doubly exploited. Even today the old colonial structures still exist. They can be described as the relation between the 'underdevelopment' of the one for the benefit of the 'development' of the other, the relation of periphery to centre, or the relation of the Third World to the countries of the industrial West. What has remained are the monocultures enforced for the benefit of the world market, which enrich the land owners. What has remained is the enforced partitioning of production. The servicing of the mountain of debt has replaced the gold and silver exports, and this means that more interest always flows from the Latin American countries to the USA and Europe than the capital which the industrial countries invest there.

The end is the Third World which is no longer needed – *which is superfluous*. The micro-electronics revolution in production is so far advanced that labour costs constitute a continually falling share of the total costs of major undertakings – in highly rationalized operations this share is already less than 10%. The cheap labour costs in developing countries accordingly offer little motivation to major foreign firms to invest there. Computers and automation are making the work force of the southern hemisphere increasingly superfluous. What the over-powerful north will need in the future are the Third World's seas, certain raw materials which are not yet replaceable, its forests, and its ecological resources. But its people will not be needed any more. 'Intelligent machines' in the industrial countries produce even more cheaply and more flawlessly than men and women workers in the low-wage countries of the Third World.[157]

It is not by chance that apocalyptic visions are emerging among the people of the Third World. They can be distinguished from the prophecies of exterminism and the general mood of doom and gloom in the countries of the West because of their precise analysis of the world that is destined to perish, and through the principle of hope for the victory of life:

'Like a huge idol, like the Beast in the Apocalypse (Rev. 13), the present economic system covers the earth with its open sewer of unemployment and homelessness, hunger and nakedness, despair and death. It destroys different ways of living and working, which are in antithesis to its own. In its hostility to the environment, it sullies nature. It enforces an alien culture on the peoples which it has conquered. In its insatiable greed for prosperity, it offers people themselves as sacrifice in a bloody holocaust, pre-eminently in the Third World but increasingly in the First World too. The Beast has become a ravening monster, armed to the teeth with tanks and guns, atomic bombs, warships with computer-guided missiles, radar systems and satellites, and it is bringing humanity to the verge of total and sudden annihilation. But in the world-wide struggles of the poor and oppressed against all forms of dehumanization, there is a sign of life and of victory. There is the believing trust in the God of life, in the Lamb who in the midst of this divided world builds up a new Jerusalem which will come down from heaven (Rev. 21.10), and who gives hope for a liberation from oppression, sin and death.'[158]

4. *Is Exterminism Apocalyptic?*

What do these barbaric end-times of modern civilization have to do with the Jewish and Christian apocalypses? Should the end-times of the modern world be interpreted apocalyptically, or do the apocalyptic hopes and visions resist the cynicism of the modern prophecies of the world's end?

In 1954, Günter Anders had recourse to the word 'apocalypse' because he declared that the nuclear end-time was the end of time in general, proceeding from a concrete analysis of the weapons of modern mass annihilation to the comprehensive conclusion that with them 'the last epoch of humanity' had begun. He consequently declared that his contemporaries were 'blind to the apocalypse' and 'apathetic towards the apocalypse', because they could not perceive, and did not want to believe, the deadly dangers which he rightly saw just as clearly as, in his own time, Karl Jaspers and Albert Schweitzer.

The ineffectiveness of his accusations then made Anders go more deeply into the matter, and study the biblical apocalypses.[159] He found unbridgeable differences between those theological apocalypses and 'our' nuclear apocalypse. The earlier apocalyptists expected that the end of the world, and judgment, would come from God, who judges and saves; our apocalyptists today expect the annihilation that is caused and made by human beings themselves. 'Then the expected end was thought to be the consequence of our own guilt. But this time the guilt can be found in the effecting of the end.'[160] The biblical apocalypses associate the expected end of this perverted world with the hope for the beginning of God's new, just world. But 'our' apocalypses are godless, knowing no judgment and no grace, but only the self-inflicted self-annihilation of humanity. The 'nuclear apocalypse' is 'a naked apocalypse, that is to say the apocalypse without a kingdom'.[161] In this respect it is really the precise reversal of the nineteenth-century modern world's faith in progress, and its belief in a kingdom of God without an apocalypse. In Christian terms this means: 'The future has already begun.' In nuclear terms it has to mean: 'Lack of future has already begun.' Günter Anders himself believed: 'The expectation at that time of the end of the world, an expectation which was not realized, was, to put it bluntly, unfounded. Today's expectation, on the other hand, is objectively justifiable.'[162] At that time the expressions 'end of the world' and 'apocalypse' were merely used metaphorically – Anders even maintains that they were 'a fiction'. 'The terms have acquired their serious and non-metaphorical sense only today, or only since the year zero (= 1945), for they now describe for the first time the end of the world that is really possible.'[163]

Anders acquired his information about the nature of Christian eschatology only from Albert Schweitzer and Rudolf Bultmann, so what he knew was confined to 'consistent eschatology', the delay of the parousia, and the disappointed expectation of an imminent end. If he had gone into the matter more precisely and in greater detail, he would have had to dispense with apocalyptic language altogether. For he would then have realized that what Jewish and Christian apocalyptic intends is not to evoke horror in the face of the end, but to encourage endurance in resistance to the powers of this world. It would then also have been clear to him that through his apocalyptic imagery he himself disguised and minimized the cruel exterminism of the modern world, and spread a religious lack of responsibility.

Anders was unsuccessful in his attempt to link nuclear exterminism and apocalyptic eschatology. 'Apocalypse' means disclosing, exposing, making manifest. The expression means the disclosure and manifestation of this world before the judgment of God – which means the becoming-true of the world in the face of its divine judge, and the becoming-manifest of the hidden God to the world in the hour of truth. The word apocalypse itself has nothing to do with 'the end of the world' or its 'extermination'. These connotations only arise because 'this perverted world' cannot before God remain what it is, once its truth is revealed. Those who, in the light of exterminism, consider that people today are 'blind to the apocalypse' are not revealing the truth about this crime of humanity. They are doing the very opposite: they are disguising it. Anyone who interprets the threatening nuclear annihilation of humanity apocalyptically as Armageddon, is pushing on to God the responsibility of human beings. That is the height of godlessness and irresponsibility. The first work of true apocalyptic eschatology must be to expose the mystifying, deluding use of apocalyptic language at the present time. It is true, however, and a revealing fact, that military, ecological and economic exterminism unmasks the true nature of the modern world: in the eyes of its victims, the perpetrators can see themselves for what they are.

§9 'THE END OF HISTORY': POST-HISTORIC PROPHETS

'The end of history' is an ancient apocalyptic theme. It takes the place of the symbol 'end of the world' once the reality of the world as a whole is comprehended as history. But what does history then mean? *Which* history is going to arrive at its end, when did it begin, and in what historical 'location' can we talk about the end of history at all? The modern post-historic tradition began in Europe with the lectures on Hegel which Alexandre Kojève gave in Paris in 1933, and which must be called individual at the very least, if not capricious.[164]

Modern culture has cut itself loose from civilization's earlier orientation towards the laws of the cosmos and the rhythms of nature, and ever since the industrial revolution has increasingly taken its bearings from human goals, projects and plans. The symbol 'history' has therefore increasingly displaced the older symbol 'nature'. To exist and work in history means that the point of orientation can only be origin or future. Origin is represented by traditions, future by visions, projects and plans. The detachment of modern civilization from nature has engendered the emotionally loaded term 'modern times', with its messianic overtones: to be liberated from their ties with nature makes human beings the free and determining subjects of their own history. On the ruins of 'the realm of necessity', modern civilization builds its carefully crafted 'realm of freedom'. 'Modern times' is a messianic term, and is a cast back to the spirit of Joachim of Fiore, as is Auguste Comte's Law of the Three Stages, according to which the religious stage of humanity, which was dominated by the priests, was followed by the metaphysical stage, with the rule of the lawyers; but now the positive stage is beginning, in which it is the sociologists who possess the knowledge required for rule, because they will master the social crises. This stage of human history is the last, because it can no longer be surpassed by any other. Consequently it is only in respect of the surmounted past that the present can be called 'modern times'; in respect of the future it is 'end-time'.[165]

The present end-time of human history is either messianically lauded or apocalyptically deplored, and both in ever new variations. The most recent ideas use for this the French neologism *post-histoire*, which goes back to Antoine Augustin Cournot,[166] although in his ideas the spirit of Auguste Comte and Saint-Simon can be detected without difficulty.

What history is supposed to be ended? In Marx it is clear: 'The history of all previous societies is the history of class conflicts,'[167] so 'the classless society' must be understood as the end of that history, or as the end of its own pre-history and the beginning of the first true history of the human race in general. 'It [i.e., communism] is the solved riddle of history and knows itself to be that solution.'[168] In the young, Left Hegelian Marx it is particularly easy to discern the emotional end-of-history fervour of German Idealism.

But is history really nothing but class struggle? Is history not also, beyond that, the experience of contingency in happening, and of freedom in the human subject's self-experience? If the experience of reality is based on experiences of contingency and freedom, then we only arrive at the end of history if chance is annihilated (this being the goal of human reason according to Wilhelm von Humboldt) and if human beings are relieved of what German calls 'the torment of choice', and no longer see themselves as responsible subjects of their own decisions. Something like this can develop if human history ends up in a huge megamachine, where everything is calculated and mastered, and human beings turn into cogs in the vast interlocking mechanism. Lewis Mumford has developed this vision of the end.[169] It is an idea which George Orwell and other science-fiction writers have elaborated. Of course the image of the great machine is inadequate. But what is meant is the organized human being who functions as he or she should, without resistance. That is 'post-historic man'.[170]

The idea of the 'administered world' which Max Horkheimer and Theodor W. Adorno developed as 'the dialectics of enlightenment'[171] certainly takes us a more realistic step forward. Liberty and autonomy are what the Enlightment promised in the sunrise of its era. In the twilight of that same era, what emerges is the total rule of 'instrumental reason', the loss of liberty and the dissolution of human subjectivity.[172] The notion that in a society no longer based on antagonism, politics will be transformed into the joint administration of 'things' really goes back to Marx and Engels – though Ernst Bloch viewed the outcome as a deficiency of any economic and political situation, and an individual 'lack of destiny'.[173]

Human beings are then no longer historical beings. Nor is it necessary that they should be, because the bureaucracies of the administered world have assumed on their behalf the mastery over contingency: events are categorized and become 'cases', which are judged according to precedent.[174]

The individual character of events is dissipated in what is general and continually recurring, and these events forfeit their uniqueness. In the administered world there are no 'special cases' and there is no 'individual treatment'. The ritualized world of the archaic, pre-historical human being returns once more in the post-historic world on a new level.

The *post-historic* human being is supposed to be a correlative to the *pre-historical* human being. Historical human beings were continually faced with alternatives between which they had to decide. The post-historic, administered world no longer leaves them any alternatives at all. All they can do is to differentiate within the framework of what is already given, and vary general rituals. There is pluralistic caprice, but nothing completely different. This, however, means that in the administered world, if what that world administers are then beings without history, no one can distinguish any more between truth and a lie, life and death, the preservation of the world and its annihilation. Once the scope of the delusion has become so total that there is 'no longer any alternative', as today's cynical phrase goes, then even 'Auschwitz' can become the sub-system of this world.

Finally, beings without history are also *beings without memory*. The history that has been experienced and will be experienced, that has been suffered and has to be decided, is historicized and its potentialities catalogued. The history that has been experienced and has to be decided is replaced by 'the museum of history', in which history is objectified and put out of commission.

Does the administered world actually end history as it really is, or does it merely make the experience of history vanish for the administered human being? Is bureaucracy the already-given 'end of history', or is it just an artificial departure from history? No one could deny that the great administrative bodies of the world make history, and certainly do not end it. The exterminism which, as we have seen, proceeds from these bodies is human history in its hitherto most dangerous form. The Roman Empire brought peace internally and a permanent state of war externally; and this is how the modern administrative worlds work too. Internally they administer, extern-ally they exterminate. It may perhaps be objected that the unfortun-ate fact is simply that the whole of humanity does not as yet live in an administered world of this kind, and that this explains why the history which the administered world has already superseded still goes on; but in answer one must then point to the ecological contradiction between the administered world and the living organ-ism of the earth, a contradiction which makes of the administered world, not 'the end of history' but at most one of the historical powers that destroy the earth, and with it humanity too.

As early as 1952, Arnold Gehlen took over the term *post-histoire* from the Belgian politician and philosopher Hendrik de Man and from Cournot, in order to predict for the perfectly organized world 'lack of surprise', 'lack of future', and hence 'lack of history'. In 'the culture of global industry' that is beginning, the genuine transmis-sion of European history will disappear. The threshold to a post-historical condition has already been crossed. In Gehlen the grounds for this prospect can be found in his negative anthropology.[175] If the human being is a 'step-child' of nature (as – like Herder – he maintains), an unfinished being and what Nietzsche called 'an as yet undetermined animal', then human beings are forced to compensate for their insufficiently sure instinct through firm social institutions. These must function without question, so that in the form of civilization they can lend a kind of second nature to the human beings who are in themselves chaotic.

In the completely organized society of the future, human beings will complete their natural incompletion and will close down their openness to the world. Their striving for security will lead them to the 'Leviathan' state, which secures them on every side. If the human being is by definition the unsecured, free, venturesome animal, unfixed and open to the world, then the denizens of the future world, who will be without history, will in this sense no longer be human beings at all. Their completely organized world is 'the end of history', and with it the end of the human being whom we here know as a historical being. The global state free of surprises and devoid of failure will then not merely bring a historical epoch to a close; it will also end the history of the human race by correcting the natural deformity of its members: the human being will become the culturally determined animal. That is Nietzsche's 'last man'. As historical and thereby incalculable beings, human beings are no longer affordable by the global society of the future. They would be too dangerous. If wars and revolutions are to disappear, human beings as free, historical individuals must be abolished first. Historical action has to be ended. As if human institutions were any less hazardous than human beings themselves!

According to Roderick Seidenberg, the pre-historical era dominated by human instincts is followed by the relatively brief time of 'history', in the conflict between instinct and reason. This leads over into 'a final post-historic phase' which corresponds more or less symmetrically to the pre-historical phase. In this final era the instincts return on the level of the completely organized society. Reason reproduces them through the medium of organization and institutionalized modes of behaviour. Then a stable global society comes into being 'not unlike that of the ants, the bees, and the termites'.[176]

The reason why animal and crystalline images suggest themselves for the positivist global state is this negative anthropology. For a long time the termite hill and the beehive were considered fascinating models. The post-historic era is to become 'the eternal return of the same thing', thus ending the linear time of history.

The 'crystallization' of history is a favourite image for the post-vital petrification of culture. Organization, Seidenberg tells us, will progress to the point of final crystallization. That is a still further step: in the post-historic condition, quasi-animal conditions first replace historical events on a new level.[177] The institutionalization of all human modes of behaviour creates reactions which are quasi-instinctively sure, and thus calculable. But in the post-historic condition life will also become lifeless compared with life as it has been hitherto. Yet lifelessness came before life and will hence be there even when the living are no more. So must human 'evolution' not necessarily proceed from the historical to the unhistorical, and then from the organic to the inorganic? The post-historic philosophers of the *post-histoire* like to take over analogies from the Darwinian theory of evolution, and enhance their prophecies of doom with the law of entropy, in order to predict – in correspondence to the death of nature through cold – a 'cold death' for human culture through the egalitarian distribution of energy in the mass society. Since the second law of thermodynamics is valid only in closed systems, to transfer it to the end of human history assumes that human culture is no longer an open system, but has become, or must be turned into, a system that is closed.

Claude Lévi-Strauss's rediscovery of 'the savage mind' also contributed to these ideas. Once the cultural 'invariants' only are investigated, human beings as the subjects of their own lives are essentially speaking dissolved.[178] Human subjectivity can now be perceived only in the variables of timeless invariants. It is not human beings who live their lives – life lives them. So subjectivity can be found only in the aberrations of life's general pattern – as the individual patient appears on the charts churned out by the medical appliances that examine him. What was for so long held cheap as primitive and 'pre-historical' or 'a-historical', proves to be what is timeless and post-historic, and 'history' is exposed as the myth of modernity.

The most recent prophet of the *post-histoire* is Francis Fukuyama, who is a member of the planning staff of the State Department in Washington. As a late pupil of Alexandre Kòjeve, and an adherent of his curious interpretation of Hegel, Fukuyama saw the year 1989 – with the events leading to the collapse of 'socialism as it really exists', to the disintegration of the Soviet Union, and to the reunification of Germany – as 'the end of history'.[179] It is the 'triumph of the West' that with the end of socialism all genuine alternatives to Western liberalism have been exhausted. After the end of fascism in the Second World War, socialism too has now been eliminated from the contest. So in 1989 we experienced not only the end of the Cold War but also 'the end of history as such'. This, that is to say, is the full stop at the end of humanity's ideological development, and the universalization of Western liberal democracy as the final form of human government. The homogeneous state, everywhere the same, 'liberal democracy', and the common satisfaction of all material needs through the 'global marketing' of everything: all these things have emerged at the end of the conflicts, wars and revolutions of history as the best solutions of all political and economic problems, and have triumphed over all other alternatives. Fukuyama demonstrates this not so much from the countries of eastern Europe and the former Soviet Union, as from the countries of East Asia, above all from the successes of postwar Japan.

Now that socialism, as capitalism's last alternative, is finished and done with, and since no other fundamental alternatives are on the horizon, we are standing at the beginning of *an era without alternatives*. It is precisely this that Hegel, according to Fukuyama, already perceived on Napoleon's entry into Jena and his victory over the Prussians there: this was to be 'the end of history' and the beginning of the post-historic age. Since 1989, we have today actually reached the goal, in Fukuyama's view. In 1990 he wrote in the *Herald Tribune* that after some thousand years of trying out different systems, we are now ending this millennium in the assurance that in pluralist-capitalist democracy we have found what we were looking for. In this post-historic condition without alternatives, it is only now a matter of making endless improvements to the system, and of endless approaches to perfection; but there are no more alternatives as far as the fundamentals are concerned.[180] There will still be reforms, but no revolutions.

For Fukuyama this 'end of history' is not a happy condition, any more than it was for his predecessors. On the contrary: 'The end of history will be a very sad time.' All historical conflicts will be superseded by economic calculations and the solution of technical problems. 'In the post-historical period there will be neither art nor philosophy, just the perpetual caretaking of the museum of human history.' Compared with the tensions of history, the post-historical condition will seem tedious, so that Fukuyama himself already looks back nostalgically to the time when history still existed. Like other prophets of the *post-histoire* too, he then ends with the illusory possibility that boredom could drive people to begin history all over again – a purely literary possibility, which Herman Hesse also tried out once before, in his *Glass Bead Game*.

As a Hegelian, Fukuyama must surely know that all earlier civilizations developed new systems for living once their inner contradictions had become unendurable. This was recognized by Left Hegelians such as Marx. But Fukuyama takes into account only the external alternatives, such as fascism, nationalism and socialism, thereby forgetting the inward contradictions inherent in the universal marketing of everything: the contradictions between market value and human dignity, between the First World and the Third, as well as between humanity and nature. These human, economic and ecological contradictions have been brought about by capitalism itself, and it is extremely doubtful whether capitalism can surmount them, since it is through capitalism that they are continually engendered, and all social and ecological corrections are always too late. The standard of living in the USA, Japan and the European Community cannot be universalized without ecologically exterminating humanity. The standard is only possible for a minority at the expense of the majority. For the mass of human beings, who have to live, not on the upper side of history but on its underside, Fukuyama's 'end of history' is not a cause for messianic rejoicing over the best of all possible worlds; it is rather a reason for apocalyptic lamentations over the lack of any alternative to their misery.[181] It will certainly not be the ennui of the children of the rich which will lead to the resurgence of history. It will be the real misery of the hungry masses and the no less real misery of the ruined system of the earth. The protest of humiliated men and women and the violated organizations of the earth will not leave the world in its present condition, for as Erich Fried said, 'the person who wants the world to remain as it is, does not want it to remain'.

The modern post-historic philosophers are not just the secular heirs of a theology based on the concept of salvation history; they are also heirs of the secularized millenarianism of modern times, with the sole difference that for them faith in progress, and the belief that history will reach its goal in a Golden Age, has switched over into the apocalypticism of an 'end of history' arrived at through the abolition of human beings. But they believe in the unity of history, and in its predetermined direction towards a goal or end. Those beliefs are their theological residue.[182] What is anti-Christian in Nietzsche's sense, on the other hand, is the notion of a necessary abolition of the historical human being, the replacement of a divine providence by biological evolution, with the final mutation of the human being into something that has nothing in common with human beings as they have hitherto been – and, not least, the admiration for a totalitarian power which will enforce the 'end of history' that is required. The European post-historic ideologists were consequently always at the same time supporters of totalitarian right- or left-wing parties. They retained this totalitarianism in their emotional evocation of the end of history. It also ruled the emotional concept of world history with which they maintained, as if by a matter of course, that their own European and 'modern' world was the world *per se*, thus generously appropriating for themselves the other human worlds too.

The post-historic philosophers expect too much of their 'end of history'. It is illogical to assume that the institutions, organizations and bureaucracies which historical people create are not themselves historical. It is illusory to maintain that the conditions which venturesome beings create in order to secure themselves against their own hazards could not be hazardous conditions. Hobbes's great Leviathan, which some of these philosophers revere so much, certainly ends 'the war of each against all' but why should it end war in general? If 'man is the wolf of man', why should the great Leviathan be a lamb and not turn into a super-wolf? Organized crime is of course the end of individual crime, but is it the end of crime in general? Is it not rather its culmination?[183]

§10 IS APOCALYPTIC ESCHATOLOGY NECESSARY?

We have distinguished between historical and eschatological millenarianism, and we are making a similar distinction between historical and millenarian apocalypticism. The apocalyptic interpretation of the catastrophes of world history, or cosmic catastrophes, is something different from the eschatological apocalypse of the powers of this world in the Judgment of God, whose purpose is the birth of a new world. The modern apocalyptic interpretations of human end-times are secularizations of biblical apocalyptic, and now have in common with it only the catastrophe, no longer the hope. They talk about the end without a beginning, and about judgment without a kingdom. They disseminate neither hope nor resistance, only paralysing anxiety and cynicism. Apocalypticism belongs to eschatology, not to history. And yet eschatology begins with apocalypticism: there is no beginning of a new world without the end of this old one, there is no kingdom of God without judgment on godlessness, there is no rebirth of the cosmos without 'the birth pangs of the End-time'. The raising of Christ from the dead presupposes his real and total death. It is from this fact that Christian apocalyptic takes its bearings: his real end was his true beginning.

Ideas about the end of the world appear only on the fringes of the Old Testament, in late prophetic writings – Isaiah 24–27, Zechariah 12–14, Daniel 2 and 7, Joel 2–3 – and then in the apocryphal books of Enoch, Syr. Baruch and II Esdras, and the so-called apocalyptic writings.[184] In the New Testament we find the 'little synoptic apocalypses' – Matthew 24, Mark 13, Luke 21 and the Book of Revelation.[185] The transitions from prophecy to apocalyptic are fluid. We talk about apocalyptic writers in distinction from the prophets when their ideas about God's future acts stand in complete discontinuity to previous history, and the crisis of God's judgment therefore acquires dimensions that extend to the whole of world history and to the cosmos. Then God's promise constitutes a new world aeon, or a new creation of all things.

Political Apocalypses can be found in the book of Daniel. In Nebuchadnezzar's dream (Dan. 2). the kingdoms of this world are crushed by a stone, but then 'the God of heaven will set up a kingdom which shall never be destroyed, nor shall its sovereignty be left to another people. It shall break in pieces all these kingdoms and bring them to an end, and it shall stand for ever.' In 'the vision of the monarchies' (Dan. 7) the kingdoms of the world rise up in bestial form out of the sea of chaos, each crueller and more repulsive than the last. But they are then burnt in the divine fire, and God gives the empire of the world to his 'Son of man' – that is, to the true human being who is in full accord with God: 'His dominion is an everlasting dominion, which shall not pass away.'

Cosmic apocalypses are to be found in the book of Enoch: 'The earth will be wholly rent in sunder, And all that is upon the earth shall perish, And there shall be a judgment upon all men' (1.7). Finally, however, the throne of God will become visible, and 'the Son of man' will come, and heaven and earth will be created anew (45.4f.). For not only human beings will be judged but the fallen angels too. According to II Peter 3.10, 12, 'On the day of the Lord the heavens will be kindled and dissolved, and the elements will melt with fire.' It is only after this, and because of it, that 'a new heaven and a new earth' are expected (3.13). According to Matt. 24.29, 'the stars will fall from heaven and the powers of the heavens will be shaken'. Only after that will the Son of man appear in the glory of God.

The *political apocalypses* of the empires of the world had their genesis in times when Israel was oppressed by the great powers. They are visions conceived by persecuted people, whose faith in God was inwardly assailed. This violent, unjust and godless world will crumble when, on his Day, God sets up his kingdom on earth. Then he will vindicate his people, who are now suffering for his Name and are refusing to submit to the powers and demons of this world.[186] With this hope the saints in Israel preserved their faith in God, and resisted: 'He who endures to the end shall be saved.'

Behind the *cosmic apocalypses* about the end of the world and the dawn of a new creation is another remembrance: the story of Noah and the Flood.[187] 'I have determined to make an end of all flesh: for the earth is filled with wickedness through them; behold I will destroy them (i.e., human beings) with the earth' (Gen. 6.13). The wickedness is the rampant violence spread by the rulers who let themselves be worshipped as 'sons of God' (Gen. 6.1). Underlying the story of Noah and the Flood is the fear that God could 'repent' of having made human beings, and that his will to create could change into the will to destroy. Only Noah is saved from the Flood, he being the archetype of the 'righteous' person. With him God makes the new covenant of creation (Gen. 8): 'Never again shall there be a flood to destroy the earth' (Gen. 9.11). The new covenant of creation embraces Noah and his family, all succeeding generations, and all living things. Behind the story of Noah and the Flood there is also the recollection of creation-in-the-beginning, which was called into existence out of the sea of chaos (Gen. 1.2) – in later terminology, *ex nihilo*. Cosmic apocalypses reveal an awareness of the world's contingency: the world is there, but it does not *have* to be there – it can be not-there too. Only God exists of himself and not from anything else.

'The end of the world' is one side of the dawn of a new world from

God, the side that is turned towards us and which we experience. Israel's apocalypses, and Christianity's too, expect that the world will end with terrors that are as yet inconceivable. But they look through these coming terrors to the beginning of a new creation of all things. That is why these apocalypses, Jewish and Christian both, reach out for the image of 'the birth pangs – the labour pains – of the End-time'. The birth of a child involves its mother's pain, and this pain goes together with 'sorrow' (John 16.21); and in the same way the pains and sorrows of the End-time – if we see them retrospectively, and in the outreach of hope – are simply the inevitable accompaniments to the new birth of the world. The downfall of this world is really already Act One of its deliverance: 'The world must founder so that it can be saved.'[188] In this unredeemed world enslaved creation is sighing for redemption, and believers who have received the first fruits of the Holy Spirit join in these sighs, according to Paul (Rom. 8.19ff.); but the 'sighings' are the groans of labour pains, birth cries of the divine Spirit which will one day be transformed into eternal joy at the rebirth of the cosmos (John 16.20). The metaphors used evidently ascribe 'the rebirth of the cosmos' (Matt. 19.28) to Yahweh's *ruach*, to God as mother (Isa. 66), God the Holy Spirit.[189]

The reason for the apocalyptic hope in the downfall of the world is pure faith in God's faithfulness. It is not optimism. God will remain faithful to his creative resolve even if the world he has created founders on its own wickedness. God's will for life is greater than his will for judgment. God's Yes outweighs God's No. 'God is faithful, for he cannot deny himself' (II Tim. 2.13). Consequently believers discern in God's No a hidden Yes,[190] and sense in judgment his coming grace, and see in the end of this world the beginning of the new world God will create.

The practical consequences are paradoxical in an almost literal sense – they are contrary, that is, to what can be seen: 'There will be signs in sun and moon and stars, and upon the earth distress of nations in perplexity at the roaring of the sea and the waves, men fainting with fear . . . Now when these things begin to take place, look up and raise your heads, because your redemption is drawing near' (Luke 21.25, 28). The end with terror makes an end of the terror without end, and brings the deliverance of those who in imprisonment and suffering here have kept the faith. In history too there are similar experiences – the end of a war, for example. In view of the destructions brought upon God's suffering people by the violent, the Jewish apocalyptists call the people to endure and to hold fast to their faith in God. They strengthen hope for the future by strengthening faith in God. This is not the active hope for the future with which Abraham went out and Moses led the people out of Egyptian captivity, but it is a resisting, enduring expectation, capable of suffering, in a situation in which nothing more can be done to avert disaster. But with this hope the attitudes and stances which always tend to emerge at human end-times can be combatted – the anger, the aggression, the depression and the self-destruction. Apathy and cynicism are forms of spiritual petrification and creeping death which go ahead of the end of the world, anticipate it, and in their own way bring it about. Apocalyptic expectation is not stolid resignation to fate. It raises up those who are cast down. True apocalyptic teaches people to 'lift up their heads', and to be open for God's new beginning in the breakdown of this world system which they perceive.

Are the apocalyptic expectations of the end *Christian*? The content of Jesus's proclamation was not characterized by apocalyptic images, though it no doubt had as its presupposition the general apocalypticism of the oppressed Israel of his time. But Jesus proclaimed the kingdom of God to the poor, and ministered in unheard-of messianic closeness *to God's kingdom*. He called God Abba, 'dear Father', and lived in this unheard-of messianic closeness *to God*. The messianic way in which Jesus talked and lived presupposed 'the last time', as the framework of reference for what he said. The New Testament always stresses that Jesus's coming, the outpouring of the Holy Spirit, the proclamation of the gospel that saves the godless, the gathering of Christ's people from all nations, and so forth, all take place in 'the last days'. The apocalyptic interpretation of time is undoubtedly the context for the early Christian sense of mission.

In content, the apostolic proclamation of the gospel to the Gentile nations is eschatological in a double sense. First, with the raising of Jesus 'from the dead' the future of the general raising of the dead and 'the life of the world to come' has already begun. Jesus is believed in as 'the first fruits of those who have fallen asleep', and experienced as 'the leader of life'. Secondly, with the exaltation, Jesus is installed as Lord of the coming divine kingdom. Through his death he has already conquered the power of sin, and through his raising God has

already broken the power of death. Compared with Jewish apocalypticism, in Christ's gospel we find a decisive shift in the different
phases: the expected 'turn of the age' does not just take place for the
first time at the end of the time of this world. It happens 'now
already', in the midst of this world-time. In the community of Christ
there is now already new creation in the midst of this unredeemed
world which is hastening towards its end. In the experience of God's
Spirit there is already here the experience of the rebirth to eternal life
in the midst of a life that has to die. The saying that 'the night is far
gone, the day is at hand' (Rom. 13.12) is an apt rendering of the
Christian sense of time, the awareness of living in the daybreak of
God's new day – in what a German hymn calls 'Morgenglanz der
Ewigkeit', the morning splendour of eternity.

Historically speaking, this *shift in the phases* of the apocalyptic
turn of the age is no doubt the reason why Christian congregations in
the first century again took up the old apocalyptic ideas about the
end of the world. On the one hand they believed that with the coming
of Christ and the outpouring of the Spirit the new creation of all
things had already begun. On the other hand they expected that
incomparable tribulations were still ahead at the end of the world
(Matt. 24.8).

Was something resurfacing in their awareness here, something
which they had repressed in the exuberance of their first enthusiasm?
Or was it their very Easter-enthusiasm that made them so oppress-
edly aware of the power and continuance of this unredeemed world?
That is not just a psychological question. It is a theological one
too.[191] The apocalyptic ideas about the end of the world in the New
Testament are clearly subordinated to the expectation of Christ's
parousia, and therefore to the completion of his salvific work. The
decisive question seems to be: does the catastrophic end of the world
bring Christ's parousia, or does Christ's parousia bring the end of
this world? In the first case, people could compel God through their
negative actions to act positively. We produce the chaos which is
necessary for the new creation. We destroy so that God may create
something new out of nothing. These are anarchistic ideas which we
can find in nineteenth-century Romanticism, but they have nothing
to do with Christian apocalypticism. In the second case, the coming
of Christ in the glory of the new creation will end the disordered and
grievous condition of this wretched world. In Christian apocalypticism, the expectation of the coming Christ outweighs the fear of the

terrors of the End-time. The question put to Christ is therefore: 'What will be the sign (first) of your coming and (second) of the end of the world?' (Matt. 24.3). A list follows of all the horrors in the world which are to come, but which 'are not yet the end', concluding with: 'the gospel of the kingdom will be preached throughout the whole world.' This is mentioned last, as 'the sign' for which people asked: only then 'will the end come' (24.14). Apocalyptically too, the hope for the coming of Christ which was active in the evangelization outweighs the experiences of the end of this world, which are anticipated in fear and terror.

And yet it remains a theological puzzle why the early Christian congregations should have expected still further final apocalyptic struggles between God and the godless powers, between the archangel Michael and the Dragon, and between Christ and the Antichrist, even though they believed in Christ's eschatological victory in his cross and his resurrection, and in their doxologies extolled the lordship of Christ over the cosmos.[192] Why does the scenario: battle, defeat, resurrection and victory, continually recur in the apocalyptic pictures of history? Why does 'the beast from the abyss' rear its head yet again? Why is the thousand years' kingdom of peace followed yet once more by a final battle with Gog and Magog?

If this is a 'return of what had been repressed' and therefore not truly surmounted,[193] then the effect of apocalypticism on Christianity would be to empty it of its inward content; fundamentally speaking, it would mean the final dissolution of the belief that Christ has already come, and that he is risen and 'will never die again' (Rom. 6.9). How can the christological 'once and for all' be reconciled with the apocalyptic expectation of new final struggles 'again and again'? Theologically, do we have to make a double – and inherently paradoxical – statement of reality, saying that 'the end is still to come *and* the new world is present'?[194] Theologically that is correct, because the Christian shift in the phases of the aeon leads to an overlapping simultaneity between the old aeon, which is still moving towards its end, and the new aeon, which has already begun with the coming of Christ and the outpouring of the divine Spirit. The Reformation formulas for Christian existence *simul iustus – simul peccator* (at once righteous and a sinner) and *iustus in spe, peccator in re* (righteous in hope, sinner in fact) are grounded on the simultaneity of the aeon that is dawning and the one that is breaking off.

And yet this does not explain why faith in end and beginning in Christ's cross and resurrection should again have picked up the notion of final apocalyptic struggles. The Christian faith stands or falls with the 'once and for all' of the Christ event, and cannot dissipate this in an 'again and again' of final struggles still to come and still undecided. Armageddon cannot replace Golgotha. But on the other hand the 'once and for all' cannot be understood in terms of linear time.[195] What is meant is Christ's eschatological uniqueness, not just his historical singularity. But the christological once-and-for-all of Christ can and will be reflected in history and the end of history. That is why baptism is once and for all, and essentially unrepeatable, just because it symbolizes a continual dying-with-Christ and rising-with-him. Against the horizon of Christian expectation the apocalyptic scenarios of the 'final battle' are just such a *reflection* or *imaging* of the messianic mission, the apocalyptic execution and the eschatological raising of Christ. In his 'catalogues of tribulations' Paul talks about being made like in form to the Christ whose apostle he is – an 'assimilation' which he has experienced and suffered; and in a similar way, in the apocalypses the Christian martyrs are made 'like in form' to the executed and victorious Christ. The whole cosmos experiences a similar assimilation. It too will be newly created, having endured death and judgment.

This imaging of the Christ event in the event of the end can also be looked at in reverse: the event of world and cosmos is drawn into the Christ event. 'The sufferings of Christ' inflicted on those who resist 'the beast' and the martyrs among them, do certainly correspond to 'the sufferings of this present time' (Rom. 8.18), which prevail everywhere in the world and are not worthy to be compared with 'the coming glory' which will be revealed to all. Apocalyptism then means that the whole creation participates in Christ's tribulation and in the light of the cross is manifested in its forsakenness and havoc, so that it may be drawn into the cosmic resurrection and new creation. 'Suffering in this cosmos is universal, because it is a suffering with the suffering of Christ, who entered this cosmos and yet burst it asunder when he rose from the dead and ascended into heaven.'[196]

Do the images about the apocalyptic end of the world *necessarily* belong to the visions of hope for the coming kingdom of God and the new creation of all things? In so far as they describe the misery, the end of which is expected, they do belong of necessity to these visions. The visions of hope for God's future are visions of deliverance from

the perils of the world which are experienced and dreaded. There is
no hope without fear. Fear is the instinct for threatening danger. In
apocalyptic images, fear perceives the truth of these dangers and tries
to give them 'a habitation and a name' in order to rob them of their
paralysing incomprehensibility.

If we were not sensitized by fear we should not notice dangers and
should be waylaid by the catastrophes. Fear wakes us up and keeps
us alert. Fear is the reverse side of hope, though hope is not the
reverse side of fear. Hope for someone can make us afraid for them,
but we do not derive any hope from mere anxiety. Fear lends hope
fore-sight, in the literal sense. Courage without foresight makes
people stupid. Foresight without courage makes them cowardly.
Anxiety makes hope wise. So the important thing is not just 'to learn
how to hope', as Ernst Bloch taught,[197] but to learn how to hope in
danger, and – as Kierkegaard thought – through anxiety to become
wise.[198]

Apocalypticism preserves the Christian doctrine of hope from
facile optimism and from false prophets who say 'peace, peace, when
there is no peace' (Jer. 8.11). Eschatology is not a doctrine about
history's happy end. In the present situation of our world, facile
consolation is as fatal as melancholy hopelessness. No one can assure
us that the worst will not happen. According to all the laws of
experience: it will. We can only trust that even the end of the world
hides a new beginning if we trust the God who calls into being the
things that are not, and out of death creates new life.

Are there grounds for any such confidence? The 'hermeneutics of
danger' means 'taking possession of a remembrance as it flashes up in
the moment of danger'.[199] In view of the deadly dangers threatening
the world, Christian remembrance makes-present the death of Christ
in its apocalyptic dimensions, in order to draw from his resurrection
from the dead hope for 'the life of the world to come', and from his
rebirth to eternal life hope for the rebirth of the cosmos. The
Indonesian word for hope means literally 'to look beyond the
horizon'. The *memoria resurrectionis Christi* lets us look beyond the
horizon of our own death into the wide space of eternal life, and
beyond the horizon of this world's end into God's new world.

Life out of this hope then means already acting here and today in
accordance with that world of justice and righteousness and peace,
contrary to appearances, and contrary to all historical chances of
success. It obliges us solemnly to abjure the spirit, logic and practice

of the nuclear system of deterrence and all other systems of mass annihilation. It means an unconditional Yes to life in the face of the inescapable death of all the living. That is the deeper meaning of the legendary Luther saying about 'the apple tree' which he would plant today even if he knew that the world was going to end tomorrow.

§11 THE RESTORATION OF ALL THINGS

1. 'The Last Judgment' and its Ambivalent Outcome

The expectation of a Last Judgment has always had a particular fascination for the imaginations of Christians. In mediaeval churches, we see the final judgment represented on the outside portals and in pictures inside: on the right hand side, angels carry the righteous away to the heaven of everlasting bliss; on the left devils drag the wicked into the hell of everlasting damnation; in the middle Christ sits on the judgment seat with the two-edged sword between his lips. In this great reckoning there are only two verdicts: eternal life or eternal death. Originally, hope for the Last Judgment was a hope cherished by the victims of world history, a hope that the divine justice would triumph over their oppressors and murderers. It was only after Constantine that Judgment – now orientated solely towards the perpetrators – was interpreted as a divine criminal tribunal where evil-doers were tried, and was understood as the prototype of imperial judicial power.

The mediaeval pictures of judgment disseminated fear and terror in order that tempted men and women should seek comfort and salvation in the means of grace provided by the church. The Reformers disseminated distress of conscience in order to awaken justifying faith through the gospel. Is there any grace except that of the judge? Who expected of the Last Judgment the final redemption of the world from evil? The expectation of judgment was a threatening and intimidating message, not a joyful and liberating one. Because psychologically it has done so much to poison the idea of God,[200] it is high time to discover *the gospel of God's judgment* and to awaken *joy in God's coming righteousness and justice*.[201]

> Dies irae, dies illa
> solvet saeclum in favilla.

Until 1969 this twelfth-century Latin sequence from the requiem

Mass was sung during the liturgy for the dead between Reading and Gospel, and it can therefore still be heard in many famous requiems. It is probably 'the most representative, the most culturally influential, and hence the most famous poem of the Latin middle ages'.[202] The cathedral scene in Goethe's *Faust* is built up round it, its first, sixth and seventh verses being interspersed there with an organ accompaniment. In books of Catholic dogmatics up to about 1960, the treatise on eschatology is constructed according to the sequence of ideas in this poem, and therefore treats first 'the eschatology of the individual', with death, judgment, purgatory and hell, and then 'the eschatology of the human race, with the Last Day, the resurrection of the dead, and final Judgment'.[203]

Protestant dogmatics really always enquire merely about the outcome of the Last Judgment. Is there a 'double outcome' – believers into heavenly bliss, unbelievers into the torments of hell? Or are all in the end redeemed, all saved, and all things brought into the new creation? Behind this question is the question about God. Does God, as their creator, go with all his created beings into life, death and resurrection – or does God as judge stand over against those he has created, detached and uninvolved, to pardon or condemn? How can the God who loves what he has created condemn not just what is evil, destructive and godless in created beings but these beings themselves?

The question: 'double outcome of judgment or universalism' is generally discussed as if it were already clear what judgment is, who the Judge is, and what the justice and righteousness is, according to which judgment is passed. But if Jesus is the judge, can he judge according to any other righteousness than the law which he himself manifested – the law of love for our enemies, and the acceptance of the poor, the sick and sinners? Can the rightousness which the Last Judgment serves be any righteousness other than the righteousness of God which creates justice and redeems, the righteousness to which the law and the prophets testify, and which the apostle Paul proclaimed in his gospel as justifying righteousness? Does theology not involve the Christian faith in inward contradictions if what is expected of the great Judgment is something different from what God has revealed in Israel's history and the history of Jesus Christ? And what is the ultimate purpose of the Last Judgment? If Judgment is just God's great final reckoning with the sinners and the saints, then this Judgment would indeed be 'the Last'. Or does it serve the revelation and establishment of God's righteousness and justice among all people and all things, so that God can build his 'new world' on lasting justice, and can therefore create for eternal peace? In that case the Last Judgment would not at all be 'the last' that can be expected of God; it would only be the 'the last but one'. 'The last' would then be his kingdom, and the new creation of all things. Just as the first thing was not sin but the primal blessing given to creation, so judgment would then not be the last thing either. What would come last would be the final blessing of the new creation in which righteousness and justice dwells.

In this chapter we shall first discuss the biblical and theological arguments for and against universalism, and shall try to solve a problem in eschatology which has been unsolved ever since Origen and Augustine. We shall then enquire about the person of the Judge, and about the righteousness and justice which he is to create. Finally we shall ask about the history of his own sufferings, and shall discover in Christ's descent into hell on the cross of God-forsakenness the most profound reason for the 'confession of hope' for the restoration of all things.

2. *The Return of the Doctrine of Universal Salvation*

'Universalism', '*apokatastasis panton*', 'universal salvation' or 'the restoration of all things' are all terms for the most disputed question in Christian eschatology. It is an eschatological question. But theologically it can be decided only in the framework of christology. The theologians of the mainline churches have always rejected these universalist doctrines and have condemned those who supported them. In his doctrine of salvation as an educative process, Origen wanted to see even the Devil ultimately redeemed; but he was unable to prevail. His doctrine was condemned in the patristic church, at the emperor's command.[204] Augustine won the day with his idea that out of all the lost – the *massa perditionis* of human beings – only a limited number of the elect (*numerus electorum*) would be redeemed. For the Lutheran churches, Article XVII of the Augsburg Confession declared: 'It is also taught among us that our Lord Jesus Christ will return on the last day for judgment and will raise up all the dead, to give eternal life and everlasting joy to believers and the elect but to condemn ugodly men and the devil to hell and eternal punishment.

Rejected, therefore, are the Anbaptists who teach that the devil and condemned men will not suffer eternal pain and torment' (in the Latin version: 'hominibus damnatis ac diabolis finem poenarum futurem esse'). The Confessio Helvetica posterior, Article XI, made a similar statement for the Calvinist churches. The Heidelberg Catechism, in answer to Question 52, adds a personal thought: '. . . to throw all his and mine enemies into everlasting pains, but to translate me with all his chosen unto himself, into celestial joys and everlasting glory.'

It was only in the seventeenth and eighteenth centuries that the rejected doctrine appeared once more in Protestantism, and when it emerged it was neither out of the humanism of the Enlightenment, nor from the Anabaptist sects, but – together with the millenarianism that had been equally rejected – out of early Pietism. It was his own biblicism, not secular humanism, that convinced the influential Württemberg theologian Johann Albrecht Bengel (1687–1752) of the truth of the doctrine of *apokatastasis*. There is certainly final judgment, and heaven and hell, but everything serves only the consummation of God's universal kingdom. Consequently the torments of hell are not everlasting; they are aeonically limited. Once God is 'all in all', there will be no more hells. Bengel's most important pupil, F. C. Oetinger (1702–1782), went on to develop both doctrines, millenarianism and 'the restoration of all things', making the whole of eschatology subject to God's resolve in Christ 'to unite all things in him, things in heaven and things on earth' (Eph.1; Col. 1). If election is the beginning of all God's ways, then the restoration of all things is its goal and end.[205] In the Hahn Community in Württemberg 'the restoration of all things' was held as 'central doctrine'. In the revival movement associated with Johann Christoph Blumhardt (1805–1880) and Christoph Blumhardt (1842–1919), universalism became 'the confession of hope'.[206] The expectation of Christ's imminent parousia, experiences of the present powers of the Spirit in healings of the sick, and hope for the whole world: all these belonged together here.[207] The Blumhardt movement in Württemberg inspired the 'religious socialists' Hermann Kutter and Leonhard Ragaz to combine hope for Christ's coming kingdom of peace on earth with active participation in the democratic, socialist, anticolonial and peace movements of the years before the First World War. They not only expected the final redemption of all human beings; they also looked for the restoration of all the things of nature in the new creation.[208]

Karl Barth took the futurist orientation of his early theology from the preaching of the Blumhardts,[209] as well as his later trend towards universalism. It was the dispute which Barth's old adversary, Emil Brunner, waged with him about universal salvation or a double outcome of judgment which brought the discussion into modern German theology: 'Barth goes far beyond all historical universalists. Scripture does not talk about universal reconciliation. On the contrary, it talks about judgment, and a double outcome of judgment: salvation or damnation. So the doctrine of universalism is the denial of judgment.'[210] Paul Althaus tried to mediate between the viewpoints: 'Christian eschatology cannot dispense with the idea of a possible double outcome of humanity's history, for Christ's sake and for the sake of conscience.' 'God's purpose with non-believers is a mystery.' Theologically it is therefore necessary, said Althaus, to preserve: first the idea and fear of being eternally lost; second, trust in the providence of God which will put everything to rights. There follows from this, thirdly, that 'We must think both thoughts, the idea of the double outcome and the idea of *apokatastasis*.[211] Gerhard Ebeling again follows Brunner when he says: 'The Bible speaks unanimously about a double outcome of the final event, using the symbols of heaven and hell . . . The idea of universal redemption, the *apokatastasis panton*, goes beyond what can be specifically said in the light of the situation before God, in favour of a harmonizing theory. What the end of evil will be is as hidden from us as is the explanation of its origin.'[212]

Before we discuss this question biblically and theologically, we must be clear about the general doubts and objections on both sides:

If *universalism* is proclaimed, is the result not the light-minded recklessness that says: why should I believe, and bother to lead a good and righteous life, if I and everyone else are going to be redeemed in any case? If we preach the redemption of all human beings, does the proclamation not really annul itself? Why is it necessary to preach what is going to happen anyway?

If *the double outcome of judgment* is proclaimed, the question is then: why did God create human beings if he is going to damn most of them in the end, and will only redeem the least part of them? Can God hate what he himself has created without hating himself? If salvation or damnation depends on a person's faith and righteousness, is God not then making his Judgment dependent on the will of human beings, thus really making himself dispensible?

3. The Dispute about the Bible:
Pro and Contra Universalism

In their dispute with Barth, Brunner and Ebeling appealed purely and simply to 'the scriptures' or 'the Bible', going on to reject the doctrine of universal salvation as speculative theology. Evangelical and fundamentalist theologians still argue in just the same way today. We shall first follow this argumentation, which claims to be 'true to the Bible', in order to see more precisely what it is saying, though without differentiating historically between the testimonies of scripture.

The expression *apokatastasis panton* is used only in Acts 3.21, where it describes 'the time for establishing all that God spoke by the mouth of his holy prophets from of old'. What is meant is the fulfilment of God's promises, but not universal salvation. Over against this, Eph. 1.10 says: '. . . to unite all things in Christ, things in heaven and things on earth', and with it Col.1.20: '. . . to reconcile to himself all things, whether on earth or in heaven, making peace by the blood of his cross.' In the cosmic christology of the Epistles to the Ephesians and the Colossians, not only all human beings and earthly creatures but the angels too – evidently the disobedient ones, since for the others it is unnecessary – will be reconciled through Christ. As reconciled, they will be gathered together under their head, Christ (who must here be understood as the personified Wisdom of Creation), and will thus be perfected. What is meant is nothing other than the restoration of all things, the homecoming of the universe in the form of what Irenaeus called the *recapitulatio mundi*.

The hymn extolling Christ in Philippians 2 also ends with the vision of the glorified universe in its peace and concord: '. . . that at the name of Jesus every knee should bow, in heaven and on earth and under the earth, and every tongue confess that Jesus Christ is Lord, to the glory of God the Father' (2.10f.). If Christ is made Pantocrator, nothing in his kingdom can be lost, all his enemies will be put under his feet (I Cor. 15.25), so that he can hand over to God the rule now consummated as his kingdom, that God may be 'all in all' (I Cor. 15.28). The great chapter on the resurrection, I Corinthians 15, makes no mention at all of a judgment with a double outcome. Paul builds up his Adam-Christ typology on the same pattern: 'As one man's trespass led to condemnation for all men, so one man's act of righteousness leads to acquittal and life for all men' (Rom.5.18), and consequently: 'As in Adam all die, so also in Christ shall all be made alive' (I Cor. 15.22). This universalism embraces 'Jews and Gentiles' without abolishing the difference between them, or reducing it to uniformity: 'God has consigned all men to disobedience, that he may have mercy upon all' (Rom. 11.32).

On the other hand the passages that talk about faith and disbelief do talk about a *double outcome of judgment*, especially in Matthew's Gospel:[213] Matt. 7.13f. distinguishes 'the way that leads to life' from 'the way that leads to destruction'. Matt. 12.32 says that 'the sin against the Holy Spirit' will not be forgiven, 'either in this age or in the age to come'. In Mark 16.16 we are told that 'he who believes and is baptized will be saved; but he who does not believe will be condemned'. Matthew 25 tells the parable of 'the wise and foolish virgins' and then presents the vision of the great Judgment of the Son of man (vv.31–46). To those on his left, the Son of man – Judge of the world says: 'Depart from me, you cursed, into the eternal fire prepared for the devil and his angels.' To those on his right he says: 'Come, O blessed of my Father, inherit the kingdom prepared for you from the foundation of the world.' The decision is made on the basis of what they have done for the poor and the hungry, for, says the Judge of the world: 'What you did to one of the least of these my brethren, you did to me.' Mark 9.45 also talks about 'hell', and Mark 9.48 speaks of the everlasting fire that 'is not quenched'. According to Luke 16.23, the rich man, Dives, goes to 'Hades, torment', whereas the poor man Lazarus is 'in Abraham's bosom'. The Gospel of John identifies faith with eternal life and disbelief with damnation: 'He who believes in the Son has eternal life: he who does not believe in the Son shall not see life, but the wrath of God rests upon him' (3.36). The person who does not believe 'will perish' (3.16). Paul also talks about a state of 'being lost' (*apoleia*) in Phil. 3.19; I Cor. 1.18; II Cor 2.15, and elsewhere.

Universal salvation *and* a double outcome of judgment are therefore both well attested biblically. So the decision for the one or the other cannot be made on the ground of 'scripture'. If one presupposes that scripture does not contradict itself, because the word of God to which it testifies is inerrant, one can then try to resolve the contradiction in the sense of the one side or the other.

Let us begin with the *resolution in the sense of the first side*, or postulate: There is indeed damnation, but is it eternal? The Greek word *aionios*, like the Hebrew word *olam*, means time without a fixed end, a long time, but not time that is 'eternal' in the absolute, timeless sense of Greek metaphysics. Consequently there are plurals *olamim* or *aiones*, which there cannot be for timeless eternity, because timeless eternity exists only in the singular. If damnation and the torments of hell are 'eternal', they are then aeonic, long-lasting, or End-time states. Only God himself is 'eternal' in the absolute sense, and 'unending' in the qualitative sense. According to Mark 9.49, hell-fire is a purifying fire – a corrective punishment. Salvation and damnation are a-symmetrical, according to Matthew 25: for the blessed, the kingdom has been prepared 'from the foundation of the world'; but fire has not been prepared for the damned 'from the foundation of the world', so it does not have to last until the end of the world either. Paul and John talk about 'being lost' only in the present tense, never in the future. So unbelievers are 'given up for lost' temporally and for the End-time, but not to all eternity. This being so, we can conclude with Walter Michaelis that what is said about judgment, damnation and 'everlasting death' is aeonic, and belongs to the End-time; it is not meant in an 'eternal' sense. For eschatologically, against the horizon of the ultimate, it is penultimate. The ultimate, the last thing is: 'Behold, I make *all things* new' (Rev. 21.5). In the new creation of heaven and earth there will be no more death, neither 'natural' death, nor 'the death of sin' nor 'everlasting death'. 'However strong or weak the testimony to universalism may be, it is the sole information which scripture offers us about the ultimate goal of God's salvific plan.'[214]

Let us try to find *the resolution in the sense of the second side*, or postulate. God certainly wants all human beings to be helped, but do they all really want to let themselves be helped? The biblical message is the proclamation of the gospel, with the goal of faith, but it is not a theory about the divine plan of salvation in world history and its possible end. We are supposed to decide, not to speculate. But if we speculate, we have to ask whether God's grace is still free grace if at the end all human beings are bound to be saved. Does this not make the decision for faith superfluous? Universalism makes God's grace cheap grace. It imposes bounds on God's freedom. It dissipates the finality of faith's decision. But 'it is appointed for men to die once, and after that comes judgment' (Heb. 9.27). If salvation is tied to faith, then all the universal statements in the New Testament must be related to God's good salvific intention, but not to the outcome of history. What is meant is the possibility of redemption, not its inevitable actuality. It is true that the word *aionios* does not mean the absolute eternity of God, but it does mean the irrevocability of the decision for faith or unbelief. Faith's experience that in the presence of the call to decision one is standing before God has as its corollary the finality of human decision. Consequently 'the double outcome' is the last word of the Last Judgment.

4. The Theological Argument about Universal Salvation or the Double Outcome of Judgment

Following a second train of thought, let us ask about the theological arguments for the one side and the other.

What speaks against a double outcome of Judgment is the experience that God's grace is more powerful than human sin. 'But where sin increased, grace abounded all the more' (Rom. 5.20). In God himself love outbalances wrath, for God is angered by human sin not *although* he loves human beings but *because* he loves them. He says No to sin because he says Yes to the sinner. He says a temporal No because in eternity he has said Yes to human beings, as the beings he has created, and his image. He judges the sins of the world so as to save the world. 'The Lord kills in order to bring to life. He brings down to hell and out again' (I Sam. 2.6). It is not his anger which is everlasting; it is his grace: 'His anger is but for a moment, and his favour is for a lifetime'(Ps. 30.5). God hates the sin, not the sinner; he loves the sinner, not the sin, said Augustine. God's judgment separates the sin from the person, condemns the sin and gives the person of the sinner a free pardon. The anger with which the righteous God condemns the unrighteousness which makes people cast themselves and this world into misery is nothing other than an expression of his passionate love.

For our problem, this means that the historical particularism of the divine election and rejection must serve the universalism of salvation. His 'Last Judgment' has no 'double outcome', but serves the universal establishment of the divine righteousness and justice, for the new creation of all things. The preponderance of God's grace over his anger, which is experienced in faith, means that Judgment and the reconciliation of the universe are not antitheses. The reconciliation of the universe comes about through the Judgment in which God reveals the righteousness that creates justice and puts things to rights, in order that he may gather all and everything into the realm of his glory.

What speaks against universalism is that – however he may deal with other creatures – the reconciling and righteous God desires to save human beings, at least, through faith. The surpassing power of God's grace is not a force of destiny, nor is it a compulsive power which disposes over people without asking them. It is the power of love which calls men and women to faith through the gospel, and entices them to free decision. God saves human beings not by overpowering them but by convincing them. In Christ and through the gospel he apparently descends to human beings to the very point of making his will to salvation dependent on their decision for faith. He lowers himself so much that he puts his glory in the hands of men and women. He is apparently dependent on mutuality, for he respects the free decision of human beings, their faith and their unfaith too, and gives to each of them in 'the Last Judgment' as they have believed – or not believed. That has nothing to do with vengeance or sadism: 'to each his own', the own that he or she has chosen – to believers salvation, to non-believers doom and disaster. The doctrine of universal salvation does not take the decision of faith as seriously as God does, when he wants to save men and women through 'the preaching of the foolishness of the cross'. Whereas universalism stresses the all-embracing totality of divine salvation, the doctrine of the double outcome of Judgment stresses the mutuality of God's salvation and human faith.

This really brings the question 'universalism or a double out-come of Judgment' down to the relationship between divine and human decision. The doctrine of universal salvation is the expression of a boundless confidence in God: what God wants to do he can do, and will do. If he wants all human beings to be helped, he will ultimately help all human beings. The doctrine of the double outcome of Judgment is the expression of a tremendous self-confidence on the part of human beings: if the decision 'faith or disbelief' has eternal significance, then eternal destiny, salvation or damnation, lies in the hands of human beings. What will happen to people in eternity really depends on their own be-haviour. God's function is reduced to the offer of salvation in the gospel, and to establishing acceptance or rejection at the Judgment. Christ becomes a person's Saviour only when that person has 'accepted' him in faith. So it is the acceptance in faith which makes Christ the Saviour of that man or that woman. But if this is so, do people not really save or damn themselves? The doctrine of the double outcome of Judgment is a relatively modern doctrine compared with the doctrine of universal salvation. It fits the modern age, in which human beings believe that they are the measure of all things, and the centre of the world, and that therefore everything depends on their decision. But what human being does this mean? Can children who die young, for example, decide for faith, or can the severely handicapped? Are they saved or lost?

Who makes the decision about the salvation of lost men and women, and where is the decision made? Every Christian theologian is bound to answer: *God* decides for a person and for his or her salvation, for otherwise there is no assurance of salvation at all. 'If God is for us, who can be against us . . .' (Rom. 8.31f.) – we may add: not even we ourselves! God *is* 'for us': that has been decided once and for all in the self-surrender and raising of Christ. It is not just a few of the elect who have been reconciled with God, but the whole cosmos (II Cor. 5.19). It is not just believers whom God loved, but the world (John 3.16). The great turning point from disaster to salvation took place on Golgotha; it does not just happen for the first time at the hour when we decide for faith, or are converted. Faith means experiencing and receiving this turning point personally, but faith is not the turning point itself. It is not my faith that creates salvation for me; salvation creates for me faith. If salvation and damnation were the results of human faith or unfaith, God would be dispensable. The connection between act and destiny, and the law of karma, would suffice to create the causal link. If, even where eternity is at stake, everyone were to forge their own happiness and dig their own graves, human beings would be their own God. It is only if a qualitative difference is made between God and human beings that God's decision and human decision can be valued and respected. God's decision 'for us', and our decisions for faith or disbelief no more belong on the same level than do eternity and time. We should be measuring God and the human being by the same yardstick if we were to ask: what, and how much, does God do for the salvation of human beings, and what, and how much, must human beings do? To see God and a human being on the same level means humanizing God and deifying the human being. 'Offer and acceptance' is a frequently used formula which brings divine grace and human decision on to the same level in just this way. The trivial slogan 'the church on offer'[215] turns God into the purveyor of a cheap offer in the religious supermarket of this society of ours, which has set out on the road to 'the global marketing of everything'. The customer is king, says a German tag. So then the customer would be God's king too.

5. Double Predestination or God's Universal Election?

To answer questions about the end with the presuppositions of the beginning was a favourite method in theology. It is therefore not surprising that the question about a double outcome of Judgment should be discussed most fully in the doctrine of predestination as it was developed in Calvinist theology. Let us look at the different answers.

(a) *Particularismus verus* (true particularism): Calvinist orthodoxy as it was taught by Beza and Gomarus, laid down in the Canons of Dort in 1618, and substantiated by the Leyden Synopsis of 1628, maintained the following doctrine: Before the creation of the world, God resolved to elect the one human being in Christ, but to reject the others because of their sins, in order to reveal in the one 'vessel' his fathomless grace, in the others his righteous wrath. Both 'vessels' serve the glorification of God.[216] But because in history who the elect are, and who the rejected, is hidden from us, God has the gospel proclaimed to all. To believers their election is *historically* revealed, as is their rejection to non-believers. At the Last Judgment the elect and the rejected will *finally* be revealed, for God's grace and his wrath will then be openly manifested. *Perseverantia usque ad finem* – perseverance to the end – therefore belongs to true faith, while real disbelief manifests a corresponding hardness of heart to the end.

According to this supralapsarian doctrine of predestination, God's decision about the salvation and damnation of human beings is not already revealed in Christ, nor is it revealed in the gospel. It is revealed provisionally in history, in faith and disbelief, but finally only at the Last Judgment. 'Experience teaches', Calvin had already argued, that the same gospel has a dual effect, evoking in the one faith, in the other disbelief, so that it divides human beings through the decision of faith. In this division God's eternal resolve becomes manifest and the double outcome of the Last Judgment anticipated, for – as Aristotle taught – what is last in execution is always the first in resolve. According to this doctrine of double predestination (*praedestinatio gemina*), God by no means desires that all human beings should be helped and that everything should be created anew; he created human beings only in order to have 'vessels' through which to reveal his grace and his anger, and thus to glorify himself in this antithetical way.

The deeper reason for this terrible doctrine of predestination is not to be found in theology at all; its location is aesthetics. Antitheses in art make for symmetry. Antitheses enhance clarity and beauty in God and human beings. That is the Aristotelian 'theorem of juxtaposition', which Augustine introduced into theology. 'Through God's decree, the beauty of the world is enhanced through contrasts. Truly, God would have created no human being, let alone an angel, whose future depravity he foresaw, had he not also known how he would use that being for the benefit of the good, in order thus to grace the order of the world, as one embellishes a poem through antitheses. What one calls antitheses are the most delightful among the adornments of language . . . Hence, just as such contrasts, when they are ranged against one another, make up the beauty of the style, so the beauty of the world is enriched through the contrasting of antitheses . . . For just as a painting has dark shadows in the proper place, so the totality of things, if we know how rightly to observe them, is beautiful even with sinners, although the sinners, if we see them for themselves, disfigure the picture through their ugliness.'[217]

If the aesthetic of juxtaposition is the inner motive for the doctrine of double predestination, then in actual fact this is a doctrine about the universalism of God's glorification. It then permits the following possibility of hearing in the No the divine Yes: The salvation of created beings is to be found solely in the glorification of God; if through disbelief I become the vessel of God's wrath, and through wrath God glorifies himself in me, then I too, castaway though I am, minister to his glorification and am, in a negative sense, in salvation. A truly Dostoievski-like, *resignatio-ad-infernum* argument![218]

(*b*) *Universalismus hypotheticus* (hypothetical universalism): This theory was developed by the Calvinist theologian Moyse Amyraut in the seventeenth century at the Huguenot Academy in Saumur.[219] He took up Calvin's idea about the *electio generalis*, according to which God has meant the gospel for everyone – that is to say has determined that everyone shall hear his word, even though he foresees that only a few will believe, and it is only believers whom he will save. The general proclamation of the gospel is a hypothetical universalism (*universalismus hypotheticus*), because the gospel can only save conditionally – that is to say, under the condition of faith. At the Last Judgment the eternal particularism of the divine election and rejection will then be manifest. God's good intention is therefore universal, but the outcome of history is particularist, as the dual effect of the gospel on believers and non-believers shows, even in the history of the universal proclamation.

(c) *Universalismus verus* (true or real universalism): This theory is maintained by the Calvinist theologian Friedrich Schleier-macher.[220] He sees the matter in exactly the opposite way: what is conditional is the particularism of the divine election of believers – what is unconditional is the universalism of salvation. The historical path to salvation proceeds by way of the divine election and rejection, but the eschatological goal is universal salvation. God *desires* to save everyone: that is the divine resolve; God *can* save everyone: that is his eternal and essential being; God *will* save everyone: that is the fulfilment of his resolve. Historical experience shows that God rejects in order to elect, that he casts into hell in order to save, that he gives people up for lost in order to gather them. He permits disbelief temporally, but his grace is in the end 'irresistible'. The human being cannot eternally maintain his unbelief contrary to God's love.[221]

(d) *Open universalism*: The new version of the doctrine of predestination put forward by Karl Barth led to a new eschatological prospect.[222] Before God chooses human beings or rejects them, he determines himself to be for these human beings their Creator, Reconciler and Redeemer. Predestination is in the first place God's determination of himself, before it becomes the determination of human beings. Consequently God's 'eternal resolve' is universal. It becomes manifest in Christ, in whom 'God in His free grace determines Himself for sinful man and sinful man for Himself. He therefore takes upon Himself the rejection of man with all its consequences, and elects man to participation in His own glory.'[223] Because this divine self-determination has taken place in eternity, this divine predestination must be understood as supralapsarian. Because in the crucified Christ God has taken upon himself the rejection of sinful men and women in order to give them his grace, this christological predestination must be understood as 'double predestination'. There is rejection and there is one who is rejected: Christ, who on the cross became sin for us and a curse, as Paul says, so that we might be saved. The resurrection of Christ manifests that universal rejection has been overcome by election, which applies equally universally to all human beings. Predestination does not mean a symmetry of Yes and No, electing and rejecting; it means the a-symmetry of a Yes, which proceeds out of the confuted No. Because Christ has borne 'the sins of the world' and the whole of rejection on the cross, all human beings are in Christ 'objectively' reconciled, whether they know it or not. Through faith they experience themselves subjectively as reconciled. It follows from this that a Christian can only view other people as those who have been reconciled in Christ. He cannot take the disbelief of others more seriously than the fact of their being reconciled with God. He can always only believe in the belief of the other person.[224]

The fundamental idea of this doctrine of universal election can already be found in Christoph Blumhardt, who strenuously resisted the compulsion towards symmetry in this question: 'They say: "If there is no everlasting torment then there is no everlasting bliss either." As if good and evil could ever be on a par with each other! Just because good is eternal, evil cannot possibly be eternal; because God's salvation is eternal, wretchedness can never be eternal . . . Because salvation is God's, everything that is not salvation comes to an end.'[225] This has a practical consequence: 'My father once wrote to me that I should make it a rule for myself at all times to view everyone as a believer, never to doubt it, and never to talk to a person in any other way. This found an echo in my own soul. If a Mohammedan comes, I call him a believer, I never accept that anyone is an unbeliever . . . Every human being believes, because God believes.'[226]

Barth's new version of the doctrine of predestination leads to an *open universalism* of salvation. There is no particularism in principle, and there is no automatic universalism. Believers expect that there will be 'an open multiplicity of the elect' and expect universal salvation for Christ's sake in 'the confession of hope'.[227] Their assurance of hope is no less than their assurance of faith; it is the other side of their assurance in Christ.

6. *Christ's Descent into Hell*
and the Restoration of All Things

If we follow the method of providing christological answers for eschatological questions, then in trying to measure the breadth of the Christian hope we must not wander off into far-off realms, but must submerge ourselves in the depths of Christ's death on the cross at Golgotha. It is only there that we find the certainty of reconciliation without limits, and the true ground for the hope for 'the restoration of all things', for universal salvation, and for the world newly created to become the eternal kingdom. It is only the person who understands what Christ suffered in his God-forsaken death who understands what, by virtue of his resurrection, is manifested in his present rule and in his future 'to judge both the quick and the dead'. In the crucified Christ we recognize *the Judge of the final Judgment*, who himself has become the one condemned, for the accused, in their stead and for their benefit. So at the Last Judgment we expect on the Judgment seat the One who was crucified for the reconciliation of the world, and no other judge. The person who in the history of Christ has experienced the righteousness of God which creates justice for those who suffer injustice, and which justifies the godless, knows what the justice is which at the Last Judgment will restore this ruined world and put everything to rights again: it is not retaliatory justice, Ulpian's *suam cuique*, to each his due – the justice that gives everyone their 'just deserts', which requites the wickedness of the wicked and repays the goodness of the good; it is the righteousness and justice of the God of Abraham, the Father of Jesus Christ, who creates justice, puts things to rights, and justifies.[228]

This means that the eschatological Last Judgment is not a prototype for the courts of kingdoms or empires. This Judgment has to do with God and his creative justice, and is quite different from the forms our earthly justice takes. What we call the Last Judgment is nothing other than the universal revelation of Jesus Christ, and the consummation of his redemptive work. No expiatory penal code will be applied in the court of the crucified Christ. No punishments of eternal death will be imposed. The final spread of the divine righteousness that creates justice serves the eternal kingdom of God, not the final restoration of a divine world order that has been infringed. Judgment at the end is not an end at all; it is the beginning.

Its goal is the restoration of all things for the building up of God's eternal kingdom.[229]

The *Christian* doctrine about the restoration of all things denies neither damnation nor hell. On the contrary: it assumes that in his suffering and dying Christ suffered the true and total hell of God-forsakenness for the reconciliation of the world, and experienced for us the true and total damnation of sin. It is precisely here that the divine reason for the reconciliation of the universe is to be found. It is not the optimistic dream of a purified humanity, it is Christ's descent into hell that is the ground for the confidence that nothing will be lost but that everything will be brought back again and gathered into the eternal kingdom of God. *The true Christian foundation for the hope of universal salvation is the theology of the cross, and the realistic consequence of the theology of the cross can only be the restoration of all things.*

In order to explain this thesis, let me take up Luther's teaching about Christ's descent into hell.

In his meditations, the young monk Luther exercised himself in profound trials such as Gabriel Biel had described and laid down. The first trial was the *tentatio de indignitate*: 'Am I, unworthy as I am, worthy of God's grace? How shall I become righteous before God?' The second trial is the *tentatio de particularitate*: 'Only a few will be chosen. Am I not one of the rejected?' In this trial, Johannes von Staupitz, the Vicar General of the Augustinian Order, to which Luther belonged, advised him that if he wished to wrestle with predestination he should begin with the wounds of Christ, after which the dispute about predestination would cease of itself: 'Si vis disputare de praedestinatione, incipe a vulneribus Christi, tunc cessabit simul omnis disputatio de praedestinatione.'[230] Luther followed this advice all his life. Even in 1542 he could still say: 'Why tormentest thou thyself with such speculations? Look upon the wounds of Christ – there thine election is assured for thee.'[231] Why? Because, according to Luther, in his forsakenness on the cross Christ suffered all the torments of hell, the rejection by God and eternal death, and did so vicariously for us, in our stead and for our benefit. The Christ dying on the cross was the most assailed and the most deeply rejected of all human beings. Because he suffered our rejection in his body, we perceive our election from his wounds.

When did Christ suffer hell for us, and what hell is it? Luther talks about Christ's descending into hell *before* his physical death on the cross, not afterwards. This is new, compared with tradition.[232] Here Calvin followed Luther.[233] The forsakenness of Christ between Gethsemane and Golgotha is the forsakenness of one who has been damned for all eternity. The prayer in Gethsemane which was not heard was the preparation for Christ's hellish torment. That is why sweat and blood fall from him on to the earth.[234] Luther says that he fell 'in gehenna et in inferno'.[235] When he was dying on the cross, what Christ experienced was not just God's present anger over the godless world, but his 'futuram iram, künftig hölle' too (future wrath, future hell).[236] Did Christ then descend to the realm of the dead after his death, in order to preach to the spirits in prison, as theological tradition said, following the Apostles' creed? Luther did not believe that hell was 'a special place'.[237] It was not a place anywhere in the world, not even in the underworld. It was an existential experience, the experience of God's anger and curse on sin and godless being. Christ suffered this hell on the cross in order to reconcile this world, damned as it is, with God. Here Luther is following Paul, for whom Christ 'was made sin' (II Cor. 5.21) for our reconciliation, and according to Gal. 3.13 even 'became a curse for us'. Those are the real 'pangs of death' (Acts 2.24) which God 'loosed' through the raising of Christ from the dead.

In the view that hell is not some remote place, but an existential experience, modern Protestant theologians follow Luther and Calvin. For Barth, the idea of Christ's descent into hell is 'the inner explanation of what happened outwardly in death and burial'.[238] According to Althaus, 'in his death [Jesus] also suffered hell, that is to say the satanic temptation of God-forsakenness, and overcame it for us, in that even here he remained the Son'.[239] Pannenberg thinks that Christ's 'descent into hell' is a way of expressing the universal significance of Jesus' accursed death, vicariously suffered.[240] I myself have said: 'Only if disaster, forsakenness by God, absolute death, the infinite curse of damnation and sinking into nothingness is gathered into God himself, is community with this God eternal salvation, infinite joy, indestructible election and divine life.'[241]

Christ's descent into hell therefore means: even in the experience of hell you are there (Ps. 139.8).

Christ's descent into hell means: you have suffered the experience of hell for us, so as to be beside us in our experiences of hell.

Christ's descent into hell means, finally: hell and death have been gathered up and ended in God: 'Death is swallowed up in victory. O

death where is thy victory? O death where is thy sting? But thanks be
to God, who gives us the victory through our Lord Jesus Christ'
(I Cor. 15.54f., 57).

In his moving 'Sermon on preparing for death' of 1519, Luther
explains: 'Thou must look upon hell and the eternity of torment, and
election too, not in thyself, not in themselves, not in those who are
damned, nor shouldst thou trouble thyself about the many in the
whole world who are not chosen . . . Look upon the heavenly picture
of Christ who for thy sake descended into hell and was forsaken by
God as one eternally damned, as he said on the cross, "O my God,
why hast thou forsaken me?" See, in that picture thy hell is
conquered, and thy uncertain election made sure . . . Seek thyself
only in Christ and not in thyself, so wilt thou eternally find thyself in
him.'[242]

By way of a deepened doctrine of Christ's descent into hell, Hans
Urs von Balthasar has tried in the spirit of Origen to mediate between
the universal assurance of salvation held by the Eastern Fathers of
the church, and the emotional emphasis on freedom of Western
theology. The godless are forsaken by God and in this sense
'damned'. They experience the hell they themselves have chosen. But
Christ's descent into hell says that even in their hell Christ is their
companion and brother. That is 'the solidarity of the dead Christ
with the dead'. 'In this way Christ disturbs the absolute solitariness
for which the sinner strives; the sinner who desires to be "damned"
away from God, finds God again in his solitariness, but God in the
absolute powerlessness of love, who in the Not-Time unpredictably
puts himself on the side of the one who damns himself.'[243] Balthasar
calls this the 'Easter Saturday* experience' of Christ, who in his
forsakenness by the Father experiences hell, because in pure
obedience he seeks the Father where he is not to be found, and
through his descent into hell takes hell and all those who are in it into
his trinitarian fellowship with the Father.[244]

Christ gave himself up for lost in order to seek all who are lost, and
to bring them home. He suffered the torments of hell, in order to
throw hell open, so that these torments are no longer without hope of
an end. Because he suffered hell, he give hope where otherwise 'all

---

*But the English name sees the 'Saturday' proleptically (in the light of Easter) and thus
does not bring out Balthasar's point. In German, Karfreitag (Good Friday) is followed
by Karsamstag – i.e., the 'Saturday' (the Roman, evil 'Saturn's day') is still under the
shadow of the cross. [Trans.]

hope must be abandoned', as Dante said. Because Christ was brought out of hell, the gates of hell are open, and its walls broken down. Through his sufferings Christ has destroyed hell.[245] Since his resurrection from his hellish death on the cross there is no longer any such thing as 'being damned for all eternity'.

What Christ *accomplished* in his dying and rising is *proclaimed* to all human beings through his gospel and will be *revealed* to everyone and everything at his appearance. What was suffered in the depths of the cross and overcome through suffering will be manifest through his parousia in glory. This inner connection between cross and parousia was already perceived by Johann Christoph Blumhardt when, in the Good Friday sermon he preached in Möttlingen in 1872, he proclaimed a 'general pardon': 'What the Lord Jesus endured there [i.e., on Golgotha] will be revealed again. For just because of this the Saviour has also acquired rights over this darkness, so that just here, here on the cross, the prospect is opened up for us that one day the point will be reached when every knee must bow, in heaven and on earth and under the earth, and every tongue confess that Jesus Christ is Lord to the glory of God the Father . . . Good Friday proclaims a general pardon to the whole world, and this general pardon is still to be revealed, for it was not for nothing that Jesus hung on the cross . . . We are moving towards a general pardon, and it will soon come! Anyone who is unable to think this greatest thing of all knows nothing about a Good Friday.'[246]

To make Christ's death on the cross the foundation for universal salvation and 'the restoration of all things' is to surmount the old dispute between the universal theology of grace and the particularist theology of faith. The all-reconciling love is not what Bonhoeffer called 'cheap grace'. It is grace through and through, and grace is always and only free and for nothing. But it is born out of the profound suffering of God and is the costliest thing that God can give: himself in his Son, who has become our Brother, and who draws us through our hells. It is costliest grace.

The question whether at the end all human beings, and even the Devil, will then really be redeemed, can receive a sure answer in 'the confession of hope':

'The confession of hope has completely slipped through the church's fingers . . . There can be no question of God's giving up anything or anyone in the whole world, either today or in eternity . . . The end has to be: Behold, everything is God's! Jesus comes as the one who has borne the sins of the world. Jesus can judge but not condemn. My desire is to have preached this as far as the lowest circles of hell, and I will never be confounded.'[247]

The eschatological point of the proclamation of 'the Last Judgment' is the redeeming kingdom of God. Judgment is the side of the eternal kingdom that is turned towards history. In that Judgment all sins, every wickedness and every act of violence, the whole injustice of this murderous and suffering world, will be condemned and annihilated, because God's verdict effects what it pronounces. In the divine Judgment all sinners, the wicked and the violent, the murderers and the children of Satan, the Devil and the fallen angels will be liberated and saved from their deadly perdition through transformation into their true, created being, because God remains true to himself, and does not give up what he has once created and affirmed, or allow it to be lost.

'The Last Judgment' is not a terror. In the truth of Christ it is the most wonderful thing that can be proclaimed to men and women. It is a source of endlessly consoling joy to know, not just that the murderers will finally fail to triumph over their victims, but that they cannot in eternity even remain the murderers of their victims. The eschatological doctrine about the restoration of all things has these two sides: *God's Judgment,* which puts things to rights, and *God's kingdom,* which awakens to new life.

IV

New Heaven – New Earth

Cosmic Eschatology

IV

New Heaven – New Earth

Cosmic Eschatology

Christian eschatology must be broadened out into cosmic eschatology, for otherwise it becomes a gnostic doctrine of redemption, and is bound to teach, no longer the redemption of the world but a redemption from the world, no longer the redemption of the body but a deliverance of the soul from the body. But men and women are not aspirants for angelic status, whose home is in heaven and who feel that on this earth they are in exile. They are creatures of flesh and blood. Their eschatological future is a human and earthly future – 'the resurrection of the dead and the life of the world to come'. According to Christian understanding, the Redeemer is no other than the Creator. He would contradict himself if he were not to redeem everything he has made. The God who created the universe will one day be 'all in all' (I Cor. 15.28). Why else should he have created everything? Cosmic eschatology is not required for the sake of some 'universalism' or other; it is necessary for God's sake. There are not two Gods, a Creator God and a Redeemer God. There is one God. It is for his sake that the unity of redemption and creation has to be thought.

In the scientific and technological civilization of modern times, the programme of a cosmic eschatology runs up against considerable difficulties, for the cosmos, both as a whole and in all its different sectors, has become the object of the natural sciences. Since these are bound to proceed agnostically in their methods, they permit no theological statements to be made within their own sphere, either about the beginning of the cosmos or about its end. It was therefore understandable that modern theology should have withdrawn from the sector 'nature' and should have concentrated on the sector 'history' and, within the sector history, should have concentrated on its innermost side, human existence. In this process nothing split apart more widely than cosmology and eschatology. But without cosmology, eschatology must inevitably turn into a gnostic myth of redemption, as modern existentialism shows.[1]

Yet the separation between the spheres of private existence on the one hand and real history on the other, and between human history and non-human nature, is an artificial split, and it cannot practically be maintained. Human existence is bodily existence and is linked, with all the senses, to the natural world on which it is dependent. Human life is participation in nature. The world of the living, of the earth, the solar system, our galaxy and the cosmos is the condition for our human world too, for it is in this world that our human world is embedded. Because there is no such thing as a soul separate from the body, and no humanity detached from nature – from life, the earth and the cosmos – there is no redemption for human beings either without the redemption of nature. The redemption of humanity is aligned towards a humanity whose existence is still conjoined with nature. Consequently it is impossible to conceive of any salvation for men and women without 'a new heaven and a new earth'. There can be no eternal life for human beings without the change in the cosmic conditions of life.

The difficulties about not just *hoping* this but *thinking* it too are considerable. We have some comprehensive attempts at thinking eschatology and cosmology together: Teilhard de Chardin brought the two into alignment with the help of the concept of evolution, and developed a purposeful metaphysics of the 'Omega Point'.[2] With his process philosophy, A.N. Whitehead offered theologians and scientists the possibility of a common philosophical platform where, for process theologians, an eschatology of world process then also became conceivable.[3] Ernst Bloch expanded his philosophy of hope, which was first historically orientated, to take in 'nature as subject', developing the Romantic philosophy of nature earlier held by F. W. J. Schelling and F. von Baader.[4] Carl Friedrich von Weizsäcker and Georg Picht worked out a scientifically verifiable and philosophically reasoned 'history of nature' in which the spheres of nature and history, which had hitherto been separated, were linked through the experience of nature in the context of time.[5] If the context or horizon of time is viewed as dominant both for the experience of history and for the experience of nature, then the question about the eschatology of time confronts us simply of itself.

In *God in Creation* I tried to understand 'creation in the beginning' as temporal, and therefore as a 'system' open to history and the future. I now have to consider the transition from the temporal to the eternal creation, in order to understand 'creation in the consummation'. In §§ 3 and 4 of the present chapter – the sections on 'The End of Time in the Eternity of God', and 'The End of Space in the Presence of God' – I am presupposing Chapter V of that earlier book on 'The Time of Creation', and Chapter VI on 'The Space of Creation'.

In *The Way of Jesus Christ*, Chapter VI, I discussed ideas about 'the cosmic Christ' and their practical consequences, so I shall not take up this cosmic christology again here, but shall presuppose it. In *The Spirit of Life* I entered in detail into the unity of the Creator Spirit and the Spirit of Creation. I am picking up this train of thought once more here, in the account of God's eschatological Shekinah: the new world as 'God's home'.

I do not propose to make the pointless attempt to develop a scientific eschatology, in order either to affirm or confute scientific ideas about the end of the world – the world's death through cold, or its collapse in the cosmic melting crucible – as religious creationism has tried to do with evolutionary theory and the notion of the Big Bang. Earlier ideas about the infinity of the universe are as far removed from theological eschatology as are more modern ideas about the end of the universe. What I should like to do, however, is to work out the tangents, or points of access, for the dialogue with scientific theories, and hope that I may be successful where the concept of time and the concept of space are concerned. Christian eschatology has its foundation in the experience of Christ's death and resurrection. Cosmic eschatology also belongs within the framework of this remembered hope for Christ: the death and raising of the universe are the prelude to the expected new creation of all things and 'the new heaven and the new earth'.

§1 THE FUTURE OF CREATION – SABBATH AND SHEKINAH

The first fundamental decision of cosmic eschatology is made in the context of the question: should redemption be understood in the light of creation, or creation in the light of redemption?[6]

In the first case creation was from the beginning perfect. Human sin spoilt it. Grace is the divine expedient designed to remedy the predicament of sin. And at the end the goodly, primal creation will be restored as it in truth always was and will be: eschatology is the doctrine of the *restitutio in integrum*, the return to the pristine beginning. In the second case, creation-in-the-beginning is the creation of a history of God's which will arrive at its goal only in 'the new creation of all things' and the universal indwelling of God in that creation. In the first case there is an eschatological hope for redemption only because of sin and its destructive consequences. In the second case the hope for the eschatological consummation of creation takes us beyond the redemption from sin and its consequences. In the first case we end up with a restorative interpretation of eschatology. In the second case we arrive at an eschatological interpretation of creation: *incipit vita nova* – here a new life begins.

It is the first interpretation of cosmic eschatology which has been passed down to us by the theological tradition of the Western church. Our very word 'creation' makes us think of a process that is finished and done with, and its result. If we hear the word 'creation', we involuntarily think of the primordial state of the world, and the beginning of all things, and we imagine a condition once-produced, finished, complete in itself, and perfect: creation means the primal state and paradise. Dogmatic tradition then also called Adam's condition in paradise the *status integritatis* – the state of virgin purity. As a being whose creation was 'very good', he possessed *iustitia et sanctitas originalis*, original righteousness and holiness.[7] The first human beings were driven out of this perfect primal condition because of their sins; to this unmarred primal condition redemptive grace will bring them back again. This idea about the final return to a lost paradise follows us even in our hymns. So at Christmas, we are exhorted in 'Christians awake!' to

> Tread in His steps, assisted by his grace,
> Till man's first heavenly state again takes place.[7a]

The Christian drama of salvation has these two sides, and we find them right down to von Balthasar's *Theo-Drama*: (1) the path of the sinner into the far country: *Paradise Lost*; (2) the return home of those who have been pardoned: *Paradise Regained*.[8] Sin perverts the good creation, grace restores it; at the end, there is creation once more, just as it was originally: 'Behold, it is very good.'[9]

But this drama of redemption is closer to the myths of origin told in many cultures than it is to Israel's story of creation. It is 'the myth of the eternal return'[10] in the form of the myth of the eternal regeneration of the time that has grown old, is worn out and dying, a myth played out in the New Year festivals. We still talk about the New Year, although it is, after all, only the 'next' year that is coming, and even if it is just the next day that is beginning, we still sing:

> Morning has broken
> like the first morning . . .[10a]

The mythical notion about the circular course of time dominated Christian theology's subconscious too: the end corresponds to the beginning, and the last to the first. That is why everything finally returns to the point of departure. It was in this sense that Aquinas wrote: 'The end of things corresponds to the beginning. For God is the beginning and end of things. Consequently the emergence of things from their beginning corresponds to the restoration of things at the end' ('Finis rerum respondet principio. Deus enim est principium et finis rerum. Ergo et exitus rerum a principio respondet reductioni rerum in finem.')[11] Just as everything proceeds from the one God, so everything returns to the one God again. Way out and way in correspond. So the time of the world as a whole takes the form of the *circulatio*, the circle. If the end corresponds to the beginning, and if this beginning returns again in the end, then the time of the world has a splendid symmetrical conformation. What happens at the end can then only be the 'restoration' of the beginning.[12]

Strictly speaking, this circle of the Christian drama of redemption would have to repeat itself to all eternity. The restoration of the original creation would have to be followed by the next Fall, and by the next redemption – the return of the same thing without end. The Stoic and Hindu cosmologies of the endlessly recurring ages of the world do in fact teach precisely that. But the uniqueness and finality of the history of Christ, which is expressed in the Pauline *ephapax*, the 'once and for all' (Rom. 6.10), disallows the idea of the eternal return of the same thing. In order to preserve this finality in cosmology, and thus to make eschatology thinkable at all, liberation, both individual and cosmic, must hold within itself the experience of an *added value* over against sin, an added value which excludes the next Fall after the restoration of creation. If where sin has increased grace 'abounds all the more' (Rom. 5.20), then this added value of grace is its power to end, not just actual sin, but even the possibility of sinning, not just actual death but even the being-able-to-die, as Augustine said.[13]

If this is correct, then the hope grounded on the experience of liberation is not directed to the 'restoration' of the original creation. What it looks for is creation's final consummation. The experience of liberation from the power of sin leads to a hope for the perfecting of creation in glory. This end does, no doubt, 'correspond' to the beginning insasmuch as the beginning is completed, and is not replaced by something different. But the end is much more than the beginning. The outreach of hope at the end extends far further than at the beginning.[14] If we call the end 'the completion' of creation, then in this light creation at the beginning appears as 'incomplete', that is to say it is a creation that has only been begun. The verdict on creation that it was 'very good' does not mean that it was in the Greek sense perfect and without any future; the Hebrew means that it was fitting, appropriate, corresponding to the Creator's will. The accounts of creation-in-the-beginning do not as yet talk about a creation in the glory of God. Only the sabbath of creation is more than 'very good'. It is 'hallowed', 'sanctified', and therefore points to creation's future glory. The sabbath is, as it were, the promise of future consummation built into the initial creation.

Through the doctrine of creation out of nothing (*creatio ex nihilo*), theological tradition has always taught the contingency of creation. But it has not stressed to the same degree that the contingent creation is *a creation in time* and must therefore be understood in the context of time. According to the *restitutio in integrum* model, history begins only with the Fall. With the Fall time begins, and when the original creation is restored, time ends. But Augustine was right when he did not see creation as beginning *in time*, but let time begin *with creation*.[15] If God created the world not *in* time but *with* time, then creation is a *creatio mutabilis*, a creation subject to change, and a system open to the future, not a closed system complete in itself. And – although Augustine did not in fact draw this conclusion – this creation is then a temporal one, not yet an eternal creation.[16] As a *temporal creation* it is projected towards a future in which it is to become an *eternal creation*.[17] Its temporality is itself the true promise of its eternity, for eternity is the fulness of time, not timelessness. If the beginning of creation is also the beginning of time, then time begins with the future out of which the present comes into being.

In *personal* eschatology the consummation of temporal creation is the transition from what is temporal into eternal life, in *historical* eschatology it is the transition from history into the eternal kingdom, and in *cosmic* eschatology it is the transition from temporal creation to the new creation of an eternal 'deified' world.[18] It is for this fulfilment that all things have been created. This consummation of what is temporal in the eternal creation includes the redemption from sin, death and annihilation, but it is not simply congruent with that, or absorbed by it. Even without sin, creation would have been completed. The completion of creation ministers to glory, in that grace liberates from the destructive power of sin.

The consummation of creation is something *new* over against creation-in-the-beginning. According to Rev. 21.4, with the 'new heaven and the new earth' 'the first things' are past. 'The first heaven and the first earth had passed away' (21.1). Thus eschatology is tuned to the keynote of 'the new thing': *incipit vita nova* – a new life begins. And yet what takes the place of heaven and earth is not something quite different. On the contrary, the new creation presupposes the old one; it is the *new* creation of all things. 'Behold, I make all things new' (21.5) means that nothing passes away or is lost, but that everything is brought back again in new form. The *creatio ex nihilo*, the creation out of nothing, is completed in the eschatological *creatio ex vetere*, the creation out of the old. In so far the keynote to which eschatology is tuned is a making-present and a return, not as a *restitutio in integrum*, a return to the beginning, but certainly as a *renovatio omnium*, a renewal of all things. The important point is to link the eschatological category *novum* with the anamnetic category of repetition in such a way that the beginning is gathered up into the end, and the consummation brings back everything that had ever been before.

What is the difference between the beginning and the consummation of creation, and what distinguishes 'the first heaven and the first earth' from 'the new heaven and the new earth'? It is the different presence of the Creator in the community of those he has created. Creation-in-the-beginning is 'finished' (Gen. 2.2) in *God's sabbath*.[19] God blesses all the works of his creation through his resting presence in them. All six days point to the seventh day, and everything that is created is created for this festival of the Creator's, and is blessed in it. But the creation is created anew so that it may embrace 'the new Jerusalem' and become the home of God's Shekinah (Isa. 65; Ezek. 37; Rev. 21).[20] The sabbath in the time of the first creation links this world and the world to come. It is *the presence of God* in the *time* of those he has created or, to put it more precisely, the dynamic presence of eternity in time, which links beginning and end, thus awakening remembrance and hope. The eschatological indwelling of God in 'the new heaven and the new earth' is *the presence of God* in the *space* of his created beings. That which went up with Israel out of bondage in Egypt, that which found a temporally restricted dwelling in Jerusalem on Mount Zion – that very same presence will fill and interpenetrate the great spaces of creation, 'heaven and earth', and will bring to all heavenly and earthly creatures eternal life and perfect justice and righteousness: God's Shekinah.

We can continue to relate the two ideas to one another: the weekly sabbath, with the sabbath year, is God's homeless Shekinah in the time of exile from Jerusalem, and in the far country of this world, estranged from God. The eschatological Shekinah is the perfected sabbath in the spaces of the world. Sabbath and Shekinah are related to each other as promise and fulfilment, beginning and completion. In the sabbath, creation holds within itself from the beginning the true promise of its consummation. In the eschatological Shekinah, the new creation takes the whole of the first creation into itself, as its own harbinger and prelude, and completes it. Creation begins with time and is completed in space. The temporality of the first creation is itself its promise, and its openness for the new, eternal creation.

The inner unity of sabbath and Shekinah is to be found in the *menuhah*, the rest to which God came on the sabbath of creation and which he seeks when he desires to dwell in his creation. It does not only mean the end of God's creative and historical unrest; it is also in the positive sense the eternal bliss and eternal peace of God himself. That is why this repose of God's is often linked with 'God's desire'. That is the divine eschatology.[21] Psalm 132.13f. shows the connection between sabbath and Shekinah: 'The Lord has chosen Zion; he has desired it for his habitation; "This is my resting place for ever; here will I dwell".'

The presence of God can be imagined in different ways: as a place of glory, as a place where God lets his name dwell, as footstool for the God who is enthroned in heaven.[22] The indwelling of God on

Zion should not be understood in an exclusive sense. Remembering the Ark of the Covenant which moved with the people, Israel always talked about God's dwelling 'in the midst of the people of Israel' (Ezek. 43.7). That is why Israel could sense the nearness of his Shekinah even in exile. It was that above all that led to the developing sanctification of the sabbath. In place of the ruined temple in Jerusalem, Israel had the sabbath as 'palace in time'.[23] The presence of God in space is transferred to his presence in time. That is why the sabbath in time thrusts forward to God's End-time Shekinah.

The New Testament's statements about the incarnation should also be understood in this framework, the framework of the remembered sabbath expectations of God's future Shekinah, which will fill heaven and earth. Gal. 4.4f. sees 'the fulfilment of time' in the sending of the Son. John 1.14 says of the same event: 'The Word became flesh and *dwelt* among us.' The indwelling of the eternal Word of God in our flesh is the fulfilment of time and, conversely, time 'fulfils itself' where this final Shekinah of God's comes about. When, according to Luke 4.18ff., in his first sermon in Nazareth, Jesus proclaims the 'fulfilment' of scripture and the messianic sabbath – 'the acceptable year of the Lord' – the authority of his proclamation is founded on the Shekinah of God's Spirit within him. It was because of this that he could call to himself 'the weary and heavy-laden' so as to 'refresh' them, and to communicate to them the divine *menuhah* which fulfils God's sabbath and his Shekinah. For the Easter community of Christians, God already 'dwells' in this godless world in the form of the crucified Christ, while in the form of the risen One he anticipates through the presence of his Spirit his universal Shekinah in the new creation. Through the forgiveness of sins and the liberation from the power of sin, men and women again become vessels for the indwelling of God's Spirit, and are filled with hope for that new creation which God will universally indwell, and in which he will be universally present.

§2 THE ANNIHILATION OF THE WORLD OR ITS CONSUMMATION?

Let us now look critically at the great ideas about the eschatology of the world held in the different Christian traditions, and then turn to the images of 'the new earth'. At first sight it is astonishing that ideas about the *consummatio mundi*, the consummation of the world, should range so widely, from the total *annihilation* of the world according to orthodox Lutheranism, its total *transformation* according to patristic and Calvinist tradition, to the world's glorious *deification*, the view of Orthodox theology. Is it just that different aspects of the end are stressed in each given case? Or is it a matter of mutually exclusive ideas? If it is the latter, we have to ask which idea corresponds to the christological interpretative framework presented by Christ's cross and resurrection.

1. The Annihilation of the World

'Transformation, not annihilation – that is the unanimously held doctrine from Irenaeus onwards, by way of Augustine and Gregory the Great, Aquinas and the whole of mediaeval theology, down to present-day Catholic dogmatics.'[24] In Lutheran orthodoxy, on the other hand, for the hundred years following the second eucharistic dispute, and with the justification provided by Johann Gerhard's theology, the unanimous view was that annihilation, not transformation, is the ultimate destiny of the world.[25] How was this exterminist annihilation of the world conceived of, and why was it taught?

'The Last Judgment will then be followed by the complete end of this world. Except for angels and human beings, everything belonging to this world will be burnt with fire and will dissolve into nothingness. What must be expected, therefore, is not the world's transformation, but a complete cessation of its substances.'[26] The biblical passage cited in evidence is II Peter 3.12. In theological justification it is explained that the blessed angels and believing human beings, as the image of God, will then be absorbed wholly into the beatific vision, in which God will be seen 'face to face'; they will therefore have no further need of the created mediations and sensory perceptions of God in parables and images.[27] They will no longer require the created environments of heaven and earth, because God himself will have become their environment, and they will be wholly in God. If God himself is the eschatological salvation of believers, and if this eschatological salvation is designed only for those created in God's image, and not for the whole creation, then blessedness must indeed be thought of as devoid of any world.[28] And the inevitable conclusion is that the world must be judged unblessed. It is a scaffolding, so to speak, and since it is no longer needed in the state of blessedness, it will be 'burnt'. Blessedness consists solely in the eternal contemplation of God. Its place is heaven. This 'heaven of the blessed' will then become the new environment for human beings. And this heaven is to be found where God is.

Which 'world' is it that is destined for eschatological annihilation? According to the apocalyptic doctrine of aeons, it must be 'this world(time)' of injustice and death. 'The form of this world passes away' (I Cor. 7.31). Those imprisoned by the powers and compulsions of 'this world(time)' will be freed by the gospel and faith. So they hope for the final destruction of the prison of 'this world(time)'. For this the New Testament uses the word 'cosmos', a word never applied to the new creation of heaven and earth.[29] If, in line with biblical usage, we distinguish between God's good creation and the world-times of this creation, we then have to ask: is *the form* of this world going to be destroyed, or will this world as God's creation perish too – is it a *form* of this world that will be annihilated, or its substance as well? The Lutheran theologians of the seventeenth century did not think just of the passing away of 'this (world)time'; they contemplated the annihilation of the earthly creation too. The world was created as heaven and earth, but all that will be left is the heaven of the saved and the hell of the damned. The earth will be dropped as irrelevant, and will be annihilated. 'Annihilation' does not just mean the destruction of a godless form of the world. It means its literal *reductio in nihilum*, its reduction to nothing, as the converse of its *creatio ex nihilo*, its creation out of nothing.[30] If creation was originally the movement from non-being to being, this eschatology becomes the movement from being to non-being. According to our vocabulary, this must be called exterminist, not apocalyptist. It has been preserved in two lines of Paul Gerhardt's which at first sight seem innocent enough: 'Himmel und Erde, die müssen das werden, / was sie vor ihrer Erschaffung gewest' ('Heaven and earth must once more be / what they were 'fore their creation'). But what were they before their creation? Just – nothing.

The following arguments may be levelled against the Lutheran doctrine of the world's annihilation:

1. The salvation of created beings is to be found in the world that accords with God and the life that accords with God, just because God himself, in his integral and undisguised presence, is their salvation. The soteriological theocentricism of Lutheran theology

must not therefore be permitted to lead to an anthropocentricism stripped of world and body, for the very reason that God would then no longer be the Creator.

2. The 'form of this world' which is destined to pass away is the God-controverting form of the creation which in itself is destined for correspondence to God. If men and women are 'freed from the godless ties of this world' then they are intended for 'grateful service to God's creatures'.[31] The annihilation of the godless powers and compulsions of 'this world(time)' therefore ministers, not to the annihilation of the world, but to its new creation in the righteousness and justice that corresponds to God. Most modern Lutheran theologians have reverted to the patristic and mediaeval hope for 'transformation, not annihilation', and thus to Luther himself.

3. Finally, the idea of 'the resurrection of the body' is lost completely if salvation is supposed to consist only of the blissful beatific vision of the disembodied soul. But once this hope is lost in eschatology, the idea of the incarnation cannot be maintained in christology either. And if that is surrendered, the Christian faith becomes a world-denying, world-despising gnosticism. Anyone who teaches the annihilation of the world eschatologically, would like to call off creation, and would seem to be more fascinated by nothingness than by existence. The covenant with Noah already speaks against this withdrawal from creation: '. . . never more shall the world be destroyed . . .' (Gen. 9.11).

2. *Transformation of the World*

Whereas the Lutheran theology of the seventeenth century maintained *God's total freedom* towards his creation and its laws, Calvinist theology in the same century held fast to *God's steadfast faithfulness* to his creation and its laws.[32] There can therefore be no annihilation of the world, only its transformation. 'After Judgment, the end of *this* world . . . will come about, inasmuch as God will destroy the present condition of that same world through fire; but that does not mean that he will annihilate the world, but that he will make out of the old world a world that is new, a new heaven and a new earth whose nature will be imperishable.'[33] Consequently it is not just the souls of believers that will be glorified, but their bodies too, since it is not just the soul that God has received into his covenant of grace but the body also. The covenant of grace in history is 'the servant form of the kingdom of God' in this world of sin and death. It will cease when sin is wholly overcome and God glorifies himself in all his fulness. That will be when the crucified Christ is manifested to all the world as the righteous One, and the servant form of God's kingdom becomes its glorified form. The raising of the dead will take place at Christ's 'second coming' and is a new creative act of God's in and for the dead which 'will reunite'[34] every soul with the body in which it lived here on earth. The Reformed tradition called the unity of innovation and identity *transformatio mundi*, the transformation of the world. It never used this term in an eschatological sense. The *annihilatio mundi*, the annihilation of the world, is comprised in its transformation, because the new creation of heaven and earth presupposes the annihilation of the world's present condition. But the transformation presupposes the world's identity as God's creation, since otherwise something quite different – or nothingness – would have to take creation's place. Correspondingly, the raising of the dead must be understood as a new, creative act of God's in and for the dead, and thus at the same time as the transformation of the dead into eternal life.

Like patristic theology, Calvinist theology sees the positive side of the eschatological transformation in *transfiguratio mundi*, the transfiguration of the world. In the new bodiliness of the saved there will be a glorification in the communication of eternal, intransient life, for they will be made like in form to 'Christ's glorious body' (Phil. 3.21). Calvinist theology sees a continuity between *the grace of Christ* experienced in history and *the glory of Christ* expected in the consummation. In individual believers too there are seeds of eternal life, which will there grow up to their fulness. Consequently even the end of the world cannot be total annihilation and new creation. It can only be a transformation out of transience into eternity. This is also indicated by the verb used in Rev. 21.5 – not *'Behold, I will create'* (Hebrew *barah*), but 'I will *make* (Hebrew *asah*) all things new'. The divine 'making' is a forming and shaping of that which has been 'created'.

In criticism of this Calvinist doctrine of the transformation of the world the following arguments have to be considered:

Is it really only the *form* of this perverted world-time *as it actually exists* that is annihilated? Surely the temporal possibility for this perversion of the form of the world must be annihilated too, if a new aeon of this world is to be created which is imperishable and no longer corruptible? But in that case the end of the world will not touch only the form of the world, but its substance too, as a temporal creation capable of sin and death. If the new creation is to be an imperishable and eternal creation, it must be new not only over against the world of sin and death, but over against the first, temporal creation too. The substantial conditions of creaturely existence itself must be changed. The expression transformation (*transformatio*) does not penetrate deeply enough for this change in the foundations of the world to be grasped. It is essential to bring out the point that the eschatological transformation of the world means a *fundamental* transformation, that is to say a transformation in the transcendental conditions of the world itself, and therefore of its very foundation: God himself changes his relationship to the world. God's *faithfulness* to his once created world cannot therefore limit his *freedom* to complete and perfect his temporal creation, making it a creation that is eternal – and thus changing creation's fundamental conditions.

3. The Deification of the World

The idea of the deification of the world maintained in the Orthodox churches of the East goes beyond Western and Calvinist ideas about the world's transfiguring transformation. Initially this idea merely extends the patristic church's so-called 'doctrine of physical redemption' to embrace the whole cosmos. 'God became human so that we human beings might be deified', says Athanasius's famous axiom.[35] This does not mean that human beings will 'become like God' in the way promised by the serpent in the Garden of Eden story. What the axiom is asserting is the divine sonship and daughterhood which Paul ascribes to believers. If being the child of God is meant in a more than metaphorical sense, it implies kinship to God. The children are of the same nature as their father and mother. Even if they are adopted, they acquire the full rights of inheritance. They become partakers of the divine nature. 'Deification' therefore does not mean that human beings are transformed into gods. It means that they partake of the characteristics and rights of the divine nature through their community with Christ, the God-human being. The divine characteristics of non-transience and immortality therefore become benefits of salvation for human beings. The conquest of death is at the centre of the patristic church's doctrine of salvation, although the conquest of sin is of course thereby included.

How does this anthropological doctrine come to be extended into a cosmological doctrine of deification? Orthodox theology has never made as rigorous a distinction between person and nature as has modern Western theology. 'According to our belief, every human person is in a certain sense a hypostasis of the whole of cosmic nature, though of course always in close association with other created beings.'[36] The consequence is a double link: on the one hand, all human persons share in the same cosmic nature; on the other hand human hypostases exist within the community of all other created beings. It follows from the hypostatic bond between person and nature that if the person is redeemed, transfigured and deified, nature is redeemed, transfigured and deified too. 'The whole of nature is destined for glory.'[37] The redemption of human beings draws in its wake the redemption of nature. The key to the hypostatic link between the human person and cosmic nature is the human body. If it is not just the soul that is created in the image of God but the body too, then salvation lies in the 'transfiguration' of the body, as Orthodox theology finds it disclosed in the light that shone on Tabor – the light that flooded Jesus on the Mount of the Transfiguration: 'His face shone like the sun, and his garments became white as light' (Matt. 17.2). Through a transfiguration of human bodiliness such as this, the whole of nature is gathered into the fellowship of transformed, transfigured humanity. 'The divine Spirit, which in all its fulness is poured out from Christ on those who believe in him, whose spirits are thereby kindled anew, does not fill only their bodies with new life, making them transparent for what is heavenly, but transforms nature and the cosmos too.'[38]

Orthodox theology did not take this further step – but the transfiguration of the cosmos really leads to the idea that the whole cosmos then becomes *imago Dei*, God's image. In the biblical tradition, being in the image of God is always bound up with the glory of God. In the sin that contraverts God, the sinner loses this divine glory (Rom. 3.23). With redemption from sin, the splendour of this glory returns. If the redemption of sighing creation from transience is also linked with the redemption from sin, then the whole redeemed creation enters into the light of God's truth and is deified. To be in the image of God is not something that divides human beings from non-human nature. It is the very thing that binds them hypostatically to all the living and the whole cosmos.

In a critical evaluation of the Orthodox idea about the deification of the cosmos, the following must be considered:

The hypostatic unity of nature and person does certainly offer a solution for the modern separation between the person as subject and nature as object. Whatever happens to the person touches nature too; whatever redeems the person, also redeems nature. Any redemption of human beings without the redemption of cosmic nature is therefore inconceivable. But the deification of the cosmos is not thought of as being a new creation of heaven and earth. It is seen as a spiritualization of the cosmos and its interpenetration by the radiance of the Spirit. That lends an element of docetism to the doctrine of cosmic deification held by the Orthodox churches, and to their spirituality. But is the 'completely spiritualized world' brought about through the union of human beings with God already 'the new earth' and the new bodiliness of God's Shekinah?

Which of these ideas about the end of the world is most in accord with the christological interpretative framework of Christ's death and resurrection? The Lutheran doctrine of the annihilation of the world seems to have as its premise a one-sided theology of the cross. The Orthodox doctrine of deification, on the other hand, corresponds to a one-sided theology of the resurrection. The Calvinist theory of transformation could be the mediation between perspectives directed severally towards the end of 'this world', and the genesis of a 'new world' that will accord with God and thus be deified. But Calvinist theology has never in its history been able to attain either to the depths of the Lutheran theology of the cross or to the heights of the Orthodox theology of deification. Nevertheless the *reductio in nihilum*, the reduction to nothingness, and the *elevatio ad Deum*, the elevation to God, belong together and are mutually complementary.

Having looked at these great pictures of the end of this world, we may now turn to the smaller images about 'the new earth': *nulla salus sine terra* – there is no salvation without an earth. But what can 'the meek' who 'will inherit the earth' (Matt. 5.5) expect of that earth, which is supposed to correspond to 'the kingdom of heaven'? We shall look at two ideas here. The one abandons eschatology and goes back to the promises of an earthly future offered by Israel's prophets; the other seeks a future for this destructible and unredeemed earth after the end of 'this world'. The first idea is put forward by Rosemary Radford Ruether, as ecofeminism. We shall take the other from the organological eschatology of Johann Tobias Beck.

4. The Good Earth: Ecofeminism

The eschatological picture of 'the new heaven and the new earth' in Revelation 21 goes back to the prophetic vision in Isaiah 65. But that chapter is not talking about a future after the end of this world. It is thinking of a real, earthly future: then there will no longer be children who die before their time, and no old people who do not fulfil their days; then people will build houses and plant vineyards and eat their fruit. 'Not immortality but a blessed longevity is the ideal realized in the resurrection.'[39] It is a golden Shalom age in the history of humanity and on this earth that is meant, not a world beyond. But that presupposes that this earth is good, and that in this promised age it will simply have to flower into a new undreamed-of fertility. It will not be annihilated and created anew. The pre-apocalyptic prophets saw a threat to Israel's life and existence, but not to the cosmos. Their visions of the blessed life presuppose a profound trust in the earth.

This trust is taken up again in modern ecofeminism as a way of bringing high, speculative (and thus 'masculine') eschatology down to earth again. The organism of the earth is good, and so is the process of life and death. To protest against death in general is pointless, and the yearning for resurrection and immortality is actually hostile to life. There is no earthly life without death, and no new generation grows up without the passing of the old one. Premature death and a life never fully lived are a curse, and must therefore be fought against, but not death itself, which is part of the eternal process of die-and-become. We should therefore revert to the doctrine of 'a natural death', and with it recognize the law of earthly life as just and good. What is going to happen to us then? 'Our existence ceases as individuated ego/organism and dissolves back into the cosmic matrix of matter/energy, from which new centers of the individuation arise.'[40] This matrix of life is 'everlasting' and remains, as the foundation of the becoming and passing away of individualized beings and planetary worlds. In accepting our death, we are identifying ourselves with this wider matrix which embraces the totality of the living. 'To the extent to which we have transcended egoism for relation to community, we can also accept death as the final relinquishment of the individuated ego into the great matrix of being.'[41] Rosemary Ruether makes this clear from the significance of our burial in the earth: our individual ego and its organization dissolve, but the components are not lost. They become the nourishment for other living things which grow out of our bones. People who have themselves buried in steel coffins are refusing to enter into this life cycle. But the earth is our mother, and all living things on earth are our kindred. From earth we came, to earth shall we return. The good earth is the great organism and replica of 'the Holy Being' of the universe, which is also called 'Holy Wisdom'.[42]

In this ecofeminism, what for the New Testament is eschatological hope turns into a pantheistic omnipresence of 'the everlasting' matrix of life. The universe is already gathered under a single head: 'That great collective personhood is the Holy Being.' The eschatological pointer or hand has already become time's eternal cycle. In the unremitting 'die and become', life regenerates itself. Individual life is mortal – collective life is immortal. But this eulogy on the good earth overlooks the fragility and destructibility of the earth's organism, and thus the earth's own need of redemption. The earth is a special creation. According to Gen. 1.11 and 1.24 it is a creation that brings forth plants and animals.[43] It was therefore rightly called 'mother of all the living' and also 'mother of the human race'.[44] In itself, this has nothing to do with pantheism. It merely respects the particular characteristic and designation of the creation 'earth'. The designation of human beings, as God's image, 'to subdue the earth' (1.28) comes up against its limits in the designation of earth, as the creation that 'brings forth' plants and animals. The earth is not just a living creation; it is a life-engendering creation too. But it is still a contingent creation, and does not turn into the eternal goddess Gaia.

Because, as Paul perceives (Rom. 8.19ff.), all earthly living things sigh under the compulsion of transience and wait for the revelation of glory, the earth itself also sighs and waits for its redemption, through which it will become 'the new earth' in the eternal creation. If *this* earth itself is supposed to redeem human beings, who is then going to redeem this earth? And if we are allegedly in safe keeping in the bosom of the earth and its supposedly eternal cycles, what will happen when the earth dies in cold, or melts in the fierce heat of the sun? Deep respect for 'the good earth' does not mean that we have to give ourselves up for burial with the consolation that we shall live on in worms and plants. It means waiting for the day when the earth will open, and the dead will rise, and the earth together with these dead will 'be raised' for its new creation. The idea of being raised *from* this earth leaves the earth behind without hope. It is therefore better to modify this idea, and to wait to be raised *with* this earth.

The hypostatic unity of person and nature maintained in Orthodox theology can be translated into the ecological unity of human being and the earth. In both cases the human body is the link, indissolubly differentiating yet conjoining. It makes little sense to sink the earth in the body, and the body in the conscious soul; but conversely it makes no sense either to dissolve the person in the earth. The hypostatic unity differentiates too – differentiates between person and nature; and the ecological unity differentiates also between the world of human beings and the organism of the earth. There is no redemption if this differentiated unity is resolved in favour of the one side or the other.

5. The New Earth: Eschatological Ecology

Johann Tobias Beck, my predecessor in Tübingen (1804–1878), considered himself to be 'a man of the Bible', but his thinking was deeply influenced by the organological ideas of the Romantics.[45] He therefore saw the eschatological 'establishment of a new world system'[46] as the rise of a new world organism. If in all sectors of the world the contradictions rooted in sin are eliminated, together with their deadly consequences, a new 'goodly order' characterized by enduring righteousness and justice will come into being. 'It is not merely a restoration of the initial state of the world, the primordial paradisal condition; the beginning has now also reached its destination.'[47] The end (*telos*) completes the beginning (*arche*), though without destroying it. The new 'organic whole' mutually unites the heavenly and the earthly, the divine and the human, and is a 'deified universe' (I Cor. 15.28).

'The Being that has found its completion in God' must by no means be thought of as non-corporeal: 'In nature and humanity, it is a heavenly transfigured bodily life', a 'natural organism' shot through by the divine Spirit. 'Fleeting, faulty and sullying pleasures are replaced by the uninterrupted inbreathing of the eternal living stream of a world filled to satiety by the divine good pleasure.'[48] The divine presence completes itself, becoming a perpetual fellowship with human beings, so that in 'the mutual immanence between God and the saved' the self can inexhaustibly develop.

In order to describe the new world-organism, Beck draws on the christological idea of mutual *perichoresis*, an idea which can also be found on the biological levels in the 'organism' thinking of the Romantics. Human beings will become 'God's temple' and God will become 'their temple'. They dwell in him in 'mutual interpenetration'. It is a 'unified interpenetration of life' such as we find in pattern form in Christ. (Beck is thinking here of the doctrine of the two natures.) Accordingly, the world's earthly sphere too is no longer divided from the heavenly one, but has itself become a heaven, inasmuch as it is 'interpenetrated by the divine manifestive life and its supreme potency'.[49] It follows from this, finally, that the 'bodiliness thus shot through with the divine Spirit' 'unites in itself both personal and natural life'.[50]

If God is 'all in all', then fellowship in God and fellowship in the world are no longer something separate or antithetical. There is then no spiritual knowing of God and enjoyment of him which is not sensory and bodily as well, and no sensory and bodily contemplation and enjoyment of the world which is not also a contemplation and 'incorporation of God'.[51]

The concept of mutual interpenetration makes it possible to preserve both the unity and the difference of what is diverse in kind: God and human being, heaven and earth, person and nature, the spiritual and the sensuous. The concomitant idea of mutual indwelling is in itself a definition of Shekinah theology.

If the expectation of a 'life of the world to come' belongs to the hope for 'the resurrection of the dead', as the Creed says, then this future life must accord with the resurrection of the dead, and be nothing other than the world in which the raised live. That must then certainly be a new world-system in which heaven and earth, reality and the potentiality of eternal life interpenetrate each other mutually. So is this to be expected only from above and from outside, or does this temporal earth itself hold within it the promise of the new earth of eternal life?

According to the prophetic idea, in that future Shalom world 'righteousness will rain down' from the heavens and the clouds and 'the earth will open and bring forth salvation' (Isa. 45.8).[52] 'Out of dry ground a shoot will grow up' (Isa. 53.2). This idea – the idea that heaven and earth will work together for the future Shalom world –

has often been interpreted in a christological sense in Christian traditions, which did not hesitate to appropriate for the purpose even Virgil's fourth Eclogue:

> Unbidden earth shall wreathing ivy bring,
> And fragrant herbs (the promise of the spring)
> As her first offering to her infant king.

(Dryden's translation)

If this potency is inherent in the earth, if there is a hidden presence of Christ in the earth of this kind, then in looking for the coming of Christ in glory our gaze cannot be directed merely to heaven, as is generally thought ('. . . from thence he shall come to judge the quick and the dead'). And then Christoph Blumhardt could be right: 'Nature is the womb of God. Out of the earth God will come to meet us again. But as yet we have no fellowship with nature. We admire her, but often trample her underfoot, using her unreasonably. Consequently nature still confronts us with icy reserve, and feels that she is alien to us. But something different must come . . . we must arrive at harmony between human beings and nature. Then both will be content. And that will be the solution for the social question.'[53]

It follows from these eschatological ideas that the earth is not *dead matter*, and not expendable material – but neither is the earth the Mother Gaia who engenders and slays. *This* earth, with its world of the living, is the real and sensorily experienceable promise of *the new* earth, as truly as this earthly, mortal life here is an experienceable promise of the life that is eternal, immortal. If the divine Redeemer is himself present in this earth in hidden form, then the earth becomes the bearer or vehicle of his and our future. But in that case there is no fellowship with Christ without fellowship with the earth. Love for Christ and hope for him embrace love and hope for the earth. For an eschatology that is christologically grounded and ecologically responsibly maintained, there is no better concept.

§3 THE END OF TIME IN THE ETERNITY OF GOD

What *the end of time* means is described by Paul in I Cor. 15.52 with the concept of the eschatological 'moment' ($ἐν ῥιπῇ ὀφθαλμοῦ$), the 'atom' of eternity ($ἐν ἀτόμῳ$). What is meant is the moment of eternity in which all the dead will be raised at once, diachronically. This last day in time is at once the present of eternity to all times. This 'last day' is 'the day of days'. There is no other way of thinking of the day of resurrection. In content it is defined as 'the day of the Lord', to which all times are simultaneous.

What *the end of time* means is described in Rev. 10.6 in the image of the mighty angel who swears 'by him who lives for ever and ever, who created heaven and what is in it, the earth and what is in it, and the sea and what is in it: time shall be no more' (χρόνος οὐσέτι ἔσται). As in Paul at 'the last trumpet', here at the trumpet call of 'the seventh angel' 'the mystery of God, as he announced to his servants the prophets will be fulfilled'. In this context, the word for time (*chronos*) means first of all the time of history, in which the prophets proclaimed the coming mystery of God; but it also means the time of creation, which has sprung from the eternity of the Creator.

The mystery of God is 'the realization and extension of God's rule over the whole world'.[54] That is to say, it is the completion of history and creation, its perfecting into the kingdom of glory in which God himself 'indwells' his creation. If God himself appears *in* his creation, then his eternity appears *in* the time of creation, and his omnipresence *in* creation's space. Consequently temporal creation will be transformed into eternal creation, and spatial creation into omnipresent creation. If the eternally living God is going to 'swallow up death for ever' (Isa.25.8) through his real presence, then what in time is 'corruptible' will perish too (II Esd. 7.31). Consequently 'time shall be no more'; it will be gathered up, fulfilled and transformed through the eternity of the new creation. This is not the absolute eternity of God himself; it is the relative eternity of the new creation, which participates in God's absolute eternity. For this the patristic and mediaeval theologians used the word *aeon* or *aevum*.

We now have to ask: what theology of time emerges from this vision of the end of time? How does time spring from eternity, and how are we to understand creation in the context of time? How does the time of history come into being, and how are we to understand the historical times? Finally, we shall ask how it is possible to think the transition from temporal to eternal creation, and shall enquire about the particular character of that aeonic time which belongs to the new creation.[55]

1. The Time of Creation

Time is perceived from changes in Being. Changeable Being is temporal Being. Changeable Being is perceived in relation to unchangeable Being, unchangeable Being in its relation to what is changeable. According to Plato, we have to make a distinction between

> that which is always real and has no becoming, and that which is always becoming and is never real.[56]

That which is always real, which neither becomes nor passes away, is divine Being; that which becomes and passes away is non-divine, earthly Being. This fundamental distinction in Greek metaphysics had to be taken up and modified by Christian theology, for the link between divine and earthly Being has not always in itself been a 'given', but emerged only out of God's free resolve to be the Creator of an earthly and temporal world different from himself. The historical understanding of God which we find in the Old and New Testaments maintains together with the freedom of the Creator the contingency of his creation. So eternity and time are not the two necessary sides of the same reality. The unity of eternity and time is not to be found in the eternal present; it lies in God's creative Word.[57]

This then suggests the question: was the world created *in time*, or was time created *with the world*? If it was created *in* time, then there was a time before creation, and we are faced with the supposedly unanswerable question: What was God doing before he created the world?[58] If time was created *with* the world, the question is then whether God is the eternal Creator of all times,[59] or whether there was ever in God a state in which he was not Creator of the world and time. So does 'the beginning' in which God created heaven and earth fall in time or in eternity? As long as Christian theology, with Plato, defines time and eternity as changeability and unchangeability, this dilemma cannot be solved. But if, as in the Christian understanding of God, God's eternity is something other than the mere negation of temporality – if it is the fulness of creative life – then it is possible to conceive an opening for time in eternity.

For this there are two models: (1) The idea of *God's creative resolve*.[60] Before God created the world, and with the world time, he resolved to be the Creator of a world different from his Being, and a time different from his eternity. 'The beginning' in which God 'created' heaven and earth is to be found in this divine self-determination. (2) The idea of *God's primordial self-restriction*.[61] In his omnipresence God makes a place for his creation, by withdrawing his presence from this primordial space. God restricts his eternity so that in this primordial time he can give his creation time, and leave it time. God restricts his omniscience in order to give what he has created freedom. These primordial self-restrictions of God's precede his creation. In Act One God acts on himself, inwards, before in Act Two he goes out of himself and creates something other than himself. Only when God withdraws himself to himself, and restricts and concentrates himself within himself, can he call into existence something other than himself and outside himself, something that is not divine in nature, and is thus not eternal and omnipresent. Both ideas really say the same thing, the first with the help of personal metaphors, the second with spatial ones. If a person resolves for himself to do something for someone else, this resolve already implies a contraction of many possibilities to this particular one. Self-determination and self-restriction are the same thing. Both presuppose a self-alteration on God's part in eternity.

The *primordial moment* is to be found before the creation of world and time in God's designation of himself to be Creator. Out of the self-restriction of God's eternity there emerges 'the time of creation'. In the primordial moment of God's creative resolve, all the possibilities which the Creator will unfurl in the time of creation are already prepared. Consequently we can talk here about a *primordial aeon*.[62]

The moment of inception for creaturely time issues from the primordial moment of the time of creation. In the act of creation, time emerges from eternity and fans out into before and after, into future, present and past. Biblically, a distinction must be made here between the beginning in which God created heaven and earth (Gen. 1.1), and the beginning of earthly time: 'And the evening and the morning were the first day' (Gen. 1.5 KJV).

Whereas for heaven and 'all who dwell in it' there is an *aeonic* time, for the earth 'and all who dwell in it' there is a *transitory* time. The differentiation lies in death, which is only earthly, not heavenly. Aeonic time can be thought of as a time corresponding to the eternity of God: a time without beginning and end, without before and after. The figure, or configuration, of time that corresponds to the one, unending eternity is *cyclical* time, which has no end. It represents the reversible, symmetrical, unending and hence timeless form of time. According to Plato 'the body of the world' is spherical, and in the same way the time of the world is 'a movable image of non-transience', 'a circle'. The earthly form of time, however, is the *time-*

hand, the pointer: future becomes present, and present past. The course of this time is not circular; it has an irreversible trend. All earthly happening is temporal happening in the sense that it is irreversible, unrepeatable and inexorable. Unlike the heavenly creation, the earthly creation belongs within the context of this temporal form of time. It is not unimportant for us to take into account this *double form of time* in creation. Earthly creation exists within the context of passing time, but this earthly time, for its part, belongs within the context of the aeonic time of 'the invisible world', continually touching it and being touched by it.

The temporal creation is by definition a creation subject to change. It resembles an open, a-symmetrical, imbalanced system which is aligned towards its future. The time of earthly creation is open for the history of its salvation and its perdition. In its constructive potentialities, earthly time is therefore *the time of promise*. The essence of its time is *futurity*, as indeed its beginning too was the future. It was created for the indwelling of its Creator, and is hence unfinished as long as it has not yet become God's home country. The seventh day, which 'finishes' creation, points to this. The sabbath rest with which the Creator blesses his creation is the promise of its consummation in God's eschatological Shekinah, a promise built as endowment into creation itself. God created everything in dualities, only the sabbath is in the singular. So the sabbath awaits her partner. According to the Jewish idea, this partner is the historical people of Israel, to whom 'Queen Sabbath' comes as bride every seventh day. Eschatologically, however, the partner is undoubtedly *God's final Shekinah* in his creation. For this Shekinah the sabbath, so to speak, keeps its place open. As the feast of creation, God's sabbath rest is the beginning of creation's consummation; God's final Shekinah is the completion of that beginning in the 'feast without end' of which Athanasius speaks. The sabbath is God's Shekinah in time. The Shekinah is God's sabbath in space.

According to the first creation account, the time pattern in creation by no means provides earthly creation only with time's irreversible flow; it also confers time that is rhythmically interrupted and ordered though the sabbath days and the sabbath years. Rhythm is at once repetition and progress. In the rhythm of the sabbath interruptions of 'time's flow', earthly creation – human beings, animals and the earth – vibrate in the cosmic liturgy of eternity. The ever-flowing stream of time regenerates itself from the presence of eternity in the sabbath rhythm of the days, the years, and the seventh year, thus preparing for the messianic sabbath of the End-time creation and, through that, for the eschatological sabbath of the eternal creation.

In its destructive possibilities, earthly time becomes *the time of transience*. *Chronos* then becomes the power of futility, the futility of everything that happens or is done in time. Chronos devours all the children whom he bears. Everything that is, will one day no longer be, for, says Mephisto in Goethe's *Faust*, 'everything that is called forth is worth destroying'. In the end everything that could be, and that was, is past, and at the end of the past stands universal death, the total non-being of all temporal things and happenings. The exit from time is not an entrance into eternity; it is the entry into Being-that-is-no-longer. Here time turns from being a form of futurity into a form of transience, and from a form of life into the form of death. The temporality of earthly creation does not reflect the presence of God – it reflects his absence. His grace is not 'new every morning' – his face is 'hidden' or turned away. Then time is experienced as the power of ageing and of death. In the language of apocalyptic, that is 'this aeon', this world-time of injustice and death, but also the time of 'this passing aeon', the world-time of evanescence, not of any abiding. It is not just what happens in time that changes; time itself changes too: primordial futurity becomes inexorable past. Consequently the direction of hope is not just that God will make all things new. Hope looks also to the future of 'a new time', the 'abiding aeon' of an 'everlasting life' (I John 1.2) in which chronos will enjoy no more efficacy (Rev. 10.6).

2. The Times of History

Present: In historical time we can distinguish between different modes of time. There is a before and an after, which divides future and past at the intersection of the present. We then understand the present as *a point in time* on a temporal line, which both distinguishes past and future and links them together.[63] This point in time is not itself a 'space of time' and has no temporal extension. It is a *punctum mathematicum*, a mathematical point.[64] Present is changeable (since this point in time passes away with time) and at the same time unchangeable (because it is always the same). In time, present lies between future and past, and is simultaneous towards future and past. Because the present point in time makes the times of past and future distinguishable, and hence constitutes them, the present is the end and beginning of the times.

The *hic et nunc* – the here and now of the present – is, as constitutive category of time, a category of eternity. It establishes the unity of time. The Now is 'the event of eternity in Being', as the mystical experience of the Deity present in the moment has always said: *nunc aeternum*, eternity in the Now. Although in linear time the present is mathematically reduced to a mere point in time, it is still ontologically the time that is distinguished in Being. In the onto-logical sense, only what is present *is*. What is future is *not yet*, what is past is *no longer*. Future and past are categories of non-Being. Only the present is a category of Being.[65] We grasp the past, which no longer *is*, only by virtue of the remembrance that makes-present. We grasp the future, which *is* not yet, only by virtue of the expectation that makes-present. Both are mediated forms of Being. Only present can be experienced as immediate existence. *Present* is the real secret of the times.

– Present constitutes, distinguishes and links past and future.
– Present is the simultaneity of past and future.
– Present is the Being between Being-that-is-not-yet and Being-that is-no-longer.
– Present is the category of eternity in time: the moment is 'an atom of eternity'.[66]

Past – Present – Future: If these three modes of time are put on to a parameter without direction, they are then, together with the movements that can be measured with the parameter, reversible and symmetrical, as the motion equations of classic and atomic physics show. If time is only a provision for measurement, then it is a matter of indifference for the tendency of movements. In complex systems, reversible time secures stability, because it is the continuous form of cyclical processes. 'Newtonian physics has the image of the stable reversible world, a world as a clock that can be wound up, a clock which can in principle be made to run backwards.'[67] The ideal symmetries are the circle and the sphere: cyclical time and the world as globe. Reversible forms of time dominate closed, symmetrical systems and systems in equilibrium – which, however, do not exist in historical reality. Reversible time is a kind of timeless time, for this form of time is itself timeless, like Newton's absolute time.

The second law of thermodynamics introduced into physics the concept of irreversible time. Entropy is not merely the measure for the loss of energy; it is a measure for the non-reversibility of processes too. Flows of energy are directional, and irreversible in time. Entropy is also a time-measure for the irreversibility of time, and hence a first step towards the perception in physics of the temporality of time itself. All changes in the world run their course according to the time-mode of irreversibility. 'No one enters the same river twice', not even an electron.

Ought we to reckon with both forms of time, reversible and irreversible time, and talk about 'the paradox of time'?[68] Or can it be proved that the ideas about a reversible time are idealizations of the more complex processes of irreversible time? Is there one sector, nature, with a reversible time structure, and another sector, history, with a time structure that is irreversible? Or is nature also involved in a history, and is there therefore a 'history of nature'?[69] If nature seriously has a history, then the paradox of time is resolved in favour of irreversible time.

In the experience of historical time, the modes of time are not entered in linear time but are assigned to *modalities of being*: past – present – future correspond to necessary – real – possible Being.[70] 'The possible corresponds wholly and entirely to what is future . . . and what is future is, for time, the possible.'[71] So the possible is what is future, the real is what is present, and the past is what has become unchangeable. Georg Picht has assigned the modes of time to the modalities of Being in this way. Because 'nothing that is past can pass away', past is necessary. 'We give the name "real" to what was once present, is present now and will be present in the future.' The possible is then the scope between that which cannot possibly be and that which has to be.[72] We can follow Ernst Bloch and make a somewhat simpler assignment: future is the sphere of the possible, past the sphere of the real, present the frontier on which the possible is either real-ized or not real-ized.[73] In either case, this arrangement creates the irreversible time-pointer or 'hand'. Out of possibility reality develops, just as out of future there will be past. The modes of time are not isomorphous. All temporal happening is irreversible, unrepeatable and inexorable. The modes of time are a-symmetrical and assigned to qualities of being which are different in kind. Potentiality and reality are distinguishable modes of being, and our dealings with them differ. Correspondingly, we deal differently with past and future. Remembered past is something other than expected future. If reality is real-ized potentiality, then potentiality must be higher ontologically than reality. If out of future there is past, but out of past never again future, then the future must have pre-eminence among the modes of time.

If time is irreversible, then *the source from which time springs* must lie in the future. But it cannot be identical with future time, for every future time passes away. Here we can follow Picht in distinguishing between the future as a mode of time, and the future as the source of time. As a mode of time, future belongs to phenomenal time, as the source of time, future is the transcendental possibility of time in general. In the transcendental sense, future is present to every time – to future, present and past time. In this respect it is also the unity of time. The future offers in a certain sense 'the whole, of which the past is merely a part'.[74]

Remembered Past – Expected Future: With the introduction of the thinking subject into the experience of time, the particular phenomena of historical time emerge: no historical experience without a subject. History is constituted by the experiences and expectations of the suffering and acting human being. This applies initially to human experience of reality, but not only to that, for every self-referential system perceives its historical time analogously.

In his psychological theory of time, Augustine relates past, present and future to their perception by the soul: through remembrance (*memoria*), the human mind makes the past present. That is the past-made-present. Through expectation (*expectatio*) the human mind makes the future present. That is the future-made-present. Through sight (*contuitus*) the human mind makes the present present. That is the present-present.[75] In the human mind, past and future are therefore present through the force of remembrance and expectation. That is a simultaneity of what is non-simultaneous. In the human mind, Being-that-is-no-longer and Being-that-is-not-yet are present through the force of remembrance and expectation. These are creative ways of making-present what is absent.

The *simultaneity*, however fragmentary in kind, of past and future in the present is a *relative eternity*, for simultaneity is one of the attributes of eternity.[76] Universal simultaneity would be absolute eternity as 'the fulness of time'. Remembered and expected present in the mind can hence be understood as a reflection, out of this fulness of the times. If through remembrances we call back to memory the

Being-that-is-no-longer of the past, if through fear or hope we have before our eyes the Being-that-is-not-yet of the future, then this is a *creative act* on what is absent, and therefore at the same time a relative eternity and a reflection in the human mind of the God who calls into being the things that are not. In these activities of the human mind Augustine glimpsed its likeness to God. To remembered past and expected future there is therefore added eternity made-present as their simultaneity. The counter-check can easily be conceived: without remembrance and without expectation we should perceive only points in time, momentary perceptions and snapshot impressions, but no connections between them. We could hear no melody and perceive no movement.

The relationships between subjective experiences of time and objective events in time make the difference between past and future even clearer. In the remembered past there is always still a difference between the past-present and the past-made-present. We remember only a little of the past, and our remembrances change with our experiences of the present and our expectations of the future. Our memory is not a video camera, and not a computer memory. It is a living organ. We try to come to terms with experiences that force themselves upon us because they are still not finished and done with. We suppress unpleasant experiences, or give them a favourable gloss. We always relate them to ourselves. What we remember always has to do with our picture of ourselves. Remembered past must therefore be corrected by historical investigation of 'the way things really were', as L. von Ranke put it, and by a comparison with the remembrances of other contemporary witnesses. Past-made-present always also includes knowledge about experience outside our own. It is also communicated through the collective memory of generations and institutions, just as, on the other hand, it will also be influenced and impaired by collectively achieved suppressions.

Reinhard Koselleck has aptly talked about a 'space of experience' in which we collect historical experiences.[77] In this 'space' these experiences are simultaneous, as archives and museums show. In expectations we make the future present to us. We do not make it present as future, but as future-present, and as possible experience. Here the difference between *future present* and *future made present* is even greater than it is in respect of the past, and it is different in kind. Experiences are collected, expectations are projected. Experience and expectation extend to different modes of being – here to reality, there to possibility – and are hence a-symetrical to one another. Instead of a space of expectation, it is useful to talk about a horizon of expectation.[78]

How are experience and expectation related to one another? On the one hand we can say that there are no expectations which are not based on particular experiences – experiences of deficiency, for example, or of superfluity. But we cannot derive our expectations entirely from our experiences. If we could, there would be nothing new under the sun, and thus nothing more to be expected either. Yet we cannot, either, draw up the project of our expectations without any relation to our experiences. If we did, all that would emerge would be utopias, which do not distinguish between what is 'really' possible and what is 'un-really' possible. The feedback which connects expectations with experiences is a necessary part of the hermeneutical process of tradition and innovation which constitutes historical time. The presence of the future in expectations is a different presence from the presence of the past in experiences. That is due to the difference between potentiality and reality. In the perception of historical time, past and future are interlaced in just such a way as are experiences and expectations in the space of experience and against the horizon of expectation.[79]

Future in the Past – Past in the Future: The interlacing of the times in historical time reaches much further than has hitherto been described. We do not just remember the past of our present in any given case; what we do remember, to be more precise, is *the past present*. But every past present, especially where earlier generations are concerned, had its own interlacing of remembrances and expectations, of past and future made present. If we call to remembrance a past present, we also perceive its own space of experience and its special horizon of expectation. We also remember the expectations and hopes of past generations, inasmuch as we exist in their traditions. With what picture of history, and with what expectations, did the young generations of Europe enter the First World War in 1914? In what space of experience and with what horizons of expectation did the Reformation begin in the sixteenth century? True tradition is always at the same time *remembered hope*. In our uncertainty about our own future we seek for future in the past, and find it in the unfulfilled hopes of past generations.

But there are also great, connected processes into which we are born and whose projects for the future we share, even if we are

personally opposed to them. 'Scientific and technological civilization' is 'the great project of modern times'. It has not yet been
realized, but neither has it as yet entirely come to grief. Every
important present-day decision intervenes in this process of modernity, which is still open and *sub judice*, as it were. Through changes in
the horizon of expectation of the project 'modernity' we can make
changes in its course. Expectations as yet unrealized have been
invested in this project. It is not yet finished and done with. We
experience our present in this project, and we experience this project
as what confronts us in our present. If we do not want our future to
become in a few decades nothing but the past, we shall have to
introduce our misgivings into the expectations of 'the modern
world'.

Where world history as a whole is concerned, it can rightly be said
that the history which we are able to survey has to be continually re-
written, because it is apparently not only present things but the
things of the past too which are in a state of flux. There is a *rebus sic
stantibus* only at the end of history: only then will things stay as they
are. Then it will be possible to make an inventory of the facts. Those
who claim to be able to do this during the process of history are
declaring history to be at an end, and are appointing themselves to be
its judge. As long as history continues and its future is open, historical judgments can be made only under the proviso *rebus sic
fluentibus*, as Ernst Bloch said – that things are still in a state of flux.

Eternity in time, finally, is nothing other than the other side of the
present, because in the mind 'present' always means a relative
simultaneity of past and future, through the force of remembrance
and expectation. If that is true for our own intellectual present in any
given case, then it applies to past presents and future presents too.
Present always makes-present past and future. Present thus always
makes-present eternity in time, since eternity is the simultaneity of
past and future. 'As long as we can say today' eternity reaches into
time. That is not the absolute eternity of the 'Wholly Other' God, but
it is, surely, the *aeonic eternity* of the invisible world of heaven,
which is bound up with the time of this visible world of the earth.

Eternity in time, however, is perceived not merely in relative
simultaneity, but also in the depth-experience of *the moment* too.
The present as a point in time, and the present as simultaneity, are
outreached by the experience of the present as *kairos*, as 'the proper
time', 'the favourable opportunity', 'the unique chance' upon which

'a second chance' never follows. In the kairological interpretation, the flux of time is non-homogeneous: there are favourable and unfavourable times. Beyond the present as kairos, there is the experience of the present as *moment*. In German, 'moment' means a mystical 'depth-dimension' of time: *nunc aeternum* – eternity is Now. In confrontation with eternity there is only one time: the present. As 'an atom of eternity', the fulfilled moment drops out of the sequence of time, interrupts time's flow, abolishes the distinction of the times in past and future, is an ecstasy that translates out of this temporal life into the life that is eternal.[80] Eternity in time is a category, not of the extensive life, but of the *intensive* life. *The presence of eternity* comes about in the wholly and entirely lived moment through undivided presence in the present. If I am wholly there – if I give myself wholly – if I expose myself wholly – if I am able to linger wholly – then I experience present eternity. It is the experience of 'the fulness of time' in the wholeness of the lived life: all time becomes present. In the midst of historical time this is, indeed, only a momentary, a moment-like experience of eternity, but an experience of eternity it is. Here eternity is not merely simultaneity but also *absolute presentness*. In the moment we experience eternity, which according to Boethius's famous definition is 'the whole boundlessness of life . . . immediate and perfect possession' ('Aeternitas . . . est interminabilis vitae tota . . . simul et perfecta possessio').[81] The whole, simultaneous and complete possession and enjoyment of life is the fulness of time in the fulness of the loved life. That too means an *aeonic eternity*, the eternity of the new life of the future world.[82]

Eternal life has nothing to do with timelessness and death, but is *full-filled life*. Because in historical time we experience fulfilled life only in the form of moment-like eternity, we develop a hunger for a wholly and completely unclouded fulness of life, and therefore for the life that is eternal. Out of this experience of present eternity arises the longing for an eternal present in which we can say to the moment, like Goethe's Faust: 'O tarry a while, thou art so fair.'

Where does reflection about time come into being? Is there an Archimedian point at which we become conscious of the temporality of life? According to the classic view, this point is death, as the exit from time into eternity or, as people have said since the beginning of modern times, into nothingness.[83] *Memento mori* teaches us to number our days. *Mors certa – hora incerta* used to be written on the clocks on church towers – death is certain, the hour uncertain. The clock was supposed to teach us that temporality is mortality. The anticipation of death in the awareness that runs ahead, makes present to us from our own bodies the limits of phenomenal time. The result is a negative theory of time. But theologically speaking, the exit from time into nothingness through death manifests only that 'at the moment when sin comes into being, temporality is sinfulness'.[84] Separation from God, the wellspring of life, leads us through our isolation to experience temporality as transience, and to see death as its universal end. The experience of temporal life is different once an exit from time in the fulfilled moment is experienced as an entry of eternity. Then eternal life already begins here and now in the midst of the life that is transitory, and makes of earthly life a prelude to itself.

3. *The Fulfilment of Time*

It was an error of presentative eschatology to identify the present *kairos* with the eschatological *moment* and not to perceive the difference.

Kierkegaard was the first to move the eschatological moment into the present of eternity, to equate it with the present kairos. 'The eternal is the present, and the present is the fulness.'[85] As present, eternity gathers into itself the 'sequence of time' which is in itself empty. For this Kierkegaard used the metaphorical expression 'moment'. 'Nothing is so swift as the glance of the eyes and yet it is appropriate for the content of the eternal.' The 'moment' means something present which no longer has any past and no longer any future, and is thus 'the perfection of the eternal'. Kierkegaard had in his mind's eye the image of Ingeborg as she looks out over the sea, in 'Frithjof's Saga'. But he also linked this with Plato's idea of the 'sudden' (τὸ ἐξαιφνῆς). Not least, however, he found in Paul, in I Cor. 15.52, a poetic paraphrase of the moment in which the world is to end 'in an atom and in a moment'. He concluded from this that time and eternity 'touch' in the moment and that this is 'the fulness of time'. With this he equated the historical and the eschatological moment, and did not pay sufficient regard to the completely different happening which takes place here in faith, and there in the raising of the dead. He was followed by Karl Barth, who in 1922, in his second interpretation of the Epistle to the Romans, drew on Kierkegaard for the interpretation of Rom. 13.11, 'This do knowing the time': 'Between the past and the future – between the times – there is a "Moment" that is no moment in time.' But every moment in time can receive the full dignity of this moment. 'This "Moment" is the eternal moment, the *Now* – when the past and the future stand still.'[86] And commenting on Rom. 13.12, 'The night is far spent, but the day is at hand', he wrote: 'Being the transcendent meaning of all moments, that eternal "Moment" can be compared with no moment in time.'[87]

He was also followed by Bultmann, when he detected in II Cor. 6.2 'the eschatological Now'. The text runs: 'Behold, now is the acceptable time; behold, now is the day of salvation.' 'The Now in which the message is proclaimed is the eschatological Now.'[88] His lectures and ideas about the relationship of history and eschatology end with 'the eschatological moment': '*The meaning in history lies always in the present*, and when the present is conceived as the eschatological present by Christian faith the meaning of history is realized . . . In every moment slumbers the possibility of being the eschatological moment. You must awaken it.'[89]

Now, in Rom. 13.11f. and II Cor. 6.2 Paul is not talking about the eschatological moment at all, as he is in I Cor. 15.52. He is talking about the 'hour' and the 'day of God' and 'the favourable time' (the kairos). He does not mean the presence of eternity in which time stands still, for in Rom. 13.12 he is looking back to a past, 'when you first believed', and forward to a future in which, out of the present dayspring colours, the full 'day of God' will dawn, and drive out the night of this world. What is meant is a present with a clearly recollected past and a distinctly expected future. Any interpretation of this 'present' as 'eschatological moment' puts too great a strain on it, and destroys it. What happens on 'the day of salvation' is not the 'sudden' transformation of time into eternity, for it is not yet the raising of the dead in that eschatological moment which does not, it is true, belong at all to time any longer. What comes about on the day of which Paul is speaking is the kairos of salvation through the call of the gospel and the rebirth in faith. What happens in this kairos is thanks to the raising of the dead Christ, and promises the eschatological raising of the dead and the life of the world to come; but it is not yet itself these things.

The present 'day of salvation' is a temporal *anticipation* of the eschatological moment. What happens in it is the beginning of that which is to be completed in the victory of life over death at the end. In the experience of the present kairos of faith, the impression of time is transformed, metaphorically speaking, from transience into futurity: it moves out of the shadows of the night of the world 'that is far gone' into the light of the dawning 'day of God'. If what happens in the present kairos of faith and the rebirth to life is the historical anticipation of what is to happen to the dead in the *eschatological moment*, then it is also the analogy to that. So there is a historical similarity, in spite of all eschatological dissimilarity; and to this the imaginative power of hope can cling.

The eschatological moment itself must be thought of, beyond the end and consummation of history, as the consummation of creation-in-the-beginning and therefore as the exit from time into eternity. It corresponds to the *primordial moment*, which we described at the beginning of this section. The end of time is the converse of time's beginning. Just as the primordial moment springs from God's creative resolve and from the divine self-restriction on which God determined in that resolve, so the eschatological moment will spring from the resolve to redeem and the 'derestriction' of God determined upon in that. God does not de-restrict himself in order to annihilate his creation, and to put himself in its place and its time; his purpose is to dwell in his creation, and in it to be 'all in all'. The primordial time and the primordial space of creation will end when creation becomes the temple for God's eternal Shekinah. The *temporal* creation will then become an eternal creation, because all created beings will participate in God's eternity. The *spatial* creation will then become an omnipresent creation, because all created beings will participate in God's omnipresence. Creation's departure from time into the aeon of glory comes about through the annihilation of death and the raising of the dead. Once death is no more, there will be no more time either, neither the time of transience nor the time of futurity. 'Death is swallowed up in victory', the victory of the life that is eternal because it has an indestructible share in the divine life. Since, as was explained earlier, the raising of the dead comprehends all the dead diachronically, from the first human being to the last, there is then a *reversion* of the time that is here *irreversible*. In 'the restoration of all things', all times will return and – transformed and transfigured – will be taken up into the aeon of the new creation. In the eternal creation all the times which in God's creative resolve were fanned out will also be gathered together. The unfurled times of history will be rolled up like a scroll, as Revelation 5 intimates. Only this can then be called 'the fulness of the times'. And of this fulness the 'fulfilled moment' – the moment full-filled entirely and wholly with life – gives only a foretaste.

The eschatological moment has two sides, in correspondence to the primordial moment of the exit of time from eternity: God completes in himself his eschatological de-restriction of himself: he appears in his creation in the splendour of his unveiled glory. He comes 'with shining countenance' so that men and women will know him 'face to face'. Through this the temporal creation experiences its transformation into the eternal creation. Just as the moment of time's inception proceeds out of the primordial moment, so in *the final moment* time passes over into eternity. So metaphorically speaking, 'the last day' is at the same time the beginning of eternity: a beginning without an end. That is the 'fulfilled time', the aeonic time, the time filled with eternity, the eternal time. However we may imagine this, it is the very opposite of 'a deathlike silence'. If we have to think of it as the time of eternal life, then we have to imagine it as the time of eternal livingness.

According to ancient ideas aeonic time is conceived of as *cyclical*, not as a time-pointer or hand. Irreversible historical time is replaced by reversible time, as a reflection of God's eternity. In the aeonic cycles of time, creaturely life unremittingly regenerates itself from the omnipresent source of life, from God. An analogy is provided by the regenerating cycles of nature, and the rhythms of the body, which already sustain life here. The purposeful time of history is fulfilled in the cyclical movements of life's eternal joy in the unceasing praise of the omnipresent God. The preferred images for eternal life are therefore dance and music, as ways of describing what is as yet hardly imaginable in this impaired life.

The new creation is defined through a new divine presence within it. The Creator no longer remains over against his creation. He dwells in it, and finds in it his rest. This makes of the new creation a sacramental world. It is interpenetrated by divine presence, and participates in the inexhaustible fulness of God's life. The indwelling of God calls into being a kind of cosmic *perichoresis* of divine and cosmic attributes. In that new aeon a mutual perichoresis between eternity and time also comes into existence, so that on the one hand we can talk about 'eternal time' and on the other about 'eternity filled with time'.

§4 THE END OF SPACE IN THE PRESENCE OF GOD

What the end of space is to be is described in Rev. 20.11. Before the
established throne of God and the unveiled face of his majesty 'earth
and sky fled away, and no place was found for them' (τόπος οὐχ
εὑρέθη αὐτοῖς). The comprehensive statement about earth and sky
shows that here *topos* does not mean a created place. It is the space of
the whole creation, conceded to it in the creative resolve. Because
God restricted his omnipresence, the *primordial place* into which he
could create heaven and earth came into being. This living space, in
which created beings could develop their potentialities, is made
accessible through a withdrawal of God's omnipresence, and hence
also through a veiling of his glory, the 'hiding of his face' (*hester
panim*). Consequently when the majesty of God himself appears in
omnipresence, heaven and earth lose the place (*topos*) conceded to
them. Before his 'revealed face' they no longer have any space in
which they could continue to exist for themselves. They lose their
own inner continuance, which they owed to the hiddenness of God.
Because God's presence changes over against his creation, the space
of his creation changes too. Heaven and earth can no longer exist in
detachment from God. They become the dwelling of God's omnipresence itself, just as the time of creation becomes the time of God's
eternity.

Here we must ask: what theology of space emerges from the vision
of the end of space in the omnipresence of God? We shall develop
further the ideas put forward in Chapter VI of *God in Creation* on
the ecological concept of space, and on the debate about 'absolute
space' pursued by Leibniz and Newton.[90] How does the space of
creation come into existence outside God's omnipresence, which
cannot know anything 'outside' itself? How do the spaces within
creation work, the spaces which created beings mutually concede to
one another? Where does God's Shekinah find the dwelling in which
it can come to rest? How are we to conceive of an end of space?

1. The Space of Creation

To some extent the theological problems of space resemble the
problems involved in the concept of time. Is space created *with*
created beings, or is creation created *in* the space of God? In the first
case, it would be a matter of created spaces; in the second case, of a

space prepared by God as the prerequisite for creation. If creation exists in a space outside God, can God then be thought of as omnipresent? But if God is omnipresent, can there be an 'outside' for him – an outside which must, after all, be assumed if we talk about the *opera Dei ad extra* (God's works for what is outside himself), as has been usual in the Western church's doctrine of God ever since Augustine?

God must undoubtedly be thought of as 'above the times'. We express this with the idea of his eternity. Correspondingly, God must also be thought of as above space.[91] We express this through the idea of his unrestricted presence. Every space is restricted, and restricts. Every space creates distance. If God is the subject of his eternity and his presence, then he is also the subject of his own restriction, through which the space for creation is constituted, a restriction which is not divine but is thought to exist with God and 'before his face'. We found that this self-restriction of God's essential omnipresence to his special presence in creation was based on God's creative resolve, from which creation proceeds. God restricts his eternity in order to take time for his creation and to leave it time. Analogously he restricts his omnipresence, in order to make room for his creation and to concede it space. From this there emerges the distance between God and creation, and God as creation's vis-à-vis, its counterpart. God withdraws himself in order to let something exist outside himself and before him.

The idea of the primordial self-restriction of God (*zimsum*) was developed in the Lurian Kabbalah.[92] 'According to the Cabala, the Infinite Holy One, whose light originally occupied the whole universe, withdrew his light and concentrated it on his own substance, thereby creating empty space.' After God, in his resolve to create the world, had completed the *zimsum*, he created 'vessels'. He set them in the 'place' which he had made free for them through his withdrawal. The vessels were destined to receive the light in which the world was to spring to life.[93] The fine distinction between place (τόπος) and vessel (σκεύη) draws attention to the fact that spaces have to be understood topologically and ecologically. Created beings do not just exist in particular places in space; they are themselves restricted spaces, destined to receive the light out of which life comes into being. This is apparently an ancient Israelite idea about the designation of created beings made in the image of God. Paul also talks about 'vessels of wrath' and 'vessels of God's mercy' (Rom.

9.22f.), and says that we have the treasure of the gospel 'in earthly vessels' (II Cor. 4.7). Beings who are created in the image of God are intended for the reception and transmission of God's radiance ($\delta \acute{o} \xi a$) in creation. They are created to be dwellings for God's Spirit.

Although, as has continually been stressed, 'the God of history' whom Jews and Christians talk about is bound to have a special relationship to time, the triune God of the Christian doctrine of the Trinity has a special relationship to space. The space that receives accords with his innermost nature. Our starting point was the essential omnipresence of God, which is restricted in the creative resolve so as to make space for a creation. But where do the three divine Persons of the Trinity exist? Is God's omnipresence their unrestricted dwelling space? Do they exist as hypostases in a divine substance, or as modes of Being in a divine subject?

According to the Christian doctrine of the Trinity, the three divine Persons exist with one another, for one another and *in one another*. They exist in one another because they mutually give each other space for a full unfolding. By existing mutually in each other, they form their unique trinitarian fellowship.[94] That is the doctrine of the trinitarian *immanentia* and *inexistentia*: *Intima et perfecta inhabitatio unius personae in aliis* – the innermost and perfect indwelling of one Person in all. If, as John 14.9–11 says, the Son exists 'in' the Father and the Father 'in' the Son, then the Father is the dwelling of the Son, and the Son the dwelling of the Father. The Spirit who 'proceeds' from the Father and 'rests' in the Son and radiates from him, finds in the Son the place of his eternal indwelling. Through their complete self-giving, the trinitarian Persons are 'beside themselves' and wholly in the others. Thus, mutually and together, they become the eternal dwelling. In the doctrine of the Trinity it is not sufficient just to talk about the divine Persons and relationships; their reciprocal indwellings must be perceived as well. Only then do we understand their trinitarian fellowship and their unique divine Being. This is perfect, requiring no other Being *in* which it can exist – not even a common divine substance. The reciprocal in-existence* constitutes the divine completion and perfection.

When the triune God restricts his omnipresence in order to permit a creation outside himself to be 'there', he does not leave behind a vacuum, as the kabbalistic doctrine of *zimsum* suggests. He throws

* 'In-' here being a preposition of location, not a prefix of negation (Trans.).

open a space for those he has created, a space which corresponds to his inner indwellings: he allows a world different from himself to exist before him, with him and *in him*. 'God called space into being thanks to a potentiality inherent in his inner-trinitarian life: he created it as a means of community between himself and us, and a means of community between human beings with one another, following the archetypal image of the community present in the Trinity, to which we too are to attain.'[95] So the space of creation is at once outside God and within him. Through his self-restriction, the triune God made his presence the dwelling for his creation. God himself is the 'broad place where there is no cramping' (Ps. 18.19; 31.8; Job 36.16). It is God's very self-withdrawal that makes it possible for those he has created to say 'In him we live and move and have our being' (Acts 17.28). 'We do not know whether God is the place of his world, or whether his world is his place', says a Jewish midrash.[96] One answer is: 'The Lord is the dwelling place of his world, but his world is not his dwelling place.' We shall see that there is another answer besides that one. But here it is sufficient to establish that 'the space of creation' is its *living space in God*. By withdrawing himself and giving his creation space, God makes himself the living space of those he has created. That space does not become 'empty space' because of his withdrawal. It is qualified and structured through the God who receives his creation. The Creator becomes the *God who can be inhabited*. God as living space of the world is a feminine metaphor, as Plato already observed. In John 17.21, in Jesus's high priestly prayer, we find precisely delineated the connection between the trinitarian indwellings of the divine Persons and their shared opening of themselves to become the living space for created beings:

> That they may all be one,
> even as thou, Father, art in me and I in thee,
> that they also may be in us.

The kairological understanding of time says: 'Everything has its time.' In *God in Creation* we accordingly developed an *ecological concept of space*: everything has its space, and every living thing has its living space. The spaces are not homogeneous. They are determined by what happens in them, comes to pass in them, or lives in them. There is no such thing as empty time without happening, and in the same way there is no empty space without objects that rest or move in it. The ecological concept of space embraces the environments of living things which are specific to their species, and in which the external conditions of their lives are embedded. Every living thing has its own living space, in which it develops. Many living things belong so closely to their living space that living thing and living space can be viewed as the inner and outer sides of that space. Only living things that can change their environments can detach themselves from them and acquire a degree of independence towards them.

We are often inclined to relate the 'environment' only to the thinking subject living in it, thus reducing the environment to a thing. Men and women tend towards anthropocentricism. They call nature – which after all is the home of many plants and animals – '*our* environment' or '*our* planetary house', as a way of appropriating it. But we see the earth as the environment for plants, animals and human beings, the sea as the environment for fish, and the air as the environment for the birds. It was ecological wisdom when the author of the first creation account talked first of all about the creation of environments, and only after that about the living things corresponding to them.

Yet this ecological concept of space is not sufficient to allow us to apprehend fully the reality of the living. The experience of space is the experience of 'being within another'. A thing can only exist in something else, because nothing in the world can exist just of its own self. Every existence is *inexistensia*, 'existence-*in*'. In his analysis of *Dasein*, existence, Heidegger described the 'Being-in-the-world' of human beings. Human 'Being-in-the-world' is always spatially conditioned. The spatiality shows 'the character of deseverance and directionality'.[97] For Heidegger, space is neither a subjective category of intuition nor an objective reality: the world 'as it really is'; space is inferred, or disclosed, through human 'Being-in-the-world'. But that is too anthropologically conceived, as if it were simply and solely 'the world' that belongs to human existence as *inexistentia*.

For human beings and mammals, the original experience of space is the experience of the foetus in the uterus. We grow nine months long 'in' the mother, then to be born and to experience the first pains of separation. When in German we talk about *Geborgenheit*, safe-keeping, we always think of safe-keeping in the mother's womb. In the experiences of separation after birth, we experience the motherly presence, hitherto permanent, as the intermittent proximity or distance of a counterpart, and we experience space as the space of movement for approach and distancing. We need not pursue the small child's experiences of space any further. But this context is important for the understanding of existence as 'in-existence'. It has a reference, not only to my existence in others, but also to the existence of others in me, as we see from the example of the mother, who becomes the physical world in which the child growing within her lives. Every human person exists in community with other people, and is also for them a living space. Every living thing is as the subject of its own life the object for other life as well. We are at once inhabitants and inhabited.

If in a community we take over responsibility for others, these others exist in a certain way *in us*, at least in our solicitude for them. That is why in Christian faith we say: because Christ *is for us* and gave himself for us, *we are in Christ*. In this relationship, *in-existence* is the other side of *pro-existence*. In a community, the pro-existent and the in-existent relationships are so multifarious that any one-sidedness is precluded. We are always there *for* other people and *in* other people, just as other people are there for us and in us. In human community we mutually open up for each other the spaces of freedom through love, or we close them through intimidation. We are presence, space and dwelling for one another. That is why the love poems say 'Thou art in me – I am in thee'. The ecological concept of space has run up against some misunderstandings, and in order to avoid these I should like to use a *perichoretic concept of space* as a way of apprehending the experience of space as I have described it – space as mutual in-existence. Perichoresis is also called *circuminsessio*, mutual indwelling, and mutual *inhabitatio*, 'habitation in'. This offers a better way of describing the warp and weft of life than ecological terms for space. The perichoretic space concept of reciprocal in-existence corresponds on the creaturely level to the concept of the eternal inner-trinitarian indwellings of the divine Persons.

Just as through their reciprocal indwellings the divine Persons also form a common space, so community on the creaturely level forms the social space of reciprocal self-development. Created beings have to exist side by side and together, and for this they need wide spaces in which they can move freely. There is no subjective *freedom* without these *free spaces* in social life, spaces opened up by respect and affection, and secured through legal systems. It is only these free spaces that make us able to approach one another and to withdraw, to open ourselves or close ourselves to others. Shared living space is the medium for human relationship and for history. This living space is formed by the interpersonal relationships of a number of people. It is 'our space' not 'my space'. It takes its impress from those present and from those absent, through proximity and distance. It is linked with landscapes and with other worlds of the living. In 'closed societies' space becomes the frontier that shuts in and shuts out. In 'open societies' the frontiers become permeable and turn into bridges of communication with others and with strangers. It is important to be mindful, not just of the historical orientation of time, but of the social and earthly order of space too.

2. Historical Spaces of God's Indwellings

Is God the space of his world or can the world also become God's space? If we assume that God is infinite but the world finite, then only God can be the space of the world, and the world cannot be God's space. And yet the Bible tells of ever new indwellings of God in the earthly world. He 'dwells' in the midst of his people, he has his dwelling on Zion, he dwells among those scattered in exile and with them returns to his dwelling. 'The Word became flesh and dwelt among us', in Christ the fulness of the Godhead 'dwells' bodily, and at the end the eternal God will 'dwell' among human beings. But how can the infinite God 'dwell' in earthly limited spaces and communities without destroying these spaces and communities through his infinity? Does he split himself up, or does he merely let a drop of the infinite sea of his deity, as it were, live among human beings on this earth? Does he transform himself and make himself small, in order to live in a temple built by human hands, and in a nation of human beings?

The Jewish doctrine of the Shekinah tries to give an answer to these questions.[98] *The Christian doctrine about the incarnation of the Logos* and the inhabitation of the Spirit is the answer in another form.[99] The two display so many parallels that we can assume that the second presupposes the first, or goes back to the same biblical presuppositions. The idea of the Shekinah links the infinite God with a finite, earthly space in which he desires to live. Shekinah theology is temple theology. Shekinah means the act of God's descent, and its consequence in his indwelling. God desires to be present and to reveal himself in a particular place. This special presence of God is not part of his general presence, but is based on a special act of descent and self-humiliation. Since God remains the subject of this self-humiliation and descent, his sovereignty is not infringed through these ideas – on the contrary: God is so sovereign that he does not have to assert himself but can give himself into the human world, becomes 'the God of Israel' and 'the Father of Jesus Christ', and in Israel and in the Son Jesus Christ is 'there'.

Rabbinic theology has tried to interpret the descent and indwelling of God with a *theory of contraction* which has to be distinguished from the later kabbalistic doctrine of *zimzum*. 'God leaves the council above and restricts (contracts) his Shekinah in the sanctuary.'[100] A concentration of this kind into an earthly localized space is not a diminution of his general presence. Even if we are told that 'God lives in heaven', this means a place in the world, the invisible side of creation. So if God's Shekinah 'lives in heaven', that is already a contraction of God which is to continue 'on earth as it is in heaven'. But if we are not prepared to accept that there can be any transformation of God, we have then to distinguish between God himself and his Shekinah. Is there here a 'self-differentiation of God', who 'is enthroned' in heaven and at the same time 'lives' in the midst of his people?[101] The rabbinic sources are evidently talking about a certain independence on the part of the Shekinah, which can come and can withdraw itself, which can journey and suffer with the people, which can even stand over against God.[102]

The Christian doctrine of the Trinity, which distinguishes divine Persons in the unity of God, was certainly in its classic form formulated in Greek and Roman terms, but in content it goes back to the Old Testament approaches of Shekinah theology, as New Testament language about the indwellings of God shows. Dogmatic christology has tried to interpret the indwelling of the fulness of the Godhead in Jesus Christ in a way that resembles contraction theology, drawing on the idea of the *kenosis* of the Logos according to Philippians 2. Through his self-humiliation and his emptying of himself, the eternal Logos 'took the form of a servant', in order, like the Shekinah, to share the sufferings of those who are his, as their Brother, and through his sufferings on the cross to redeem them. In order to save the concept of God's unalterability, later christology replaced the idea of kenosis by the idea of the *assumption* of human nature by the eternal Logos. Both ideas lead to the conception of a unique community of the indwelling God with human nature and its history, which he indwells; and both thus deepen Shekinah theology.

In rabbinic writings, the presence and appearance of the Shekinah in history is described as 'the history of the liberations or redemptions of God' and of Israel's special community with God. No fixed system of salvation history is associated with this idea, but there are times when the Shekinah is far off, and times when it descends. Thus the Shekinah dwelt in the Garden of Eden, and departed from human beings step by step with the Fall. From Abraham to Moses, we again see a step-by-step descent of the Shekinah on Israel. Together with Israel, the Shekinah departed from Egypt, delivering the people at the Reed Sea. It appeared to Moses in the burning bush on Sinai. It rested on the Ark of the covenant, and found a dwelling place in the temple on Zion. After the destruction of Solomon's temple in 587 it either returned to heaven or went into captivity with the people. The utterances about the Shekinah which suffers and journeys with the people in their exile are among the most moving testimonies of Jewish faith. 'Every redemption is followed by a return of the people to the promised land, and hence a return of the Shekinah to the sanctuary.'[103] There are two different images for the Shekinah in history: (1) The descent into the tabernacle of the present – the ascent from the first sanctuary – the return at the End-time; (2) The defeat – the exile – the redemption of the Shekinah from exile.

In both cases hope for the homecoming of the Shekinah, whether it be from heaven or from exile, puts its mark on exilic theology. The remembrance of the destruction of the city of God, the temple and the king's palace by the Babylonians changes into the hope that God and his glory will return to the temple of the future, in order there 'to dwell for ever in the midst of the Israelites', as Ezekiel 40–48 puts it in the great closing vision. The promise that the dwelling will be 'for ever' makes this hope an eschatological hope. The link between Shekinah and *kabod* stresses the unity of God's indwelling and his manifestation. The End-time revelation of God's glory is linked with the final return of the Shekinah, which is no longer under threat. The glory which fills heaven and earth is identical with the Shekinah which dwelt in the sanctuary.[104]

This hope means that the time of history is experienced as exile, as the far country and remoteness from God, as existence under God's 'hidden countenance'. If the Shekinah returned to heaven after the destruction of God's city, then the time of history is without it, and has therefore been forsaken by God's presence. But if the Shekinah journeyed with the captive people into Babylonian exile, then it remains 'in the midst of the Israelites', but as the exiled Shekinah, as a divine presence without a home. The Shekinah participates in the persecutions, and sufferings, and dying of the people, and together with that exiled people waits for its redeeming homecoming. Through shared suffering, God and the people remain bound to one another and wait for their redemption. This idea about God's 'redemption of himself' only sounds strange if we fail to distinguish between God and his Shekinah, and assume in God only a single subject. It is not the undifferentiated 'suffering of God', but the suffering of *the Shekinah*, God's com-passionate indwelling in the suffering of the people, which is 'the *means* through which Israel is redeemed: God himself is "the ransom" for Israel.'[105]

Israel's eschatological hope for the final indwelling of God is the foundation of the Christian hope for the 'new heaven and the new earth'. Ezekiel 37.27 returns once more in the promise of Rev. 21.3:

> I will dwell with them,
> and I will be their God,
> and they shall be my peoples.

That is 'the tabernacle – the dwelling – of God with human beings', God's sanctuary among them 'for ever': the new Jerusalem.

In this fundamental idea of exilic and later rabbinic Shekinah theology it is not difficult to discern the presuppositions of Christian christology and pneumatology. We find the combination of indwelling and the manifestation of glory in the Gospel of John (1.14). In his use of the temple metaphor for the community of Christ and for the body, Paul combines Shekinah and Spirit (I Cor. 6.19). What is said about the dwelling of God in his people Israel is transferred to the dwelling of the fulness of God in Christ (Col. 2.9). It is not Jesus as a historical individual that is meant here; it is Jesus as the messianic representative of God and Israel for the peoples of the earth. It is therefore not surprising that the patterns of Shekinah theology should put their impress on the eschatological expectation of Christians too. The One who here among men and women is hidden beneath the cross will be revealed in glory – whether it be that he 'comes again' from heaven, or whether he emerges from his hidden presence and fills everything with his radiance.

And yet there is one particular Christian contribution to Shekinah theology. This is the idea of the mutual Shekinah of God and human beings 'in Christ'. 'In Christ' is God himself, God who has 'reconciled the world with himself' (II Cor. 5.19). Those who are 'in Christ' are 'a new creation' (II Cor. 5.17). 'In Christ' we find a double dwelling: the indwelling of God and the indwelling of believers. This double indwelling becomes the foundation for the eschatological and universal hope of Christians for the new creation of all things.

The difference between Shekinah theology and christology is that although – especially among the rabbis – God's Shekinah, as Israel's co-sufferer and its companion on the way, can take on human features, it has not yet specifically 'become flesh' and as messianic person 'dwelt among us'.[106] The difference between Shekinah eschatology and Christian eschatology is the difference between the new temple in the earthly Jerusalem, and the new Jerusalem that comes down from heaven and which has no temple. Ultimately, in the redemption, God and his Shekinah will be indistinguishably one. God's 'self-differentiation' will be ended. According to the Christian idea, Christ will hand over the kingdom to the Father, so that God may be 'all in all', but the Son does not therefore make himself superfluous, and there is no self-dissolution of the Son in the Father. In glory too, God is still the triune God.

3. The Fulfilment of Space in the Presence of God

Through the space conceded by God, creation is given detachment from God and freedom of movement over against him. If God were omnipresent in the absolute sense, and manifested in his glory, there would be no earthly creation. In order to make himself endurable for his earthly creatures, God has to veil his glory, since 'he who looks upon God must die'. Remoteness from God and spatial distance from God result from the withdrawal of God's omnipresence and 'the veiling of his face'. They are part of the grace of creation, because they are conditions for the liberty of created beings. It is only for sinners, who cut themselves off from God, that they become the expression of God's anger towards them in their God-forsakenness. If God himself enters into his creation through his Christ and his Spirit, in order to live in it and to arrive at his rest, he will then overcome not only the God-forsakenness of sinners, but also the distance and space of his creation itself, which resulted in isolation from God, and sin;

for redemption can only mean that with sin itself the potentiality for sin has also been surmounted; otherwise redemption would not be final. What does that mean for the space of created beings?

We said first that the space of creation is both the space in which created beings can move, and the dwelling space in God conceded to them: 'The Lord is the dwelling space of his world.' If we follow the exposition of Jewish and Christian Shekinah theology, we now have to expand this and say: And creation is destined to be the dwelling space for God. The history of God's indwellings in people and temple, in Christ and in the Holy Spirit, point forward to their completion in the universal indwelling of God's glory and its manifestation: 'The whole earth is full of his glory' (Isa.6.3). Through the historical process of indwelling and its eschatological completion, the distanced contraposition of the Creator *towards* his creation becomes the inner presence of God *in* his creation. To the external presence of God *above it* is added the inner presence of God *within it*. To the transcendence of the Creator towards his creation is added the immanence of his indwelling in his creation. With this the whole creation becomes the *house of God*, the *temple* in which God can dwell, the *home country* in which God can rest. All created beings participate directly and without mediation in his indwelling glory, and in it are themselves glorified. They participate in his divine life, and in it live eternally. Once God finds his dwelling place in creation, creation loses its space outside God and attains to its place in God. Just as at the beginning the Creator made himself the living space for his creation, so at the end his new creation will be his living space. A mutual indwelling of the world in God and God in the world will come into being. For this, it is neither necessary for the world to dissolve into God, as pantheism says, nor for God to be dissolved in the world, as atheism maintains. God remains God, and the world remains creation. Through their mutual indwellings, they remain unmingled and undivided, for God lives in creation in a God-like way, and the world lives in God in a world-like way.

The mutual indwellings then issue in a cosmic *communicatio idiomatum*, a communication of idioms, to use a scholastic phrase – that is to say, mutual participation in the attributes of the other. Created beings participate in the divine attributes of eternity and omnipresence, just as the indwelling God has participated in their limited time and their restricted space, taking them upon himself. This means that for those God has created, the time (*chronos*) of remoteness from God and of transience ceases, and eternal life in the divine life begins. It means that for those God has created, the space (*topos*) of detachment from God ceases, and eternal presence in the omnipresence of God begins. God's indwelling eternity gives to created beings eternal time. God's indwelling presence gives to created beings for ever the 'broad space in which there is no more cramping'.

§5 THE COSMIC TEMPLE: THE HEAVENLY JERUSALEM

The visions of the heavenly Jerusalem in Rev. 21.1–22.5 must be understood as prophetic encouragement given to resisting men and women in this world of Babylon/Rome, which is anti-God. But the visions offer the cosmic image of a different world which accords wholly with God, because he himself dwells in it. The city of God is the centre of the new creation. It is not easy to decipher the picture language, and to elucidate all the references and allusions, for this is the 'secret revelation' (as the book is also called) or, as we should say today, underground literature, with an encoded message. John on Patmos is writing for Christians who in the discipleship of the crucified Christ are resisting Rome's political demon-service, and are exposing themselves to the risk of martyrdom. Curiously enough, he writes in such a way that the Jewish resistance can also find itself in his visions of the new Jerusalem. We shall try to arrive at an interpretation in the perspectives of political and cosmic eschatology.

1. The Earthly and the Heavenly Jerusalem

For the first Christians, *the earthly Jerusalem* had an ambivalent significance. Jerusalem was the city of Jesus's crucifixion and the place of his Easter appearances at his tomb. Jerusalem was *the place of terror*, and the place where godless powers plotted against God's Messiah. Here Jesus was abandoned by the Jewish authorities of his people, if not spurned. Here he was tortured by the Roman occupying power under the procurator Pontius Pilate and murdered through crucifixion. For the first Christians, 'Jerusalem' and 'Rome' were bound to blend into one another, as powers hostile to Christ. Jerusalem was the place of Christ's suffering and 'abuse'. That is why the Epistle to the Hebrews exhorts the Christians: 'So Jesus also suffered outside the gate . . . Therefore let us go forth to him outside the camp, and bear the abuse he endured' (13.12f.)

But Jerusalem was also *the place of hope*. It was there that the risen One appeared to the women who had come with him from Galilee and had held out at his cross, when the disciples had run away. They had heard the message: 'He is not here. He is risen' (Matt. 28.6). The Easter appearances were the sure sign of the Messiah. That is why the disciples who had fled returned to Jerusalem when they heard the message from the women, although any other place in the world would surely have offered them more protection. They had to reckon with prosecution by the Romans, and their rejection by the men and women of their own people. But apparently they had lost their fear of death and were prepared to suffer the same fate as their Master. If there is a historically strong 'proof' of the resurrection of Jesus, it is not the empty tomb; it is this death-defying return of the disciples. Why did they go back to Jerusalem? Because according to prophetic promise it is in Jerusalem that the Messiah will appear, in order once more to establish Israel from Zion, and so as to bring justice and righteousness among the nations and on earth. 'The Deliverer will come from Zion, he will banish ungodliness from Jacob' (Rom. 11.26). So it was in Jerusalem that the first Christian community awaited the messianic kingdom, gathering round the twelve apostles, who represented the twelve tribes of Israel.

Up to the year 65, when the Jewish-Christian James 'the Just' was murdered ('Just' meaning faithful to the Torah), this first Jerusalem congregation was the spiritual centre of the Christian congregations that grew up in the Mediterranean area. They evidently saw a messianic mission to the Gentiles going hand in hand with the expectation of a final conversion of Israel. That is why the missionary apostle Paul collected money in the Christian congregations, in Rome too; it was a collection for 'the poor among the saints in Jerusalem' (Rom. 15.26), as a sign that the church is the vanguard of the nations who will make a pilgrimage to Zion so as there to receive the righteousness and peace of God of which the gospel of Christ has given them testimony. Large sections of the early Christian congregations saw themselves as a messianic movement of peace, in which the prophetic promise was fulfilled (Isa. 2.4; Micah 4.1–3).[107]

When Jerusalem was destroyed by the Romans in the year 70, the earthly centre of the Christian congregations was destroyed too.

Jesus's criticism of the temple, and Stephen's prophecy that the temple would be destroyed, were seen as a reference to this. But mourning for the loss of the earthly Jerusalem was increasingly pushed out by the ancient apocalyptic image of hope, *the heavenly Jerusalem* (Zech. 12.1–14; Tob. 1.4–7; 2 Esd. 8.52 and other passages).[108] This idea stems from the Israelite inclination (reinforced by Platonic influences) to assume that religious objects on earth have heavenly archetypes (cf. Ex. 25.40). 'The Jerusalem above is free, and she is our mother', writes Paul in Gal. 4.26. The antithesis to 'the present Jerusalem' (4.25) indicates that he understands 'the Jerusalem above' not platonically but eschatologically. If Jerusalem is 'our mother', then he views her 'in the Holy Spirit', seeing in the communities of Christ her provisional realization in time. Isa.54.1 also points to the renewed people of God. As distinct from 'Hagar – Sinai – earthly Jerusalem', Paul means 'the heavenly commonwealth to which the Christians already belong here on earth'.[109] Qumran also saw itself as the community of the heavenly Jerusalem.[110]

The practical consequence is the call to freedom, the call too to live as strangers in this world. Christians are citizens of the coming kingdom of God, which is symbolized in 'the heavenly Jerusalem' and 'the city to come'. They are therefore refugees in all the kingdoms of the world. Because they wait for the redemption of this whole perverted world in the coming eternal kingdom, they feel that in this world, estranged from God as it is, they are strangers. The 'heavenly Jerusalem' becomes for them the symbol of the hoped-for new creation of the world, God's dwelling, and an anti-symbol to this world's godless metropolises, such as Babylon and Rome. When the writer of the Epistle to the Hebrews wrote 'We have here no lasting city, but we seek the city which is to come' (13.14), what he said was probably directed first against the earthly Jerusalem, but then and above all against murderous Rome. 'Lasting city' (πόλις μένουσα) is the promise of all holy metropolises: *Roma aeterna*, eternal Rome. For apocalyptically hoping Christians, however, there is no 'lasting city' in the transitory time of this world, and in the godless time of this world no 'holy city'. If Christ is really risen, then his tomb is empty. Consequently for Christians there are no longer any 'holy places' which have to be visited or cherished. Those who worship him are to 'worship him in spirit and in truth' (John 4.24), nowhere else. Because they live wholly in the expectation of the coming kingdom, for these people 'every home country becomes a foreign land and every foreign land a home' as the Epistle to Diognetus says (ch. 6). Christians belong to no nation and therefore come from all nations. In the Roman empire they knew themselves to be *tertium genus*, literally 'a third race or gender', belonging nowhere.

2. *Jerusalem and Babylon/Rome*

'The new Jerusalem' has a forerunner in the past and its antithesis in the present. The forerunner is the earthly Jerusalem, with the temple on Zion; the antithesis is 'Babylon', a code word for the metropolis Rome in the Roman empire. The colours with which the future city of God are painted are taken from both cities. The Christian world for which the book of Revelation was written was the world of cities.[111] The Christians were city-dwellers, 'the heathen' were called *pagani*, villagers.

In the urban world, the cities usually had feminine names and symbols. Turning these symbols upside down was a way of expressing criticism and judgment. The metropolis Rome is not called *Dea Roma* (the goddess Rome) but 'the great harlot' (17.1) who has dominion over the kings on earth (17.18) and seduces the nations through the splendour of her power and wealth. She is 'the mother of harlots and of all earth's abominations'. She sits on a scarlet beast full of blasphemous names, clothed in purple and scarlet, gold and pearls, with the 'golden cup' which makes all the world drunk (Jer. 51.7), and she herself is drunk with the blood of the saints and Jesus's witnesses (17.6). She is 'the beast from the abyss', the city that dominates the world.

'The new Jerusalem', the city of God, is also symbolized as a woman. She is 'the Lamb's bride' (19.7; 21.2). Her forerunner is the heavenly woman who gives birth to the Messiah and hides him from the dragon in the wilderness (12.2ff.): a woman 'clothed with the sun, with the moon under her feet, and on her head a crown of twelve stars'. She is the mother of Jesus and of Christians, of earthly Israel and the 'Jerusalem above', symbol for the Holy Spirit.[112] This female figure is the precursor of the holy city. The divine alternative of resisting and persecuted Christians should not be looked for just in the eschatological future; hidden and persecuted, it is already coming into being now, in the present-day of Roman imperial rule. Rome is called 'Babylon' because its godless claim to universal rule corresponds to the tower of Babel, and because in 70 AD Rome destroyed the city and temple of God, as neo-Babylon had done once before, in 587 BC. Rome's empire is the satanic parody of God's sovereignty over the world. So Rome must fall, in order that the new Jerusalem, as true city of God, can take its place. Revelation makes this clear through antitheses and correspondences between 'Babylon' and 'Jerusalem':

Here Jerusalem, the pure bride of the Lamb (21.2) – there Rome, the great whore with whom the kings on earth have fornicated (17.2); here 'the nations' walk in her light and kings on earth will 'bring their glory into her' (21.24) – there 'she has dominion over the kings of the earth' (17.18) and her 'merchants were the princes on earth' (18.23); this city's fame is 'the glory of God' (21.23) – that city's fame is her 'wealth' (18.17), which comes from the exploitation of her empire; this city contains 'the water of life' (22.1) – while the other makes the nations drunk through her wine (18.3). Here there is 'life and healing' (22.1f.) – there blood and death (17.6; 18.24). Like Rome, the city of God is also radiant with the splendour of precious stones and pearls (21.18–21). Just as the harlot has written her name on the brows of those who are hers, so people in the New Jerusalem bear 'God's name on their foreheads' (22.4); their names are written in 'the book of life' (21.27). The new Jerusalem is the dwelling place of the true God, while Babylon/Rome is the dwelling place of demons (18.1–3).

Here we have a counter-image of hope for those who resist Rome's theo-political claim to universal rule, an image which is nevertheless fed by the splendour of Babylon and Rome. The tower of Babel was the attempt of godless human beings to storm heaven. The city of God, in contrast, comes down from heaven to earth, and out of grace fulfils the wish of human beings for God's presence. Thus in the book of Revelation the heavenly Jerusalem appears in many dimensions as the Rome whose perversion has been put to rights. But it belongs to those who have born 'the abuse of Christ' because they have not submitted to Rome's religious claim and its world-wide political and economic domination. That is the antithesis that lies in the parallels between the metropolis of Rome and the city of God, Jerusalem. The present citizens of the coming city of God are not just the Christian martyrs; they are the murdered prophets and saints as well, and, beyond those, 'all who have been slain on earth' (18.24), whose blood can be found in the city of the damned. This widening out of 'the abuse of Christ' to take in Christians and Jews, and the resistance of the peoples too, is important for the vision of the people of the heavenly Jerusalem (cf. already Heb.11.26).

3. *The City of God: Crystal Temple and Garden City*

As city of God, the new Jerusalem is paradise, at once the holy city and the cosmic temple. As paradise, it contains 'the water of life' and 'the tree of life' (22.1f.) and gives eternal life 'without payment' (21.6). As holy city, it fulfils the ideal of the ancient city, as a place where heaven and earth meet, at earth's central point, the point from which God rules his world and his humanity, not through power but through the force of attraction. The heavenly city of God descends upon the 'great and high mountain' (21.10), which according to ancient mythology is the dwelling place of the gods, and according to Ezek. 40.2 joins heaven and earth. Mount Zion, on which the Jerusalem temple stood, is in reality a comparatively low hill. In the prophetic visions it is immeasurably elevated, becoming 'the joy of all the earth' (Ps. 48.2). The temple becomes the place of God's indwelling presence, the place where the face of God can be seen. From it the glory of God will radiate and illuminate the cosmos. 'The throne of God' will no longer be in heaven; it will stand in this cosmic temple, which binds together heaven and earth.

The material used in the vision of the heavenly Jerusalem in chapters 21 and 22 of the book of Revelation is taken from Ezekiel 37 to 48.[113] But John expands the Ezekiel vision with material from Isaiah, and takes up the apocalyptic ideas about the new Jerusalem. He also draws in the ancient traditions of the *polis*, the city state. If we compare John with Ezekiel, we notice that he describes not merely the city but its walls and gates too (which Ezekiel does not mention), and does so particularly lovingly. Moreover he describes only the city, not the temple, whereas Ezekiel describes the temple but hardly the city. John puts 'the throne of God and of the Lamb' at the centre. 'The Lamb', as name for the crucified Christ, is naturally missing in Ezekiel. The city of God is set at the centre of the new world, in accordance with the ancient idea.

Whereas the city of God is described in cosmic dimensions, the city walls with the city gates symbolize the people of God, Jews and Gentiles. Into the twelve gates are chiselled the names of the twelve tribes of Israel (21.12), the walls rest on the foundation stones of

Christ's twelve apostles (21.14). With the dominant number 'twelve' we can also think of the twelve signs of the zodiac in Babylon. The foundations correspond to the precious stones on the breastplate of the Jewish high priest (2.19ff.) – a way of symbolizing the priestly people of God. The distinction between the city walls and the city itself draws attention to the curious measurements with which John describes the relation between them. 'An enormous discrepancy exists between the size of the city and the size of the walls.'[114] Whereas the city is 12,000 stadia in breadth and length (about 1,200 miles), the walls are only 144 cubits (rather more than 200 feet). Unless John was just working with symbolic figures, the discrepancy must be meant to express the immeasurable degree to which the cosmic new creation of the world exceeds the magnitude of the Jewish and Christian people of God. The Christian community is not one particular religious community among others. It is a small, resisting and steadfast witness to the coming reshaping of the whole present world system, like the Jewish community too.

The whole city radiates God's glory like jasper – a rare precious stone – and clear as crystal (21.11). Like jasper shines the One who sits upon the throne in heaven (4.3), and the crystal sea before the heavenly throne reflects his glory. This picture has been the inspiration of painters, poets and city architects down to the present day.[115] The crystal city is a true 'city of light'. Since her streets are of pure gold (21.21), she is 'the golden city'. Since her gates are never closed day or night, she is 'the open city'.[116] Is the crystal palace an appropriate symbol for the kingdom of God, or has a myth which we also find in many fairytales been taken over from an astral religion? As a petrified future, crystal is by no means a good symbol for eternal life, but as transparency for the omnipresent light of God, and as abolition of spacial borderlines and distances, it is appropriate enough.

The city of God is the perfect 'garden city'. In it the abundance of life and the beauty of the Garden of Eden return, but it is more than just paradise regained. As city, it fulfils the need and longing of men and women to build a living place of their own for human fellowship and culture. As the perfect city, it fulfils the history of human civilization, which according to the biblical saga began when Cain, the city-builder (Gen. 4.17), murdered his brother Abel, the nomadic shepherd. The new Jerusalem holds within itself the Garden of Eden (22.1ff.) and is an image of perfect harmony between civilization and nature. It thereby also consummates the history of earthly nature with human beings. The city of God lives in nature, and nature lives in the city of God. 'The garden city' was an ancient ideal of the *polis* for many peoples. It is the ideal of ecological city civilization too, and modern mass cities offend against it at the cost of the death of nature, and later of human beings as well.

Finally, it has always been noticed that the city of God has no temple, whereas in Ezekiel's vision the new temple is the main thing. It is a city devoid of religion and cult. Of course this does not mean that it is a 'secular city'.[117] The new Jerusalem has no need of a temple as a special house of God, because the whole city is filled with the immediate presence of God and Christ. It is the city of God's kingdom without religion, because it is religion's fulfilment and end. The city of God is itself the temple city for the indwelling of his glory (21.22). Whereas the temple always stands in a closed-off precinct ($\tau\acute{\epsilon}\mu\epsilon\nu o\varsigma$), so as to separate the sacred from the profane, in the eschatological city of God this separation is ended. God's Shekinah is omnipresent and traverses all spatial borderlines. That is the reason for the astonishing cubic form of the heavenly Jerusalem: its breadth, length and height are the same (21.16). In this respect the city resembles no earthly city, and no earthly temple either. But it does correspond to the Holy of Holies in Israel's temple, the inner sanctuary (I Kings 6.17–20). The innermost heart of the vision of the new Jerusalem and the new creation of heaven and earth is nothing other than the immediate, omnipresent and eternal indwelling of God and of Christ.

4. The Peoples of God

The significance of 'the holy city', the new Jerusalem, which descends from heaven, lies in the new divine covenant:

> Behold, the dwelling of God is with men;
> and he will dwell with them.
> and they shall be his peoples,
> and God himself will be with them
> and be their God (21.3).

That is Israel's ancient covenant formula, which in Ezek. 37.27 is associated with the new temple. But here the covenant with Israel is extended to human beings ($\dot{\alpha}\nu\theta\rho\dot{\omega}\pi o\iota$). All nations ($\dot{\epsilon}\theta\nu\acute{\eta}$) will be

God's peoples (λαοί). In the new Jerusalem, John sees God's covenant with human beings, and uses for the nations the word *laos*, which otherwise is used only for the people of God. Curiously enough most translators miss this point. But it means: 'Now that the covenant people have fulfilled their role of being a light to the nations, all nations will share in the privileges and promises of the covenant people.'[118]

This eschatological universalization of the particularism of salvation history can be viewed under two perspectives: (1) The nations will be gathered into the covenant relationship of Israel and the church; (2) God's covenant relationship with Israel and the church will be extended. In the first case Israel's historical privilege is retained; in the second, Israel has fulfilled its historical mission and enters into the eschatological covenant of its God with humanity. As we have seen, Israel and the church are the foundation stones for the gates and the walls of the holy city, but not for the city itself, which rises into cosmic dimensions. But the covenant formula is repeated in 21.7, in order to single out the men and women martyrs who 'have overcome'. They will serve God and the Lamb, will see his face and bear his name on their foreheads (22.3, 4) and reign with him in eternity (22.5). The Jewish high priest was permitted to enter the Holy of Holies only once a year, but they live in it continually. Moses saw the face of God only once, they see it always. In the new Jerusalem, the martyrs will become priests and priestesses and kings and queens. The nations will walk in the light of God in the holy city, and 'the kings of the earth', who were subjugated by Babylon/Rome, will come into the holy city of their own free will, in order to bring 'their glory' into it. Their cultural pluralism will not be ended – it is desired. What is the relation between the particularism of the *people* of the covenant and the eschatological universalism of the *peoples* of the covenant?

Because John is writing for the resistance, for the persecuted and the martyrs, he sees between Israel and the peoples the throng of men and women from Israel and the Christian congregations who have born 'the abuse of Christ', and whose eschatological future he wishes to paint (cf. ch. 7). These are the people who have been 'sealed' from the twelve tribes of Israel, and the throng of the resisting and the redeemed out of all nations. They serve God eternally. God will dwell above them. They receive the water of life and God will wipe away their tears (7.15, 17). Whereas the twelve tribes of Israel and the twelve apostles form the gates and walls of the holy city, the sealed men and women martyrs seem to constitute the throng of the city's royal priesthood. The nations of humanity will become God's covenant peoples (21.3) and have free access to the holy city. Historical Israel and the historical church no longer receive any special mention. It is not that the people of the covenant live in the city, while the nations come with their gifts and go with their light; nor is it that Israel now belongs to the new peoples of the covenant, and therefore enters the holy city from outside. From this we can only conclude that the historical tasks and privileges of the covenant people – Jewish and Christian both – will be gathered up in the eschatological Jerusalem, arriving at their fulfilment and their end. The eschatological covenant with God makes all nations covenant peoples, and brings the nearness of God to them all: 'All nations shall come and worship thee' (15.4). Only unrepentant sinners have no access to the new Jerusalem. No one who shares in the godless power of Babylon and clings to it enters God's holy city. This does not just mean Rome's lack of morals. It is referring much more to the demonic character of the metropolis, politically and economically, the outcome of which is lack of morality.

This, then, is the picture we are given of the people of God: Israel and the church form the walls of the city and its gates. The holy city itself is open for the new peoples of God's covenant. In the city, the men and women martyrs of Israel and the church who have resisted the empire of Rome and its idols pray and reign together with Christ, the Lamb.

5. God's Cosmic Shekinah

The most important thing about the new Jerusalem and the new peoples of God is God's new presence, which consists of the indwelling of his unmediated and direct glory. The indwelling presence makes heaven and earth new, and is also the really new thing in the new Jerusalem. God will 'dwell' among them. That is *the cosmic Shekinah*. What in history was experienced only among the people of God and in the temple, in Christ and in the Holy Spirit, and was expected of God's future, is there fulfilled: God's immediate presence interpenetrates everything. For that reason we shall be able to look upon his face without perishing. For that reason his throne will move from the heavens above the earth into that holy city which joins heaven and earth – or rather brings heaven down to earth. What was present in the earthly temple in restricted form and mediated through priests will then be unrestricted and in need of no mediation. The eschatological indwelling of God in all things has two characteristics: holiness and glory.

Holy is God himself, and everything that belongs to God will be holy, because he has created and redeemed it, and made it the vessel of his indwelling. That is why the city of God is 'the holy city'. Everything unholy must be excluded from it. The godless and murderous metropolis Babylon/Rome is unholy. What belongs to her, what lives from her and worships her has no place in God's city, for it cannot become the vessel of the divine light. The antithesis between holy and unholy is a comprehensive one, and must be understood politically, economically and morally.

The *glory* lies in the unfolding of the divine splendour and its inexhaustible beauty. The precious stones, the pearls and crystal reflect God's light through their own beauty, which begins to shine only in the divine light that falls on them. Everything that is ugly is excluded from the beauty of God's city. The indwelling presence of God is the source of the light that interpenetrates everything and makes it shine. The light that shines through everything is a visible sign of the all-interpenetrating presence of God, and of the perichoresis which does not destroy created beings but full-fills them. The countless and multifariously bright reflections of the divine light show the richness and the eternal participation of created beings in the present glory of God.

The holiness and the glory of the eternal indwelling of God is the eschatological goal of creation as a whole and of all individual created beings. This gives cosmic eschatology a theological dimension and an aesthetic one.

Talk about 'the throne of God' makes the image of the new Jerusalem a political one, related to the forms of domination of the time. Seen as counter-image to the throne of the caesars, it is noticeable that the throne of God is accessible to everyone, and is surrounded by no heavenly household and no bodyguards. Remarkably enough, even the angels of Heb. 12.22 are not mentioned, just as the heaven of Revelation 21 ceases to have any significance of its own. All who enter the holy city have direct access to God. There are no special priests or kings who rule with him. All who serve him will also reign with him for ever and ever (22.3 and 5). God's rule over them is simultaneously their participation in that rule. That can be regarded as the reconciliation of the sovereignty of God and human freedom. Rule through the mutual give and take of power is the other counter-image to the power of the Roman caesars, who subjugate through violence. The eschatological power of God is not characterized by suppression and subjugation. It is typified by the well and the tree of life (22.1–2). The presence of the divine life becomes the inexhaustible source of creaturely life, which thereby becomes the life that is eternal.

In the final visions of the book of Revelation, heaven descends to earth. The earth becomes the city which holds paradise within itself. This city becomes the place open to all. In this place God's Shekinah finally comes to rest. In its rest, all created beings find their eternal happiness. For this 'the Spirit and the Bride' call in the unrest of history and in the sufferings of this present time (Rev. 22.17).

V

Glory

Divine Eschatology

V

Glory

Divine Eschatology

The final article in dogmatics, especially the dogmatics of Calvinist orthodoxy, has to do with *the glorification of God*: Soli Deo gloria – to God alone be the glory. The glorification of God is the ultimate purpose of creation. Consequently the supreme goal of human beings is 'to glorify God and to enjoy him forever'.[1] 'Since the glorification of God is the purpose of all things, and since God, as the primordial source of all bliss, desires to glorify himself in believers, these believers are called by the Father, not merely to the enjoyment of Christ's grace, but also to the enjoyment of Christ's glory, although in its whole perfection this will be conferred on the elect only after death.'[2] In history and in this life believers experience 'the servant form of God's kingdom' in the suffering Christ. But in his parousia they will with him experience God's kingdom in its form of glory. To 'glorify' God means to love God for his own sake, and to enjoy God as he is in himself. The idea of *enjoying* God in the glorification of God derives from Augustine: sinners 'make use' of God in order to 'enjoy' the world, but believers 'make use' of the world in order to 'enjoy' God.[3] So to 'glorify' God means to rejoice in God's existence and one's own, and to express this joy in thanksgiving and praise, in the joy of living and in celebration.

This means that all moral purposes are excluded from the glorification of God, as is every economic utility. The praise of God has no purpose and no utility – if it had, God would not be praised for his own sake. It is simply meaningful in itself. The glorification of God has this in common with the child's self-forgetting delight in its game. Free human self-expression is an echo of the Creator's good pleasure in the creations of his love. Consequently the simplest glorification of God is the demonstrative joy in their existence of those he has created.[4] It is impossible to stress sufficiently the significance of the glorification of God for the inward and outward liberation of men and women from the plans and purposes of their workaday world. Ethical existence is gathered up and perfected in the aesthetic existence of doxology.

In this chapter, however, we shall turn the question upside down, and ask about the meaning *for God himself* of his glorification by human beings and all his creatures. 'What does God get from the world?'[5] Is the world a matter of indifference for him, because he suffices for himself? Does he need it, in order to complete himself? Does it perhaps give him pleasure, because he rejoices in the echo of those he has created? Is there also a kind of divine eschatology in the glorification of God, so that in his glorification God arrives at his goal, and in his goal arrives at himself? We shall consider a number of theses which have been put forward in the course of the history of theology, and shall discuss their consequences: Does glory consist

1. in the self-glorification of God?
2. in the self-realization of God?
3. In the interactions between divine and human activity?

True glory is:

4. The fulness of God and the feast of eternal joy.

§1 THE SELF-GLORIFICATION OF GOD

A first answer emphasizes God's sovereignty and his self-sufficiency. There is no glorification of God which does not proceed from God himself, does not take place through God himself, and is not related to God himself: all glorification of God through others is God's self-glorification in others. God's self-glorification consists in God's *self-glory*. God exists through himself. God is sufficient for himself. God is in himself complete. God is in himself blissful. So God does not need the world, but the world needs him. The world does not exist through itself. It finds continuance only in God. Nothing in the world is ever sufficient for itself, and therefore finds sufficiency only in God. Nothing in the world can be happy in itself. God himself is the eternal happiness of all non-divine living beings. God moves all things without himself moving, for as perfect beauty he draws the Eros of all the living to himself.[6] Like a magnet, the Deity attracts through himself, drawing to himself everything that is transitory and scattered. The Deity who is in himself complete, self-sufficing and blissful, is also the complete, self-sufficing and in itself blissful *self-love*. This causes all living things to join in the divine self-love when they begin to love God and find their happiness in him.

But if God does not need the world, why did he create it? If God is sufficient for himself in his untouched glory, why does he then seek the echo of his self-glory in his glorification through other beings who are not divine? This thesis explains neither the creation of a world out of God, nor the consummation of this creation in God. It makes all thanksgiving, all praise, and all glorification of God by those he has created superfluous. If the world has no significance for God – if, that is, God 'gets nothing' from the world – is this not a declaration that creation, the incarnation, cross and resurrection of Christ, the indwelling of the divine Spirit, and the kingdom of God are meaningless? Is the world, its misery and its praise not inevitably a matter of complete indifference for a God who is sufficient for himself? So does this thesis about the immanent self-glorification of God not actually abolish the glorification which it is supposed to substantiate and explain?

We can only escape this dilemma if we distinguish between God's *essential nature* and his *will*. It is then possible to say: 'God could have remained satisfied with Himself and with the impassible glory and blessedness of His own inner life. But He did not do so. He elected man as a covenant partner.'[7] In his innermost nature God is complete and does not need those he has created for his completion or his enrichment. The foundation of their existence and their extolling joy in existence is an unprovoked overflow of his goodness and his eternal love. Creation, reconciliation and redemption come from God's free will, not out of his eternal nature; and yet they are not just arbitrary, random acts, for God wills and does that which pleases him and in which he find his good pleasure. In what God wills, he accords with his essential nature. He is faithful, he cannot deny himself (II Tim. 2.13). It is not out of inner necessity, it is out of overflowing love, that God goes out of himself and wills the existence of other beings, not divine, who will be in accord with his divine bliss through their joy in existence.

This distinction between God's essential nature and his will permits the link to be made between God's self-sufficiency and his affirmation of the world that is not divine, his self-glory and his joy in being glorified through others. But it introduces into God himself a contradiction or a reversal of love: essential *self-love* must become the creative love for the other, that is to say *selfless love*. In the sense of self-love God needs no one; in the sense of selfless love he seeks out everyone. In the sense of self-glory he is self-sufficing; in the sense of selfless love he is not self-sufficing. Are there then two natures in God? Can there be a contradiction such as this between God's nature and his will? Which is stronger in the end? Moreover, with this distinction is God not thought of as a super-narcissist in his deity, for whom not even his self-love is enough, but who requires world-wide applause for it in addition? Is God then to be thought of in the image of the absolutist and vainglorious Sun King Louis XIV, a God who merely 'graciously condescends' to accept the homage of his subjects 'out of grace', not for his own sake but for theirs?

According to this thesis of God's self-glorification, there is no divine eschatology, for there cannot be anything which God could still wish, hope or seek for himself. It is only in a trinitarian concept of God that selfless love and divine completion can be thought together without contradiction: the three divine Persons love one another mutually in complete, selfless love. By virtue of their love the Father is wholly in the Son, the Son is wholly in the Father, and the Spirit is wholly in the Father and the Son. Through their mutual self-giving, they together form the perfect and complete divine life which through self-giving communicates itself. We shall come back to this presently.

§2 THE SELF-REALIZATION OF GOD

The history of the world, according to Hegel's idealistic system, is the process of 'the self-realization of absolute Mind'. Its goal is that God should be in everything, and that everything should be in God. That is to say, this divine eschatology maintains that it is only at the end that God arrives at himself. According to this German Idealist thesis (which was initiated by Fichte and elaborated by Schelling and Hegel) the history of the world is nothing less than a mighty 'theogonic' process.[8] The history of the world is itself 'the becoming God', as the conception of history held in the Goethe era declared, with the help of a transference of Spinoza's pantheistic equation: *Deus sive natura* (God equals nature) into *Deus sive historia* (God equals history).[9] God is in everything that happens, and everything that happens is in God. God and world interpenetrate each other in mutual perichoresis. Consequently, not only does God affect all happening; all happening, conversely, also has an effect on God. Deity and humanity are mutually related and mutually dependent. The Deity has its importance for the destiny of humanity, but humanity also has its importance for the destiny of the Deity.

To explain this bold concept, we shall confine ourselves to a glance at a few of Hegel's ideas, for it was he who gave conceptual form to this world of thought belonging to the Goethe era.

When God creates something that is not the same as himself, but is different from himself, while yet corresponding to himself wholly and entirely, God then goes out of himself and expresses himself in this 'other' of his own self.[10] To this other he communicates existence, life and consciousness, and makes the other's world part of his own existence, life and consciousness. Consequently the history of his world becomes 'the course taken by his own life'.[11] His own infinity and the finitude of his world are eternally distinguished by their difference; but in this difference they are at the same time eternally united. In his early period Hegel called the unity of difference and oneness the primal phenomenon of love, and saw in it the primal phenomenon of religion: 'Religion is one with love. The beloved is not our opposite, he is one with our being; we see in him only ourselves – and yet again he is not we – a marvel that we are unable to grasp.'[12] Hegel's original conception of the dialectic of life – oneness in separation, separation in oneness – goes back to a poem of Hölderlin's, the friend of his youth:

> Alles Getrennte findet sich wieder
> und Friede ist mitten im Streit
> ('All that are sundered find back to each other, and there is peace in the midst of strife').

If, now, God's 'other', the world, becomes estranged from God and contradicts him instead of corresponding to him, while God, notwithstanding, desires to remain true to his creation and hence to himself, then God must empty himself into the estrangement of this world and take upon himself the absolute pain of dichotomy in order to bring about the reconciliation of what is separated from him. This is what happens in God's incarnation, for inherent in the incarnation is the resolve for the unity of the divine with human nature. This incarnation of God's prolongs itself in God's self-emptying to the point of death on the cross. Following the primal image of the hymn on Christ in Philippians 2, Hegel describes the history of the world's salvation as the self-humiliation and exaltation of the absolute Mind – that is to say, as the history of God himself. Just as God *expresses* himself in the other, so he *expends* or empties himself into what is opposite to himself, absolute death. The death of Christ manifests 'the death of God'. Consequently we have to understand *Jesus*'s 'historical Good Friday' as the primordial image for *God's* 'speculative Good Friday'. World history itself is 'the Golgotha of the absolute Mind'.[13] To view the cross of Jesus on Golgotha 'speculatively' – and that simply means in the context of the whole of the history of God – is to perceive that here God has made death in God-forsakenness, his absolute opposite, an aspect of his own eternal life and his own eternal love. If 'God himself' dies on the cross, and if in this dying he still remains the eternal God, then the death of Christ is 'the death of this death itself, the negation of negation . . . It is infinite love that God has made himself identical with what is alien to himself, in order to kill it.'[14] In 'the Spirit of the community' which perceives God in the death of Christ, the absolute Mind comes to knowledge of itself, and thus, out of its non-identity, arrives at its identity. Hegel called this 'the kingdom of Mind': 'Through death God has reconciled the world and eternally reconciles it with himself. This coming back from estrangement is his return to himself, and through it he is Mind, and this Third is for the reason that Christ is risen. The negation is thereby overcome, and the negation of negation is thus an aspect of the divine nature.'[15] The goal of world history in the history of God is for God his total self-realization, which dialectically also includes the negative, which it gathers into itself. For the world, the goal is the total and eternal reconciliation with God which can no longer be negated by anything at all.

After this brief account of Hegel's concept of world history in the history of God, let us look at the objections which have been brought against his trinitarian-sounding philosophy of reconciliation.

1. If reason grasps only that whose necessity it perceives, then according to Hegel the creation of the world and the incarnation are for God 'essential to his nature'. It is essential to the absolute Idea that it should enter into finitude, that it should sink itself in its opposite, should eternally rise out of it again, and should come to itself. Does this imply a 'disregard of God's freedom'? Is God then made 'his own prisoner', as Karl Barth mistrustfully suspected?[16]

This familiar theological charge against Hegel once again introduces the distinction between God's *nature* and his *will*, a distinction which cannot be maintained, even if one starts from God's will, in order to stress the undeserved grace of his incarnation and reconciliation with men and women. For God's grace is neither an arbitrary caprice nor a divine hand-out, an act of charity.[17] Is God not beyond every kind of polarity between freedom and necessity which human beings experience?[18] If this is so, then in making God's freedom the starting point, we have to remember the inner necessity of his love, and in proceeding from the love of God, which is his essential nature, we must remember his unconstrained freedom.

Let us test this against the theology of the cross. The theology of the cross explains why Christ died on the cross, and for what purpose. But does that mean that it actually transforms the reality of the cross into the word of the cross? If history is supposed to be nothing other than 'Mind expended into time', then for those who perceive history in Mind 'time is effaced'.[19] But there is something in the cross of Christ which resists every attempt to absorb it into its theological concept: and that is the pain of Christ and his death cry: 'My God, why . . .?' No theology of the cross can answer this cry, because it is not adequately answered by any explanation of his death, but only through his resurrection from death and the Easter jubilation of the raised. In the cross of Christ elements of the fortuitous character of history and its inner contradictions remain, elements which cannot be absorbed into any theory and thereby ended. This also limits the optimistic total claim of historical reason which Hegel propounded: what is 'reasonable' is not yet 'actual', and what is 'actual' is by no means therefore 'reasonable'.[20]

2. This already indicates the lines of the second reproach. In Hegel's world, which is objectively already wholly 'reconciled', the eschatological future is missing.[21] If the world is 'objectively speaking' already reconciled in the history of God, then it requires nothing more than the subjective knowledge of its reconciliation. The Hegel critic Karl Barth already made this point, in good Hegelian fashion, in his 'theology of reconciliation'. All that the future can still bring is the 'disclosure' of the world's objective state of reconciliation, but nothing which, over against the reconciliation, can be called 'new'. In Hegel there is no unknown future. According to Hegel nothing new can happen. But how can we describe this 'unredeemed world' as already reconciled in God without waiting

and hoping for its redemption, which has not yet taken place? Even a reconciled world is not yet the new world, but at best its beginning in the unsolved contradictions of history. Unless this is so, the reconciliation of the world turns into the justification of its suffering, and the result is an illusory world.[22] But if reconciliation is by no means already the eschatology of the world, then it cannot hold within itself the divine eschatology either. As 'the Spirit of the resurrection', the 'Spirit of the community' is no more than the down-payment or advance pledge of glory; it is not yet glory itself. The God who in Christ reconciles the world to himself is the *God on the way* to his glory and to the new creation of the world in his kingdom. Hegel's 'reason in history' was the provisional millenarian attempt to end history in the midst of history, and its effect on life in the historical catastrophes of the twentieth century was disastrous.

3. Finally, Hegel's idea of the self-realization of the absolute Mind is not really conceived in trinitarian terms, although it was put forward with the claim to restore the Christian doctrine of the Trinity. There is only *a single* divine Subject who expresses and expends himself, and who must therefore out of the negation of himself restore himself through negation of this negation. According to Philippians 2, it is the Son of God who empties himself to the point of death on the cross, but it is God the Father who raises him and exalts him over all things; whereas in Hegel it is only a single divine Subject who shows himself in these two movements. Hegel's triadic consideration of the Absolute is modalism in extreme form: the one divine Subject passes through the stages of 'the kingdom of the Father', 'the kingdom of the Son' and 'the kingdom of the Spirit'. This makes a divine eschatology inconceivable.

§3 INTERACTIONS BETWEEN DIVINE AND HUMAN ACTIVITY

Whether we talk about God's self-glorification, his self-realization or his self-communication, the glorification of God is always supposed to proceed solely from God himself. But this does not have to be so. God can also be glorified through an interaction between God and the world, God and human beings, or between the trinitarian divine Persons. We shall put forward three sequences of ideas which lead in this direction, and shall consider them critically.

(*a*) The idea of the co-workings of several subjects in the glorification of God presupposes that God is involved both actively and passively, both as giver and receiver, as both speaking and listening. A.N. Whitehead offers an interesting conception for this when he distinguishes between two natures in God, his *primordial* nature and his *consequent* nature.[23] In his primordial nature God is the subject of all his potentialities. Unmoved by the course of things, he determines and orders everything. In this primordial nature, God is the principle of what Whitehead calls 'concrescence' and of concretion, and in this respect is also the organ of the new. In his second, consequent nature, however, God is touched by the course of things, and perceives them in his own way. 'The "consequent nature of God" represents this reacting, physically sentient, sustaining and – as Whitehead also says – saving activity of God's.'[24] God 'experiences the world'. It is only in this receptive sense that we can talk about a consciousness in God. In respect of his first nature God creates the world, in respect of his second nature the world 'creates' God, because it puts its mark on him.[25] In God's consequent nature, every real event finds its permanent fulfilment, because it remains in him eternally. This second nature of God's preserves time and whatever has appeared in it. What is past has not vanished but has become immortal in the perceiving consequent nature of God. 'The consequent nature of God is the fluent world become "everlasting" by its objective immortality in God.'[26] It is true that in our awareness things succeed each other in time, and pass away with time. But if all worldly happening is perceived by God in his consequent nature, then in him everything is also simultaneous and in a certain sense eternal. The presently experienced moment acquires ineffaceability in God. That is Whitehead's impressive doctrine about 'objective immortality'. Using other terminology, we could also talk about *the memory of God*, for which nothing is lost and in which everything is preserved.

When we look more closely at this doctrine about God's two natures, we find that as far as his consequent nature is concerned, the process of reality really does make God ever richer.[27] If God lets the world affect him, then with every day he experiences more of it and his consequent nature becomes ever wider and ever fuller. Should the process of reality one day arrive at a completion, then God also arrives at his fulfilment in respect of his consequent nature. If a completion is arrived at, then God – as far as his consequent nature is concerned – is wider and richer than he was at the beginning. If that is called 'glory', then the whole of world history is present in it by virtue of its objective immortality in God: an 'apotheosis of the world'. But, if we follow Whitehead's concept, are we bound to conceive of an eschatology of the process of reality, and with it a divine eschatology? There can be an end of this kind, but there does not have to be. Since in Whitehead's view the process of reality has no beginning, it does not have to have an end either. And are all catastrophes, all crimes and all sufferings in the world really supposed to be 'eternalized' in God's consequent nature?

Although Whitehead uses personal metaphors, such as 'experience', 'perceive' and 'remember', his concept of God is conceived in curiously impersonal terms. The consequent nature of God, in which the objective immortality of all events is to be found, resembles an unfeeling monitor, which registers and records everything, rather than a human memory which can transform, forgive and forget. Not all happening in the world which the consequent nature of God experiences and preserves contributes to God's glory. On the contrary: most events contribute rather to God's scorn and his grief. It is only if the consequent nature of God itself works creatively on the experiences of happening in the world that we could put our trust in a divine mercy, where these destructive happenings in the world are concerned – as is suggested in the call for God's remembrance in the psalms: 'Remember us according to thy mercy.' Whitehead by no means excludes this, but himself inclines to the personal view when he writes: 'God is the great companion – the fellow-sufferer who understands.'[28]

(*b*) Every idea about the co-workings of created beings with God for the purpose of God's glorification presupposes a *self-restriction* on God's part, out of which the freedom and the free responses of created beings spring.[29] According to Jewish insights, God puts the sanctification of his Name, the doing of his will, and hence the coming of his kingdom in the hands of men and women. He waits for his glorification through the people of his choice. God's Name does not mean anything external to God, for according to the ancient idea God himself is present in his Name. In the sanctification of his Name, God arrives at his identity and his recognition in his world. In his Name, God emerges from his mystery and manifests himself. In the sanctification of his Name God experiences the response and the correspondence of human beings to his manifested presence in the world.

Kiddush ha-shem, the sanctification of the Name, takes place according to Jewish conviction in the Sh'ma Israel, the Jewish acknowledgment of the One, the Only God (Deut. 6.4f.), so that it can be said that the Name of God is One. But there is also a *kiddush ha-shem* in the sacrifice of a person's own life, and this is manifested in the death of Israel's martyrs. Those who go to their deaths with the acknowledgment of the One God are therefore called 'Israel's saints'. Through them the promise of redemption is affirmed, the redemption not only of the world but of God too. When one day no other name stands over against the name of God any longer, when the One is the All One, and all created being acknowledges only him and him alone, then 'the act of sanctification has arrived at its rest', then everything has become holy.

But is God himself in need of sanctification, and in this sense also in his own way in need of redemption? If the necessity of sanctifying his Name springs from God's primordial self-restriction, then God has made himself in need of redemption through human beings, We can make this clear to ourselves with the help of Franz Rosenzweig's Shekinah theology. The Shekinah, the descent and dwelling of God among human beings, originally in the Ark of the Covenant and in the temple on Zion, can be imagined as a self-differentiation in God.[30] God does not just restrict himself in order to concede human beings freedom; he differentiates himself from himself in order to be beside them in their wanderings. He whom the heaven of heavens cannot contain dwells among his people and goes with his people into exile. Consequently every utterance of the Sh'ma Israel does not merely acknowledge the One God; it also 'unites' God and brings his Shekinah out of the far country home to the Eternal One: 'To acknowledge God's unity – the Jew calls it *uniting* God. For this unity is, in that it becomes; it is a Becoming Unity. And this Becoming is laid on the soul of human beings and in their hands.'[31]

Without Shekinah theology the redemption of God through human beings in the *kiddush ha-shem* can also be interpreted in a highly titanic sense. Ernst Bloch ended his book 'The Spirit of Utopia' (*Geist der Utopie*, 1918), with the following words: 'For only the wicked exist through their God, but the righteous – God exists through them, and in their hands is laid the sanctification of the Name, the naming of God himself, the God who moves and ferments within us, surmised gateway, darkest question, rapturous within: in the hands of our God-invoking philosophy and of truth as prayer.'[32] But that which 'moves and ferments within us' is 'the darkness of the lived God'. Is that not again, after all, God's Shekinah?

But if God's glorification and the sanctification of his Name are made to depend on the acts of human beings, is there then a divine eschatology? Because the acts of human beings, as far as they are known to us in history, are always ambiguous, this question remains open. The complete and universal sanctification of God's name is not to be expected of human beings: we must rather expect the complete and universal de-sanctification of the divine Name. Only trust in the indwelling Shekinah of the holy God himself, and its wanderings with us, offers a well-founded hope for the final redemption of God and of human beings by God.

(c) This brings us face to face with the third possibility: to think of the co-workings which lead to glorification *in trinitarian terms*.[33] A comprehensive point of departure can be found in the Johannine theology of transfiguration: 'Father, the hour has come: glorify thy Son that the Son may glorify thee . . . I glorified thee on earth, having accomplished the work which thou gavest me to do; and now, Father, glorify thou me in thy own presence with the glory which I had with thee before the world was made' (John 17.1, 4f.; cf. also 13.31). And chapter 16 says about 'the Spirit of truth': 'He will glorify me, for he will take what is mine and declare it to you' (16.14). Jesus 'glorifies' God the Father though his perfect obedience in life and death. He is the Messiah who sanctifies God's name and does God's will and thereby brings God's kingdom. His own 'glorification', in its turn, is expected of the Father, and according to John, as I think, takes place in the raising of the One crucified in obedience, through the glory which the Son had with the Father before he became human. The resurrection glory corresponds to that primordial glory of the Son with the Father. Its light also falls retrospectively on the Christ who sanctifies the name of God in his death on the cross, and in his obedience, so that the difference between cross and raising is absorbed into the reciprocal glorification of the Son and the Father. The Paraclete, for his part, will then glorify Christ, the Son, by spreading his knowledge and his love. He proceeds from the Father and illumines the Son (John 14.16, 26).

This trinitarian interpretation of the process of God's glorification in the history of Christ's self-surrender, raising and presence in the Spirit, must clearly be understood not exclusively but inclusively. The fellowship between Christ and God in the process of mutual glorification is so wide open that the community of Christ's people can find a place in it: ' . . . that they also may be in us.' In view of the cosmic dimensions of this divine eschatology of the mutual glorification of the Father and the Son and the Spirit, it will even be permissible to say that the mutual relationships of the Trinity are so wide open that in them the whole world can find a wide space, and redemption, and its own glorification.[34]

Paul apparently also conceives of the divine eschatology as a trinitarian process. The process of resurrection began with the raising of Christ and continues in the experience of the Spirit of the resurrection, who is efficacious in the present. This process is to end with the raising of all the dead and the annihilation of death. Then Christ will have completed his rule and can hand over 'the kingdom' as consummated sovereignty to God the Father, 'so that God may be all in all' (I Cor. 15.20–28).[35] Christ 'rules' as the leader of life. His sovereignty will be completed in the world of the resurrection. His 'last enemy' is death. Paul otherwise avoids the word βασιλεία, kingdom, which in the synoptic Gospels is the quintessence of Jesus's message; but he uses it here to designate the eschatological process of 'the handing over of the kingdom'. In his language, this is also the perfecting of 'the obedience of the Son' (I Cor. 15.28). If we ask why, then, the rule of God was committed to Christ, we come in Paul upon Christ's living 'obedience', which realizes the messianic *kiddush ha-shem*, while in Matthew we encounter the astonishingly trinitarian passage, Matt. 11.27f.: 'All things have been delivered to me by my Father; and no one knows the Son except the Father, and no one knows the Father except the Son and any one to whom the Son chooses to reveal him. Come to me, all who labour and are heavy laden, and I will give you rest.' The eschatological 'handing over of the kingdom' by the Son to the Father is evidently an inner-trinitarian process too, and an expression of the divine eschatology.

Over against the tradition about God's self-glorification, the consummation according to John and Paul is more than the beginning: in the beginning creation – at the end the kingdom; in the beginning God in himself – at the end God all in all. In this divine eschatology God acquires through history his eternal kingdom, in which he arrives at his rest in all things, and in which all things will live eternally in him.

Over against Hegel's idea about God's self-realization, the history of Christ's self-emptying and glorification is here not thought of modalistically; it is seen in trinitarian terms, as the co-workings of the Father, the Son and the Spirit. This leads neither to a dialectical pantheism nor to an apotheosis of the world. Its consequence is rather that all created beings are drawn into the mutual relationships of the divine life, and into the wide space of the God who is sociality.

Over against the Jewish *kiddush ha-shem*, faith and the discipleship of Christ awaken a strong assurance that through Christ the name of God is sanctified, that in him God's will is done, and that with him, therefore, God's kingdom will come. The trinitarian ideas about the co-workings of the Son and the Father and the Spirit of truth had their genesis in close spiritual proximity to Jewish Shekinah theology.

§4 THE FULNESS OF GOD AND THE FEAST OF ETERNAL JOY

'From his fulness (πλήρωμα) have we all received, grace upon grace' (John 1.16). The approach by way of *the fulness of God* (Eph. 3.19) which 'dwells bodily' in Christ leads us beyond the traditional ideas about the self-glorifying *will of God* and the self-realizing *nature of God* and makes the *interplay* of all blessing and praising, singing, dancing and rejoicing creatures in the community of God more comprehensible.[36]

In order to grasp *the fulness of God*, we are at liberty to leave moral and ontological concepts behind, and to avail ourselves of aesthetic dimensions. The fulness of God is the rapturous fulness of the divine life; a life that communicates itself with inexhaustible creativity; an overbrimming life that makes what is dead and withered live; a life from which everything that lives receives its vital energies and its zest for living; a source of life to which everything that has been made alive responds with deepest joy and ringing exultation. The fulness of God is radiant light, light reflected in the thousand brilliant colours of created things. The glory of God expresses itself, not in self-glorying majesty, but in the prodigal communication of God's own fulness of life. The glory of God is not to be found, either, in his laborious self-realization by way of his self-emptying, but follows upon that on the eternal day of resurrection.[37]

The glory of God is the feast of eternal joy, and the Gospels therefore continually compare it with a wedding feast: 'Enter into the joyful feast of your master' (Matt. 25.21). Jesus's friends are wedding guests (Mark 2.19; Matt. 9.15; Luke 5.34), because they are people belonging to God's kingdom. Their final fulfilment is imagined in Rev. 19.7 as 'the marriage of the Lamb'. Even 'the heavenly Jerusalem' comes down from heaven to human beings 'like a bride adorned for her husband', according to Rev. 21.2. In Luke, the announcement of Christ's birth is proclaimed as 'news of a great joy' (Luke 2.10). According to John, Jesus's joy will remain in those who are his, so that their joy 'may be full' (John 15.11). For the coming of Christ is the arrival of God's kingdom, and the first human reaction to it is profound joy.

The resurrection of Christ means the overcoming of death's power and the appearance of imperishable, eternal life.[38] The first human reaction to this is unrestrained Easter jubilation. Here the divine life opens and communicates itself. The Bible calls this *charis*. The divine life communicated is also eternal life, life in participation in the divine life. But it is not just life in 'the world beyond', 'life after death'; it is an awakening, a rebirth, already here and now, and the endowment of earthly life with new vital energies.

The *charis* communicates itself in countless *charismata*. These are not just 'gifts' of grace. They are new living energies as well. We are interpreting *charis* too narrowly if we only relate grace in a legalistic way to indicted sinners. *Charis* is life drawn from the fulness of God, and it shows itself in new livingness and exuberant joy. The reaction to *charis* is *chara*, joy. It is this joy that is called 'true faith'.

For human beings who desire to live and have to die, everything draws to a point in death. If death is the end, then all delight in living is as transitory as earthly life itself. But if life comes from the fulness of God, then this life is divine life, and manifests itself in us in the resurrection life. Consequently for Christian faith the resurrection of Christ was from the very beginning the open plenitude of God, and the joy that is called faith was Easter rejoicing.

> The day of resurrection, let us be light on this feast. And let us embrace one another. Let us speak to those who hate us. For the resurrection's sake we will forgive one another everything. And so let us cry: Christ is risen from the dead (Orthodox Easter Liturgy).[39]

In joy over the open fulness of God, out of which we receive not just 'grace upon grace' but also – as we can now say – life upon life, the life we live here and now is already transfigured and becomes a *festive* life, life in celebration. The joy brings music and imagination into this life, so that it is not just lived but is also shaped and given expression. Then life does not just *go* forth, it is *set* forth and moulded by God and human beings. Lived life itself becomes a song of praise. Even in pain and fear, community with the crucified Christ brings into life sparks of trust and candles of hope.

Do believers have this joy for themselves in a world hostile to them and to life? No, for them the transfiguration of life in Easter joy which they experience is no more than a small beginning of the transfiguration of the whole cosmos. The risen Christ does not come just to the dead, so as to raise them and communicate to them his eternal life; he draws all things into his future, so that they may become new and participate in the feast of God's eternal joy:

> Through thy resurrection, O Lord, the universe is illumined . . .
> the whole creation praises thee, day by day offering thee a hymn
> (Orthodox Easter Liturgy).[40]

Out of the resurrection of Christ, joy throws open cosmic and eschatological perspectives that reach forward to the redemption of the whole cosmos. A redemption for what? In the feast of eternal joy all created beings and the whole community of God's creation are destined to sing their hymns and songs of praise. This should not be understood merely anthropomorphically: the hymns and praises of those who rejoice in the risen Christ are, as they themselves see it, no more than a feeble echo of the cosmic liturgy and the heavenly praise and the uttered joy in existence of all other living things.

The feast of eternal joy is prepared by the fulness of God and the rejoicing of all created being. If we could talk only about God's nature and his will, we should not do justice to his plenitude. Inappropriate though human analogy is bound to be, in thinking of the fulness of God we can best talk about the inexhaustibly rich *fantasy of God*, meaning by that his creative imagination. From that imagination life upon life proceeds in protean abundance. If creation is transfigured and glorified, as we have shown, then creation is not just the free decision of God's will; nor is it an outcome of his self-realization. It is like a great song or a splendid poem or a wonderful dance of his fantasy, for the communication of his divine plenitude. The laughter of the universe is God's delight. It is the universal Easter laughter.

Soli Deo Gloria

NOTES

I The Coming God

1. Ch. III §6 will discuss in detail the messianic spirit of 'modern times'. The secularization of Christian eschatology was the secularization of Christian millenarianism, i.e., the expectation of the 'Thousand Years' empire' in history before its end.

2. E. L. Tuveson, *Redeemer Nation. The Idea of America's Millennial Role*, Chicago 1968. American political messianism will be discussed in detail in Ch. III §4.

3. E. Sarkisyanz, *Russland und der Messianismus des Orients. Sendungsbewusstsein und politischer Chiliasmus des Ostens*, Tübingen 1955; H. Schaeder, *Moskau – das Dritte Rom*, Darmstadt 1963.

4. M. Begzos, *Die Eschatologie in der Orthodoxie des 20. Jahrhunderts*, Athens 1989.

5. Cf. W. Kreck, *Die Zukunft des Gekommenen. Grundprobleme der Eschatologie, A: Die Haupttypen der Eschatologie*, Munich 1961, 14–76; J. Moltmann, *Theology of Hope*, trans. J. W. Leitch, London and New York 1967, Ch. 1: Eschatology and Revelation, 37–94; C. H. Ratschow, 'Eschatologie' in *TRE*[3].

6. G. Möller, 'Föderalismus und Geschichtsbetrachtung im 17. und 18. Jahrhundert', *ZKG* 50, 1931, 397ff.; J. Moltmann, 'Jacob Brocard als Vorläufer der Reich-Gottes-Theologie und der symbolisch-prophetischen Schriftauslegung des Johann Coccejus', *ZKG* 71, 1960, 110–129, with the following quotations there cited.

7. G. Menken, *Über Glück und Sieg der Gottlosen. Eine politische Flugschrift aus dem Jahre 1795* in *Schriften* VII, Bremen 1858, 82.

8. A. Schweitzer, *The Quest of the Historical Jesus*, trans. W. Montgomery, London 1910 (= ET of 1st German edition [1906], which was published under the title *Vom Reimarus zu Wrede*), 397.

9. Ibid., 396.

10. J. Weiss, *Jesus' Proclamation of the Kingdom of God* (1892), trans. R. H. Hiers and D.L. Holland, London 1971, also perceived that Jesus's 'eschatological-apocalyptic' message was diametrically opposed to the moral and religious concept of the kingdom of God held by his father-in-law A. Ritschl. He recognized the profound contradiction between the culture-Christianity of his own day, and Jesus and early Christianity; and

contrary to his own better knowledge he decided in favour of the culture-Christianity of his own day. Cf. p. 135: 'We no longer pray, "May grace come and the world pass away" but we pass our lives in the joyful confidence that *this* world will increasingly become the showplace of the people of God' (trans. slightly altered).

11. A. Schweitzer, *Quest*, 250.

12. Ibid., 389.

13. R. Bultmann, 'New Testament and Mythologie' (1941) in H. W. Bartsch (ed.), *Kerygma and Myth*, trans. R. H. Fuller, London 1953, 5: 'Mythical eschatology is untenable for the simple reason that the parousia of Christ never took place as the New Testament expected. History did not come to an end, and, as every sane person knows, it will continue to run its course' (trans. slightly altered).

14. A. Schweitzer, *Geschichte der Leben-Jesu-Forschung*, 6th ed., Tübingen 1951, 636 (the passage is not included in the English translation, which was based on the 1st German edition; see n.8 above).

15. A. Schweitzer, *Geschichte der Leben-Jesu-Forschung*, 640 (not included in the English translation; see previous note).

16. A. Schweitzer, *Quest*, 397.

17. O. Cullmann, *Christ and Time*, trans. F. V. Filson, revised ed., London 1962; also his *Salvation in History*, trans. S. G. Sowers *et al.*, London 1967.

18. O. Cullmann, *Christ and Time*, 81ff.

19. Ibid., 87.

20. Ibid.; cf. 85, 141. Thus also K. Barth, *CD* II/2, 688f.: the Devil is already 'checkmate', but he does not know it and goes on playing.

21. O. Cullmann, *Christ and Time*, 97.

22. Ibid.

23. Ibid., 51ff.

24. Ibid., 107.

25. Ibid., ix (trans. altered).

26. On the following passage see F. Holmström's comprehensive work *Das eschatologische Denken der Gegenwart. Drei Etappen der theologischen Entwicklung des 20. Jahrhunderts*, Gütersloh 1935.

27. K. Barth, *The Epistle to the Romans*, trans. from 6th German ed. by E. C. Hoskyns, London 1933, 498.

28. Ibid., 497.

29. Ibid., 501.

30. Ibid., 500.

31. Ibid., 499f.

32. I am also drawing on C. H. Dodd, *The Parables of the Kingdom*, London 1955, not for the sake of completeness, but because he supports Barth's argument.

33. Ibid., 50: 'This declaration that the Kingdom of God has already come necessarily dislocates the whole eschatological scheme in which its expected coming closes the long vista of the future. The *eschaton* has moved

from the future to the present, from the sphere of expectation into that of realized experience. It is therefore unsafe to assume that the content of the idea "The Kingdom of God" as Jesus meant it, may be filled in from the speculations of apocalyptic writers. They were referring to something in the future, which could be conceived only in terms of fantasy. He was speaking of that which, in one aspect at least, was an object of experience.'

34. Ibid., 61. The heritage of contemporary Cambridge Platonists is also implicit in this interpretation.

35. P. Althaus, *Die letzten Dinge*, 1st ed., Gütersloh 1922, 64.

36. Ibid., 84.

37. Ibid., 86.

38. Quoted in C. Hinrichs, *Ranke und die Geschichtstheologie der Goethezeit*, Göttingen 1954, 165. For a fuller comment on Ranke's philosophy of history, see J. Moltmann, *Theology of Hope*, 245–253. The dictum quoted by no means represents the whole of Ranke's philosophy of history.

39. Cf. K. Barth, *CD* II/1, 624f.

40. P. Althaus, *Die letzten Dinge*, 174.

41. K. Barth, *CD* II/1, 635.

42. Cf. K. Barth, *CD* III/2, §47: Man in his Time, 437ff.

43. E. Brunner, *Das Ewige als Zukunft und Gegenwart*, Zürich 1953. (The title of the [1954] ET, however, is *Eternal Hope*.)

44. R. Bultmann, 'The Christian Hope and the Problem of Demythologizing', trans. C. Bonifazi, *Expository Times* 65 (1954) 228–230 and 276–278; *History and Eschatology* (Gifford Lectures 1955; first published in English) Edinburgh 1957.

45. R. Bultmann, *Theology of the New Testament* vol. 1, trans. K. Grobel, London 1952, 21.

46. R. Bultmann, 'History and Eschatology in the New Testament', *New Testament Studies* I (1954; first published in English) 16.

47. R. Bultmann, *History and Eschatology*, 155. One is reminded of the poem of Goethe's in which he urges that happiness be grasped in the present:

Warum in die Ferne schweifen, / Sieh, das Gute liegt so nah.

Lerne nur das Glück ergreifen, / Denn das Glück ist immer da.

48. In H.-W. Bartsch (ed.), *Kerygma und Mythos. Ein theologisches Gespräch*, 4th ed., Hamburg 1960, 131.

49. M. Heidegger, *Being and Time*, trans. J. Macquarrie and E. Robinson, London 1962: Division 2, I: Dasein's Possibility of Being-a-Whole, and Being-towards-Death, 279ff.

50. J. Weiss, *Jesus' Proclamation*, 135f.

51. F. Schleiermacher, *On Religion: Speeches to its Cultured Despisers*, trans. J. Oman (London 1893; reissued New York 1958) 101.

51a. Ich selbst bin Ewigkeit, wenn ich die Zeit verlasse und mich in Gott und Gott in mich zusammenfasse.

52. J. B. Metz, *Faith in History and Society*, trans. D. Smith, London 1980, 171: 'The shortest definition of religion: interruption.' But I entirely

share his criticism of the homogeneous, linear concept of time in the modern logic of evolution.

53. E. Peterson already pointed this out; see 'Von den Engeln' in his *Theologische Traktate*, Munich 1951, 334, By the coming God I do not mean Hölderlin's unknown, new but 'coming God', whose name is Dionysius. Cf. M. Frank, *Der kommende God. Vorlesungen über die neue Mythologie*, Frankfurt 1982.

54. E. Bloch, *Das Prinzip Hoffnung*, Frankfurt 1959, 1457f. (ET *The Principle of Hope* trans. N. and S. Plaice and P. Knight, Cambridge, Mass. and Oxford 1986, 1236).

55. Thus rightly W. Pannenberg, 'Der Gott der Hoffnung' in S. Unseld (ed.), *Ernst Bloch zu ehren. Beiträge zu seinem Werk*, Frankfurt 1965, 209–225.

56. J. Moltmann, *The Way of Jesus Christ. Christology in Messianic Dimensions*, trans. Margaret Kohl, London and New York 1990, 322.

57. J. Moltmann, *God in Creation. An Ecological Doctrine of Creation* (Gifford Lectures 1984–85), trans. Margaret Kohl, London and New York 1985, 132ff. Theories about time will be considered in more detail in Ch. IV §3: The End of Time in the Eternity of God.

58. This is the inner tension in Bloch's *Principle of Hope*, which tried to formalize messianic ideas with Greek concepts of time. His ontology of 'not-yet-Being' fails to provide a foundation for hope because it inescapably has to become the ontology of Being-that-is-no-longer'. If future arises from the tendencies and latencies of the historical process, the future cannot bring anything surprisingly new, and never a *novum ultimum*. Eschatology is then only possible as teleology. But, as Bloch knew, teleology runs aground on death.

59. G. Picht, *Hier und Jetzt: Philosophie nach Auschwitz und Hiroshima*, vol. I, Stuttgart 1980, 362ff.

60. R. Bultmann, 'Liberal Theology and the Latest Theological Movement' in *Faith and Understanding*, trans. L. Pettibone Smith, London 1968, 35.

61. G. von Rad, *Old Testament Theology* II, trans. D. M. G. Stalker, Edinburgh and London 1965, 1.

62. J. Moltmann, 'Die Kategorie Novum in der christlichen Theologie' in *Ernst Bloch zu ehren*, 243–263. Otherwise the *remembrance* that resists forgetting has always been, and still is, the pre-eminent and particular characteristic of Jewish religiosity: 'Remembrance hastens the redemption.'

63. For more detail here see S. Mosès, *Der Engel der Geschichte. Franz Rosenzweig, Walter Benjamin, Gershom Scholem*, Frankfurt 1994 (trans. from the French *L'ange de l'histoire*, Editions du Seuil 1992); also the biographies by M. Susman, *Ich habe viele Leben gelebt. Erinnerungen*, Stuttgart 1964, and G. Scholem, *From Berlin to Jerusalem*, New York 1980; also his *Tagebücher, Aufsätze und Entwürfe*, 1st half-volume: 1913–1917, Frankfurt 1994.

64. E. Bloch, *Geist der Utopie*, revised edition of the second, 1923

version (*Gesamtausgabe* 3), Frankfurt 1964, 11. There is no English translation of this book, but it is referred to in the body of the present text as *The Spirit of Utopia*.

65. E. Bloch, *Durch die Wüste. Frühe kritische Aufsätze*, Frankfurt 1964, 122–140 (no English translation, but referred to in the body of the present text as *Through the Wilderness*). In old age, Bloch always brushed aside questions about his Judaism somewhat brusquely, and talked about Martin Buber more ironically than seriously. We are indebted to D. Krochmalnik for evidence that this did not accord with his own history between 1911 and 1913; see D. Krochmalnik, 'Ernst Blochs Exkurs über die Juden' in *Bloch Almanach* 13, Ludwigshafen 1993, 39–58. I have based what I have said here on his work, which in its turn rests on A. F. Christen, *Ernst Blochs Metaphysik der Materie*, Bonn 1979.

66. E. Bloch, *Durch die Wüste*, 125.

67. Ibid., 140.

68. This is the way M. Landmann characterizes Bloch's *Prinzip Hoffnung* (1959) in *Jüdische Miniaturen* I, Bonn 1982, 172.

69. E. Bloch, *Subjekt – Objekt. Erläuterungen zu Hegel*, Berlin 1949.

70. E. Bloch, *Geist der Utopie*, 254.

71. Ibid., 347.

72. E. Bloch, *Das Prinzip Hoffnung*, §53, 1392ff. (ET *The Principle of Hope*, 1183ff.).

73. I am here initially following the account in S. Mosès, *Der Engel der Geschichte*, 25ff.

74. G. W. F. Hegel, *Grundlinien der Philosophie des Rechts* (1821), §§341ff., esp. §347, §352 and §358 (PhB 124, ed. J. Hoffmeister), 4th ed., Berlin 1956, 293ff. (*Hegel's Philosophy of Right*, trans. T. M. Knox, London 1967).

75. G. W. F. Hegel, *Die Vernunft in der Geschichte. Einleitung in die Philosophie der Weltgeschichte* (PhB 171a, ed. G. Lasson), 40 (*Lectures on the Philosophy of World History, Introduction: Reason in History*, trans. H. B. Nisbet, Cambridge 1975). Lasson writes in his introduction (1917): 'The "Ideas of 1914" undoubtedly derive from Hegel's view of history and his doctrine of the state.' They were the 'ideas' of Protestant nationalism and 'German civilization' and were directed against the 'ideas' of 1789 and the civilization of the Western European democracies. Cf. F. W. Graf, 'Schmerz der Moderne, Wille zur Ganzheit. Protestantismus 1914 – und was davon geblieben ist', *Lutherische Monatshefte* 28, 1989, 458–463.

76. S. Mosès, *Der Engel der Geschichte*, 70.

77. Ibid., 81.

78. F. Rosenzweig, *Der Stern der Erlösung*, 3rd ed., Heidelberg 1954, Part III, Book 1, 63ff. (*The Star of Redemption*, trans. W. W. Hallo, London 1971).

79. Ibid., Part II, Book 3, 170.

80. S. Mosès, *Der Engel der Geschichte*, 59.

81. F. Rosenzweig, *Der Stern der Erlösung*, Part II, Book III, 170. Cf. here

also K. Löwith, 'M. Heidegger und F. Rosenzweig, ein Nachtrag zu "Sein und Zeit" in his *Gesammelte Abhandlungen. Zur Kritik der geschichtlichen Existenz*, Stuttgart 1960, 68–92. Löwith praises particularly highly Rosenzweig's eternity concept.

82. G. Scholem, *From Berlin to Jerusalem*.

83. G. Scholem, 'Zur Neuauflage des "Stern der Erlösung"' in his *Judaica* I, Frankfurt 1963, 226ff.

84. Ibid., 232.

85. Ibid.

86. S. Mosès, *Der Engel der Geschichte*, 163.

87. G. Scholem, 'Zum Verständnis der messianischen Idee im Judentum' in his *Judaica* I, 25.

88. Ibid., 20.

89. Ibid., 10ff., 13.

90. Ibid., 73.

91. Ibid., 8. Cf. here my discussion of this argument against the Christian faith (an argument which fundamentally speaking also calls Judaism in question) in J. Moltmann, *The Way of Jesus Christ*, Ch. I, §3: Messianic Categories, 21ff.

92. W. Benjamin, *Illuminationen. Ausgewählte Schriften*, Frankfurt 1961, 9. (Cf. *Illuminations*, trans. H. Zohn, with an introduction by Hannah Arendt, London 1970, reprinted 1992. This selection, in spite of its title, is not identical in content with the German volume. It includes a translation of *Theses on the Philosophy of History*, but not the *Theological-Political Fragment*. Quotations in the present text are translated directly from the German.)

93. W. Benjamin, *Illuminationen*, 268–279. A comparable profound theological text can be found in J.B. Metz, *Faith in History and Society*, 169–183.

94. W. Benjamin, *Illuminationen*, 270f.

95. Ibid., 271f.

96. Ibid., 276.

97. Ibid., 278.

98. Ibid., 279.

99. Ibid., 280f.

100. T. W. Adorno, *Minima Moralia. Reflections from damaged life*, trans. E. F. N. Jephcott, London 1974, 247.

101. K. Löwith, *Weltgeschichte und Heilsgeschehen*, Stuttgart 1952, Vorwort 7 (this preface to the German edition does not appear in its English predecessor, *Meaning in History*, for which see the text and n. 104).

102. J. Taubes, *Abendländische Eschatologie, Mit einem Anhang*, 2nd ed., Munich 1991, 15f.

103. Ibid., 213.

104. K. Löwith, *Meaning in History*, Chicago 1949, 191.

105. Ibid., 192.

106. Cf. K. Löwith, *Gesammelte Abhandlungen. Zur Kritik der Ge-*

schichtlichen Existenz, Stuttgart 1960; also his *Vorträge und Abhandlungen zur Kritik der christlichen Überlieferung*, Stuttgart 1966.

II Eternal Life

1. L. Wittgenstein, *Tractatus-logicus philosophicus*, 6.4311, *Schriften* I, Frankfurt 1960, 81 (ET by D. F. Peas and B. F. McGuinness, London and New York 1962; reprint 1994).
2. Here I am picking up ideas which H.-E. Mertens has gathered together from English theology in 'Tendenzen in de engelstalige Eschatologie', *TTh* 21, 1981, 407–421 (German in *ThG* (B) 25, 1982, 242–253).
3. D. Bonhoeffer, *Letters and Papers from Prison*, trans. R.H. Fuller. (4th) enlarged ed., London and New York 1971, 157: 'It is only when one loves life and the earth so much that without them everything seems to be over that one may believe in the resurrection and a new world.'
4. Cf. U. Beck, *Risikogesellschaft. Auf dem Weg in eine andere Moderne*, Frankfurt 1986.
5. T. W. Adorno, *Negative Dialectics*, trans. E. B. Ashton, New York and London 1973, 370.
5a. Ina Seidel, 'Die tröstliche Begegnung'.
6. W. Biermann, 'Das kann doch nicht alles gewesen sein (Lied vom donnernden Leben)' in *Preussischer Ikarus. Lieder. Balladen. Gedichte. Prosa*, Cologne 1978, 93.
7. A. Champdor, *Das äyptische Totenbuch in Bild und Deutung*, ed. M. Lurker, trans. from French, Bern, Munich and Vienna 1977, 151: 'As far as their souls were concerned, the Egyptians imagined them in the form of a bird with the face of the dead person.' (See the Egyptian Book of the Dead.)
8. Thus rightly R. F. Beerling, quoted by H.-E. Mertens 'Tendenzen', *ThG* (B) 25, 244, contrary to the Letter of the Congregation for the Doctrine of the Faith Regarding Certain Questions of Eschatology (*Epistula ad Venerabiles Praesules Conferentiarum Episcopalium de quibusdam quaestionibus ad Eschatologiam spectantibus . . . die 17 Maii 1979*) (AAS Aug. 1979).
9. J. Moltmann, *God in Creation. An Ecological Doctrine of Creation* (Gifford Lectures 1984–85), trans. Margaret Kohl, London and New York 1985, 260ff.
10. Helen Oppenheimer, 'Life after Death', *Theology* 82, 1979, 333.
11. J. Moltmann, *The Spirit of Life. A Universal Affirmation*, trans. Margaret Kohl, London and Minneapolis 1992, esp. 83ff.
12. J. Moltmann, 'Liebe – Tod – Ewiges Leben. Entwurf einer personalen Eschatologie' in J. Becker, B. Einig and P. Ullrich (eds), *Im Angesicht des Todes. Ein interdisziplinäres Kompendium* II (Pietas Liturgica 4), St Ottilien 1987, 837–854.
13. P. Ariès, *Geschichte des Todes*, Munich 1980; W. Fuchs, *Todesbilder in der modernen Gesellschaft*, Frankfurt 1969; H. Schnoor and K. Sendzik,

Die Bedeutung des Todes für das Bewusstsein vom Leben. Ansätze in Psychologie, Soziologie und Philosophie, Frankfurt 1986.

14. N. Elias, *Über die Einsamkeit der Sterbenden in unseren Tagen*, Frankfurt 1982; G. Schmied, *Sterben und Trauern in der modernen Gesellschaft*, Munich 1988.

15. A. and M. Mitscherlich *The Inability to Mourn*, trans. B.R. Placzek, New York 1975; W. Lepenies, *Melancholie und Gesellschaft*, Frankfurt 1969.

16. For the interpretation cf. R. Guardini, *The Death of Socrates*, trans. B. Wrighton, London 1948; J. Pieper, *Death and Immortality*, trans. R. and C. Wilson, New York 1969.

17. Plato, *Phaedo*, trans. D. Gallop, World's Classics, Oxford and New York 1993, 72e.

18. Ibid., 75bff.

19. Ibid., 80e, 81a.

19a. *The Bhagavad-Gita*, trans. and ed. by R.C. Zaehner, Oxford 1969, II, 20.

20. Thus E. Bloch, *Das Prinzip Hoffnung*, Frankfurt 1959, 1390 (ET *The Principle of Hope*, trans. N. and S. Plaice and P. Knight, Cambridge, Mass. and Oxford 1986, 1181).

21. Plato, *Phaedo*, 80e.

22. Cf. M. Pohlenz, *Die Stoa. Geschichte einer geistigen Bewegung*, 2nd ed., Göttingen 1959, 151ff.

22a. *The Bhagavad-Gita* 11, 15, 17.

23. J. G. Fichte, *Ausgewählte Werke* I, ed. F. Medicus, Darmstadt 1962, 250.

24. Ibid., IV, 449; V, 200.

25. Ibid., V, 200.

26. Ibid., 187.

27. Ibid., 260.

28. Ibid., III, 133.

29. Ibid., I, 224.

30. E. Bloch, *Das Prinzip Hoffnung*, 1385–1391 (ET *The Principle of Hope*, 1178–1182). The following quotations are taken from this section. Cf. here J. Moltmann, '"Where There is Hope, There is Religion" (Ernst Bloch). The Philosophy and Theology of Hope' in *History and the Triune God: Contributions to Trinitarian Theology*, trans. J. Bowden, London 1991, 143ff.

31. The saying is reminiscent of the Christian liturgy: 'In te, Domine, speravi, non confundar in aeternum' ('In thee, Lord, have I put my hope, let me never be confounded') – only Bloch (ibid. 1388, ET, 1180) leaves out the main clause.

32. E. Bloch, *Das Prinzip Hoffnung*, 1391 (ET *The Principle of Hope*, 1182).

33. Cf. ibid., 1409, ET 1197.

34. E. Bloch, *Experimentum Mundi. Frage, Kategorien des Herausbrin-*

gens, Praxis in *Gesamtausgabe* 15, Frankfurt 1975.

35. C. Barth, *Die Errettung vom Tode in den individuellen Klage- und Dankliedern des Alten Testaments,* Zollikon 1947.

36. J. Moltmann, *The Way of Jesus Christ. Christology in Messianic Dimensions,* trans. Margaret Kohl, London and New York 1990, Ch. V, 213ff. Cf. also K. Rahner, 'The Resurrection of the Body', *Theological Investigations* II, trans. K.-H. Kruger, London and Baltimore 1963, 203–216.

37. I pointed to this dilemma in *The Way of Jesus Christ,* Ch. VII, §5, 3, 336ff.

38. W. Pannenberg, *The Apostles' Creed in the Light of Today's Questions,* trans. Margaret Kohl, London 1972, 172. Thus also M. Welker, *Gottes Geist. Theologie des Heiligen Geistes,* Neukirchen 1992, 300ff. (*God the Spirit,* trans. J. Hoffmeyer, Minneapolis 1994).

39. With this I am going beyond the alternative in the *Theology of Hope* (trans. J.W. Leitch, London 1967).

40. The alternative is stressed by O. Cullmann, ET *Immortality of the Soul or Resurrection of the Dead?* London and New York 1958. For a more differentiated view, see now H. Sonnemans, *Seele. Unsterblichkeit – Auferstehung. Zur griechischen und christlichen Anthropologie und Eschatologie* (FThSt 128), Freiburg 1984. On pp.370ff. Sonnemans puts together these arguments very cogently. Cf. also G. Greshake and J. Kremer, *Resurrectio Mortuorum. Zum theologischen Verständnis der leiblichen Auferstehung,* Darmstadt 1986, 240ff.

40a. A well-known hymn of Paul Gerhardt's says the same thing:

Kann uns doch kein Tod nicht töten,

sondern reiss

unsern Geist

aus viel tausend Nöten.

41. J. Moltmann, *God in Creation,* Ch.IX: 219ff., 232ff.

42. I am here using the concept of Spirit which I have developed in *The Spirit of Life.*

43. K. Barth, *CD* III/2, 344–366, calls the Spirit 'the basis of soul and body'. 'Spirit in His being *ad extra* is neither a divine nor a created something, but an action and attitude of the Creator in relation to His creation' (356). 'The whole man is of the Spirit, since the Spirit is the principle and power of the life of the whole man' (363). 'When the subject dies, He [i.e., the Spirit] returns to God who gave Him. In distinction from the human subject, He is immortal' (364). Cf. here H. Wohlgschaft, *Hoffnung angesichts des Todes. Das Todesproblem bei Karl Barth und in der zeitgenössischen Theologie des deutschen Sprachraums* (BÖT 14), Paderborn 1977, 85ff. I agree with his criticism that in Barth the difference between the immortal Spirit and the mortal human subject remains unsatisfactory, and welcome his suggestion when he says: 'If we (were to understand) the relation to God which is not destroyed in death and which preserves the human being as *person . . .* as the total principle of God's

personhood, then we should do *substantial* justice to Barth's concern . . .'
(86).

44. K. Rahner, 'The Secret of Life', *Theological Investigations* VI, trans.
K.-H. and B. Kruger, London and Baltimore 1969, 141–152.

45. A. N. Whitehead, *Process and Reality. An Essay in Cosmology*, New
York 1941, 523, 532. Cf. here M. Welker, *Universalität Gottes und
Relativität der Welt. Theologische Kosmologie im Dialog mit dem ameri-
kanischen Prozessdenken nach Whitehead*, Neukirchen 1981, 109ff.

46. C. Hartshorne, *The Logic of Perfection*, London 1963. Similarly N.
Pittenger, *After Death – Life in God*, London and New York 1980.

47. A. N. Whitehead, *Process and Reality*, 532.

48. Following C. Stange, *Das Ende aller Dinge. (Die christliche Hoffnung, ihr Grund und ihr Ziel)*, Gütersloh 1930, 137ff. 1930, 138ff., P.
Althaus, *Die letzten Dinge, Lehrbuch der Eschatologie*, 7th ed., Gütersloh
1957, 110ff., made relational immortality the basis of his personal
eschatology: 'Death is the limit of what we know as life. It is not the limit of
our relationship to God, however, but a moment in it' (110). H. Thielicke
also made this idea the content of his eschatology: see his *Leben mit dem
Tod*, Tübingen 1980, esp. 198ff. (*Living with Death*, trans. G. W. Bromiley,
Grand Rapids 1983) and *Der Evangelische Glaube. Grundzüge der
Dogmatik* III, Tübingen 1978, 512ff. (*The Evangelical Faith*, trans. G. W.
Bromiley, Grand Rapids and Edinburgh 1982).

49. M. Luther, *Genesisvorlesung* (1535–45), WA 43, 481, quoted in P.
Althaus, *Die Letzte Dinge*, Gütersloh 1922, 110; also by H. Thielicke, 274.
J. Ratzinger, *Eschatologie, Tod und ewiges Leben* (*Kleine Katholische
Dogmatik* IX), Regensburg 1977, 127ff., also says that the Christian
understanding of immortality has 'the character of dialogue'.

50. In the *Theology of Hope*, 179f., I called resurrection a *creatio ex nihilo*
(creation from nothing) and a *nova creatio* (new creation), my purpose being
to point to the creative God and the eschatologically new character of his
activity. This gave rise to misunderstandings, which I hope my present
exposition has cleared away.

51. P. Althaus, 'Auferstehung', *RGG*³ I, 697.

52. For the anthropological significance of the name, cf. J. Moltmann,
God in Creation, 262.

53. On the connection between the Spirit and 'the light of God's
countenance', cf. J. Moltmann, *The Spirit of Life*, 45f.

54. E. Jüngel, *Death: the riddle and the mystery*, trans. I. and U. Nicol,
Edinburgh 1975, 115f.

55. N. Elias, *Über die Einsamkeit der Sterbenden*, 100.

56. E. Jüngel, *Death*, 115.

57. Thus also H. Küng, *Eternal Life?*, trans. E. Quinn, London 1984,
140ff.

58. Thus the Preface in the Catholic Requiem Mass.

59. H. Gese, 'Der Tod im Alten Testament' in *Zur biblischen Theologie.
Alttestamentliche Vorträge*, Munich 1977, 31–54.

60. G. von Rad, *Old Testament Theology* I, trans. D.M.G. Stalker, Edinburgh and London 1962, 276ff., 369f.

61. Thus M. Luther, *Psalmenvorlesung* (1519–21), WA 5, 166; AWA 2, 303, who calls this trust the 'spes purissima in purissimum Deum', the purest hope in the purest God.

62. This already struck Ernst Bloch, *Prinzip Hoffnung*, 1323 (ET *Principle of Hope*, 1125): 'It is surprising that for a very long time the Jews did not think about the ultimate anxiety at all, and cast no dream over it. This people lived as entirely in this world as the Greeks, and yet its life was incomparably more directed towards the future and towards future goals.' G. von Rad, *Theology* I, 369, n.33, makes a similar observation; 'Jahwism showed a particular intransigence over against death. Death definitely separated a man from Jahweh.' Israel 'radically demythologized and desacralized death', says von Rad (ibid., 277).

63. O. Weber, *Grundlagen der Dogmatik* I, Neukirchen 1955, 684.

64. H. Denzinger and A. Schönmetzer, *Enchiridion Symbolorum*, 16th ed., Freiburg 1965, 101 (*The Sources of Catholic Dogma*, trans. by R. J. Deferrari from Denzinger, 13th ed.; St Louis and London, 1955).

65. Ibid., 175.

66. Ibid., 788, 789.

67. Augustine, *Enchiridion*, 107.

68. H. Schmid, *Die Dogmatik der evangelisch-lutherischen Kirche, dargestellt und aus den Quellen belegt*, 7th ed., Gütersloh 1993, 461ff.

69. J. Gerhard, cited ibid. 396.

70. F. Schleiermacher, *The Christian Faith*, trans. H.R. Mackintosh and J.S. Stewart from the 2nd ed., Edinburgh 1928, reprint Philadelphia 1976, §75.1, cf. §§75–77. Thus also more recently P. Althaus, 'Tod. Dogmatisch', *RGG*³ VI, 917: 'Theology cannot derive physical death as such, as biological event, as it were causally from sin, from the Fall, and understand it as a punitive intervention by God in the original constitution of his creation. It cannot teach an original condition free of death, in the sense of a never-ending natural life, and death as sign of "the fallen creation".' Similarly E. Brunner, *Das Ewige als Zukunft und Gegenwart*, Zürich 1953, 115ff. (ET *Eternal Hope*, 1954). Brunner draws for help on the simple distinction between 'God's perspective' and 'the world's perspective'. Also H. Thielicke, *Tod und Leben, Studien zur christlichen Anthropologie*, 2nd ed., Tübingen 1946.

71. F. Schleiermacher, *The Christian Faith*, §75.

72. Cf. O. Kirn, 'Tod', *RE*³, 801–805.

73. K. Barth, *CD* III/2, 632. Cf. the comments by H. Wohlgschaft, *Hoffnung angesichts des Todes. Das Todesproblem bei K. Barth*, 73ff.

74. K. Barth, *CD* III/2, 625–6.

75. Ibid., 638.

76. Ibid., 639.

77. Ibid., 633. Thus also E. Jüngel, *Death*, 120: 'It is as finite that man's infinite life is *made eternal*. Not by endless extension – there is no

immortality of the soul – but through participation in the very life of God. Our life is *hidden* in his life. In this sense the briefest form of the hope of resurrection is the statement: "God is my eternity"'. 121: 'Resurrection from the dead means then that it is the life we have actually lived that is gathered into community, made eternal and made manifest' (trans. slightly altered). But eternalizing without a putting to rights, a transformation, a completion and a transfiguration would be no favourable hope. The last sentence must surely read 'resurrection of the dead', not 'from the dead' – or are the others supposed to remain dead?

78. H. Schmid, *Dogmatik*, §32, 211f.

79. P. Tillich adopted the doctrine of 'natural death' and assigned death, suffering and fear to the essence of finite life. But it death is the natural end of a finite being, then according to Tillich death, suffering and fear must be essentialized in eternal life too. Attention has been drawn to this problem in Tillich's system by E. Schmalenberg, 'Der Sinn des Todes', *NZSTh* 14, 1972, 233–249; also I.C. Henel, 'Paul Tillichs Begriff der Essentifikation und seine Bedeutung für die Ethik', *NZSTh* 10, 1968, 1–17.

80. This image is used by Hildegard of Bingen; see her *Lieder*, Salzburg 1969, 229, 235, 287. Cf. also C. Blumhardt, *Ansprache, Predigten, Reden, Briefe II: 1865–1971. Neue Texte aus dem Nachlass herausgegeben von J. Harder*, Neukirchen 1978, 295f.: 'Nature is the womb of God. Out of the earth God will come to meet us again. But as yet we still have no fellowship with nature. We admire her, yet often tread her underfoot, use her in a way contrary to reason. So nature still confronts us with icy reserve, and feels alien to us. Something else must come . . . The harmony between human beings and nature must come. Then both will be content. And that will be the solution of the social question.'

80a. Annette von Droste-Hülschoff, 'Die ächzende Kreatur'. For the German text see *God in Creation*, 331 n.33.

81. D. Staniloae, *Orthodoxe Dogmatik* I, Gütersloh 1985, 291ff.

82. *The Way of Jesus Christ*, Ch. IV §2, 160ff.; Ch. V §5, 252.

83. Elaine Pagels, *Adam, Eve, and the Serpent*, New York and London 1988, xxiii, 42ff. As she shows, the pre-Constantinian Fathers of the church interpreted the story of creation in the light of the command given to human beings to rule, as a designation for moral autonomy (*autexousia*), and understood it politically in a sense critical of domination. After Constantine, this positive anthropology is changed into the negative anthropology of original sin, in order to justify a positive political theology of power, and ecclesiastical authority. Because human beings cannot rule themselves but, according to the law of the wild, 'eat or are eaten', they need for protection from themselves and each other a strong state and an authoritarian church. That is the political side of the doctrine of original sin. I myself have departed from Augustine's interpretation of Genesis 3 and have defined sin as 'acts of violence', in accordance with Genesis 6 – as wickedness against life. See *The Way of Jesus Christ*, 127ff.

84. T. W. Adorno, *Negative Dialectics*, 362 (trans. slightly altered).

85. M. Heidegger, *Being and Time*, trans. J. Macquarrie and E. Robinson, London 1962, §§49–53.

86. K. Löwith, *Das Individuum in der Rolle des Mitmenschen*, Munich 1928; E. Jüngel, *Death*, Ch. II: The Death of the Other Person (Death as a Social Fact).

87. M. Schmaus, *Katholische Dogmatik* IV/2, 2nd ed., Munich 1941, 151–173; on the development of the idea of purgatory cf. J. Le Goff, *Die Geburt des Fegefeuers*, Stuttgart 1984; further literature includes: H.-J. Vogels, *Christi Abstieg ins Totenreich und das Läuterungsgericht an den Toten*, Freiburg, Basle and Vienna 1976; H. Vorgrimler, 'Das Fegefeuer' in J. Feiner and M. Löhrer (eds), *Mysterium Salutis. Grundriss heilsgeschichtlicher Dogmatik V, Zwischenzeit und Vollendung der Heilsgeschichte*, Zürich, Einsiedeln and Cologne 1976, 453–457; J.B. Walz *Die Fürbitte der armen Seelen und ihre Anrufung durch die Gläubingen auf Erden. Ein Problem des Jenseits*, 2nd ed., Würzburg 1933; A. Winklhofer, 'Die Lehre der katholischen Kirche vom Leben nach dem Tod mit der neuesten Auffassung über Fegfeuer und Tod' in G. Hildmann (ed.), *Jenseits des Todes. Beiträge zur Frage des Lebens nach dem Tod*, Stuttgart 1970, 30–48.

88. The classic text is the Council of Trent, Sessio XXV, in H. Denzinger/A. Schönmetzer 1820–1835 (ET R.J. Deferrari). Cf. F. Diekamp, *Katholische Dogmatik nach den Grundsätzen des heiligen Thomas* III, 13th, newly revised ed. by K. Jüssen, Freiburg 1962, 404–497; M. Schmaus, *Katholische Dogmatik* IV/2, 70–252.

89. Benedict XII, Constitution *Benedictus Deus* (1336) in H. Denzinger/A. Schönmetzer 1000–1002.

89a. *Dante's Paradise*, trans. M. Musa, Bloomington 1984, Penguin, Harmondsworth 1985.

90. *Katholische Erwachsenen-Katechismus. Das Glaubensbekenntnis der Kirche*, Bonn 1985, 424.

91. Letter of the Congregation for the Doctrine of the Faith Regarding Certain Questions of Eschatology (see n.8) 4 (AAS Aug. 1979, p.941).

92. M. Luther, 'Widerruf vom Fegefeuer'(1530), WA 30, II, 360–390.

93. J. Calvin, *Institutio Christianae Religionis* III, 5, 6 (ET *Institutes of the Christian Religion*, ed. J.T. McNeill, London and Philadelphia 1961).

94. Letter of the Congregation for the Doctrine of the Faith Regarding . . . Eschatology, 3 (AAS Aug. 1979, p.941).

95. O. H. Pesch, 'Theologie des Todes bei Martin Luther' in J. Becker, B. Einig and P. Ullrich (eds), *Im Angesicht des Todes* II, St. Ottilien 1987, 709–789; cf. P. Althaus, *Letzte Dinge* 141ff.; also his *Die Theologie Martin Luthers*, 3rd ed., Gütersloh 1972, 343–349 (esp. 346f.).

96. M. Luther, 'Predigt am 16. Sonntag nach Trinitatis (im Hause)' (1533), WA 37, 151; also his 'Predigt am 24. Sonntag nach Trinitatis' (1532), WA 36, 349; also 'Epistelauslegung Petr und Jud' (1523/24), WA 14, 70f. Thus also the Qur'an, Sure 10, 46ff.; 46, 35: Because the time between death and final judgment is without consciousness, the person raised has the impression that judgment takes place immediately after death.

97. M. Luther, WA 36, 547. Cf. Luther's hymn 'Christ lag in Todes-banden', the third verse of which runs: Jesus Christus, Gottes Sohn an unser Statt ist kommen / und hat die Sünde abgetan, damit dem Tod genommen / all sein Recht und sein Gewalt; da bleibt nichts denn Tod's Gestalt, / den Stachel hat er verloren. / Halleluja.'

98. M. Luther, WA 36, 548.

99. K. Rahner, 'Purgatory', *Theological Investigations* XIX, trans. E. Quinn, London 1984, 181–193; also 'The Intermediate State' in *Theological Investigations* XVII, trans. Margaret Kohl, London 1981, 114–124; G. Greshake and G. Lohfink, *Naherwartung – Auferstehung – Unsterblichkeit* (QD 71) 4, and expanded edition Freiburg 1982; J. Ratzinger, *Eschatologie – Tod und Ewiges Leben*: H. Vorgrimler, *Hoffnung auf Vollendung. Aufriss der Eschatologie* (QD 90), Freiburg 1980.

100. *Glaubensverkündigung für Erwachsene. Deutsche Ausgabe des Holländischen Katechismus*, Nijmegen and Utrecht 1968, 525.

101. C. Schütz, 'Vollendung' in J. Feiner and L. Vischer (eds), *Neues Glaubensbuch. Der gemeinsame christliche Glaube*, 15th ed., Freiburg 1979, 541f.

102. *Letter of the Congregation for the Doctrine of the Faith Regarding . . . Eschatology*, 5 (AAS Aug. 1979, p.941).

103. K. Rahner, 'The Intermediate State', 115.

104. G. Lohfink, 'Geschichte und Vollendung' in G. Greshake and G. Lohfink, *Naherwartung*, 97. It is noteworthy that for their doctrine about 'resurrection in death', Greshake and Lohfink use, not the eschatological concept about the resurrection *of* the dead, but the chiliastic concept of resurrection *from* the dead. That can only mean that the others remain in death and that only believers will be raised.

105. I should like to draw attention to the New Testament essays by W. Thüsing, *Per Christum in Deum. Studien zum Verhältnis von Christozentrik und Theozentrik in den paulinishen Hauptbriefen* (NTA. NS 1), Münster 1965; P. Hoffmann, *Die Toten in Christus. Eine religionsgeschichtliche und exegetische Untersuchung zur paulinischen Eschatologie*, 3rd expanded edition, Münster 1969.

106. E. Käsemann, 'On the Subject of Primitive Christian Apocalyptic' in *New Testament Questions of Today*, London 1969, 108ff., who has taken over these ideas from E. Peterson. Cf. B. Nichthweiss, *Erik Peterson. Neue Sicht auf Leben und Werk*, Freiburg 1992, 228.

107. Thus Paul Gerhardt's hymn verse:

Ich hang und bleib auch hangen an Christo als ein Glied;
wo mein Haupt durch ist gangen, da nimmt er mich auch mit.
Er reisset durch den Tod, durch Welt durch Sünd, durch Not,
er reisset durch die Höll, ich bin stets sein Gesell.

108. W. Benjamin, *Illuminationen* (*Ausgewählte Schriften* I), Frankfurt 1961, 270f. 'The enemy' is the Antichrist: 'For the Messiah comes not only as the Redeemer; he comes as the overcomer of the Antichrist.'

109. On the following passage see 'Unsere Hoffnung. Ein Beschluss der

Gemeinsame Synode der Bistümer in der Bundesrepublik Duetschland' in *Gemeinsame Synode der Bistümer in der Bundesrepublik Deutschland. Beschlüsse der Vollversammlung. Offizielle Gesamtausgabe* I, Freiburg 1976, esp. 88ff.; also the comment by J. B. Metz, *Faith in History and Society*, trans. D. Smith, London 1980, Part II.6, 100–118.

110. M. Horkheimer, *Die Sehnsucht nach dem ganz Anderen. Ein Interview mit Kommentar von H. Gumnior*, Hamburg 1970, 61f.

111. This section relates to the theses in J. Stott, *Evangelical Essentials. A liberal-evangelical Dialogue* Downer Groves, Ill., 1988, 312ff., and the balanced response by S. J. Grenz, *Theology for the Community of God*, Nashville, Tn., 1994, 831ff. For the further discussion of questions about the divine judgment and hell, see Ch. III, §11.6 below.

112. G. MacGregor, *Reinkarnation und Karma im Christentum* I, Munich 1985; R. Hummel, *Reinkarnation. Weltbilder des Reinkarnationsglaubens und das Christentum*, Mainz and Stuttgart 1988; H. Küng, *Eternal Life?*, 81–94.

113. J. Moltmann, *Creating a Just Future*, trans. J. Bowden, London and Philadelphia 1989, esp. 87ff.

114. R. Hummel, *Reinkarnation*, 29; H. Küng, *Eternal Life?*.

114a. *The Bhagavad-Gita*, trans. and ed. R.C. Zaehner, Oxford 1969.

115. Quoted in R. Hummel, ibid., 57.

116. Quoted ibid., 42.

117. E. Kübler-Ross, *On Life after Death*, Berkeley, Ca., 1991.

118. A. Kardec, *Das Buch der Geister*, Freiburg 1987.

119. Thus H. von Glasenapp and H. von Stietencron, quoted in R. Hummel, *Reinkarnation*, 43f.

120. G. Greshake, 'Seelenwanderung oder Auferstehung? Ein Diskurs über die eschatologische Vollendung des Heils' in *Gottes Heil – Glück der Menschen*, Freiburg 1983, 241f.

121. J. Zink, *Sieh nach den Sternen – gib acht auf die Gassen. Erinnerungen*, Stuttgart 1992, 393.

122. Of the extensive literature I have drawn on the following: Y. Spiegel, *The Grief Process*, Nashville and London 1977; V. Kast, *Trauern. Phasen und Chancen des psychischen Prozesses*, Stuttgart 1982; J. Bowlby, *Verlust, Trauer, Depression*, Frankfurt 1983; M. Leist, *Kinder begegnen dem Tod*, Gütersloh 1979; G. Schmied, *Sterben und Trauern in der modernen Gesellschaft*, Munich 1988; S. Kahl-Passoth, S. Dille and A. von Walther, *Nimmt das denn nie ein Ende? Mit Trauer leben lernen*, Gütersloh 1992.

123. C. Lasch, *The Culture of Narcissism. American Life in an Age of Diminishing Experience*, New York 1978; also his *The Minimal Self. Psychic Survival in Troubled Times*, London and New York 1984.

124. S. Kahl-Passoth et al., *Nimmt das denn nie ein Ende?*, 26ff.

125. Y. Spiegel, *The Grief Process*.

126. Smalcald Articles III, 4.

127. D. Bonhoeffer, *Letters and Papers from Prison*, 176 (letter of Christmas Eve, 1943; trans. slightly altered).

128. S. Kahl-Passoth *et al.*, *Nimmt das denn nie ein Ende?*, 40f.

129. S. Freud, 'Mourning and Melancholia', trans. J. Riviere, in *Collected Papers of Sigmund Freud*, IV, London 1925, 152–170.

130. Ibid., 153.

131. Ibid. (trans. slightly altered).

132. M. de Unamuno, *The Tragic Sense of Life*, ET London and Princeton, N.J., 1972, with the comment by J. Moltmann in *The Trinity and the Kingdom of God*, trans. Margaret Kohl, London 1981 (= *The Trinity and the Kingdom*, New York 1981), 21ff.

133. T. Rees, *Hymns and Psalms*, Methodist Publishing House 1983, No. 36, verse 2. One may also remember P. Gerhardt's verse in 'O sacred head sore wounded . . .': 'Wenn mir am allerbängsten / wird um das Herze sein, / dann reiss mich aus den Ängsten, / kraft deiner Angst und Pein.' ('And when my heart must languish / Amidst the final throe, / Release me from mine anguish / By Thine own pain and woe.')

134. This is stressed by Luther in 'Ein Sermon von der Bereitung zum Sterben' (1519), WA 2, 685–697.

135. J. Moltmann, *The Way of Jesus Christ*, 100.

III The Kingdom of God

1. A. von Harnack, *What is Christianity?*, trans. T. B. Saunders, London 1901; 5th ed., 1958, 49.

2. P. Althaus, *Die letzten Dinge*, 1st ed., Gütersloh 1922, 231: 'Eternal Life is nothing other than life in God's kingdom. No one has eternal life without and before the coming of the kingdom. The coming of the kingdom – that is the all-embracing hope of Christians.' See also M. Welker's programmatic essay, 'Das Reich Gottes', *EvTh* 52, 1992, 497–512.

3. J. Moltmann, *Theology of Hope*, trans. J.W. Leitch, London and New York 1967, Ch. IV: Eschatology and History, 230ff.; also *God in Creation. An Ecological Doctrine of Creation* (Gifford Lectures 1984–85), trans. Margaret Kohl, London and New York 1985, Ch. V: The Time of Creation, 104ff.; also *The Way of Jesus Christ. Christology in Messianic Dimensions*, trans. Margaret Kohl, London and New York 1990, Ch. V, §2: History and the Resurrection of Christ: the Theological Problem, 227ff.

4. C. Schmitt, *Politische Theologie. Vier Kapitel zur Lehre von der Souveränität*, 2nd ed., Munich and Leipzig 1934, 49; P. Tillich, *Systematic Theology* III, Chicago 1963, London 1964, 346f.

5. J. Assmann, *Politische Theologie zwischen Ägypten und Israel*, ed. Heinrich Meier (C. F. von Siemens-Stiftung Themen LII), Munich 1992, 35ff.

6. K. Löwith, *Meaning in History*, Chicago 1949, 2; J. Taubes, *Abendländische Eschatologie* (1947), 2nd ed., Munich 1991; E. Voegelin, *Die neue Wissenschaft der Politik. Eine Einführung* (1959), Freiburg 1991.

7. K. Löwith, ibid., 18.

8. Cf. K. Löwith, *Gesammelte Abhandlungen. Zur Kritik der geschicht-*

lichen Existenz, Stuttgart 1960; also his *Vorträge und Abhandlungen. Zur Kritik der christlichen Überlieferung*, Stuttgart 1966. Here Löwith shows himself to be a prophet of the ecological crisis and a precursor of ecological thinking.

9. W. Pannenberg *et al.* (ed.), *Revelation as History*, trans. D. Granskou and E. Quinn, London and Sydney, New York 1969. Of fundamental importance for Pannenberg was Klaus Koch's interpretation of Daniel 7 as universal history; see K. Koch, 'Spätisraelitisches Geschichtsdenken am Beispiel des Buches Daniel', *HZ* 193, 1961, 7–32. The apocalyptic interpretation was thereby overlaid.

10. G. Picht, *Die Erfahrung der Geschichte*, WuG 19, Frankfurt 1958; see also G. Cunico, *Da Lessing a Kant. La storia in prospettiva escatologica*, Genoa 1992.

11. J. Moltmann, 'The End of History' in *Hope and Planning*, trans, Margaret Clarkson, London 1971, 155ff.

12. K. Löwith, *Meaning in History*, 18.

13. F. Fukuyama, *The End of History and the Last Man*, New York and Toronto 1989.

14. R. Bultmann, 'New Testament and Mythology' in H.-W. Bartsch (ed.), *Kerygma and Myth*, trans. R. H. Fuller, London 1953, 5 (altered).

15. I am indebted here to J. Ebach, 'Apokalypse. Zum Ursprung einer Stimmung' in *Einwürfe 2*, 2ff. The subversive import of revelation is also stressed by C. Rowland, *The Open Heaven. A Study of Apocalyptic in Judaism and Early Christianity*, London and New York 1982, and A. Boesak, *Comfort and Protest. Reflections on the Apocalypse of John of Patmos*, Philadelphia 1987.

16. On the philosophical level, this corresponds to the difference between the messianic thinking of E. Bloch, *Das Prinzip Hoffnung*, Frankfurt 1959 (ET *The Principle of Hope*, trans. N. and S. Plaice and P. Knight, Cambridge, Mass. and Oxford 1986) and T. W. Adorno, *Negative Dialectics*, trans E. B. Ashton, New York and London 1973.

17. This idea goes back to G. von Rad, *Old Testament Theology*, trans. D. M. G. Stalker, Edinburgh and London, 1962–65. At present it has been adopted particularly by liberation theology. Cf. G. Gutiérrez, *A Theology of Liberation*, trans. C. Inda and J. Eagleson, Maryknoll, New York, 1973, London 1974; 2nd ed. 1985, 155ff., 163ff.

18. G. von Rad later became aware of this and corrected himself; cf. his *Wisdom in Israel*, trans. J. D. Martin, Nashville 1972, London 1975.

19. J. Ebach, *Apokalypse*.

20. R. Radford Ruether, *Gaia and God. An Ecofeminist Theology of Earth Healing*, San Francisco 1992, London 1993, 205ff., sees an antithesis between eschatological expectation and the sabbath tradition. She seems to think that eschatology is purposeful and masculine, and that the rhythmical healing of the world in the sabbath is feminine. This is a typically modern misunderstanding of eschatology.

21. J. Ebach, *Apokalypse*.

22. F. Rosenzweig, *Der Stern der Erlösung, Gesammelte Schriften* II, The Hague 1976, 244 (*The Star of Redemption*, trans. W. W. Hallo, London 1971).

23. R. Koselleck, *Vergangene Zukunft. Zur Semantik geschichtlicher Zeiten*, Frankfurt 1979, esp. 349ff.

24. K. Löwith, *Meaning in History*, 6.

25. E. Bloch, *Das Prinzip Hoffnung* 7 (ET *The Principle of Hope*, 8f.): 'The rigid separations between past and future thus collapse of themselves, unrealized future becomes in the past visible, avenged and inherited, mediated and fulfilled past in the future.' Seen messianically, the statement in the second part of the sentence is correct; seen apocalyptically it is false.

26. Cf. here G. Menken, 'Das Monarchienbild' (1802), *Schriften* 7, Bremen 1858, 105ff. He relates the four kingdoms of the world to the four 'chief revolutions', latterly the French one, in order to announce the imminent coming of the all-embracing, eternal 'universal monarchy of God'.

27. P. Tillich, *Systematic Theology* III, 341f.

28. J. Moltmann, *Christoph Pezel und der Calvinismus in Bremen*, Bremen 1958, Beilage I: Von der philippistischen Geschichtswissenschaft zum apokalyptisch-heilsgeschichtlichen System des Coccejus, 167ff.; also 'Jacob Brocard als Vorläufer der Reich-Gottes-Theologie und der symbolisch-prophetischen Schriftauslegung des Johann Coccejus', *ZKG* 71, 1960, 110–129.

29. P. Schäfer, 'Die Torah der messianischen Zeit', *ZNW* 65, 1974, 27ff.

30. P. Toon (ed.), *Puritans, the Millennium and the Future of Israel: Puritan Eschatology 1600 to 1660*, Cambridge and London 1970, esp. 42ff. on Johann Heinrich Alsted; R. Bauckham, *Tudor Apocalypse. Sixteenth century apocalypticism, millenarianism and the English Reformation: from John Bale to John Foxe and Thomas Brightman*, Oxford 1975, 166. Deserving of special attention is A. Osiander, *Conjecturae de ultimis temporibus, ac de fine mundi, ex Sacris literis* (1544) which was already translated into English in 1545, and M. Luther, *Supputatio annorum mundi* (1541, 1545), WA 53, 22–182.

31. See here M. Reeves, *The Influence of Prophecy in the Later Middle Ages. A Study in Joachimism*, Oxford 1969; H. de Lubac, *La postérité spirituelle de Joachim de Fiore* I: *De Joachim à Schelling*; II: *De Saint-Simon à nos jours*, Paris 1979, 1980; H. Mottu, *La manifestation de l'Esprit selon Joachim de Fiore, Herméneutique et théologie de l'histoire d'après le 'Traité sur les quatres Evangiles'*, Neuchatel and Paris 1977; J. Moltmann, 'Christliche Hoffnung: Messianisch oder transzendent? Ein theologisches Gespräch mit Joachim von Fiore und Thomas von Aquin', *MThZ* 4, 1982, 241–260.

32. This is what H. de Lubac maintained, evidently without being familiar with the *Liber Figurarum*.

33. Thus M. Hahn, *Brief von der ersten Offenbarung Gottes durch die ganze Schöpfung bis an das Ziel aller Dinge, oder das System seiner Gedanken*, 2nd ed., Tübingen 1839, 467, 492ff., 484.

34. G. Menken, 'Über Glück und Sieg der Gottlosen' (1795), *Schriften* 7, Bremen 1858, 82.

35. G. van den Honert, *Inst. theol. typ* 3, 422, 394, quoted in G. Möller, 'Föderalismus und Geschichtsbetrachtung im 17. und 18. Jahrhundert', *ZKG* 50, 1931, 419: G. Sauter, 'Die Zahl als Schlüssel zur Welt. Johann Albrecht Bengels "prophetische Zeitrechnung" im Zusammenhang seiner Theologie', *EvTh* 26, 1966, 1–36.

36. G. Lampe, *Geheimnis des Gnadenbundes* IV, Bremen 1712, 124: 'Since we daily make new discoveries in nature (through telescopes), why should we be amazed that through increasing effort in the investigation of the divine Word new discoveries should also be made, and the promised increase in knowledge of the Last Times (Dan. 12.4, Ezek.47.4) should more and more begin to be fulfilled?'

37. Cf. F. Calixt, *De Chiliasmo cum antiquo tum pridem renato. Tractatus theologicus*, Helmstedt 1692; H. Corrodi, *Kritische Geschichte des Chiliasmus*, Frankfurt and Leipzig 1781–83; E. Waldstein, 'Die eschatologische Ideengruppe: Antichrist – Weltsabbat – Weltende und Weltgericht in den Hauptmomenten ihrer christlich-mittelalterlichen Gesamtentwicklung', *ZWTh* 38, 1895, 538–616; 39, 1896, 251–293; F. Gerlich, *Der Kommunismus als Lehre vom tausendjährigen Reich*, Munich 1920; L. Radvanyi, *Der Chiliasmus. Ein Versuch zur Erkenntnis der chiliastischen Idee und des chiliastischen Handelns*. Diss. Heidelberg 1923; M. Katz, *Messianismus; Chiliasmus und Eschatologie in der deutschen Dichtung des 17. Jahrhunderts*, Diss. Vienna 1938; W. Nigg, *Das ewige Reich. Geschichte einer Hoffnung*, Zürich 1944; H. Bietenhard, *Das Tausendjährige Reich. Eine biblisch-theologische Studie*, Zürich 1955; E. Sarkisyanz, *Russland und der Messianismus des Orients. Sendungsbewusstsein und politischer Chiliasmus des Ostens*, Tübingen 1955; J. L. Talmon, *The History of Totalitarian Democracy: 2: Political messianism. The romantic phase*, London and New York 1960; W. E. Mühlmann, *Chiliasmus und Nativismus. Studien zur Psychologie, Soziologie und historischen Kasuistik der Umsturzbewegungen*, Berlin 1961; W. Veit, *Studien zur Geschichte des Topos von der goldenen Zeit von der Antike bis zum 18. Jahrhundert*, Diss. Cologne 1961; G. Scholem, 'Zum Verständnis der messianischen Idee im Judentum', *Judaica* I, Frankfurt 1963, 7–74; E. L. Tuveson, *Redeemer Nation. The Idea of America's Millennial Role*, Chicago 1968; N. Cohn, *The Pursuit of the Millennium. Revolutionary millenarians and mystical anarchists of the middle ages*, London 1957; revised and expanded ed., 1970 ; R.G. Clouse (ed.), *The Meaning of the Millennium. Four Views*, Downers Grove 1977; M.D. Bryant and D.W. Dayton, *The Coming Kingdom. Essays in American Millennialism and Eschatology*, New York 1983. More recent American writings on millennialism are treated in R. Williamson (ed.), *The End in Sight? Images of the End and Threats to Human Survival*, Uppsala 1993. Of the French literature cf. J. Le Goff, 'Millénarisme', *Enc. Univ.* XI, Paris 1968, 30ff.; H. Desroche, *Dieu d'hommes. Dictionnaire des messianismes et des millénarismes de l'ère*

chrétienne, Paris 1969; De La Platine, *Les trois voix de l'imaginaire, le messianisme, la possession et l'utopie*, Paris 1974; C. Duquoc, *Messianisme de Jésus et Discretion de Dieu*, Geneva 1984.

38. Between 1800 and 1820 more than 20,000 people emigrated from Württemberg to Russia for chiliastic reasons, hastening to meet the coming Lord and to find on Ararat in the Caucasus the place of refuge in the end of the world. Johann Albrecht Bengel had calculated that Christ would come again and that the Thousand Years' empire would dawn on Sunday, 18 June 1836. The 'brotherly emigration harmonies' emptied the villages round Tübingen. See the *Schwäbisches Tagblatt* of 4 April 1985.

39. Cf. R. R. Ruether and H. J. Ruether, *The Wrath of Jonah. The Crisis of Religious Nationalism in the Israeli-Palestinian Conflict*, San Francisco 1989, 74ff.

40. See R. Bauckham. *Tudor Apocalypse*, 15f.; G. Fackre, *The Religious Right and Christian Faith*, Grand Rapids 1982, 90ff.

41. J. Katz, 'Israel and the Messiah', *Com.* 73, 1982, 34–41.

42. Consequently the *Confessio Helvetica Posterior* 1566, Article 11, condemned millenarianism as Jewish dreams (*'judaica somnia'*) and as the notion of 'an age of gold' (*'seculum aureum'*).

43. Thus also G. Scholem on 'Die messianische Idee in Judentum', 21.

44. As Scholem maintains, ibid. 20.

45. As J. T. Beck, *Glaubenslehre* II, Gütersloh 1887, 709, emphatically points out.

46. Cf. here E. Peterson, *Zeuge der Wahrheit*, Leipzig 1937, 33ff.

47. Thus rightly R. Bauckham, *The Theology of the Book of Revelation*, Cambridge 1993, 107f.

48. Irenaeus, *Adv. haeres.* 5.32.

49. P. Althaus's judgment in *Die letzten Dinge*, 314.

50. The new apocalypticism of American fundamentalists such as Hal Lindsey, *The Late Great Planet Earth*, New York 1970, distributed in millions of copies, works with science-fiction elements and is hardly more serious than Batman fantasies. Cf. A.G. Mojtabai, *Blessed Assurance. At Home with the Bomb in Amarillo, Texas*, London 1987, 181 ' . . . When you leave here in the Rapture of the church, you're going to be travelling 186,000 miles a second . . . Lord, when the trump of God sounds we're going to clear out of here in one split second . . . And we'd sing on our way like a meteor! Right up into the firmament above Amarillo, Texas. Amen! And we can look back down to the houses where we live and we can say: "Goodbye, you piece of junk! Goodbye, old shack!" Amen – you can look back at your automobile and say: "Goodbye, old paint, hah! Goodbye! Goodbye!" Look back down to your job there and say "Goodbye, fellas! I'm headed out of here! Goodbye, Goodbye!" Aha! Oh yes, and then pretty soon you'd be seeing the lights of Dallas and the lights of Houston, and you'd look away over to the west and you'd see the lights of Los Angeles. And you'd say: "Goodbye, Dallas! Goodbye, Houston! Goodbye, Los Angeles! Goodbye world! Goodbye!"' Billy Graham has tried to lay stress on the love of God,

contrary to this delight in the nuclear Armageddon and the 'Apocalypse 2000': *Approaching Hoofbeats. Four Horsemen of the Apocalypse*, New York 1983. Only he is really unable to decide: cf. 221ff.

51. A. von Harnack, *Lehrbuch der Dogmengeschichte* I, 4th ed., Tübingen 1909, 187, n.1.

52. Eusebius of Caesarea, *Hist. eccl.* 10.4.

53. The second Article of the Nicene Creed already says of the lordship of Christ that his 'kingdom shall have no end', whereas in I Cor. 15.28 Paul assumes that at the end the Son will pass over the kingdom to the Father, so that God may be all in all. Even today, Orthodox theology rejects the assumption that there will be a messianic kingdom of Christ which will serve to prepare for the eternal kingdom of the Father. Cf. *Gemeinsam den eine Glauben bekennen*, Frankfurt 1991, 76.

54. H. Preuss, *Die Vorstellung vom Antichrist im späten Mittelalter, bei Luther und in der konfessionellen Polemik*, Leipzig 1906; H.A. Obermann, *Luther. Man between God and the Devil*, trans. E. Walliser–Schwarzbad, London 1989.

54a. Translation by T. G. Tappert in *The Book of Concord. The Confessions of the Evangelical Lutheran Church*, Philadelphia 1959.

55. R. Bauckham, *Theology of the Book of Revelation*, Ch. 11: The Millennium, 208ff.

56. D. Cantimori, *Italienische Häretiker der Spätrenaissance*, Basle 1949.

57. Cf. G. Schrenk, *Gottesreich und Bund im älteren Protestantismus vornehmlich bei Johannes Coccejus* (1923), Giessen and Basle 1985; G. Weth, *Die Heilsgeschichte. Ihr universeller und ihr individueller Sinn in der offenbarungsgeschichtlichen Theologie des 19. Jahrhunderts*, Munich 1931.

58. Bengel's eschatology is characterized by dichiliasm. He distinguishes the 'thousand years' mentioned in Rev. 20.2 and Rev. 20.4 from each other as the earthly and the heavenly millennium, and expects *two* thousand years' kingdoms at the end of world history, which are supposed to last from the year 5777 1/9 to 7777 1/9, counting from the creation of the world, or from 1836 to 3836 according to our calendar. According to this 'the Day of Christ' will be 'the Last Day', or Last Judgment, in time.

59. F. C. Oetinger, 'Hoffnung, Elpis' in *Biblisches und Emblematisches Wörterbuch*, Stuttgart 1776, 330.

60. The idea goes back to Johann Albrecht Bengel: ' . . . The more dangerous a time, the greater the help which is offered against it in prophecy.' Cf. R. Breymayer, '"Anfangs glaubte ich die Bengelsche Erklärung ganz . . ." Philipp Matthäus Hahns Weg zu seinem wiederentdeckten "Versuch einer neuen Erklärung der Offenbarung Johannis" (1785)', *JGP* 15, 1989, 182, n. 51. Also P. H. Gaskill's comments in 'Meaning in History: "Chiliasm" in Hölderlin's "Patmos"', *Colloquia Germanica* 11, 1978, 19–52.

61. J. M. Lochman, *Comenius*, Freiburg 1982, 45f.

62. F. Gerlich, *Der Kommunismus*, has described precisely the transition from theological to philosophical chiliasm in the eighteenth century. His chiliastic interpretation of Marxism, on the other hand, is weak. His book was influenced by the *Räterepublik*, the Workers' and Soldiers' Councils set up in Munich in 1920.

63. G. Fackre, *Ecumenical Faith in Evangelical Perspective*, Grand Rapids 1993, esp. 21ff.: Political Fundamentalism: Distinctions and Directions.

64. H. Berkhof, *Die Theologie des Euseb von Caesarea*, Amsterdam 1939.

65. E. Peterson, 'Monotheismus als politisches Problem' in his *Theologische Traktate*, Munich 1951, 90.

66. Ibid. 89, quoting Eusebius VII, 2.22.

67. Eusebius, *Praep. ev.* 1.4–5. similarly *Hist. Eccl.* X 4.53. Cf. G. Podskalsky, *Byzantinische Reichseschatologie*, Munich 1972.

68. Eusebius, *Laus Constantini* X, 7, with the comments in H. Berkhof, *De Kerk en de Keizer*, Amsterdam 1946 (German trans., *Kirche und Kaiser. Eine Untersuchung der Entstehung der byzantinischen und der theokratischen Staatsauffassung im vierten Jahrhundert*, Zurich 1947, 83 ff., esp. 101. H. Dörries, *Konstantin der Grosse*, Stuttgart 1958, 147 (*Constantine the Great*, trans. R. H. Bainton, New York and London 1972).

69. H. Dörries, *Konstantin*, 146 ff. (*Constantine the Great*).

70. J. Weiss, *Jesus' Proclamation of the Kingdom of God* (1892), trans. R. H. Hiers and D. L. Holland, London 1971, 135.

71. H. Dörries, *Konstantin*, 127 ff. (*Constantine the Great*); K. Steffen, *Drachenkampf. Der Mythos vom Bösen*, Stuttgart 1984.

72. K. Steffen, ibid., 220.

73. Ibid., 227.

74. F. G. Maier (ed.), *Byzanz* (*Fischer Weltgeschichte* 13), Frankfurt 1973, esp. 66 ff.

75. Ibid., 21f.

76. R. Stählin, 'Geschichte des christlichen Gottesdienstes von der Urkirche bis zur Gegenwart' in *Leiturgia. Handbuch des evangelischen Gottesdienstes* I, Kassel 1954, 25ff.

77. H. Schaeder, *Moskau – das Dritte Rom. Studien zur Geschichte der politischen Theorien in der slawischen Welt*, Darmstadt 1963.

78. Cf. here A. Schmemann, 'The Problem of the Church's Presence in the World in Orthodox Consciousness' in S. C. Agourides, *Procès-Verbaux du Deuxième Congrès de Théologie Orthodoxe*, Athens 1978, 236–249.

79. R. Rothe, *Theologische Ethik* III, §447, Wittenberg 1848, 1010f.: 'If we wish to find our way about the present state of the Christian faith, the necessary premise is the recognition that the ecclesiastical stage of Christianity's historical development is past, and that the Christian spirit has already entered upon its moral, that is to say its political, age. If the church is the essential form in which Christianity exists, then – that we must honestly admit – this same church is in our days in a lamentable condition, and that

not merely since yesterday . . . But then at heart Christianity wishes to reach out beyond the church, it wishes to make as its organism nothing less than the total organism of human life, which is to say the state. Its intention is essentially to become more and more of the world, that is to say to divest itself of the ecclesiastic form which it was forced to assume on its entry into the world, and to put on the generally human, in actual fact moral form of life.' For by secularizing itself, Christianity gives moral form to society. By moving from the particular ecclesiastic form of life to its general political form, the church humanizes politics. In this transition from ecclesiasticism to morality, from hierarchy to world-wide Christianity, from religion to life, and from faith to political responsibility, the kingdom of God is approached. God ultimately desires the state, the perfected state, the moral divine state, because he desires responsible human beings. Once that is attained, the church will have become dispensible, as a temporary educational institution. Its goal has been reached, since it is there, not for itself and its own expansion, but for the divine kingdom. 'The pious church-goer is a thing of the past.' There is now only the Christian as citizen of the perfected kingdom of morality and civilization. Because the idea of morality is a star that has risen in world history, today 'the Christian spirit', which is 'the exalted Christ' himself, is in the process of 'surrendering its religious and ecclesiastical formation, and of acquiring its general, moral and political form.'

80. J. B. Metz has rightly drawn attention to this in *Zeit der Orden? Zur Mystik und Politik der Nachfolge*, Freiburg 1977, 78ff.: 'Ordensexistenz als Hoffnungsexistenz mit apokalyptischem Stachel.'

81. W. Goez, *Translatio Imperii. Ein Beitrag zur Geschichte des Geschichtsdenkens und der politischen Theorien im Mittelalter und in der frühen Neuzeit*, Tübingen 1958.

82. K. Breuning, *Die Vision des Reiches. Deutscher Katholizismus zwischen Demokratie und Diktatur (1929–1934)*, Munich 1969.

83. C. Schmitt, *Politische Theologie*, 2nd ed., Berlin 1934, 49f.; *Römischer Katholizismus und politische Form*, Hellerau 1927, 74–78. Carl Schmitt's ideological counterpart was in his own opinion Michail Bakunin, the Russian anarchist. In the End-time struggle between atheistic anarchism and state sovereignty, both were concerned about theo-political unity 'ni Dieu – ni maitre'. See here H. Meier, *Die Lehre Carl Schmitts. Vier Kapitel zur Unterscheidung Politischer Theologie und Politischer Philosophie*, Stuttgart 1993; also G. Meuter, *'Der Katechon': Zu Carl Schmitts fundamentalistischer Kritik der Zeit*, Berlin 1994.

84. B. Diaz del Castillo, *The True History of the Conquest of Mexico* (1632), trans. M. Keatinge, London 1800, 1928.

85. L. Abramowski, 'Der Bamberger Reiter. Vom Endzeitkaiser zum heiligen König Stephan von Ungarn', *ZKG* 98, 1987, 2, 206–229. On the myth of the End-time emperor, see also N. Cohn, *The Pursuit of the Millennium*, 54ff. Cohn points to the Byzantine ideas which were used by the French monk Adso.

86. R. N. Bellah, *Civil Religion in America*, Daedalus 1967, 331ff.; also

his *The Broken Covenant. Civil Religion in Time of Trial*, New York 1975. Cf. also E. L. Tuveson, *Redeemer Nation. The Idea of America's Millennial Role*, Chicago 1968.

87. Extensive collections of historical material on America's political faith can be found in C. Cherry (ed.), *God's New Israel. Religious Interpretation of American Destiny*, Eaglewood Cliff, NJ, 1971, E.A. Smith (ed.), *The Religion of the Republic*, Philadelphia 1971; W.S. Hudson (ed.), *Nationalism and Religion in America. Concepts of American Identity and Mission*, New York 1970. Cf. also the extracts from presidential inaugural addresses collected in F. C. Packard Jr (ed.), *They Spoke for Democracy. Classic Statements of the American Way*, New York 1958.

88. Ronald Reagan in an interview with Marvin Kalb for the *Jerusalem Post*, October 1983, and the comments in 'Armaggedon and the End time' in *Time*, 5 November 1984; R. Jewett, 'Coming to terms with the doom boom', *MOR* 3/4, 1984, 9–22.

89. This is rightly called 'the dark side of the myth'. Cf. R. Benne and P. Hefner, *Defining America. A Christian Critique of the American Dream*, Philadelphia 1974, 32. America's famous poetical myth is H. Melville's *Moby Dick*. In *Whitejacket* he wrote: 'And we Americans are the peculiar chosen people – the Israel of our time; we bear the ark of the liberties of the world . . . Long enough have we been sceptics with regard to ourselves, and doubted whether, indeed, the political Messiah had come. But he has come in *us*, if we would but give utterance to his promptings.' The white whale Moby Dick is the prototype of evil, and Captain Ahab is the tragic hero. America's messianic dream becomes a tragic myth. That gives *Moby Dick* its profondity. R. Jewett, *The Captain America complex. The Dilemma of Zealous Nationalism*, Philadelphia 1973, writes (27): 'As Winthrop S. Hudson puts it, "the New England story was viewed as a continuation of John Foxe's narrative of the pitched battles between Christ and Anti-Christ that had marked the course of human history from the beginnings."' Cf. also C. Cherry (ed.), *God's New Israel*, 21f.

90. M. Walzer, *The Revolution of the Saints. A Study in the Origins of Radical Politics*, Cambridge, Mass., 1965.

91. E. L. Tuveson, *Redeemer Nation*, 55.

92. J. F. Maclear, 'The Republic and the Millennium' in E. A. Smith (ed.), *The Religion of the Republic*, 183ff.; also C. Cherry (ed.), *God's New Israel*, 23.

93. W. S. Hudson (ed.), *Nationalism and Religion in America*, 93ff.

94. E. L. Tuveson, *Redeemer Nation*, VIII.

95. R. Jewett, *The Captain America Complex*, 148.

96. C. Cherry (ed.), *God's New Israel*, 1ff.: Two American Sacred Ceremonies.

97. Ibid., 4f.

98. W. S. Hudson, *Nationalism and Religion in America*, 19ff.

99. H. N. Smith, *Virgin Land. The American West as Symbol and Myth*, New York 1950; A. K. Weinberg, *Manifest Destiny*, Gloucester, Mass.,

1958; E. L. Tuveson, *Redeemer Nation*, Ch. IV: When did Destiny become manifest?, 91ff.

100. C. Cherry (ed.), *God's New Israel*, which I am following in this section.

101. J. M. Swomley Jr (ed.), *American Empire. The Political Ethics of Twentieth-Century Conquest*, London 1970.

102. C. Cherry (ed.), *God's New Israel*.

103. I have pointed to these ambiguities and the particularist-universal dilemma in *On Human Dignity. Political Theology and Ethics*, trans. M. D. Meeks, Philadelphia and London, 1984, Ch. 8: 'America as Dream', 147ff., esp. 148f. For a different view see W. Pannenberg, 'Das christliche Imperium und das Phänomen einer politischen Religion im Christentum' in *Die Bestimmung des Menschen*, Göttingen 1978, 61ff., esp. 82f.

104. *New York Times*, January 1993.

105. S. Schreiner, 'Die Säkularisierung der messianischen Idee. Jüdischer und polnischer Messianismus im 19. Jahrhundert', *EvTh* 54, 1994, 45–60.

106. H. Schaeder, *Moskau – das Dritte Rom*, 12ff.

107. Cf. M. Kehl's agreeably self-critical Catholic ecclesiology, *Die Kirche. Eine katholische Ekklesiologie*, Würzburg 1992, esp. 364ff.

108. Constitution on the Church, *Lumen Gentium*, I, 5; VII, 48.

109. P. Tillich, *Systematic Theology* III, 345.

110. Augustine, *De civ. Dei*, XX, 9: 'Quod sit regnum sanctorum cum Christo per mille annos et in quo discernatur a regno aeterno.' 'Interea dum mille annis ligatus est diabolus, sancti regnant cum Christo etiam ipsis mille annis, eisdem sine dubio et eodem modo intellegendis, id est isto iam tempore prioris eius adventus.' Translation in the text taken from *The City of God*, trans. G.G. Walsch and D.J. Honan, Washington D.C., 1954, 205. See here W. Kamlah's detailed study, *Christentum und Geschichtlichkeit. Untersuchungen zur Entstehung des Christentums und zu Augustins 'Bürgerschaft Gottes'*, Stuttgart 1951; also U. Duchrow, *Christenheit und Weltverantwortung. Traditionsgeschichte und systematische Struktur der Zweireichelehre*, Stuttgart 1970, 259ff.

111. H. Küng and J. Moltmann (eds), *Mary in the Churches, Concilium* 168, 1983; Catherine Keller, 'Die Frau in der Wüste. Ein feministisch-theologischer Midrasch zu Offb 12', *EvTh* 50, 1990, 414–432.

112. W. Kamlah, 'Ecclesia und regnum Dei bei Augustin', *Philologus* 53, 1938, 251.

113. Cf. *Christliche Erneuerung der menschlichen Gesellschaft. Die Sozialenzykliken der Päpste Leo XIII., Pius XI. und Johannes XXIII und die Pfingstansprache La Solennità Pius XII: Mit einer Einführung von O. v. Nell-Breuning*, Aschaffenburg 1962.

114. Thus Thomas Aquinas, contrary to Joachim of Fiore, *STh* II, CVI, a IV: 'Utrum lex nova sit duratura usque ad finem mundi?'

115. G. Greshake, 'Zur Bedeutung der Trinitätslehre', *Pastoralblatt* 42, 1990, 39; *The Trinity and the Kingdom of God*, trans. Margaret Kohl, London 1981 (= *The Trinity and the Kingdom*, New York 1981), 200ff.;

L. Boff, *Trinity and Society*, ET New York and London 1988.

116. M. Volf, *Wir sind die Kirche! Eine ökumenische Untersuchung über Kirche als Gemeinschaft*, postdoctoral thesis, Tübingen 1994.

117. Emphatic attention was already drawn to this a long time ago by F. Gerlich in *Der Kommunismus als Lehre vom tausendjährigen Reich*, Munich 1920, 142ff.

118. Gershom Scholem, *Sabbatai Sevi. The Mystical Messiah*, revised and augmented trans. from Hebrew, Princeton and London 1983.

119. R. Bauckham, *Tudor Apocalypse. Sixteenth-century apocalypticism, millenarianism, and the English Reformation*, Oxford 1975; W. Philipp, *Das Zeitalter der Aufklärung*, Bremen 1964, LVff., 42ff., treats the philosemitism of the early English Enlightenment under the heading 'Messianismus und Resettlement Israels'. On the one hand it is a matter of the messianic justification of the readmittance of Jews to England under Cromwell, which was justified by the Chief Rabbi of Amsterdam, Manasseh ben Israel, on the grounds that the Messiah would first appear as Lord of the Thousand Years' empire when Israel was dispersed throughout every country – i.e., England too. This led to a national English identification with the ten lost tribes of Israel and the English claim to rule over the world in the millennium. The complete dispersion was to be followed by Israel's return home to Zion, and the coming of the Messiah-Christ to the glorious kingdom of Zion.

120. T. Todorov, *Die Eroberung Amerikas. Das Problem des Anderen*, Frankfurt 1985.

121. I. Kant, Preface to the 2nd edition of the *Critique of Pure Reason* (1787).

122. F. Gerlich, *Kommunismus*, 150: 'The reshaping of the Christian chiliastic idea about the return of the Messianic kingdom into a philosophical idea about the realization of a moral world-order is not Lessing's work either, nor is it the work of any "free thinker". It is the work of a chiliastic Pietist.'

123. G. E. Lessing, *The Education of the Human Race*, trans. F.W. Robertson 1872, reprinted London and New York 1927 (trans. slightly altered).

124. I. Kant, *Idee zu einer allgemeinen Geschichte in weltbürgerlicher Absicht*, *Werke* VI, 45.

125. I. Kant, *Der Streit der Fakultäten*, *Werke* VI, 357, cf. also 361.

126. I. Kant, *Zum ewigen Frieden*, *Werke* VI, 195–251.

127. I. Kant, *Werke* VI, 45.

128. I. Kant, *Religion within the Limits of Reason Alone*, trans. T. M. Greene and H. H. Hudson, London and Chicago 1934, 122.

129. Ibid.

130. As R. Guardini maintained: see *The End of the Modern World. A search for orientation*, trans. J. Theman and H. Burke, London 1957.

131. P. Althaus, *Die letzten Dinge*, 318.

132. W. Kreck, *Die Zukunft des Gekommenen. Grundprobleme der Eschatologie*, Munich 1964, 188.

133. K. Barth, 'The Problem of Ethics Today' (1922) in *The Word of God and the Word of Man*, trans. D. Horton, London 1928, reprinted New York 1957, 158, 160.

134. W. Pannenberg, *Jesus – God and Man*, trans. L. C. Wilkins and D. A. Priebe, London 1968, 53ff.

135. I have made a first attempt in this direction in P. Lapide and J. Moltmann, *Israel und Kirche: ein gemeinsamer Weg?*, Munich 1980, 24ff.

136. C. Auberlin, quoted in P. Althaus, *Die letzten Dinge*, 306, n.3. See also A. A. van Ruler, *Die christliche Kirche und das alte Testament*, Munich 1955, 82ff. (*The Christian Church and the Old Testament*, trans. G. W. Bromiley, Grand Rapids 1971).

137. See J. Moltmann, *The Way of Jesus Christ*, 28ff.

138. O. Hofius, 'Das Evangelium und Israel. Erwägungen zu Römer 9–11', *ZThK* 83, 1986, 297–324, talks about 'faith'; but that is not mentioned here and in the case of 'life from the dead' can also hardly be presupposed among the dead.

139. J. T. Beck, *Die Vollendung des Reiches Gottes. Separatabdruck aus der Christlichen Glaubenslehre*, Gütersloh 1887, 63f.

140. Ibid., 58.

141. Ibid, 35. Cf. also M. Theunissen, *Negative Theologie der Zeit*, Frankfurt 1991, 314ff.

142. G. Lohfink, *Wem gilt die Bergpredigt? Beiträge zu einer christlichen Ethik*, Freiburg 1988, 99ff.

143. E. P. Thompson, 'Exterminismus als letztes Stadium der Zivilisation', *Befreiung* 19/20, 1981, 12ff.

144. L. Reinisch, *Das Spiel mit der Apokalypse*, Freiburg 1984; G. M. Martin, *Weltuntergang. Gefahr und Sinn apokalyptischer Visionen*, Stuttgart 1984.

145. K. Jaspers, *The Future of Mankind*, trans. E. B. Ashton, Chicago 1961; G. Anders, *Die atomare Drohung*, 4th ed. of *Endzeit und Zeitende* (1959), Munich 1983; G. D. Kaufmann, *Theology for a Nuclear Age*, New York 1985; G. C. Chapman, *Facing the Nuclear Heresy. A Call to Reformation*, Elgin, Ill., 1986. J. Moltmann, *Creating a Just Future. The Politics of Peace and the Ethics of Creation in a Threatened World*, trans. J. Bowden, London and Philadelphia 1989.

146. G. Anders, *Die atomare Drohung*, 55ff.

147. Cf. here G. Anders' vision of 'the end of history' through the abolition of the historical human being in G. Anders, *Die Antiquiertheit des Menschen*, 3rd ed., Munich 1984.

148. The annual reports of the Worldwatch Institute, Washington DC, speak a sober and impressive language. Attention must also be explicitly drawn to the publications of the Club of Rome. The reports of the many national and regional institutes cannot be listed here. A pessimistic view can be found in G. Fuller, *Das Ende. Von der heiteren Hoffnungslosigkeit im Angesicht der ökologischen Katastrophe*, Leipzig 1993.

149. Cf. R. Arce Valentin, 'Die Schöpfung muss gerettet werden. Aber:

Für wen? Die ökologische Krise aus der Perspektive lateinamerikanischer Theologie', *EvTh* 51, 1991, 565–577.

150. See here *God in Creation*, Ch. II.

151. E. Williams, *Capitalism and Slavery*, Chapel Hill, 1944; D. P. Mannix and M. Cowley, *Black Cargo. A History of the Atlantic Slave Trade*, New York 1962.

152. D. P. Mannix and M. Cowley, ibid., 287. It should, however, be said that a bill abolishing the slave trade within the British dominions was passed by parliament in 1807. Though this was at first frequently violated, a second bill passed in 1811 which declared the traffic to be a felony punishable with transportation proved effective. A measure abolishing slavery itself in the British colonies was passed in 1833.

153. E. Galeano, *Die offenen Adern Lateinamerikas*, Wuppertal 1981; T. Todorov, *Die Eroberung Amerikas. Das problem des Anderen*; B. de las Casas, *Kurzgefasster Bericht von der Verwüstung der Westindischen Länder*, Frankfurt 1981 (cf. a selection of his writings, trans. G. Sanderlin, New York 1971); G. Gutiérrez, *Las Casas. In Search of the Poor of Jesus Christ*, trans. R. R. Barr, Maryknoll N.Y. 1993; F. Mires, *Im Namen des Kreuzes. Der Genozid an den Indianern während der spanischen Eroberung. Theologische und politische Diskussionen*, Fribourg 1989.

154. See G. Gutiérrez, *La Casas*.

155. E. Galeano, *Die offenen Adern*, 34.

156. Ibid., 122.

157. H. Assmann and F. J. Hinkelammert, *Götze Markt*, Düsseldorf 1992.

158. *Herausgefordert durch die Armen. Dokument der Ökumenischen Vereinigung von Dritte-Welt Theologen 1976–1986*, Freiburg 1990, 156f.

159. G. Anders, *Die atomare Drohung*, 241ff.: Exkurs über christliche und atomare Apokalypse.

160. Ibid., 219.

161. Ibid., 207.

162. Ibid., 218.

163. Ibid., 214.

164. A. Kojève, *Introduction to the reading of Hegel . . . Lectures on the Phenomenology of Spirit*, trans. J.H. Nichols Jr, New York and London 1969; also the critical comment in R.K. Maurer, *Hegel und das Ende der Geschichte. Interpretationen zur 'Phänomenologie des Geistes'*, Stuttgart 1964, 139ff. and L. Niethammer, *Posthistoire. Has History come to an End?*, trans. P. Cammiller, London and New York 1992, 63ff., 73ff. Was Kojève being serious or ironical when he said that the OECD, where he worked, was the end of European history? What would he have said about the war in Bosnia?

165. For more detail see J. Moltmann, 'The End of History', in *Hope and Planning*, trans. Margaret Clarkson, London 1971, 155ff.

166. A. Gehlen, 'Ende der Geschichte?' in *Einblicke*, Frankfurt 1975, 115ff.; L. Niethammer, *Posthistoire*, 16ff.

167. K. Marx, *Frühschriften*, ed. S. Landshut, Stuttgart 1953, 525.

168. Ibid., 235.

169. L. Mumford, *Technics and Civilization*, New York 1934; *The Transformation of Man*, New York 1956, London 1957.

170. R. Seidenberg, *Post-historic Man. An Inquiry*, Chapel Hill, NC., 1950.

171. M. Horkheimer and T. W. Adorno, *Dialectic of Enlightenment*, trans. J. Cumming, London 1973.

172. M. Horkheimer, *Kritische Theorie* I and II, Frankfurt 1968.

173. E. Bloch, *Naturrecht und menschliche Würde*, Frankfurt 1961, 310.

174. This took place first of all in church service books and handbooks, in which birth, marriage and death turned from being unique, individual events into 'cases' (*casus*) which have to be 'dealt with' according to fixed rituals. On the ritualization of history and the bureaucratization that followed, cf. *God in Creation*, Ch.V: The Time of Creation, 105ff.

175. A. Gehlen, *Urmensch und Spätkultur*, Bonn 1956, esp. 47ff.

176. R. Seidenberg, *Post-historic Man*, 179, and the pertinent comment by L. Niethammer, *Posthistoire*, 143: 'Crystallization also entails the end of freedom and meaning, and therefore a reanimalization of man.'

177. Cf. here the valuable survey in L. Niethammer, *Posthistoire*, 24ff.

178. C. Lévi-Strauss, *The Savage Mind*, London 1966, with K. Homann's comment in 'Geschichtsphilosophie', *HWP* 2, 300.

179. F. Fukuyama, 'The End of History?' in *The National Interest* 16, 1989, 3–18; also his 'Reply to my Critics', ibid. 18, 1989/90, and his already cited book *The End of History and the Last Man* (see n. 13).

180. None of his critics has called in question Fukuyama's 'liberal principles', as he rightly remarks in his reply to them (see n.179). But of course that does not mean that these principles are proved with regard to the end of history.

181. It is astonishing that these outside perspectives on their own system play only a minor role among the prophets of the *post-histoire*. For Fukuyama too they are not particularly important. But before one speculates about a *post-histoire*, it would be more realistic to take into view the existing *sub-histoire*.

182. L. Niethammer, *Posthistoire*, 135ff.

183. J. Moltmann, 'Covenant or Leviathan? Political Theology for Modern Times', *Scottish Journal of Theology*, 47/1, 1994, 19–41.

184. On the rise of Jewish apocalyptic see P. D. Hanson, *The Dawn of Apocalyptic. The Historical and Sociological Roots of Jewish Apocalyptic Eschatology*, Philadelphia 1979.

185. Elisabeth Schüssler Fiorenza, *Revelation. Vision of a Just World*, Minneapolis 1991, Edinburgh 1994; J. Roloff, *Die Offenbarung des Johannes*, Zürich 1984; R. Bauckham, *The Theology of the Book of Revelation*, Cambridge 1993.

186. A. Boesak, *Comfort and Protest, The Apocalypse from a South African Perspective*, Philadelphia 1987, lends this an impressive topical

reference in his South African context. In his own way J. Ellul does the same thing in *Apocalypse. Die Offenbarung des Johannes – Enthüllung der Wirklichkeit*, Neukirchen 1981.

187. G. M. Martin has drawn attention to this in *Weltuntergang. Gefahr und Sinn apokalyptischer Visionen*, Stuttgart 1984. Cf. also here U.H.J. Körtner's extensive and informative work *Weltangst und Weltende. Eine theologische Interpretation der Apokalyptik*, Göttingen 1988, esp. 155ff.: Weltuntergänge.

188. G. M. Martin, ibid., 63.

189. Cf. here Christine Gerber, 'Das Pneuma weht, wo es will' in Elisabeth Moltmann-Wendel (ed.), *Die Weiblichkeit des Heiligen Geistes*, Gütersloh 1995, 38–56.

190. This is ancient Jewish tradition. Cf. Nedarim 11a: 'Out of the Nay you hear the Yay.'

191. G. M. Martin, *Weltuntergang* 101ff., makes this clear, in dispute with J. Metzner, *Persönlichkeitszerstörung und Weltuntergang*, Tübingen 1976.

192. Because Karl Barth made this the sole point of departure for his *Church Dogmatics*, the apocalyptic dimension is missing in his eschatology.

193. G. M. Martin, *Weltuntergang* 101ff. cf. also his 'Apokalypse in Film' in *ZOOM, Zeitschrift für Film*, December 1993, 6–15.

194. G. M. Martin, *Weltuntergang* 102.

195. O. Cullmann, *Christ and Time*, trans. F.V. Filson, revised ed., London 1962.

196. E. Peterson, 'Zeuge der Wahrheit' in *Theologische Traktate*, Munich 1951, 188.

197. E. Bloch, *Das Prinzip Hoffnung*, Frankfurt 1959, 1f. (ET *The Principle of Hope*, 1f.).

198. S. Kierkegaard, *The Concept of Dread*, ET Princeton and Oxford 1944.

199. W. Benjamin, *Geschichtsphilosophische Thesen* VI in *Illuminationen. Ausgewählte Schriften*, Frankfurt 1961, 270 (*Illuminations*, trans. H. Zohn, London 1970, reprinted 1992; for full reference see also Ch. I n.92).

200. T. Moser, *Gottesvergiftung*, Hamburg 1976.

201. Cf. *The Way of Jesus Christ*, Ch. VII §5: '. . . To judge both the quick and the dead', 334ff.

202. F. Rädle, 'Dies irae' in H. Becker *et al.* (eds), *Im Angesicht des Todes. Ein interdisziplinäres Kompendium* I, St Ottilien 1987, 331ff.

203. H.-J. Klauck, Introduction to H.-J. Klauck (ed.), *Weltgericht und Weltvollendung. Zukunfsbilder im Neuen Testament*, QD 150, Freiburg 1994, 11f.

204. DS 211: 'Si quis dicit aut sentit, ad tempus esse daemonum et impiorum hominum supplicium, eiusque finem aliquando futurum, sive restitutionem et reintegrationem fore daemonum aut impiorum hominum,

Anathema sit.' The Fifth Ecumenical Council of Constantinople (553) confirmed this edict of the Emperor Justinian.

205. F. Groth, *Die 'Wiederbringung aller Dinge' im württembergischen Pietismus. Theologiegeschichtliche Studien zum eschatologischen Heilsuniversalismus württembergischer Pietisten des 18.Jahrhunderts,* Göttingen 1984. Paul Gerhardt's well known Christmas hymn 'Iche stehe an deiner Krippen hier' also contains consoling lines in which Christ promises that he 'will restore all things': 'Lasst fahren, O liebe Brüder, / was euch fehlt, / was euch quält, / ich bring' alles wieder.' For Bonhoeffer's personal and moving comment on the verse see his letter to Bethge of 18 December 1943, in *Letters and Papers from Prison,* ed. R. Bethge, trans. R. H. Fuller, enlarged ed., London and New York 1971.

206. F. Groth, 'Chiliasmus und Apokatastasishoffnung in der Reich-Gottes-Verkündigung der beiden Blumhardts' in M. Brecht (ed.), *Pietismus und Neuzeit,* Jahrbuch zur Geschichte des neueren Protestantismus 9, Göttingen 1983, 56–116.

207. This is also brought out in a well-known hymn from the same period written by Isaac Watts (1674–1748):

Jesus shall reign where e'er the sun
Doth his successive journeys run,
His kingdom stretch from shore to shore,
Till moons shall wax and wain no more.

Where he displays his healing power
Death and the curse are known no more;
In him the tribes of Adam boast
More blessings than their father lost.

208. On the history and theology of universalism cf. the recent German post-doctoral theses by H. Rosenau, *Allversöhnung. Ein transzendental-theologischer Grundlegungsversuch,* Marburg 1991, and C. Janowski, *Apokatastasis panton – Allerlösung. Annäherungen an eine entdualisierte Eschatologie,* Tübingen 1993.

209. K. Barth, 'Vergangenheit und Zukunft. Friedrich Naumann und Christoph Blumhardt' (1919) in J. Moltmann (ed.), *Anfänge der dialek-tischen Theologie* I, Munich 1962, 37–49.

210. E. Brunner, *Dogmatik* I, Zürich 1946, 359 (*The Christian Doctrine of God. Dogmatics,* vol.I, trans. O. Wyon, London 1949). The last sentence, it must be said, is illogical, since universal reconciliation could, after all, be the result of judgment.

211. P. Althaus, *Die letzten Dinge,* 187, 194, 195.

212. G. Ebeling, *Dogmatik des christlichen Glaubens* I, Tübingen 1979, 527f. Similarly C. H. Ratschow, 'Eschatologie', *TRE* 10, 357: 'Of course judgment as judgment only has a point if through it the one enters into the glory of God's kingdom while the others are condemned to the everlasting fire.' The intellectual compulsion to dualism needs antitheses such as God

372   *Notes to pages 239 to 249*

and the devil, heaven and hell, blessedness and damnation, because the negative seems to be required for the enhancement of the positive. The emotional weight of decision necessarily results in the dualism of a separation between friend and enemy, which is what Carl Schmitt demanded in his antidemocratic politology.

213. Cf. U. Luz, *Das Evangelium nach Matthäus*, Evangelisch-katholischer Kommentar, vol. 1 chs 1–7, vol. 2 chs 8–17, Zürich, Einsiedeln and Cologne 1985, 1990 (ET of vol. 1: *Matthew 1–7. A Commentary*, Minneapolis and Edinburgh, 1989).

214. W. Michaelis, *Die Versöhnung des Alls. Die frohe Botschaft von der Gnade Gottes*, Bern 1950, 151.

215. That was the motto for the Synod of the Evangelical Church in Germany (EKD) in 1993.

216. Cf. the splendid scheme drawn up by Theodore von Beza, *Summa totius Christianismi* in H. Heppe and E. Bizer, *Die Dogmatik der evangelisch-reformierten Kirche*, Neukirchen 1958, 119.

217. I am indebted for this reference and the quotation to C. Janowski, *Apokatastasis panton*, 30; Augustine, *De Civ.*, XI, 18 and 21.

218. The young Luther also drew on this mystical doctrine of the *resignatio ad infernum*, the purpose of which was to be saved through conformity with God's will to condemn; see his lectures on Romans, 1515/16. Cf. *Luthers Werke in Auswahl* V, Berlin 1933, 271–279.

219. J. Moltmann, 'Prädestination und Heilsgeschichte bei Moyse Amyraut', *ZKG* 4, III, 65, 3, 270–303.

220. F. Schleiermacher, *Über die Lehre von der Erwählung* (1819).

221. J. A. T. Robinson, *In the End God*, New York 1968, Ch. XI: All in All, 119ff., sees the problem of universalism in the encounter between human freedom and divine love. For human freedom the alternative between heaven and hell continues to exist, but for divine love the universe must be won; otherwise God would not be God. 'Hell, so limitless to the man who has chosen it, is still bounded by the "nevertheless" of divine love. And that love must win' (132). He does, certainly quote Charles Wesley's verse:

> I yield, I yield,
> I can hold out no more;
> I sink by dying love compelled
> To own thee conqueror!

But what he really finds convincing is Origen's legendary saying that Christ hangs on the cross as long as there is still a sinner in hell. God will in the end be all in all, not because God's love overcomes the very last unbeliever, but because the shadows of Christ's cross dissolve hell.

222. K. Barth, *CD* II/2.

223. Ibid., §33, 94ff.

224. Ibid., 295f.

225. C. Blumhardt, *Ansprachen, Predigten, Reden, Briefe: 1865–1917*, ed. J. Harder, Neukirchen 1978, 134f.

226. Ibid., 133.
227. Ibid., 130f.
228. On the difference between the Roman and the biblical idea of justice, cf. the article '*sdq*' in E. Henni (ed.), *Theologisches Handwörterbuch zum Alten Testament* II, 507–523. and G. von Rad, *Old Testament Theology* I, 377: 'No references to the concept of a punitive *sdaqah* can be adduced – that would be a *contradictio in adiecto*.' Here one may think particularly of Ps. 31.1: 'Through thy righteousness deliver me.'
229. P. Stuhlmacher, *Biblische Theologie* I, Tübingen 1992, 326; 308: 'From Isaiah 25 . . . and Daniel 7 . . . we can see very well that the final Judgment is not an end in itself, but has a positive goal, and points beyond the act of judgment: God's rule and justice will finally be made to prevail, Israel will be delivered from its oppressors, death will be destroyed, and the messianic community of the saints will be established.' For Paul too, typically, 'final judgment is not an act of divine retaliation, but the event – and the longed for event – of the final establishment of God's justice, which creates salvation, over against all the powers of evil.'
230. See here E. Wolf, *Staupitz und Luther*, Berlin 1927; E. Vogelsang, *Der angefochtene Christus bei Luther*, Berlin 1932, esp. 30ff.: Die Anfechtung der Erwählung und die Hölle.
231. M. Luther, *Tischreden* I, 1017 (ET *Table Talk*, London 1833, and frequently, at least in selection).
232. For the theology of Christ's descent into hell in general cf. W. Maas, *Gott und die Hölle. Studien zum Descensus Christi*, Einsiedeln 1979; H. U. von Balthasar, *Abstieg zur Hölle*, ThQ 150, 1970, 193–201; also his *Mysterium Paschale* in *Mysterium Salutis* III/2, Einsiedeln, Zürich and Cologne 1969, 227ff.: Der Gang zu den Toten (Karsamstag); H. Vorgrimler, *Geschichte der Hölle*, Munich 1993; J. L. Walls, *Hell. The Logic of Damnation*, Notre Dame and London, 1992.
233. Calvin, *Inst.* II, 16, 10 (J. T. McNeill, ed., *Institutes of the Christian Religion*, trans. F. L. Battles, London and Philadelphia 1961).
234. M. Luther, *Genesisvorlesung* (1544).
235. M. Luther, WA 44, 523.
236. Luther, WA 46, 312.
237. Luther, WA 19, 225.
238. K. Barth, *Dogmatik im Grundriss im Anschluss an das apostolische Glaubensbekenntnis*, Stuttgart 1947, 126f. (*Dogmatics in Outline*, trans. G. T. Thomson, London 1949).
239. P. Althaus, *Die christliche Wahrheit*, 6th ed., Gütersloh 1962, 485.
240. W. Pannenberg, *Jesus – God and Man*, 269 ff.
241. J. Moltmann, *The Crucified God*, trans. R. A. Wilson and J. Bowden, 2nd ed., London 1973, 246 (trans. slightly altered).
242. M. Luther, 'Sermon von der Bereitung zum Sterben' (1519), WA 2, 685–697, esp. 691.
243. H. U. von Balthasar, 'Über Stellvertretung' in *Pneuma und In-*

stitution, Einsiedeln 1974, 408; cf. here M. Kehl, Eschatologie, Würzburg 1986, 297f.

244. H. U. von Balthasar, Mysterium Paschale, 246ff.; see here W. Maas, Gott und die Hölle, 244ff.

245. According to the Armenian view, Christ 'per suam passionem destruxit totaliter infernum'. I believe that this is correct, although this opinion was condemned by the patristic church. Cf. DS 1011.

246. J. C. Blumhardt, Gesammelte Werke II, 190.

247. C. Blumhardt, Ansprachen, Predigten, Reden, Briefe II, 131.

IV New Heaven – New Earth

1. H. Jonas, Gnosis und spätantiker Geist, 2nd ed., Göttingen 1954.

2. P. Teilhard de Chardin, Werke, Olten and Freiburg 1963ff.

3. A. N. Whitehead, Process and Reality. An Essay in Cosmology (1929), New York 1953, with the comment by M. Welker, Universalität Gottes und Relativität der Welt. Theologische Kosmologie im Dialog mit dem amerikanischen Prozessdenken nach Whitehead, Neukirchen 1981.

4. E. Bloch, Das Prinzip Hoffnung, Frankfurt 1959 (The Principle of Hope, trans. N. and S. Plaice and P. Knight, Cambridge, Mass., and Oxford 1986). Cf. here A. Schmidt, Der Begriff der Natur in der Lehre von Karl Marx, bes. Postscriptum 1971, 2nd ed., Frankfurt 1971, 207ff.

5. C. F. von Weizsäcker, The History of Nature, trans. F. D. Wieck, London 1951; also his Die Einheit der Natur, Munich 1971; G. Picht, Hier und Jetzt, Philosophieren nach Auschwitz und Hiroshima I, Stuttgart 1980. Cf. here C. Link, Schöpfung. Schöpfungstheologie angesichts der Herausforderungen des 20. Jahrhunderts, Handbuch Systematischer Theologie 7/2, Gütersloh 1991.

6. Cf. J. Moltmann, 'Creation as an Open System' in The Future of Creation, trans. Margaret Kohl, London 1979, 115–130.

7. Thus in a summing up of mediaeval doctrines about the primal condition CA II, BSLK 53.

7a. We find the same idea in a well-known German Christmas hymn 'Lobt Gott, ihr Christen alle gleich':

Heut'schleusst er wieder auf die Tür
Zum schönen Paradeis,
Der Cherub steht nicht mehr dafür:
Gott sei Lob, Ehr und Preis!

8. The same pattern is reflected in K. Barth's doctrine of reconciliation: 1. The Way of the Son of God into the Far Country (CD IV/1, §59, 157ff.); 2. The Homecoming of the Son of Man (CD IV/2, §64, 20ff.).

9. This radically Anselmian solution was maintained by A.A. van Ruler, of whose systematic work unfortunately only the small contribution, Gestaltwerdung Christi in der Welt, Neukirchen 1956, is available in German, and even that not in English.

10. M. Eliade, *The Myth of the Eternal Return*, trans. W. R. Trask, London 1955.

10a. Cf. the German hymn that begins: 'Gott Lob, der Sonntag kommt herbei, / Die Woche wird nun wieder neu!'

11. Thomas Aquinas, *STh* I, 90, q3 ad2; I. Sent. d 14 q2 ad2.

12. Under the impression of this myth, R. Bultmann wrote: 'So what meaning has the divine righteousness, the forgiveness of sins? . . . Its meaning is *that the original* relationship of creation will be restored' ('Der Begriff der Offenbarung im Neuen Testament', *Glauben und Verstehen* III, Tübingen 1960, 26). The reduction of the divine righteousness to the forgiveness of sins is restoratively conceived and is not in accord with Pauline thinking.

13. Augustine, *Enchiridion*, 106.

14. E. Bloch, 'Die Formel Incipit vita nova' in *Tübinger Einleitung in die Philosophie* II, Frankfurt 1964, 151–169. Cf. J. Moltmann, 'Die Kategorie Novum in der christlichen Theologie' in S. Unseld (ed.), *Ernst Bloch zu ehren, Beiträge zu seinem Werk*, Frankfurt 1965, 243–264.

15. Augustine, *De civ. Dei* XI, 6.

16. Augustine, *Conf.* XI, 30, 40. If God is *creator aeternus*, then his creation must also be eternal. But that contradicts its temporality. Cf. my proposed solution in *God in Creation. An Ecological Doctrine of Creation* (Gifford Lectures 1984–85), trans. Margaret Kohl, London and New York 1985, Ch. V §3: The Time of Creation, 112ff.

17. D. Staniloae, *Orthodoxe Dogmatik* I, Ökumenische Theologie 12, Gütersloh 1984, 297ff., esp. 303ff. on 'time, aeon and aeonic eternity'.

18. Ibid., 293ff.: 'The world, as work of God's love, destined to be deified.'

19. On the theology of the sabbath, see A.J. Heschel, *The Sabbath. Its Meaning for Modern Man*, 7th ed., New York 1981. This wonderful study does not take into account the ecological significance of the sabbath. See here J. Moltmann, *God in Creation*, Ch. XI: The Sabbath: The Feast of Creation, 276ff.

20. A. M. Goldberg, *Untersuchungen über die Vorstellung von der Schekhina in der frühen rabbinischen Literatur – Talmud und Midrasch –*, Studia Judaica V, Berlin 1969; B. Janowski, '"Ich will in eurer Mitte wohnen." Struktur und Genese der exilischen Schekhina-Theologie', *BTh* 2, Neukirchen 1987, 165–193. On the connection between Shekinah and God's Spirit, cf. J. Moltmann, *The Spirit of Life*, trans. Margaret Kohl, London and Minneapolis 1992, Ch. II §3: God's Spirit and His Shekinah, 47ff.

21. Cf. J. Moltmann, *The Spirit of Life*, Ch. V: The Liberation for Life, 99ff.

22. B. Janowski, ' "Ich will in eurer Mitte wohnen" ', 180ff.

23. A. J. Heschel, *The Sabbath*, 11ff.

24. P. Althaus, *Die lezten Dinge*, 1st ed., Gütersloh 1922, 350.

25. Althaus was unable to explain this development in Lutheran

orthodoxy. The riddle has meanwhile been solved through K. Stock's excellent historical study *Annihilatio Mundi. Johann Gerhards Eschatologie der Welt*, FGLP 10/42, Munich 1971. It was not due to the influence of any gnostic thinking or a-cosmic mysticism, but was a result of the Lutheran doctrine of the Real Presence as formulated in the second eucharistic dispute.

26. H. Schmid, *Die Dogmatik der evangelisch-lutherischen Kirche, dargestellt und aus den Quellen belegt*, 10th ed., Gütersloh 1983, 407.

27. J. Gerhard, *Loci Theologici*, ed. H. Preuss, 2nd ed., Leipzig 1885, IX, 163: 'In vita aeterna beati Deum videbunt a facie ad faciem, ergo non opus habebunt creaturarum magisterio.' This means that the existence of other created beings has no justification other than to lead human beings to the knowledge of God. Once they have attained this knowledge, other creatures are superfluous. They therefore exist solely for the sake of human beings.

28. This is the conclusion drawn by P. Althaus, *Die letzten Dinge*, 355, and K. Stock, *Annihilatio Mundi*, 185.

29. C. H. Sasse, 'κόσμος' *TDNT* III, 884f.

30. Quenstedt (IV, 638): 'Forma consummationis huius non in nuda qualitatum immutatione, alteratione seu innovatione, sed in ipsius substantiae mundi totali abolitione et *in nihilum reductione* (Ps. CII, 27. 2 Petr III, 10. Ap. XX, 11. Es XXXIV, 4. Luk XXI, 33. Iob XIV, 12) consistit.' Quoted in H. Schmid, *Die Dogmatik der evangelisch-lutherischen Kirche*, 407.

31. Thus the Barmen Theological Declaration, Thesis 2 (text ed. A. Bürgsmüller and R. Weth, Neukirchen-Vluyn 1983).

32. H. Heppe and E. Bizer, *Die Dogmatik der evangelisch-reformierten Kirche, Locus XXVIII: De glorificatione*, 2nd ed., Neukirchen 1958, 557ff.

33. Ibid., 560.

34. Ibid., 557.

35. Athanasius, *De inc.*, ch. 54. D. Staniloae, *Orthodoxe Dogmatik* I, 359: 'This maximal union with God in which the person is interpenetrated by God's fulness without being absorbed into it, means at the same time the deification of the human being.'

36. D. Staniloae, ibid., 294.

37. Ibid.

38. Ibid., 369.

39. R. Radford Ruether, *Sexism and God-Talk. Towards a Feminist Theology*, Boston and London 1983, 239, Cf. also her *From machismo to mutuality: essays on sexism and woman–man liberation*, New York 1979, and 'Frauenbefreiung und Wiederversöhnung mit der Erde' in E. Moltmann-Wendel (ed.), *Frauenbefreiung. Biblische und theologische Argumente*, 4th ed., Munich 1986, 192–202 (this is a translation of 'Women's Liberation and the Reconciliation with the Earth', a paper: Office of Women's Affairs, Berkeley, CA). For a comprehensive account and discussion of her theology cf. C. Rehberger, *Humanisierung des Menschen und die Wiederversöhnung mit der Erde. Die Befreiungstheologie Rosemary Radford Ruethers und ihre systematisch-theologischen Grundlagen*, Diss. Tübingen 1993, esp. 273.

40. R. Radford Ruether, *Sexism and God-Talk*, 257.

41. Ibid., 257f.

42. Ibid., 258. Her notion of replacing Christian eschatology by sabbath theology fails to appreciate the origin of biblical eschatology in the theology of the sabbath and the Shekinah.

43. E. Moltmann-Wendel, 'Rückkehr zur Erde' and J. Moltmann, 'Die Erde und die Menschen. Zum theologischen Verständnis der Gaja-Hypothese', both in *EvTh* 53, 1993, 406–419 and 420–438 respectively. On the Gaia hypothesis and its religious evaluation cf. also R. Radford Ruether, *Gaia and God. An Ecofeminist Theology of Earth Healing*, New York 1992 and London 1993.

44. Gregory of Nazianzus, *Die fünf theologischen Reden* (the Five Theological Orations), ed. J. Barbel, Düsseldorf 1963, 32, 10.

45. Cf. A. Schlatter, *Becks theologische Arbeit.* Gütersloh 1904; K. Barth, *Protestant Theology in the Nineteenth Century*, trans. B. Cozens . . . J. Bowden, London 1972, Philadelphia 1973; Pae, Kyung-Sik, *Eschatologie bei J. T. Beck*, Diss. Tübingen 1988.

46. J. T. Beck, *Die Vollendung des Reiches Gottes. Separatabdruck aus der Christlichen Glaubenslehre*, Gütersloh 1887, 95ff.

47. Ibid., 96.

48. Ibid., 101.

49. Ibid., 103.

50. Ibid., 102.

51. Ibid., 103f.

52. For a detailed exposition here see E. Moltmann-Wendel, 'Rückkehr zur Erde', *EvTh* 53, 1993, 406–420.

53. C. Blumhardt, *Ansprachen, Predigten, Reden, Briefe* II, *Neue Texte aus dem Nachlass*, ed. J. Harder, Neukirchen-Vluyn 1978, 295f.

54. E. Schüssler Fiorenza, *Revelation. Vision of a Just World*, Minneapolis 1991; Edinburgh 1994, 75.

55. I am thus developing further the theology of time which I began to work out in *God in Creation*, Ch. V §3: The Time of Creation, 104ff., and in *The Way of Jesus Christ. Christology in Messianic Dimensions*, trans. Margaret Kohl, London and New York 1990, Ch. VII §3: 'The Day of the Lord', 326ff.

56. Plato, *Timaeus*, trans. J. Warrington, London 1965, 27d, with the comments by G. Böhme, *Zeit und Zahl. Studien zur Zeittheorie bei Platon, Aristoteles, Leibniz und Kant*, Frankfurt 1974; S. Toulmin and J. Goodfield, *The Discovery of Time*, New York 1965; G. J. Whitrow, *Time in History: the evolution of our general awareness of time and temporal perspective*, Oxford 1988.

57. This is the new point of departure in Augustine, *Conf.* XI. Cf. *God in Creation*, 112f.

58. Augustine, *Conf.* XI, 12, 14.

59. Thus Augustine, *Conf.* XI, 30, 40.

60. K. Barth, *CD* II/2, 88ff., 120ff., 161ff., esp. 166f.

61. G. Scholem, 'Schöpfung aus Nichts und Selbstverschränkung Gottes', *Eranos* 25, 1956, 87–119, esp. 117f.

62. D. Staniloae, *Orthodoxe Dogmatik* I, 303: 'Saint Maximus Confessor distinguishes between aeon and eternity, and thinks that the aeon is eternity which is filled with the experiences of time; or that it is time filled up with eternity. There is a final aeon in which all time is summed up, and there is a first aeon, which includes all the possibilities thought of in God which will be developed in time. The non-temporal laws of creation, the time-ideas, form such an aeon.'

63. Aristotle, *Physics*, 114f.

64. C. W. Thomsen and H. Holländer (eds), *Augenblick und Zeitpunkt. Studien zur Zeitstruktur und Zeitmetaphorik in Kunst und Wissenschaften*, Darmstadt 1984.

65. This idea derives from Parmenides, Fragment B 8,5: 'It never was, nor will it ever be, since it is now simultaneously a unified, continuous whole' (for the translation see F.M. Cornford, *Plato and Parmenides*, London and New York 1939, 30f.). See the comment by G. Picht, 'Die Epiphanie der ewigen Gegenwart' in H. Höfling (ed.), *Beiträge zu Philosophie und Wissenschaft. Festschrift für W. Szilasi*, Munich 1960, 244: 'The Now is neither a point in time nor is it extension; it is, rather, the unity of time. In this sense the "Now", if the word is permissible, is the event of eternity in Being.'

66. S. Kierkegaard, *Der Begriff der Angst* (1944), *Werke* I, ed. I. Richter, Hamburg 1960, 82 (ET *The Concept of Dread*, Princeton and Oxford 1944).

67. F. Cramer, *Der Zeitbaum. Grundlegung einer allgemeinen Zeittheorie*, Frankfurt 1993, 40. Cf. also W. Kaempfer, *Die Zeit und die Uhren*, Frankfurt 1991.

68. I. Prigogine and I. Stengers, *Time, Chaos and the Resolution of the Time Paradox* (in preparation); German trans. from the English manuscript: *Das Paradox der Zeit. Zeit, Chaos und Quanten*, Munich 1993.

69. C. F. von Weizsäcker, *The History of Nature*.

70. G. Picht, *Hier und Jetzt*, Ch. V, 17: Die Zeit und die Modalitäten, 362ff.

71. S. Kierkegaard, *Der Begriff der Angst*, 99 (ET *The Concept of Dread*).

72. G. Picht, *Hier und Jetzt*, 371.

73. E. Bloch, *Das Prinzip Hoffnung*, 224ff. (ET *The Principle of Hope*, 195ff.).

74. S. Kierkegaard, *Der Begriff der Angst*, 85 (ET *The Concept of Dread*).

75. Augustine, *Conf.* XI, 20, 26.

76. Ibid., XI, 11, 13, 14, 17.

77. R. Koselleck, *Vergangene Zukunft. Zur Semantik geschichtlicher Zeiten*, Frankfurt 1979, 349ff.

78. Ibid., 354ff.

79. Cf. J. Ebach, *Ursprung und Ziel. Erinnerte Zukunft und erhoffte Vergangenheit. Biblische Exegesen, Reflexionen, Geschichten*, Neukirchen-Vluyn 1986.

80. S. Kierkegaard, *Der Begriff der Angst*, 80f. (ET *The Concept of Dread*).

81. Boethius, *De consolatione philosophiae*, V. 6. Thus also Thomas Aquinas, *STh* I, q 10 a 1.

82. Cf. here M. Theunissen, *Negative Theologie der Zeit*, Frankfurt 1991, 309ff.

83. Thus also G. Picht, *Hier und Jetzt* 403, following Heidegger: 'In the first stage of transcendence the human being was translated from his mere present into the unity of time. The second stage of transcendence is opened up when in the expectation of death he anticipates the exit from time in general, and thus perceives the unity of time.'

84. S. Kierkegaard, *Der Begriff der Angst*, 85 (ET *The Concept of Dread*).

85. Ibid., 80f. The following quotation on p.81.

86. K. Barth, *Epistle to the Romans*, trans. from the 6th German ed. by E. Hoskyns, London 1933, 497.

87. Ibid., 498.

88. R. Bultmann, 'Geschichte und Eschatologie im Neuen Testament' in *Glauben und Verstehen* III, Tübingen 1961, 106.

89. R. Bultmann, *History and Eschatology*, the Gifford Lectures for 1955, Edinburgh 1957, 154.

90. J. Moltmann, *God in Creation*, Ch.VI: The Space of Creation, 140ff.

91. D. Staniloae, *Orthodoxe Dogmatik* I, 182f.

92. See here G. Scholem, *Die jüdische Mystik in ihren Hauptströmungen*, Frankfurt 1967, 285ff. on the zimzum doctrine of Isaak Luria and his school. (This book is based on the 3rd US edition of *Major Trends in Jewish Mysticism*, New York 1954, London 1955; see there 260ff.)

93. M. Jammer, *Concepts of Space*, Cambridge, Mass., 1954, Oxford 1955, 35; cf. G. Scholem, *Sabbatai Sevi. The Mystical Messiah*, Princeton and London 1973 (revised and augmented translation from the Hebrew), 31f.

94. J. Moltmann, *The Trinity and the Kingdom of God*, trans. Margaret Kohl, London 1981 (= *The Trinity and the Kingdom*, New York 1981), Ch. V §3.2: The Life of the Trinity, 171ff.

95. D. Stanliloae, *Orthodoxe Dogmatik* I, 189.

96. Quotation from the midrash Rabbah Genesis in M. Jammer, *The Concept of Space*, 28.

97. M. Heidegger, *Being and Time*, trans. J. Macquarrie and E. Robinson, London 1962, 145. Cf. also O. F. Bollnow's phenomenological description in *Mensch und Raum*, 7th ed., Stuttgart 1994.

98. The standard work is A. M. Goldberg, *Untersuchungen über die Vorstellung von der Schekhinah in der frühen rabbinischen Literatur*, Berlin 1969. There is also a wealth of material in P. Kuhn, *Gottes Selbsternied-*

rigung in der Theologie der Rabbinen, Munich 1968, For the interpretation cf. G. Scholem, *Von der mystischen Gestalt der Gottheit*, Frankfurt 1973, Ch. IV: Shechina: das passiv-weibliche Moment in der Gottheit, 135ff.

99. J. Moltmann, *The Spirit of Life*, Part I, Ch. 2, §3: God's Spirit and His Shekinah, 47ff.

100. A. M. Goldberg, *Vorstellung von der Schekhinah*, 477.

101. F. Rosenzweig, *Der Stern der Erlösung*, 3rd ed., Heidelberg 1954, 192ff. (*The Star of Redemption*, trans. W. W. Hallo, London 1971).

102. P. Kuhn, *Gottes Selbsterniedrigung*, 106.

103. A. M. Goldberg, *Vorstellung von der Schekhinah*, 523.

104. Ibid., 468ff.

105. P. Kuhn, *Gottes Selbsterniedrigung*, 90.

106. Ibid., 108.

107. G. Lohfink, ' "Schwerter zu Pflugscharen": Die Rezeption von Jes 2, 1–5 par Mi 4, 1–5 in der Alten Kirche und im Neuen Testament', *ThQ* 166, 1986, 184–209.

108. E. Schüssler Fiorenza, *Revelation*, 110; Cf. the old standard work, W. Bousset, *Die Offenbarung Johannis*, 6th ed., Göttingen 1906, 442ff.; H. Kraft, *Die Offenbarung des Johannes*, Tübingen 1974; O. Böcher, *Die Johannesapokalypse*, Darmstadt 1975.

109. F. Mussner, *Der Galaterbrief*, Freiburg 1974, 319ff.; G. Ebeling, *Die Wahrheit des Evangeliums. Eine Lesehilfe zum Galaterbrief*, Tübingen 1981, 318.

110. G. Jeremias, *Der Lehrer der Gerechtigkeit*, Göttingen 1963, 245–249. Cf. also E. Lohse, 'Zion-Jerusalem', *ThWNT* VII, 324f. and 336f.

111. R. Bauckham, *The Theology of the Book of Revelation*, Cambridge 1993, 126ff., on which I have drawn considerably here.

112. C. Keller, 'Die Frau in der Wüste. Ein feministisch-theologischer Midrasch zu Offb 12', *EvTh* 50, 1990, 414–432.

113. On the following see E. Schüssler Fiorenza, *Revelation*, 110ff. On Ezekiel, cf. W. Zimmerli, *Ezekiel* II (24–48), trans. J. D. Martin (Hermeneia Commentaries), Philadelphia 1983.

114. E. Schüssler Fiorenza, *Revelation* 112, points to this.

115. L. Mumford, *The City in History. Its Origins, its Transformations, and its Prospects*, London 1961, 42: 'Beginning as a representation of the cosmos, a means of bringing heaven down to earth, the city became a symbol of the possible. Utopia was an integral part of its original constitution.' And 63: 'The city, as it took form around the royal citadel, was a man-made replica of the universe. This opened an attractive vista: indeed a glimpse of heaven itself. To be a resident of the city was to have a place in man's true home, the great cosmos itself, and this very choice was itself a witness of the general enlargement of powers and potentialities that took place in every direction. At the same time, living in the city, within sight of the gods and their king, was to fulfil the utmost potentialities of life.'

116. E. Bloch, *Das Prinzip Hoffnung*, Frankfurt 1959, 819ff. (ET *The Principle of Hope*, 699ff.) cites for his description of 'the architectonic

utopias' the mediaeval hymn: 'Urbs Jerusalem beata/Dicta pacis visio/Quae construitur in coelis/Vivis ex lapidibus' [cf. the hymn 'Jerusalem the golden']. He pursues the 'crystal' metaphor particularly. Cf. 863ff. (ET 738ff.); 'Town plans, ideal cities, and again true clarity: interpenetration of crystal with fulness.'

117. H. E. Cox, *The Secular City. Secularization and Urbanization in Theological Perspective*, New York 1965.

118. R. Bauckham, *Theology of the Book of Revelation*, 137.

V Glory

1. Westminster Catechism, of 1647, in answer to the question: 'What is the chief end of man?'

2. H. Heppe and E. Bizer, *Die Dogmatik der evangelisch-reformierten Kirche*, 2nd ed., Neukirchen 1958, 557.

3. Augustine, *De doctrina christiana*, I, 5 and I, 12.

4. J. Moltmann, *Theology of Play*, trans. R. Ulrich, New York 1972 (= *Theology and Joy*, London 1973).

5. This rather too stringently economic question is put by H. Urs von Balthasar, *Theodramatik* IV: *Das Endspiel*, Einsiedeln 1983, 463 (*Theo-Drama: a theological dramatic theory*, trans. G. Harrison, San Francisco 1988, Vol. V [German vol. IV]: The Last Act).

6. Aristotle, *Metaphysics* XII, 107b. See also Augustine, *Confessions* X, 27: 'Late have I loved Thee, thou beauty, eternally old and eternally new, late have I loved Thee.'

7. K. Barth, *CD* II/2, 166. I have entered into a detailed critical discussion of Barth's understanding of God's freedom in *The Trinity and the Kingdom of God*, trans. Margaret Kohl, London 1981 (= *The Trinity and the Kingdom*, New York 1981), 52ff.

8. Of the extensive literature, I may draw attention to K. Löwith, *Von Hegel zu Nietzsche. Der revolutionäre Bruch im Denken des neunzehnten Jahrhunderts*, 4th ed., Stuttgart 1958; M. Theunissen, *Hegels Lehre vom absoluten Geist als theologisch-politischer Traktat*, Berlin 1970; M. Frank, *Der kommende Gott. Vorlesungen über die Neue Mythologie*, Frankfurt 1982. For the theological interpretation see W. Kasper, *Das Absolute in der Geschichte. Philosophie und Theologie der Geschichte in der Spät-philosophie Schellings*, Mainz 1965, and H. Küng, *The Incarnation of God: an introduction to Hegel's theological thought*, trans. J. R. Stephenson, Edinburgh 1987.

9. H. A. Korff, *Geist der Goethezeit. Versuch einer ideellen Entwicklung der klassisch-romantischen Literaturgeschichte* I-IV, 4th ed., Leipzig 1957; C. Hinrichs, *Ranke und die Geschichtstheologie der Goethezeit*, Göttingen 1954.

10. I am here following G. W. E. Hegel, *Philosophie der Religion* II

(*Sämtliche Werke* XVI, ed. H. Glockner), 3rd ed., Stuttgart 1959, 218f. (*Lectures on the Philosophy of Religion*, trans. E. B. Speirs and J. B. Sanderson, 3 vols, London 1968).

11. Ibid., 296.

12. G. W. F. Hegel, *Theologische Jugendschriften*, ed. H. Nohl, Tübingen 1907, 377 (*Early Theological Writings*, trans. T. M. Knox, Chicago 1948).

13. G. W. F. Hegel, *Glauben und Wissen* (1802/3), PhB 62b, ed. G. Lasson, 124; *Phänomenologie des Geistes* (1807), PhB 114, ed. J. Hoffmeister, 6th ed., Hamburg 1952, 564 (*Phenomenology of Mind*, trans. J. B. Baillie, 2nd ed., London and New York 1931).

14. G. W. F. Hegel, *Philosophie der Religion* (*Philosophy of Religion*). Cf. also 306: ' "God himself is dead" says the Lutheran hymn; this awareness expresses the fact that the human, the finite, the fragile, the weak, the negative is itself a divine aspect, is in God itself; that the otherness, the finite, the negative is not outside God, that as otherness it does not prevent the unity with God: it knows itself to be the otherness, the negation as aspect of the divine nature itself. The supreme perception about the nature of the idea of Mind can be found here.'

15. Ibid., 304. Cf. also 300: 'God has died. God is dead . . . But the course of things does not stand still here; now comes the antithesis; for God receives himself in this process, and this process is only the death of death. God rises again to life: things therefore change into their opposite' (*Lectures on the Philosophy of Religion*).

16. K. Barth, *Protestant Theology in the Nineteenth Century*, trans. B. Cozens . . . J. Bowden, London 1972, Philadelphia 1973, §10: Hegel.

17. As H. Urs von Balthasar seems to assume when he stresses the 'gratuity' of grace so strongly, as a way of avoiding any kind of pantheism. Cf. H. Urs von Balthasar, *Theodramatik*, IV, 464f. (*Theo-Drama*, V).

18. This is rightly stressed by P. Tillich, *Systematic Theology* I, Chicago 1951, London 1953, 179.

19. G. W. F. Hegel, *Phäenomenologie des Geistes*, 558f. (*Phenomenology of Mind*).

20. G. W. F. Hegel, *Grundlinien der Philosophie des Rechts*, Vorrede, 14 (*Hegel's Philosophy of Law*, trans. T. M. Knox, London 1967).

21. His theological contemporary C. H. Weisse already noticed this. Cf. T. Koch, *Differenz und Versöhnung. Eine Interpretation der Theologie G. W. F. Hegels nach seiner 'Wissenschaft der Logik'*, Gütersloh 1967, 21.

22. Cf. here W. D. Marsch, *Gegenwart Christi in der Gesellschaft. Eine Studie zu Hegels Dialektik*, Munich 1965, and P. Cornehl, *Die Zukunft der Versöhnung. Eschatologie und Emanzipation in der Aufklärung, bei Hegel und in der Hegelschen Schule*, Göttingen 1971. The first interprets Hegel in a more Left Hegelian sense, the second rather in a Right Hegelian sense. My own criticism of Hegel is along the lines of the Left Hegelians.

23. A. N. Whitehead, *Process and Reality. An Essay in Cosmology* (1929), New York 1960, 521–533. For the interpretation cf. M. Welker,

Universalität Gottes und Relativität der Welt. Theologische Kosmologie im Dialog mit dem amerikanischen Prozessdenken nach Whitehead, Neukirchen 1981, esp. 112ff. and 117ff.

24. M. Welker, ibid., 119.

25. A. N. Whitehead, *Process and Reality*, 528.

26. Ibid., 527; 'The consequent nature of God is the fluent world become "everlasting" by its objective immortality in God.'

27. P. Tillich also several times considered the idea that God's eternal life may be 'enriched' through the life-processes of finite life. Cf. his *Systematic Theology* III, 400f., 417, 422f.

28. A. N. Whitehead, *Process and Reality*, 532.

29. G. Scholem, *Von der mystischen Gestalt der Gottheit*, Frankfurt 1973, 115ff.

30. F. Rosenzweig, *Der Stern der Erlösung*, 3rd ed., Heidelberg 1954, Book III, 192ff. (*The Star of Redemption*, trans. W.W. Hallo, London 1971).

31. Ibid., 194.

32. E. Bloch, *Geist der Utopie* (1918), *Gesamtausgabe* 3, revised ed. of the second version of 1923, Frankfurt 1964, 346.

33. H. U. von Balthasar has considered this complex of ideas in detail, making it a central theme: cf. *The Glory of the Lord. A Theological Aesthetics*, ET Edinburgh 1982ff., I-III. See also here V. Spangenberg, *Herrlichkeit des Neuen Bundes. Die Bestimmung des biblischen Begriffs der 'Herrlichkeit' bei Hans Urs von Balthasar*, Tübingen 1993. I am grateful to Balthasar for many stimulating ideas, especially in his literary interpretations, but I am not always able to go along with his theological speculations.

34. H. Urs von Balthasar finds himself able to say that creation is a gift of each of the divine Persons involved to the other two, as a way of 'increasing' the glory of the others. See his *Theodramatik* IV, 464 (*Theo-Drama* V). He thereby takes the *opera trinitatis ad extra* into the inner Trinity, making them *opera ad intra*. It then becomes difficult to conceive that the community of creation corresponds to the one community of the Tri-unity, and not to the inner 'threefold God'.

35. See here W. Thüsing, *Per Christum in Deum. Studien zum Verhältnis von Christozentrik und Theozentrik in den paulinischen Hauptbriefen*, 2nd ed., Münster 1968.

36. H. Rahner, *Man at Play*, trans. B. Battershaw and E. Quinn, London 1965; J. Moltmann, *Theology of Play* (= *Theology and Joy*).

37. We are thereby heeding Hegel's warning in his Preface to the *Phänomenologie des Geistes*: 'The life of God and divine intelligence, then, can, if we like, be spoken of as love disporting with itself; but this idea falls into edification and even sinks into insipidity, if it lacks the seriousness, the suffering, the patience, and the labour of the negative' (G. W. F. Hegel, *Phenomenology of Mind*, trans. J. B. Baillie, 2nd ed., London and New York 1931, 81).

38. Cf. N. A. Nissiotis, 'Die österliche Freude als doxologischer Aus-

druck des Glaubens' in *Gottes Zukunft, Zukunft der Welt. J. Moltmann zum 60. Geburtstag*, Munich 1986, 78–88. This wonderful text was the last thing he wrote before his fatal accident.

39. K. Kirchoff, *Osterjubel der Ostkirche* I: *Hymnen aus der fünfzigtägigen Osterfeier der byzantinischen Kirche*, 2nd ed., Münster 1961, 24.

40. Ibid., 25.

Index of Names